SWAMP THING

the saga of the swamp thing

ALAN MOORE STEVE BISSETTE
JOHN TOTLEBEN

TATJANA WOOD
COLORIST

JOHN COSTANZA TODD KLEIN
LETTERERS

SWAMP THING CREATED BY LEN WEIN
AND BERNI WRIGHTSON

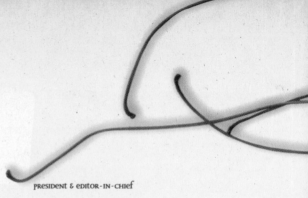

the saga of the swamp thing published by dc comics. cover, introduction and compilation copyright ©1987 dc comics. all rights reserved. originally published in single magazine form as saga of the swamp thing #21-27. copyright © 1983, 1984 dc comics. all rights reserved. all characters, their distinctive likenesses and related indicia featured in this publication are trademarks of dc comics. the stories, characters, and incidents featured in this publication are entirely fictional. dc comics, 1700 broadway, new york, ny 10019. a division of warner bros. - an aol time warner company. printed in canada. fourth printing. isbn: 0-930289-22-6. cover illustration by michael zulli. publication design by louis prandi.

table of contents

acknowledgments

alan moore, steven bissette,
john totleben, co-plotters on:
"the sleep of reason..."
"...a time of running..."
"...by demons driven!"

stephen bissette and
rick veitch, co-pencillers:
"the anatomy lesson"
"...a time of running..."
"...by demons driven!"

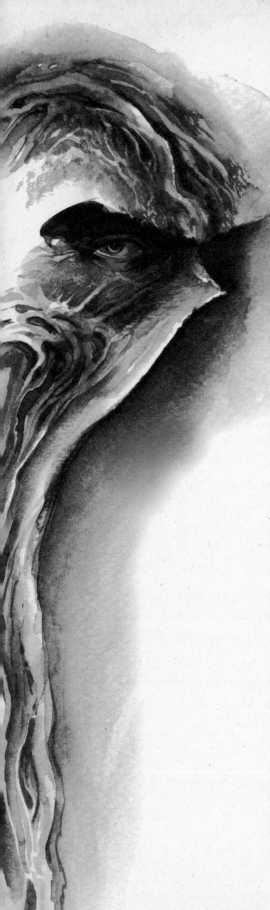

foreword by ramsey campbell

"It's raining in Washington tonight. Plump, warm summer rain that covers the sidewalks with leopard spots. Downtown, elderly ladies carry their houseplants out to set them on the fire escapes, as if they were infirm relatives or boy kings."

I didn't write that, but I would be happy to have done so. These are the opening lines of Alan Moore's first SWAMP THING story in this book, and I think they demonstrate that Moore needs no special pleading at all. Let me explain what I mean. Back in the late sixties a change overtook many of the comic books on the shelves; even familiar series became harsher, more cutting, more willing to take on reality in ways that, when the Comics Code was at its most suffocating, would have been unthinkable. Some of the loudest applause was mine. Still, when I look back now at some of the comics I praised, it seems to me that for all their seriousness about issues such as heroin addiction and racial intolerance, they weren't necessarily very well-written: too shrilly and melodramatic, perhaps, or too given to dull Hollywoodish preaching in the dialogue; characters intoning lines that would be groaned off the screen in a movie. It's possible, as with the rock music of those years that used classical themes or was played from scores, that some of us—especially those like myself who hadn't previously been drawn to the field— tended to overrate what we found unexpected. But then again, without the progress made in those years, we might not have comics written by Alan Moore, in which case we would be a good deal poorer.

In some ways, his merits are those of the finest tradition of comics: his ear for dialogue, his talent for concise, clear storytelling, his unerring sense of pace and timing. In other ways, he and his collaborators, Stephen Bissette and John Totleben, pretty well lead the field, especially in building a sense of terror. You'll find a hint of this on the first page of "The Anatomy Lesson," a promise gruesomely kept by the finale of the story. But it's the uncompromising radicalism of "The Anatomy Lesson" that announces most clearly this team is a force to be respected. There surely can't be many writers who, having taken over an established character, would begin by demonstrating (in the autopsy scene) that the character has never made sense as he was presented and is in fact something far less human than even he himself believed. Moore, Bissette, and Totleben take Swamp Thing apart in order to rebuild him.

It's a moving and disturbing process, illuminated by the resurrection of a minor DC villain, the Floronic Man, to represent the dark side of identification with the vegetable kingdom, Swamp Thing's darker self. Jason Woodrue is all the more disconcerting for expressing genuine ecological concerns; he's more articulate than monsters usually are—since Frankenstein's, anyway (though comic books are more prepared than most fiction to let their monsters have their say). He is given some of the best and most unsettling lines, and a poignant farewell. "If there's one thing I despise, it's the sound of steak sobbing," he muses, and later sums up humanity as "screaming meat," a phrase one could use to summarize splatter movies: maybe they are the revenge of vegetables, and Woodrue seems to acknowledge this by wielding a chainsaw.

Meanwhile we're taken on a hallucinatory journey by Swamp Thing's changing consciousness, introduced by the extraordinary image of Swamp Thing's face filling up with rain. (Here I restrain myself from raving on about the visual inventiveness of the comic, preferring to let you discover that pleasure for yourself in your own time, but let me take the opportunity to celebrate Tatjana Wood's coloring, especially effective in the mental landscapes.) Here as else-where, Moore's language and imagery is simultaneously comic and horrifying, as is the way with horror fiction. Horror fiction at its best is in the business of pushing back the barriers, of risking the absurd in order to reach the sublime, just as Jason Woodrue does by eating a tuber of Swamp Thing's. By this stage no reader can doubt that here is a story prepared to go to the end of itself, whatever it may find there or on the way.

One troubling character it finds is Abby Arcane, still under-standably suffering from all she went through, and not only in previous issues: one nightmarish childhood memory, powerfully depicted, seems to have no immediate narrative significance. Perhaps it stands for the horror that underlies the world of these stories and can break through at any time without warning: a world where one may buy a panel from a Francis Bacon crucifixion study as a poster, or be the life of the party by turning one's friends into zombies, or where all the pupils at a school for autistic children may suddenly draw the same monster. But perhaps it also means that Abby has suffered enough to be able to reach the children. We can only hope.

Having passed through the vegetable consciousness, with his own skull playing Yorick to his Hamlet and getting the best lines, Swamp Thing is resurrected in an awesome full-page panel. From here on the comic becomes what I would call a poetic reinvention of the super-hero, not only Swamp Thing but the Justice League (one of whom is brilliantly epitomized as "a man who moves so fast that his life is an endless gallery of statues") and later, Jack Kirby's Demon. It seems to me that this creates a real problem in sustaining a tale of terror: after all, if the terror only needs a handy super-hero to thump it into submission, we might as well not lose any sleep about it. But Alan Moore's terrors are too profound to be gotten rid of so easily. They are rooted deeper in the characters than a super-hero can reach.

Len Wein and Berni Wrightson's *Swamp Thing* was a remarkable fusion of the super-hero comic and the horror story, but I should like to claim even more for the new *Swamp Thing*. "All I knew were the suburbs of fear...and now here I am, in the big city." Indeed. The notion of the horror that can take the form of the victim's deepest fear is hardly new, but I have never seen a more terrifying image of it than the one that visits Jessica in "...A Time of Running..." One test of art is that it is deeply felt, and can anyone doubt that this is? I believe that at its best, the new *Swamp Thing* can stand beside the finest works of contemporary horror fiction. I believe horror fiction is capable of encompassing a great range of human experience— comedy, tragedy, terror, and awe—and now it is beginning to do so. It is all the richer for Messrs. Moore, Bissette, and Totleben. Long may they continue to light up our darkest dreams.

Ramsey Campbell has won numerous awards for horror fiction. He has received the British Fantasy Award for his novels The Parasite, Incarnate, The Hungry Moon, The Influence, Midnight Sun *and is also the recipient of the World Fantasy Award. Ramsey is also an accomplished editor, having put together many collections of his fellow writers' work. Most recent of his anthologies,* Uncanny Banquet, *includes literature out of print since 1914.*

INTRODUCTION BY ALAN MOORE

In a century packed to the bursting point with paradoxes, one of the most puzzling must surely be the meteoric ascent of horror as a genre in literature, cinema, and even music, all at a time when each day seems to make us just a little more conscious and aware of the real-life horrors unfolding all around us. While the faces of missing children stare from milk cartons, lines for the latest dead teenager movie are stretching 'round the block. While the AIDS virus sweeps through society with a chilling ease, born upon a colossal wave of ignorance and prejudice, the shelves of our bookstores creak beneath the weight of plagues and infestations filling the pages they're forced to support—whether they be the plagues of rats, slugs, crabs, or centipedes that characterize the nastier end of the market or the real thing, as presented in Stephen King's *The Stand*. While radioactive clouds blow west and test-ban treaties go up in a mushroom of poisonous smoke, punk bands gob out splatter-movie imagery with a ferocity that at best signals hopeless defiance and at worst a perverse and nihilistic acceptance of the situation.

Like it or not, horror is part of our media, part of our culture, part of our lives—none of which answers the question of why an entire society should stand around engrossed, reading *Dracula* while up to their jugulars in blood. Do we immerse ourselves in fictional horror as a way of numbing our emotions to its real-life counterpart? Is it some sort of inoculation...a tiny dose of something frightening with which we hope to ward off a more serious attack in later life? Could it even represent a useful, if not vital tool with which we enable ourselves to investigate and understand the origins of horror without exposing ourselves to physical or mental harm? Whatever the answer, the fact still stands: horror fiction of one form or another is a major totem of the twentieth century. We've all seen it. We know what to expect from it, its general content and the rules that it plays by. It is the very familiarity of horror in our culture, however, that makes this introduction necessary: Whatever kind of horror you've chanced across in your various readings and viewing to date, *Swamp Thing* isn't that kind of horror. I'm not saying that it's better, or that it's worse, just that it's different. You'd do well to bear this in mind as you proceed.

The reason for this dissimilarity is that the artifact you currently hold in your hands collects some examples of a rather rarefied strand of *comic book* horror. Comic book horror, spawned from the same roots as any other variety but grown in specific and unusual conditions, has many strange quirks and appendages not shared by other strains within the same genre. The *reasons* for these eccentricities are obscure, complex, and probably not terribly interesting to anyone not utterly infatuated with comics as a medium. If you *really* want to know, there are numerous books and fanzines that I'm sure can provide the answer. For my part, though, I intend to simply describe the effect these differences have wrought upon the comic book horror landscape, while leaving the causes to more capable and academic hands than mine.

The very first thing that anyone reading a modern horror comic should understand is that there are great economic advantages in being able to prop up an ailing, poor-selling comic book with an appearance by a successful guest star. Consequently, all the comic book stories produced by any given publisher are likely to take place in the same imaginary universe. This includes the brightly colored costumed adventurers populating their super-hero titles, the shambling monstrosities that dominate their horror titles, and the odd grizzled cowpoke who's wandered in from a western title through a convenient time warp. For those more familiar with conventional literature, try to imagine Dr. Frankenstein kidnapping one of the protagonists of *Little Women* for his medical experiments, only to find himself subject to the scrutiny of a team-up between Sherlock Holmes and Hercule Poirot. I'm sure that both the charms and the overwhelming absurdities of this approach will become immediately apparent, and so it is in comic books: Swamp Thing exists in the same universe as Superman, the same world as Batman and Wonder Woman and all the other denizens of the cosmos delineated within the pages of DC Comics' various publications.

As I said above, this approach has both its charms and absurdities. The absurdities are obvious: to work properly, horror needs a delicate and carefully sustained atmosphere—one capable of being utterly ruined by the sudden entrance of a man in green tights and an orange cloak, especially if as a character, he's fond of puns. The charms are much harder to find, but once revealed, can actually be rewarding. The continuity-expert's nightmare of a thousand different super-powered characters coexisting in the same continuum can, with the application of a sensitive and sympathetic eye, become a rich and fertile mythic background with fascinating archetypal characters hanging around, waiting to be picked like grapes on the vine. Yes, of course, the whole idea is utterly inane, but to let its predictable inanities blind you to its truly fabulous and breathtaking aspects is to do both oneself and the genre a disservice.

Imagine for a moment a universe jeweled with alien races ranging from the transcendentally divine to the loathsomely Lovecraftian. Imagine a cosmos where the ancient gods still exist somewhere and where whole dimensions are populated by anthropomorphic funny animals. Where Heaven and Hell are demonstrably real and even accessible, and where angels and demons alike seem to walk the earth with impunity. Imagine a planet where exposure to dangerous radiation granted the gift of super-speed rather than bone cancer, and where the skies were thus filled by flying men and women threatening to blot out the sun. Imagine a place where people were terribly good or terribly bad, with little room for the mediocre in between. No, it certainly wouldn't look very much like the world we live in, but that doesn't mean it couldn't be every bit as glorious, touching, sad or scary. With this kind of perspective, the appearance in these pages of the Justice League of America or vintage DC super-villain Jason Woodrue should be less unnerving than it might otherwise have been to the uninitiated.

The other major factor separating comic book horror from its more respectable cousins is *duration*. The stories here don't end—not in the way a movie ends or a book ends. Oh, the current menace may be averted or triumphed over, but there'll be something else along in a month's time, sure as eggs is eggs. The character will continue indefinitely until poor sales or some other factor dictates his comic book's cancellation. Even then, the dispossessed protagonist will probably find himself enough guest slots in other characters' comics to avoid total limbo. The story rarely ends, even when the books carrying it cough blood and drop dead at its feet. Nor, unless you are lucky enough to spot a hit series when it first comes out or rich enough to buy the back issues later, does the story ever begin. Anyone picking up a comic book for the first time is almost certain to find themselves in the middle of a continuum that may have commenced before the reader's birth, and will quite possibly continue long after his or her demise. *Swamp Thing* is no exception to this rule. Created in 1972 by writer Len Wein and artist Berni Wrightson, *Swamp Thing* was originally the story of an idealistic young scientist named Alec Holland and his young wife, Linda, working together on a plant-growth-promoting "bio-restorative" formula out in the Louisiana bayou. The experiment is sabotaged with a bomb, and the blazing, staggering body of Alec Holland, drenched in his own untested compounds, reels out into the swamp and vanishes beneath its murky waters. As is often the way in comic books, this apparently fatal episode turns out to be merely temporary. Before very long, rising from the waters of the swamp, draped in moss and weed, we see the half-humanoid/half-vegetable figure Alec Holland has presumably become. With the murder of his wife, the risen swamp creature embarks upon a series of adventures that take him through the book's first successful run. Traveling to Europe he meets archvillain Anton Arcane, a techno-sorcerer obsessed with cheating death — perhaps by usurping Swamp Thing's invulnerable body. Though Arcane seemed to perish in this first appearance, his innocent and beautiful niece Abigail became a regular member of *Swamp Thing's* supporting cast, and, along with tough private investigator Matthew Cable, the monster's confidant.

After the cancellation of the book's first run, *Swamp Thing* lay dormant for a few years before surfacing again under the new team of writer Marty Pasko and artist Tom Yeates. Picking up where the old stories left off, this new run continued Swamp Thing's forlorn search for some means to retrieve his lost humanity while simultaneously introducing a new cast of supporting characters to play alongside the now married Abby Arcane and Matt Cable. These included a young couple named Liz Tremayne and Dennis

Barclay, and, on the villainry side, a sinister corporation headed by one General Sunderland, his company having strong and suspicious ties to a clandestine government "dirty tricks" agency called the D.D.I.

This new lineup held the stage for the first twenty issues of the new run, climaxing in a rematch with Anton Arcane, now a hideous half-spider thing as his quest for godhood led him deeper into monstrosity. Planning to take control of Swamp Thing's body by some sort of mind transplant, Arcane is thwarted at the last moment and left to fade away and perish as a disincarnate intelligence with no hope of finding a body. Abby and Swamp Thing escape as Arcane's dragonfly-shaped craft crashes into the mountains of West Virginia, but their problems do not end there. For one thing, Abby's husband, Matt, thanks to some D.D.I.-sponsored medical treatment, has developed bizarre mental powers that make his innermost thoughts and fears physically manifest themselves.

Since Matt is battling with a drinking problem at this time, the creatures boiling up live and tangible from his subconscious are both frightening and dangerous. In a private bout of wrestling with his problem, however, Matt learns to control it. Having immense power at his fingertips, his drink-damaged psyche can think of no more deserving a use for his talents than the creation of erotic homunculi who will perform their puppet show entertainments for his eyes only. Abby remains unaware as her husband's tastes slide from the pathetic to the nightmarish, having plenty of other things to occupy her mind, not least being a sudden last-ditch assault by the combined forces of the D.D.I. and the Sunderland corporation, who have finally located Swamp Thing and his friends in West Virginia. Intent upon retrieving the swamp creature's body in the hope of discovering the secret of the bio-restorative formula and also intent upon removing any witnesses, Sunderland carries out a covert military exercise in Virginia during which he believes that he has killed both the Cable couple and Liz and Dennis. In actuality, they have all escaped, fleeing to their various places of safety, unaware of each other's survival.

Swamp Thing is not so fortunate. Surrounded in a thicket by troops with searchlights, flamethrowers, and high-powered rifles, Swamp Thing is driven out of cover and into a hail of withering gunfire that blasts huge holes in his torso before a lucky armor-piercing shot explodes his skull. The great moss-covered body falls, twitches, and lies still. Emerging from hiding, the troops examine it and pronounce it dead, which is the point at which the volume you hold in your hands begins.

Hopefully, with the above information, you should be able to read this saga with as much enjoyment and comprehension as those readers who snapped it up first time around as part of the original continuing series. Commencing with my first attempts to take *Swamp Thing* in a slightly new direction that would characterize the book's subsequent run to date, it represents as sensible a place to start as any. Your punt is about to nose silently out into new backwaters of horror where the trees are heavy with untried fruits that look both beautiful and poisonous. Though unused to the currents here, I hope you don't get lost, and the vivid and toxic delicacies on display are to your tastes.

BOOK ONE

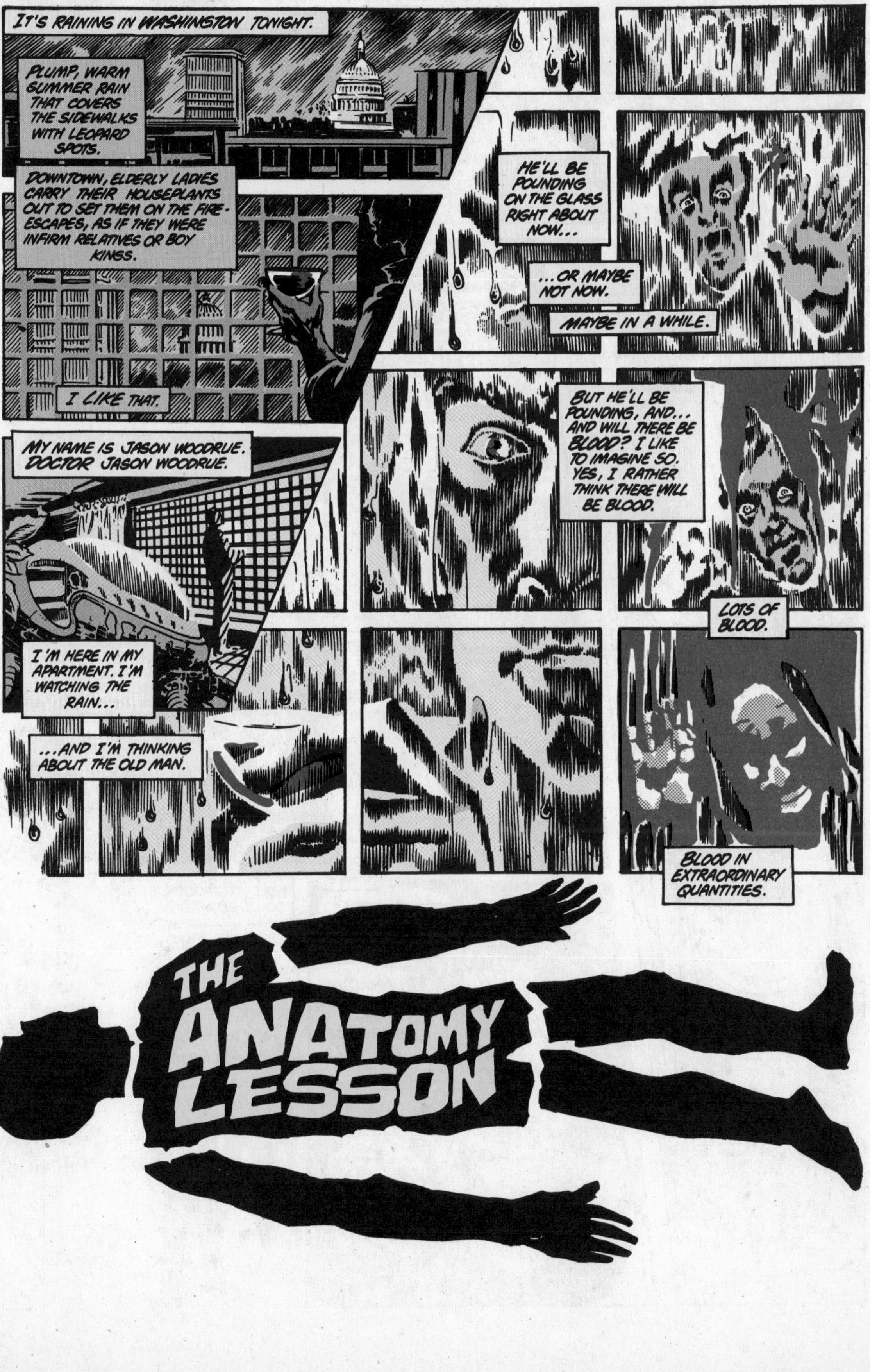
IT'S RAINING IN WASHINGTON TONIGHT.
PLUMP, WARM SUMMER RAIN THAT COVERS THE SIDEWALKS WITH LEOPARD SPOTS.
DOWNTOWN, ELDERLY LADIES CARRY THEIR HOUSEPLANTS OUT TO SET THEM ON THE FIRE-ESCAPES, AS IF THEY WERE INFIRM RELATIVES OR BOY KINGS.
I LIKE THAT.
HE'LL BE POUNDING ON THE GLASS RIGHT ABOUT NOW...
...OR MAYBE NOT NOW.
MAYBE IN A WHILE.
MY NAME IS JASON WOODRUE. DOCTOR JASON WOODRUE.
I'M HERE IN MY APARTMENT. I'M WATCHING THE RAIN...
...AND I'M THINKING ABOUT THE OLD MAN.
BUT HE'LL BE POUNDING, AND... AND WILL THERE BE BLOOD? I LIKE TO IMAGINE SO. YES, I RATHER THINK THERE WILL BE BLOOD.
LOTS OF BLOOD.
BLOOD IN EXTRAORDINARY QUANTITIES.
THE ANATOMY LESSON

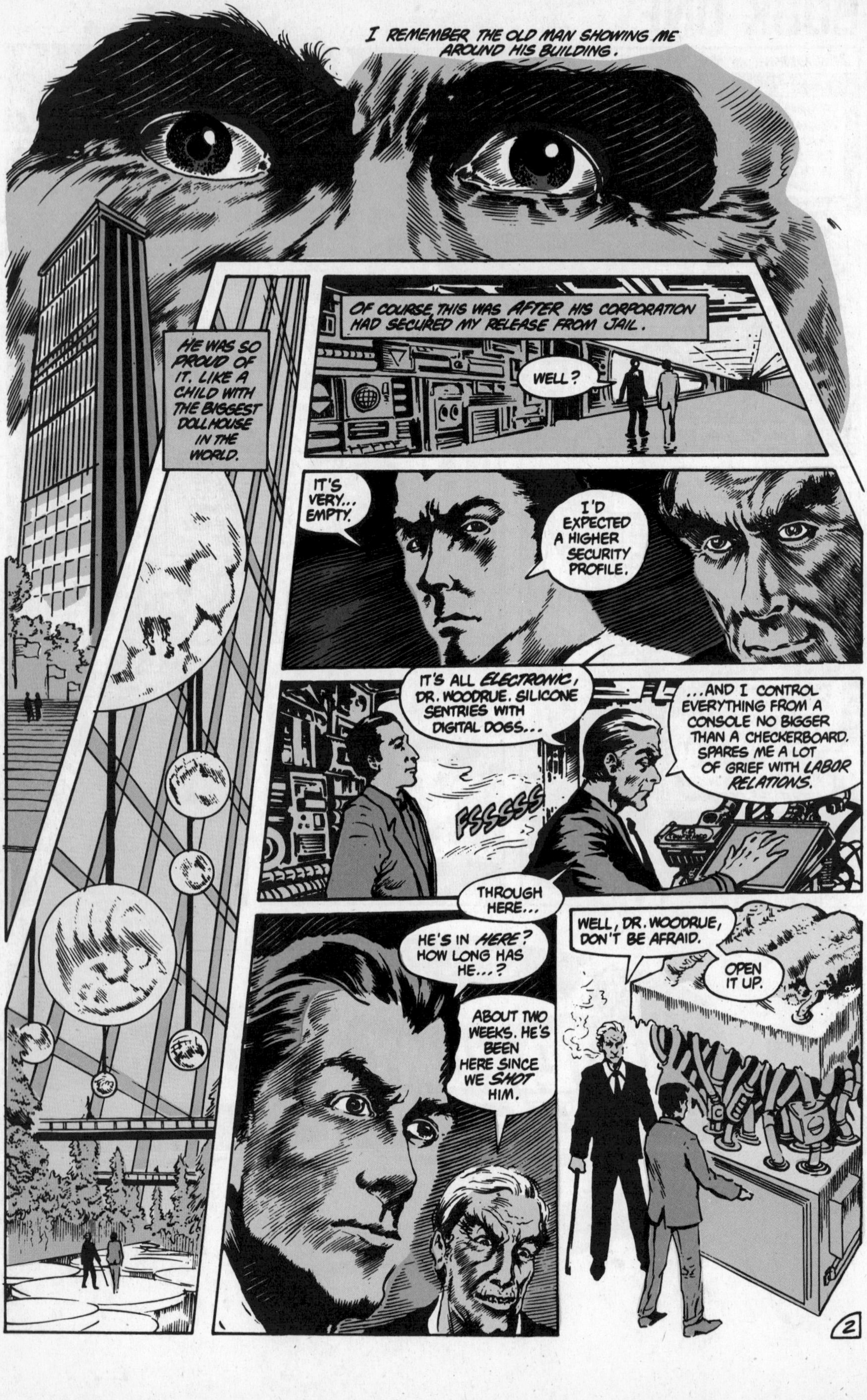
I REMEMBER THE OLD MAN SHOWING ME AROUND HIS BUILDING.
HE WAS SO PROUD OF IT. LIKE A CHILD WITH THE BIGGEST DOLLHOUSE IN THE WORLD.
OF COURSE, THIS WAS AFTER HIS CORPORATION HAD SECURED MY RELEASE FROM JAIL.
WELL?
IT'S VERY... EMPTY.
I'D EXPECTED A HIGHER SECURITY PROFILE.
IT'S ALL ELECTRONIC, DR. WOODRUE. SILICONE SENTRIES WITH DIGITAL DOGS...
...AND I CONTROL EVERYTHING FROM A CONSOLE NO BIGGER THAN A CHECKERBOARD. SPARES ME A LOT OF GRIEF WITH LABOR RELATIONS.
FSSSSS
THROUGH HERE...
HE'S IN HERE? HOW LONG HAS HE...?
ABOUT TWO WEEKS. HE'S BEEN HERE SINCE WE SHOT HIM.
WELL, DR. WOODRUE, DON'T BE AFRAID.
OPEN IT UP.
2

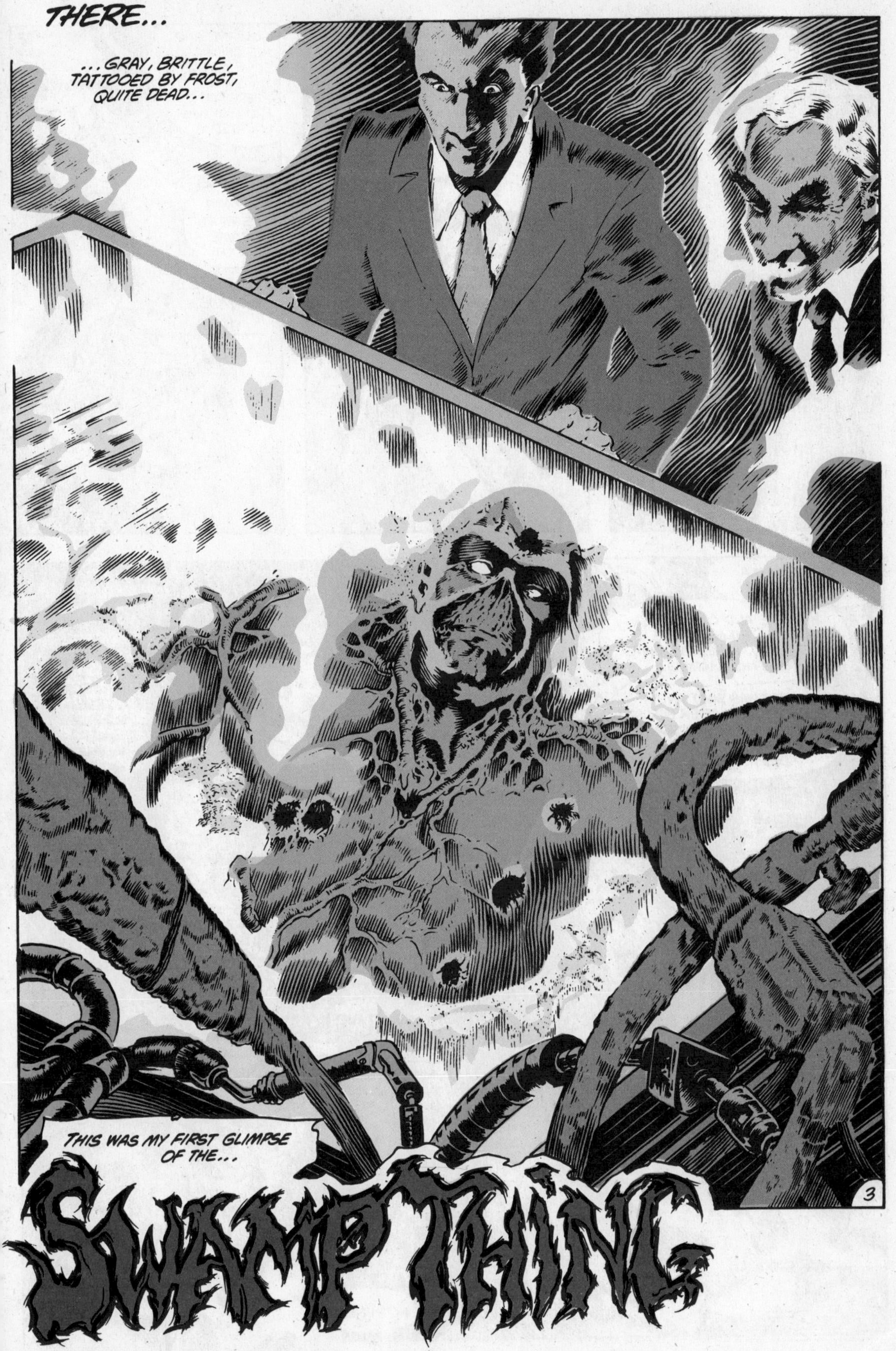
THERE...
...GRAY, BRITTLE, TATTOOED BY FROST, QUITE DEAD...
THIS WAS MY FIRST GLIMPSE OF THE...
SWAMP THING
3

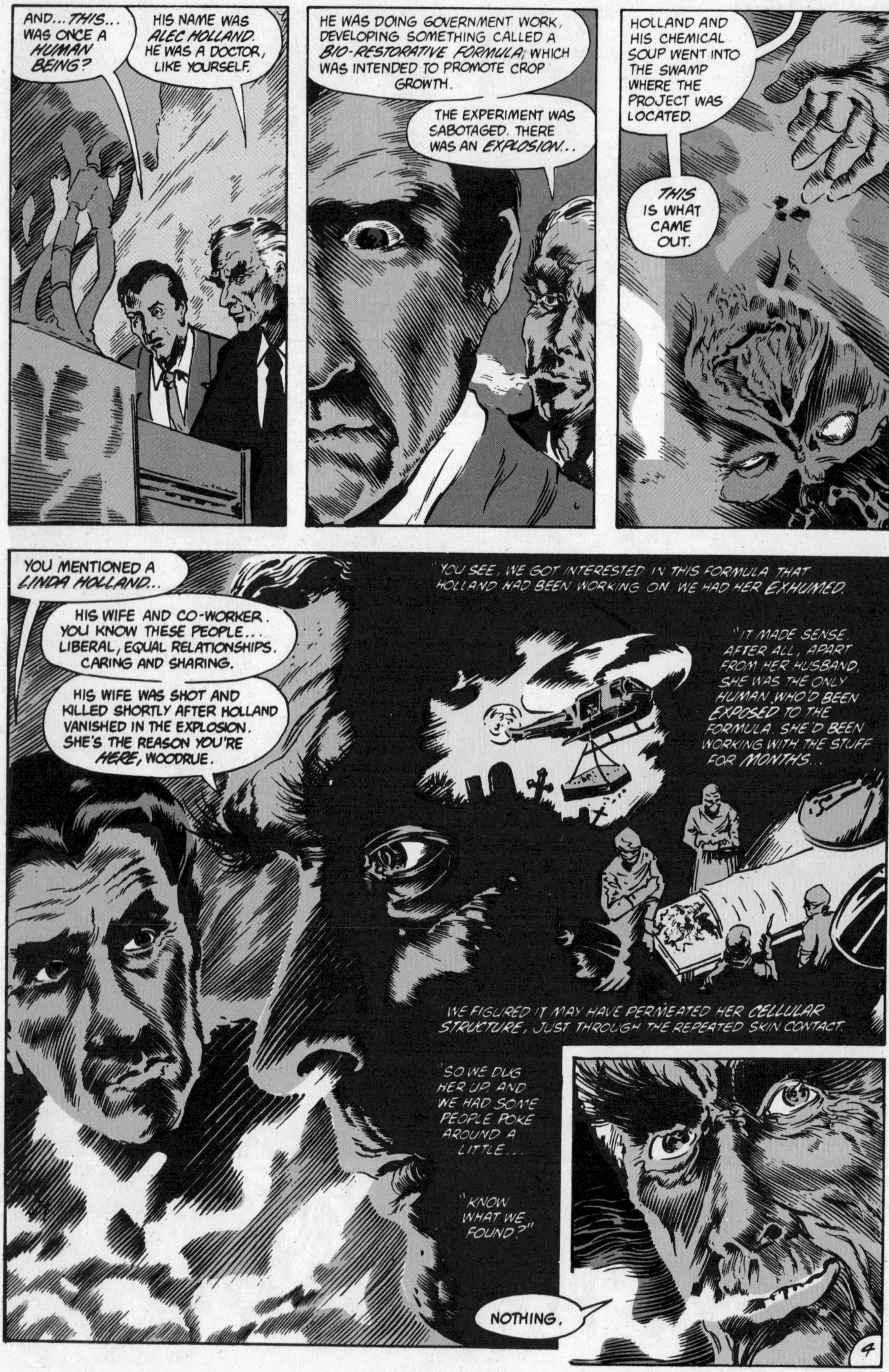
AND... THIS... WAS ONCE A HUMAN BEING?
HIS NAME WAS ALEC HOLLAND. HE WAS A DOCTOR, LIKE YOURSELF.
HE WAS DOING GOVERNMENT WORK, DEVELOPING SOMETHING CALLED A BIO-RESTORATIVE FORMULA, WHICH WAS INTENDED TO PROMOTE CROP GROWTH.
THE EXPERIMENT WAS SABOTAGED. THERE WAS AN EXPLOSION...
HOLLAND AND HIS CHEMICAL SOUP WENT INTO THE SWAMP WHERE THE PROJECT WAS LOCATED.
THIS IS WHAT CAME OUT.
YOU MENTIONED A LINDA HOLLAND...
HIS WIFE AND CO-WORKER. YOU KNOW THESE PEOPLE... LIBERAL, EQUAL RELATIONSHIPS. CARING AND SHARING.
HIS WIFE WAS SHOT AND KILLED SHORTLY AFTER HOLLAND VANISHED IN THE EXPLOSION. SHE'S THE REASON YOU'RE HERE, WOODRUE.
"YOU SEE, WE GOT INTERESTED IN THIS FORMULA THAT HOLLAND HAD BEEN WORKING ON. WE HAD HER EXHUMED.
"IT MADE SENSE. AFTER ALL, APART FROM HER HUSBAND, SHE WAS THE ONLY HUMAN WHO'D BEEN EXPOSED TO THE FORMULA. SHE'D BEEN WORKING WITH THE STUFF FOR MONTHS...
WE FIGURED IT MAY HAVE PERMEATED HER CELLULAR STRUCTURE, JUST THROUGH THE REPEATED SKIN CONTACT.
"SO WE DUG HER UP AND WE HAD SOME PEOPLE POKE AROUND A LITTLE...
"KNOW WHAT WE FOUND?"
NOTHING.
4

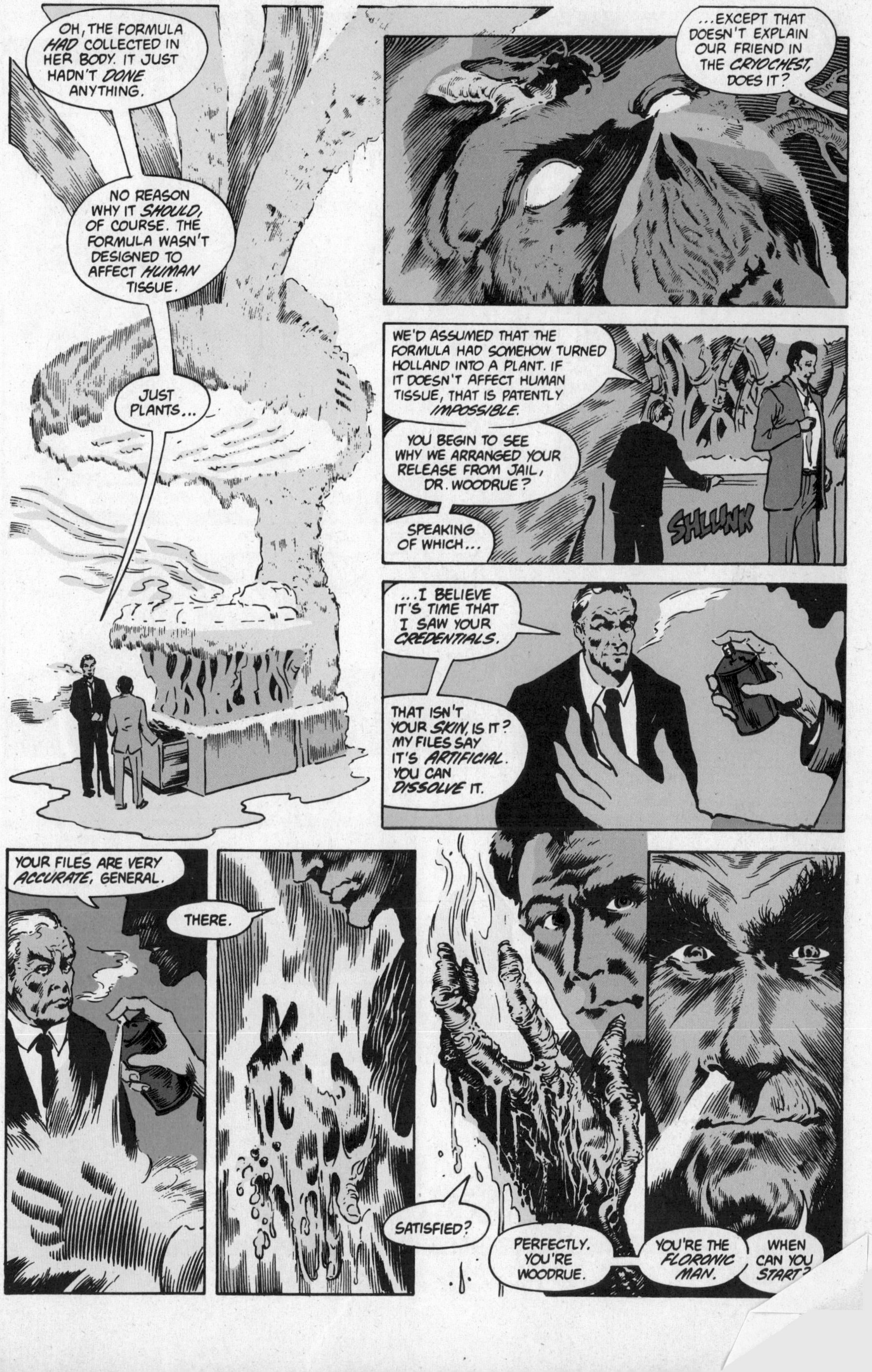
OH, THE FORMULA HAD COLLECTED IN HER BODY. IT JUST HADN'T DONE ANYTHING.
NO REASON WHY IT SHOULD, OF COURSE. THE FORMULA WASN'T DESIGNED TO AFFECT HUMAN TISSUE.
JUST PLANTS...
...EXCEPT THAT DOESN'T EXPLAIN OUR FRIEND IN THE CRYOCHEST, DOES IT?
WE'D ASSUMED THAT THE FORMULA HAD SOMEHOW TURNED HOLLAND INTO A PLANT. IF IT DOESN'T AFFECT HUMAN TISSUE, THAT IS PATENTLY IMPOSSIBLE.
YOU BEGIN TO SEE WHY WE ARRANGED YOUR RELEASE FROM JAIL, DR. WOODRUE?
SPEAKING OF WHICH...
SHLUNK
...I BELIEVE IT'S TIME THAT I SAW YOUR CREDENTIALS.
THAT ISN'T YOUR SKIN, IS IT? MY FILES SAY IT'S ARTIFICIAL. YOU CAN DISSOLVE IT.
YOUR FILES ARE VERY ACCURATE, GENERAL.
THERE.
SATISFIED?
PERFECTLY. YOU'RE WOODRUE.
YOU'RE THE FLORONIC MAN.
WHEN CAN YOU START?

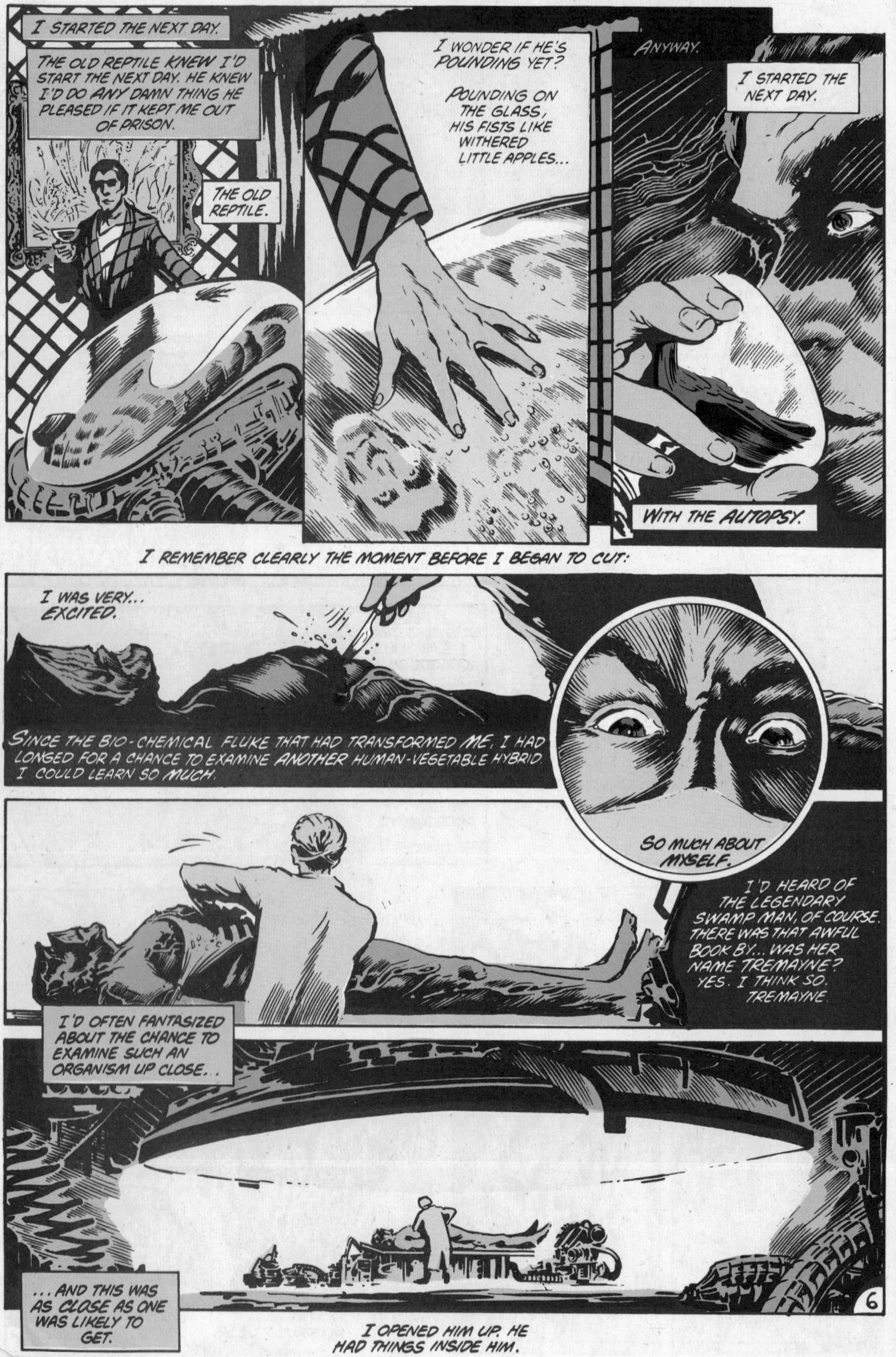
I STARTED THE NEXT DAY.
THE OLD REPTILE KNEW I'D START THE NEXT DAY. HE KNEW I'D DO ANY DAMN THING HE PLEASED IF IT KEPT ME OUT OF PRISON.
THE OLD REPTILE.
I WONDER IF HE'S POUNDING YET?
POUNDING ON THE GLASS, HIS FISTS LIKE WITHERED LITTLE APPLES...
ANYWAY.
I STARTED THE NEXT DAY.
WITH THE AUTOPSY.
I REMEMBER CLEARLY THE MOMENT BEFORE I BEGAN TO CUT:
I WAS VERY... EXCITED.
SINCE THE BIO-CHEMICAL FLUKE THAT HAD TRANSFORMED ME, I HAD LONGED FOR A CHANCE TO EXAMINE ANOTHER HUMAN-VEGETABLE HYBRID. I COULD LEARN SO MUCH.
SO MUCH ABOUT MYSELF.
I'D HEARD OF THE LEGENDARY SWAMP MAN, OF COURSE. THERE WAS THAT AWFUL BOOK BY... WAS HER NAME TREMAYNE? YES. I THINK SO. TREMAYNE.
I'D OFTEN FANTASIZED ABOUT THE CHANCE TO EXAMINE SUCH AN ORGANISM UP CLOSE...
...AND THIS WAS AS CLOSE AS ONE WAS LIKELY TO GET.
6
I OPENED HIM UP. HE HAD THINGS INSIDE HIM.

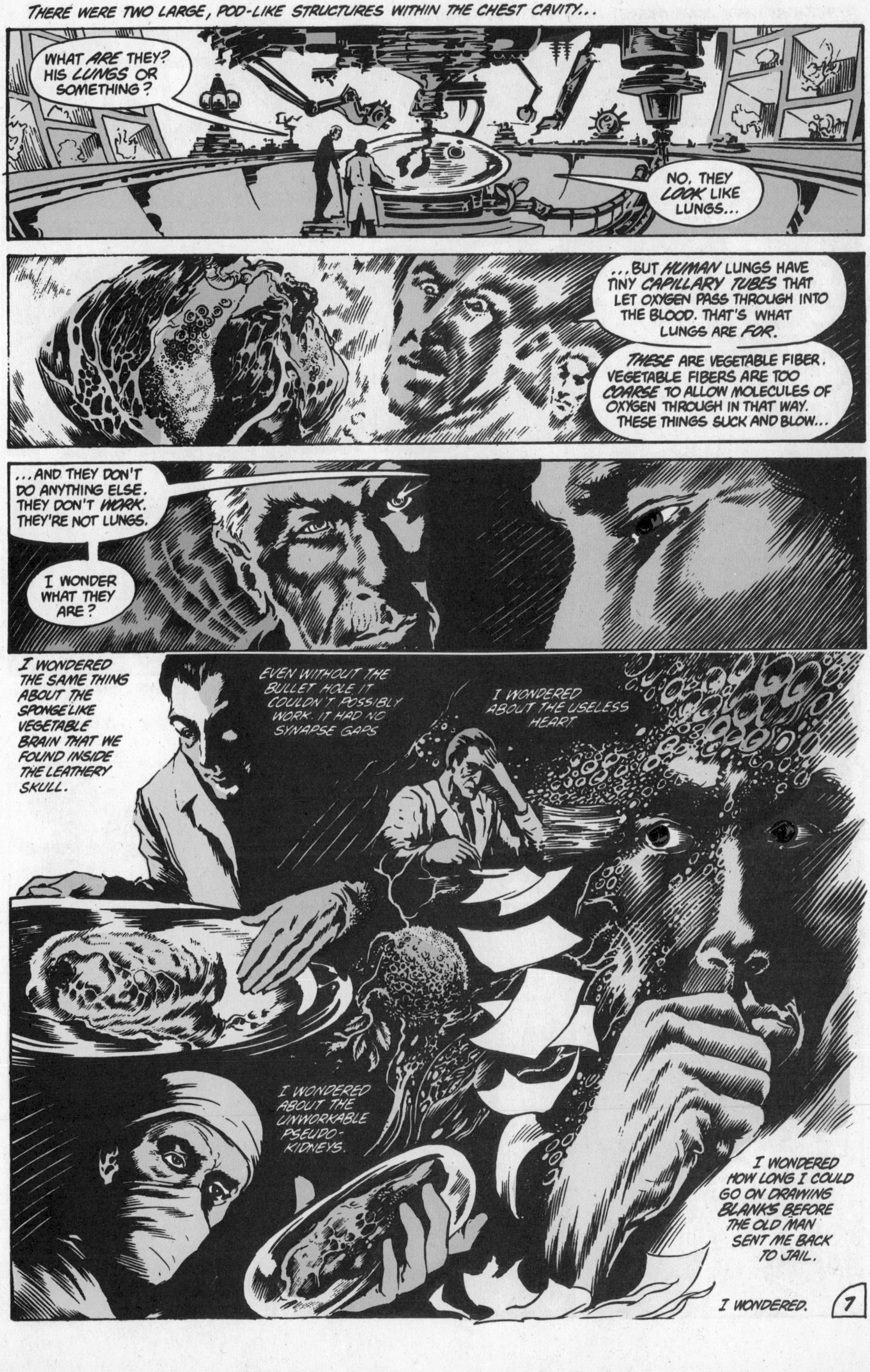
THERE WERE TWO LARGE, POD-LIKE STRUCTURES WITHIN THE CHEST CAVITY...
WHAT ARE THEY? HIS LUNGS OR SOMETHING?
NO, THEY LOOK LIKE LUNGS...
...BUT HUMAN LUNGS HAVE TINY CAPILLARY TUBES THAT LET OXYGEN PASS THROUGH INTO THE BLOOD. THAT'S WHAT LUNGS ARE FOR.
THESE ARE VEGETABLE FIBER. VEGETABLE FIBERS ARE TOO COARSE TO ALLOW MOLECULES OF OXYGEN THROUGH IN THAT WAY. THESE THINGS SUCK AND BLOW...
...AND THEY DON'T DO ANYTHING ELSE. THEY DON'T WORK. THEY'RE NOT LUNGS.
I WONDER WHAT THEY ARE?
I WONDERED THE SAME THING ABOUT THE SPONGE-LIKE VEGETABLE BRAIN THAT WE FOUND INSIDE THE LEATHERY SKULL.
EVEN WITHOUT THE BULLET HOLE IT COULDN'T POSSIBLY WORK. IT HAD NO SYNAPSE GAPS.
I WONDERED ABOUT THE USELESS HEART.
I WONDERED ABOUT THE UNWORKABLE PSEUDO-KIDNEYS.
I WONDERED HOW LONG I COULD GO ON DRAWING BLANKS BEFORE THE OLD MAN SENT ME BACK TO JAIL.
I WONDERED.
7

THOSE WERE LONG WEEKS. LONG AND FRUITLESS.

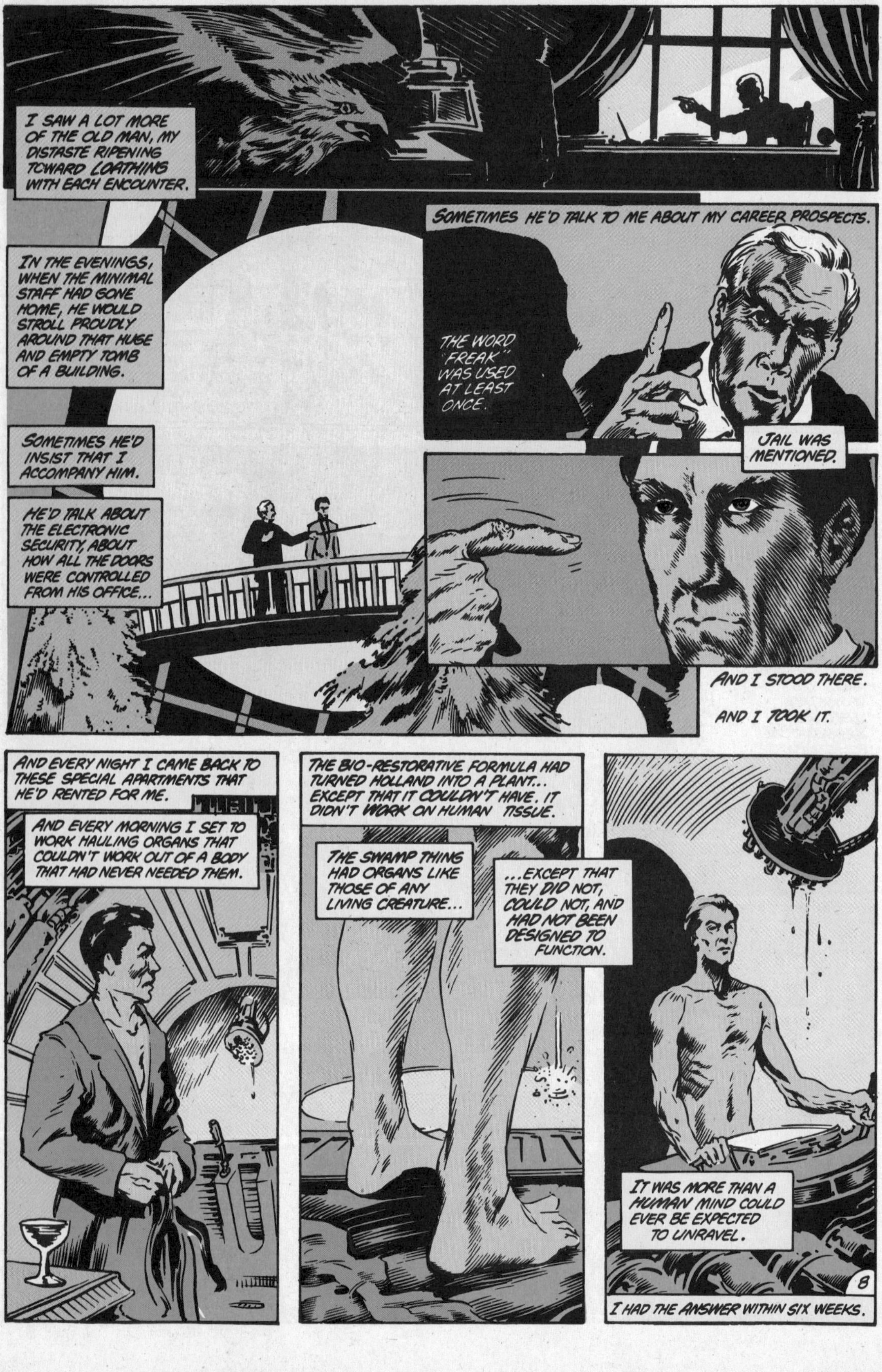
I SAW A LOT MORE OF THE OLD MAN, MY DISTASTE RIPENING TOWARD LOATHING WITH EACH ENCOUNTER.
IN THE EVENINGS, WHEN THE MINIMAL STAFF HAD GONE HOME, HE WOULD STROLL PROUDLY AROUND THAT HUGE AND EMPTY TOMB OF A BUILDING.
SOMETIMES HE'D INSIST THAT I ACCOMPANY HIM.
HE'D TALK ABOUT THE ELECTRONIC SECURITY, ABOUT HOW ALL THE DOORS WERE CONTROLLED FROM HIS OFFICE...
SOMETIMES HE'D TALK TO ME ABOUT MY CAREER PROSPECTS.
THE WORD "FREAK" WAS USED AT LEAST ONCE.
JAIL WAS MENTIONED.
AND I STOOD THERE.
AND I TOOK IT.
AND EVERY NIGHT I CAME BACK TO THESE SPECIAL APARTMENTS THAT HE'D RENTED FOR ME.
AND EVERY MORNING I SET TO WORK HAULING ORGANS THAT COULDN'T WORK OUT OF A BODY THAT HAD NEVER NEEDED THEM.
THE BIO-RESTORATIVE FORMULA HAD TURNED HOLLAND INTO A PLANT... EXCEPT THAT IT COULDN'T HAVE. IT DIDN'T WORK ON HUMAN TISSUE.
THE SWAMP THING HAD ORGANS LIKE THOSE OF ANY LIVING CREATURE...
...EXCEPT THAT THEY DID NOT, COULD NOT, AND HAD NOT BEEN DESIGNED TO FUNCTION.
IT WAS MORE THAN A HUMAN MIND COULD EVER BE EXPECTED TO UNRAVEL.
8
I HAD THE ANSWER WITHIN SIX WEEKS.

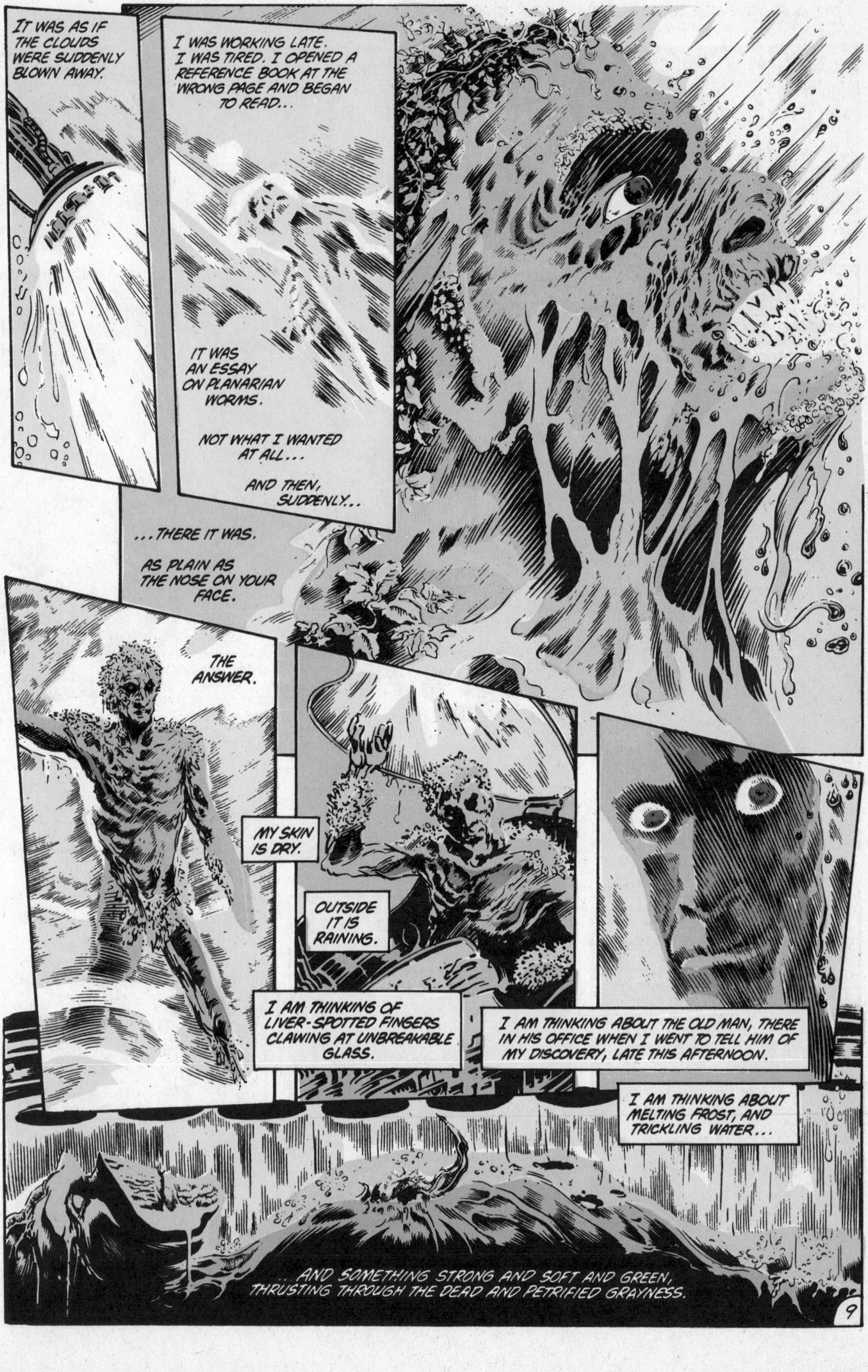
IT WAS AS IF THE CLOUDS WERE SUDDENLY BLOWN AWAY.
I WAS WORKING LATE. I WAS TIRED. I OPENED A REFERENCE BOOK AT THE WRONG PAGE AND BEGAN TO READ...
IT WAS AN ESSAY ON PLANARIAN WORMS.
NOT WHAT I WANTED AT ALL...
AND THEN, SUDDENLY...
...THERE IT WAS.
AS PLAIN AS THE NOSE ON YOUR FACE.
THE ANSWER.
MY SKIN IS DRY.
OUTSIDE IT IS RAINING.
I AM THINKING OF LIVER-SPOTTED FINGERS CLAWING AT UNBREAKABLE GLASS.
I AM THINKING ABOUT THE OLD MAN, THERE IN HIS OFFICE WHEN I WENT TO TELL HIM OF MY DISCOVERY, LATE THIS AFTERNOON.
I AM THINKING ABOUT MELTING FROST, AND TRICKLING WATER...
...AND SOMETHING STRONG AND SOFT AND GREEN, THRUSTING THROUGH THE DEAD AND PETRIFIED GRAYNESS.
9

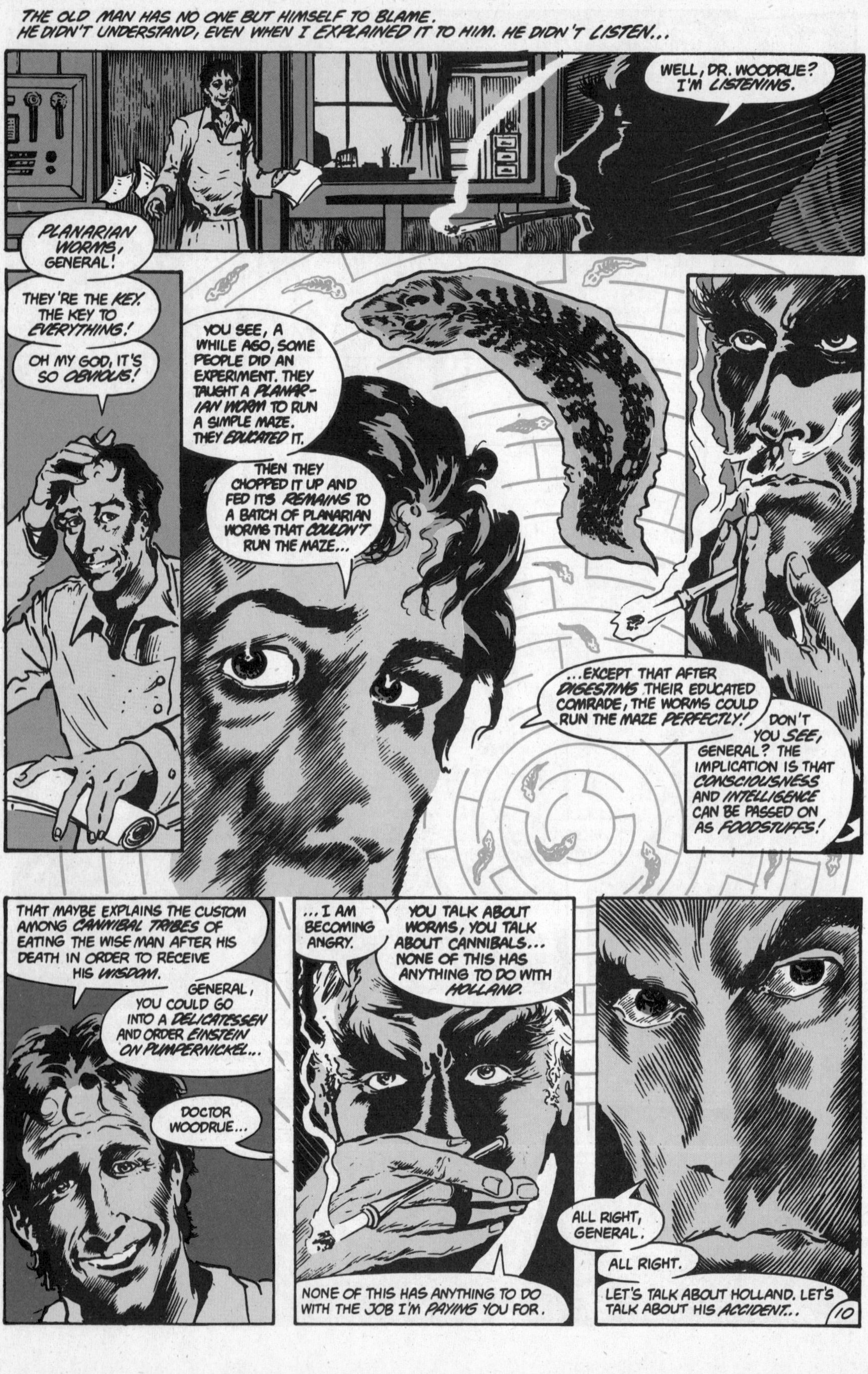
THE OLD MAN HAS NO ONE BUT HIMSELF TO BLAME.
HE DIDN'T UNDERSTAND, EVEN WHEN I EXPLAINED IT TO HIM. HE DIDN'T LISTEN...
WELL, DR. WOODRUE? I'M LISTENING.
PLANARIAN WORMS, GENERAL!
THEY'RE THE KEY. THE KEY TO EVERYTHING!
OH MY GOD, IT'S SO OBVIOUS!
YOU SEE, A WHILE AGO, SOME PEOPLE DID AN EXPERIMENT. THEY TAUGHT A PLANARIAN WORM TO RUN A SIMPLE MAZE. THEY EDUCATED IT.
THEN THEY CHOPPED IT UP AND FED ITS REMAINS TO A BATCH OF PLANARIAN WORMS THAT COULDN'T RUN THE MAZE...
...EXCEPT THAT AFTER DIGESTING THEIR EDUCATED COMRADE, THE WORMS COULD RUN THE MAZE PERFECTLY!
DON'T YOU SEE, GENERAL? THE IMPLICATION IS THAT CONSCIOUSNESS AND INTELLIGENCE CAN BE PASSED ON AS FOODSTUFFS!
THAT MAYBE EXPLAINS THE CUSTOM AMONG CANNIBAL TRIBES OF EATING THE WISE MAN AFTER HIS DEATH IN ORDER TO RECEIVE HIS WISDOM.
GENERAL, YOU COULD GO INTO A DELICATESSEN AND ORDER EINSTEIN ON PUMPERNICKEL...
DOCTOR WOODRUE...
...I AM BECOMING ANGRY.
YOU TALK ABOUT WORMS, YOU TALK ABOUT CANNIBALS... NONE OF THIS HAS ANYTHING TO DO WITH HOLLAND.
NONE OF THIS HAS ANYTHING TO DO WITH THE JOB I'M PAYING YOU FOR.
ALL RIGHT, GENERAL.
ALL RIGHT.
LET'S TALK ABOUT HOLLAND. LET'S TALK ABOUT HIS ACCIDENT...
10

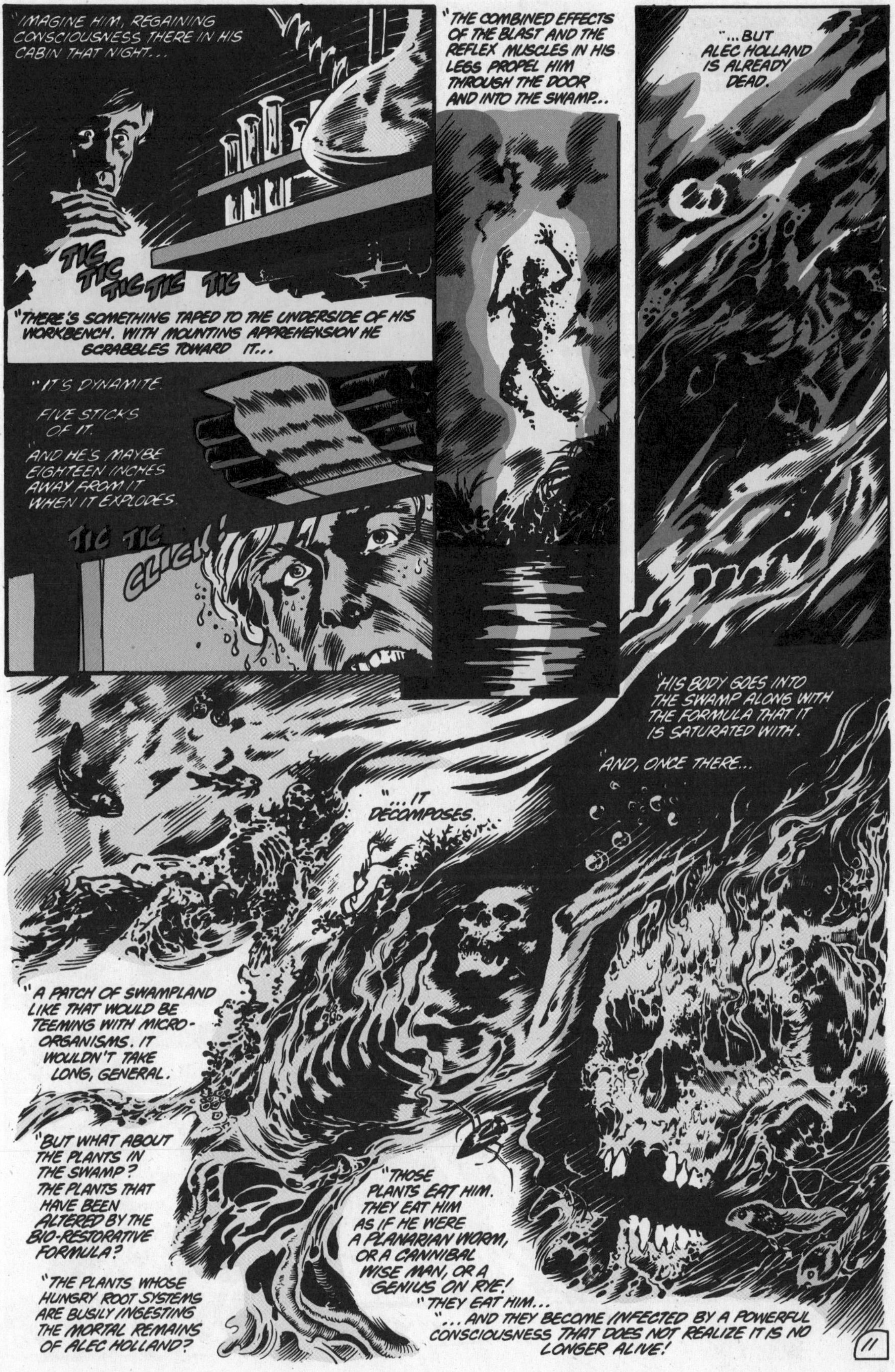
"IMAGINE HIM, REGAINING CONSCIOUSNESS THERE IN HIS CABIN THAT NIGHT...
TIC TIC TIC TIC TIC
"THERE'S SOMETHING TAPED TO THE UNDERSIDE OF HIS WORKBENCH. WITH MOUNTING APPREHENSION HE SCRABBLES TOWARD IT...
"IT'S DYNAMITE.
FIVE STICKS OF IT.
"AND HE'S MAYBE EIGHTEEN INCHES AWAY FROM IT WHEN IT EXPLODES.
TIC TIC
CLICK!
"THE COMBINED EFFECTS OF THE BLAST AND THE REFLEX MUSCLES IN HIS LEGS PROPEL HIM THROUGH THE DOOR AND INTO THE SWAMP...
"...BUT ALEC HOLLAND IS ALREADY DEAD.
"HIS BODY GOES INTO THE SWAMP ALONG WITH THE FORMULA THAT IT IS SATURATED WITH.
"AND, ONCE THERE...
"...IT DECOMPOSES.
"A PATCH OF SWAMPLAND LIKE THAT WOULD BE TEEMING WITH MICRO-ORGANISMS. IT WOULDN'T TAKE LONG, GENERAL.
"BUT WHAT ABOUT THE PLANTS IN THE SWAMP? THE PLANTS THAT HAVE BEEN ALTERED BY THE BIO-RESTORATIVE FORMULA?
"THE PLANTS WHOSE HUNGRY ROOT SYSTEMS ARE BUSILY INGESTING THE MORTAL REMAINS OF ALEC HOLLAND?
"THOSE PLANTS EAT HIM. THEY EAT HIM AS IF HE WERE A PLANARIAN WORM, OR A CANNIBAL WISE MAN, OR A GENIUS ON RYE!
"THEY EAT HIM...
"...AND THEY BECOME INFECTED BY A POWERFUL CONSCIOUSNESS THAT DOES NOT REALIZE IT IS NO LONGER ALIVE!
11

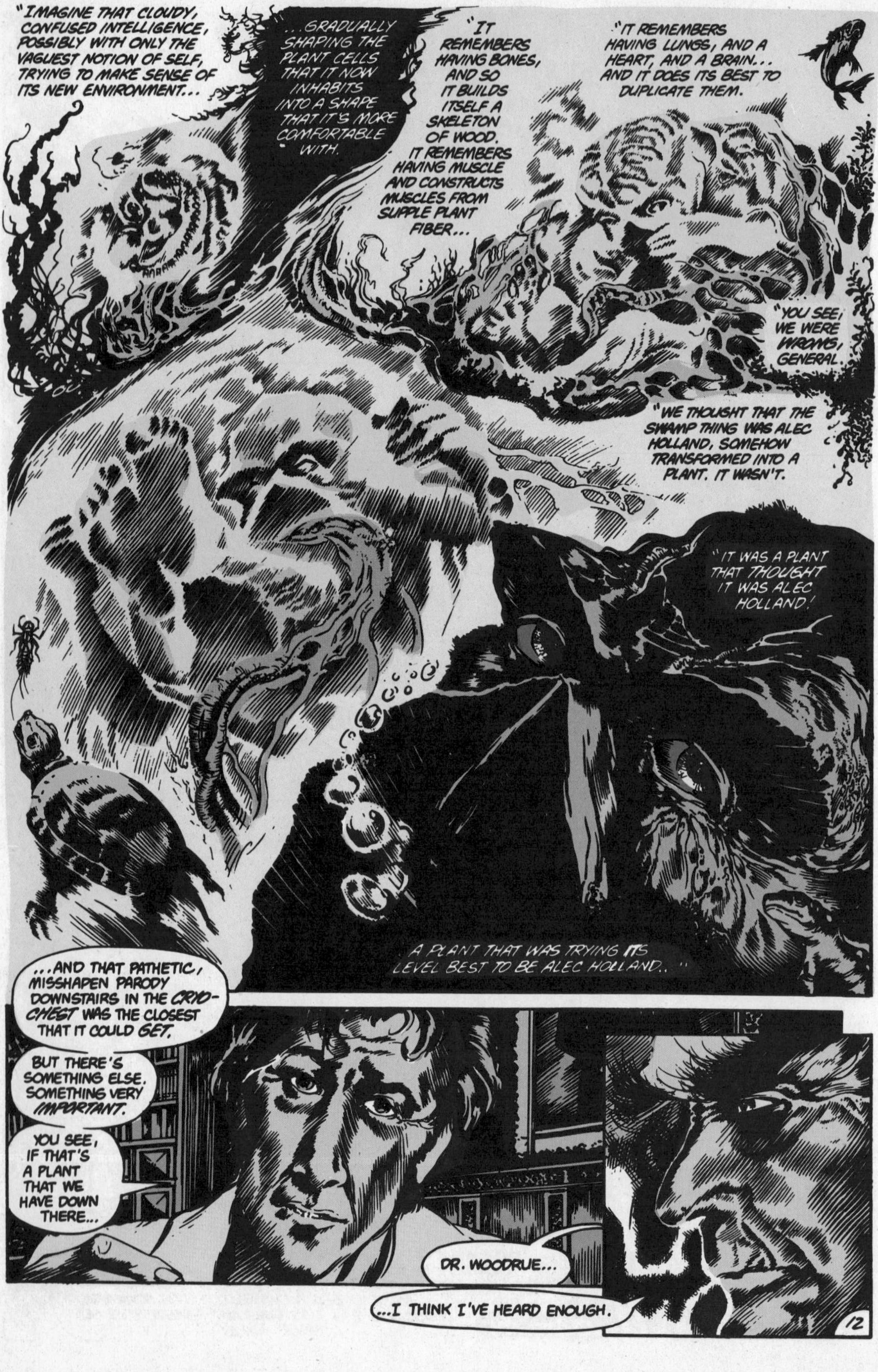
"IMAGINE THAT CLOUDY, CONFUSED INTELLIGENCE, POSSIBLY WITH ONLY THE VAGUEST NOTION OF SELF, TRYING TO MAKE SENSE OF ITS NEW ENVIRONMENT...
...GRADUALLY SHAPING THE PLANT CELLS THAT IT NOW INHABITS INTO A SHAPE THAT IT'S MORE COMFORTABLE WITH.
"IT REMEMBERS HAVING BONES, AND SO IT BUILDS ITSELF A SKELETON OF WOOD. IT REMEMBERS HAVING MUSCLE AND CONSTRUCTS MUSCLES FROM SUPPLE PLANT FIBER...
"IT REMEMBERS HAVING LUNGS, AND A HEART, AND A BRAIN... AND IT DOES ITS BEST TO DUPLICATE THEM.
"YOU SEE, WE WERE WRONG, GENERAL.
"WE THOUGHT THAT THE SWAMP THING WAS ALEC HOLLAND, SOMEHOW TRANSFORMED INTO A PLANT. IT WASN'T.
"IT WAS A PLANT THAT THOUGHT IT WAS ALEC HOLLAND!
A PLANT THAT WAS TRYING ITS LEVEL BEST TO BE ALEC HOLLAND.."
...AND THAT PATHETIC, MISSHAPEN PARODY DOWNSTAIRS IN THE CRYO-CHEST WAS THE CLOSEST THAT IT COULD GET.
BUT THERE'S SOMETHING ELSE. SOMETHING VERY IMPORTANT.
YOU SEE, IF THAT'S A PLANT THAT WE HAVE DOWN THERE...
DR. WOODRUE...
...I THINK I'VE HEARD ENOUGH.
12

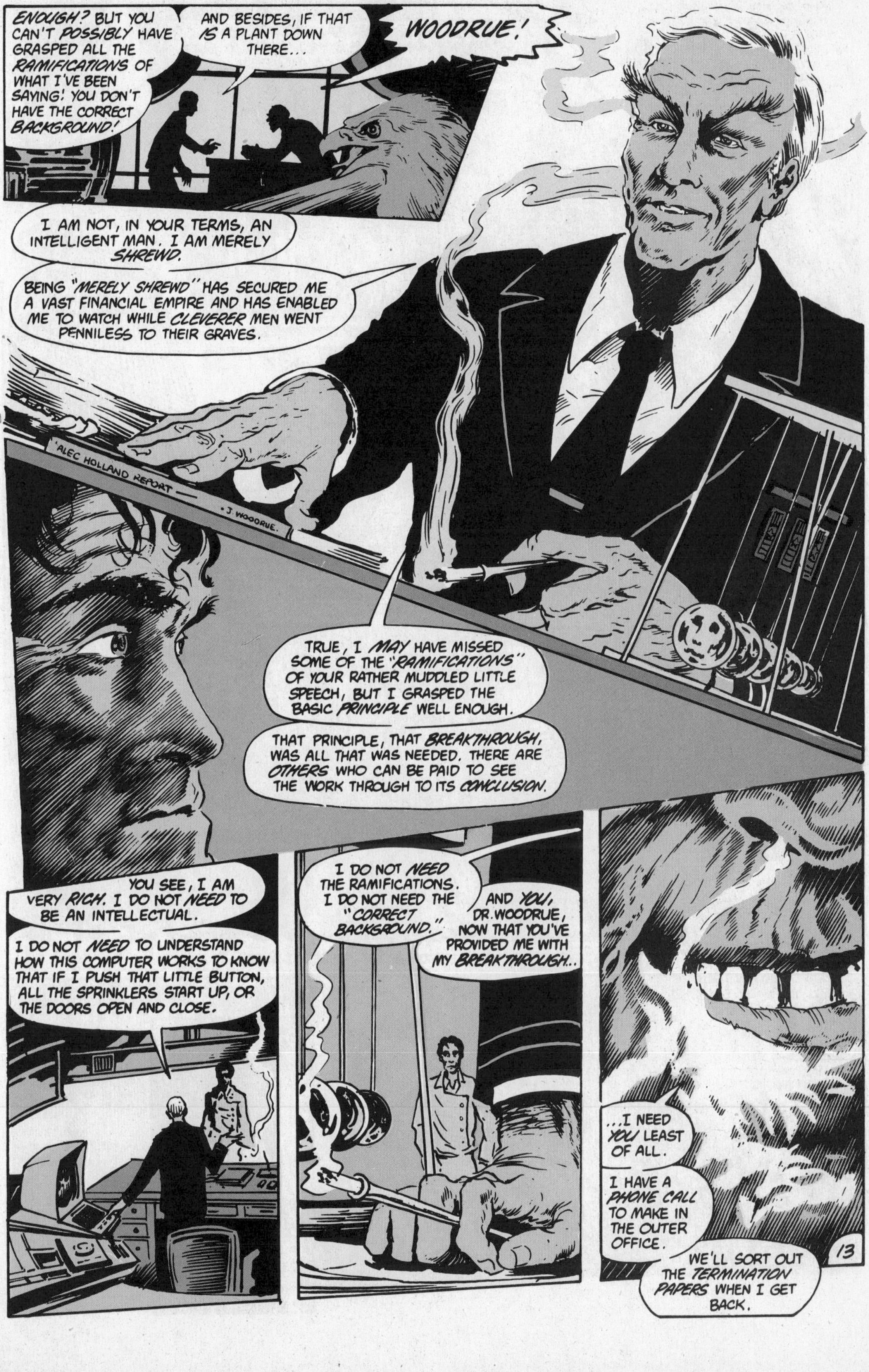
ENOUGH? BUT YOU CAN'T POSSIBLY HAVE GRASPED ALL THE RAMIFICATIONS OF WHAT I'VE BEEN SAYING! YOU DON'T HAVE THE CORRECT BACKGROUND!
AND BESIDES, IF THAT IS A PLANT DOWN THERE...
WOODRUE!
I AM NOT, IN YOUR TERMS, AN INTELLIGENT MAN. I AM MERELY SHREWD.
BEING "MERELY SHREWD" HAS SECURED ME A VAST FINANCIAL EMPIRE AND HAS ENABLED ME TO WATCH WHILE CLEVERER MEN WENT PENNILESS TO THEIR GRAVES.
ALEC HOLLAND REPORT — J. WOODRUE.
TRUE, I MAY HAVE MISSED SOME OF THE "RAMIFICATIONS" OF YOUR RATHER MUDDLED LITTLE SPEECH, BUT I GRASPED THE BASIC PRINCIPLE WELL ENOUGH.
THAT PRINCIPLE, THAT BREAKTHROUGH, WAS ALL THAT WAS NEEDED. THERE ARE OTHERS WHO CAN BE PAID TO SEE THE WORK THROUGH TO ITS CONCLUSION.
YOU SEE, I AM VERY RICH. I DO NOT NEED TO BE AN INTELLECTUAL.
I DO NOT NEED TO UNDERSTAND HOW THIS COMPUTER WORKS TO KNOW THAT IF I PUSH THAT LITTLE BUTTON, ALL THE SPRINKLERS START UP, OR THE DOORS OPEN AND CLOSE.
I DO NOT NEED THE RAMIFICATIONS. I DO NOT NEED THE "CORRECT BACKGROUND."
AND YOU, DR. WOODRUE, NOW THAT YOU'VE PROVIDED ME WITH MY BREAKTHROUGH...
...I NEED YOU LEAST OF ALL.
I HAVE A PHONE CALL TO MAKE IN THE OUTER OFFICE.
WE'LL SORT OUT THE TERMINATION PAPERS WHEN I GET BACK.
13

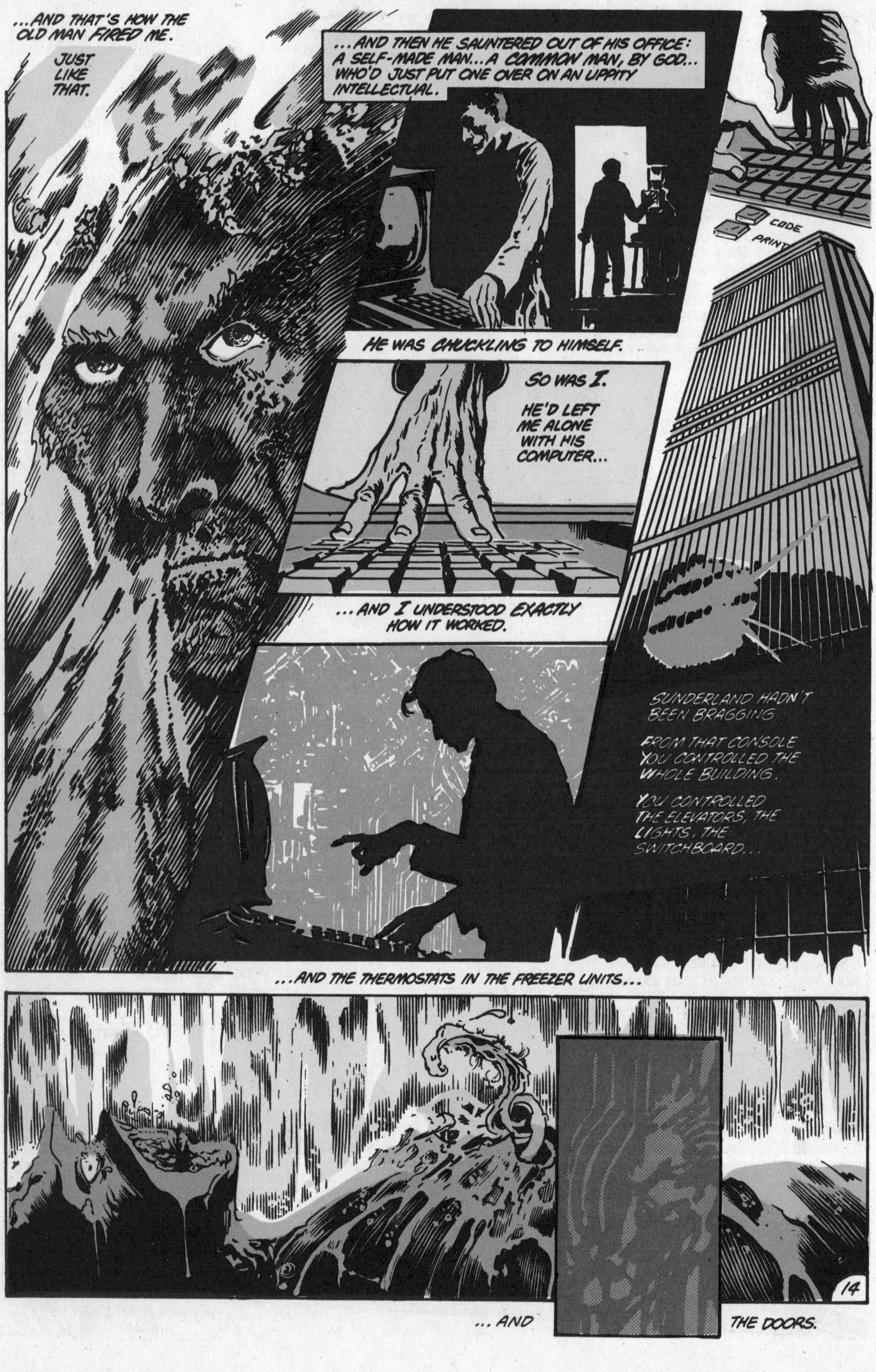
...AND THAT'S HOW THE OLD MAN FIRED ME.
JUST LIKE THAT.
...AND THEN HE SAUNTERED OUT OF HIS OFFICE: A SELF-MADE MAN... A COMMON MAN, BY GOD... WHO'D JUST PUT ONE OVER ON AN UPPITY INTELLECTUAL.
CODE
PRINT
HE WAS CHUCKLING TO HIMSELF.
SO WAS I.
HE'D LEFT ME ALONE WITH HIS COMPUTER...
...AND I UNDERSTOOD EXACTLY HOW IT WORKED.
SUNDERLAND HADN'T BEEN BRAGGING.
FROM THAT CONSOLE YOU CONTROLLED THE WHOLE BUILDING.
YOU CONTROLLED THE ELEVATORS, THE LIGHTS, THE SWITCHBOARD...
...AND THE THERMOSTATS IN THE FREEZER UNITS...
14
...AND
THE DOORS.

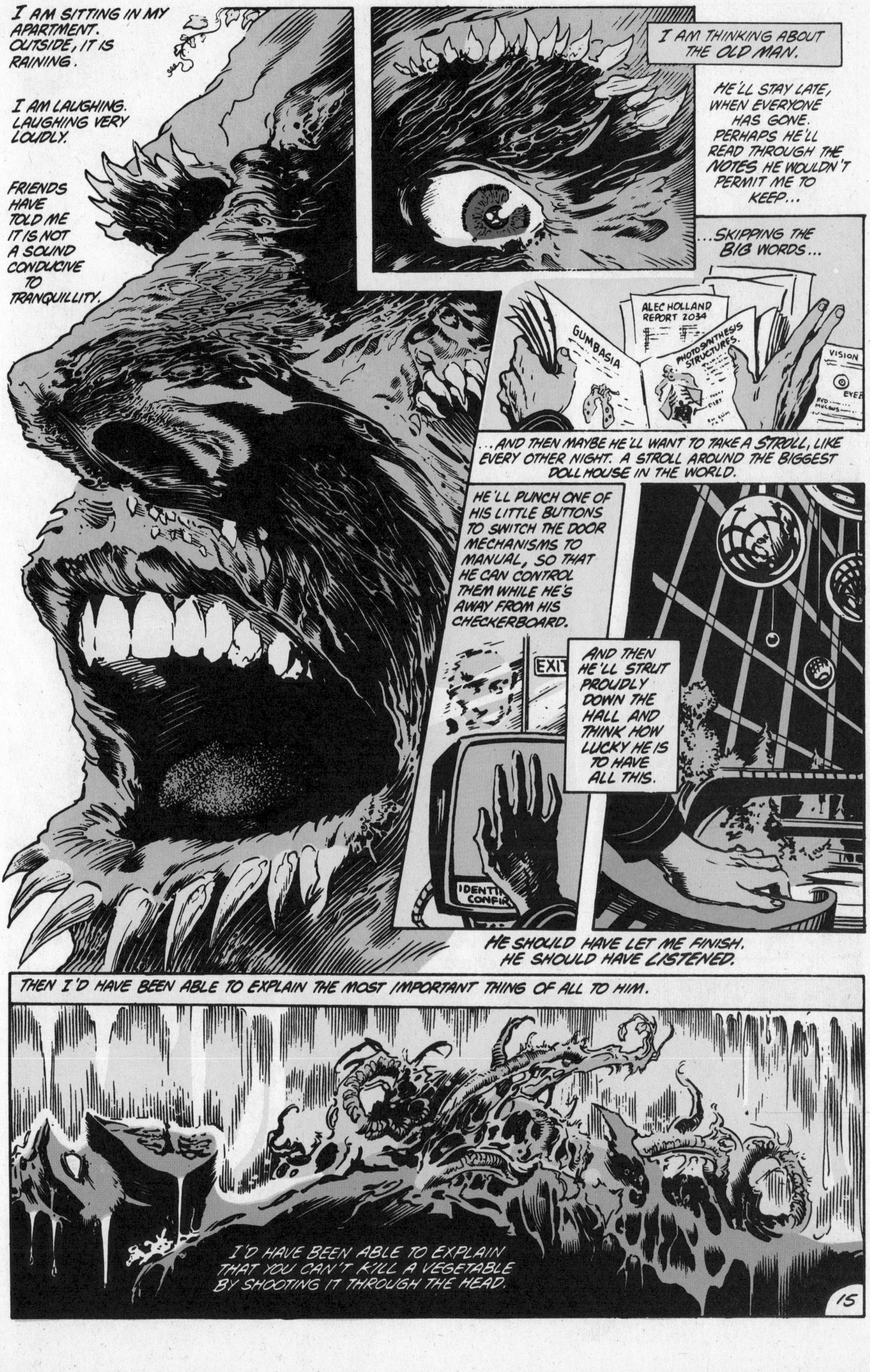
I AM SITTING IN MY APARTMENT. OUTSIDE, IT IS RAINING.
I AM LAUGHING. LAUGHING VERY LOUDLY.
FRIENDS HAVE TOLD ME IT IS NOT A SOUND CONDUCIVE TO TRANQUILLITY.
I AM THINKING ABOUT THE OLD MAN.
HE'LL STAY LATE, WHEN EVERYONE HAS GONE. PERHAPS HE'LL READ THROUGH THE NOTES HE WOULDN'T PERMIT ME TO KEEP...
...SKIPPING THE BIG WORDS...
ALEC HOLLAND REPORT 2034
GUMBASIA
PHOTOSYNTHESIS STRUCTURES
VISION
...AND THEN MAYBE HE'LL WANT TO TAKE A STROLL, LIKE EVERY OTHER NIGHT. A STROLL AROUND THE BIGGEST DOLL HOUSE IN THE WORLD.
HE'LL PUNCH ONE OF HIS LITTLE BUTTONS TO SWITCH THE DOOR MECHANISMS TO MANUAL, SO THAT HE CAN CONTROL THEM WHILE HE'S AWAY FROM HIS CHECKERBOARD.
EXIT
AND THEN HE'LL STRUT PROUDLY DOWN THE HALL AND THINK HOW LUCKY HE IS TO HAVE ALL THIS.
HE SHOULD HAVE LET ME FINISH. HE SHOULD HAVE LISTENED.
THEN I'D HAVE BEEN ABLE TO EXPLAIN THE MOST IMPORTANT THING OF ALL TO HIM.
I'D HAVE BEEN ABLE TO EXPLAIN THAT YOU CAN'T KILL A VEGETABLE BY SHOOTING IT THROUGH THE HEAD.
15

OH, YOU COULD GIVE IT SUCH A SHOCK THAT IT WOULD PLUNGE INTO A CELLULAR COMA. YOU COULD KEEP IT IN THAT STATE BY PLACING IT IN A FREEZER UNIT...

...BUT YOU COULDN'T KILL IT.

REALLY, THE OLD MAN COULD HAVE WORKED THAT OUT FOR HIMSELF.

CRYOGE
WARNING — D

HE JUST DIDN'T HAVE THE CORRECT BACKGROUND.

I WONDER WHAT HE'S DOING NOW?

I WONDER HOW LONG HE'LL BE ABLE TO RESIST GOING DOWN THERE AND TAKING A LOOK?

HOLLAND

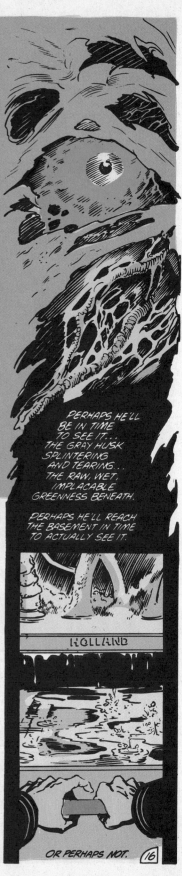

PERHAPS HE'LL BE IN TIME TO SEE IT... THE GRAY HUSK SPLINTERING AND TEARING... THE RAW, WET, IMPLACABLE GREENNESS BENEATH.

PERHAPS HE'LL REACH THE BASEMENT IN TIME TO ACTUALLY SEE IT.

HOLLAND

OR PERHAPS NOT.   16

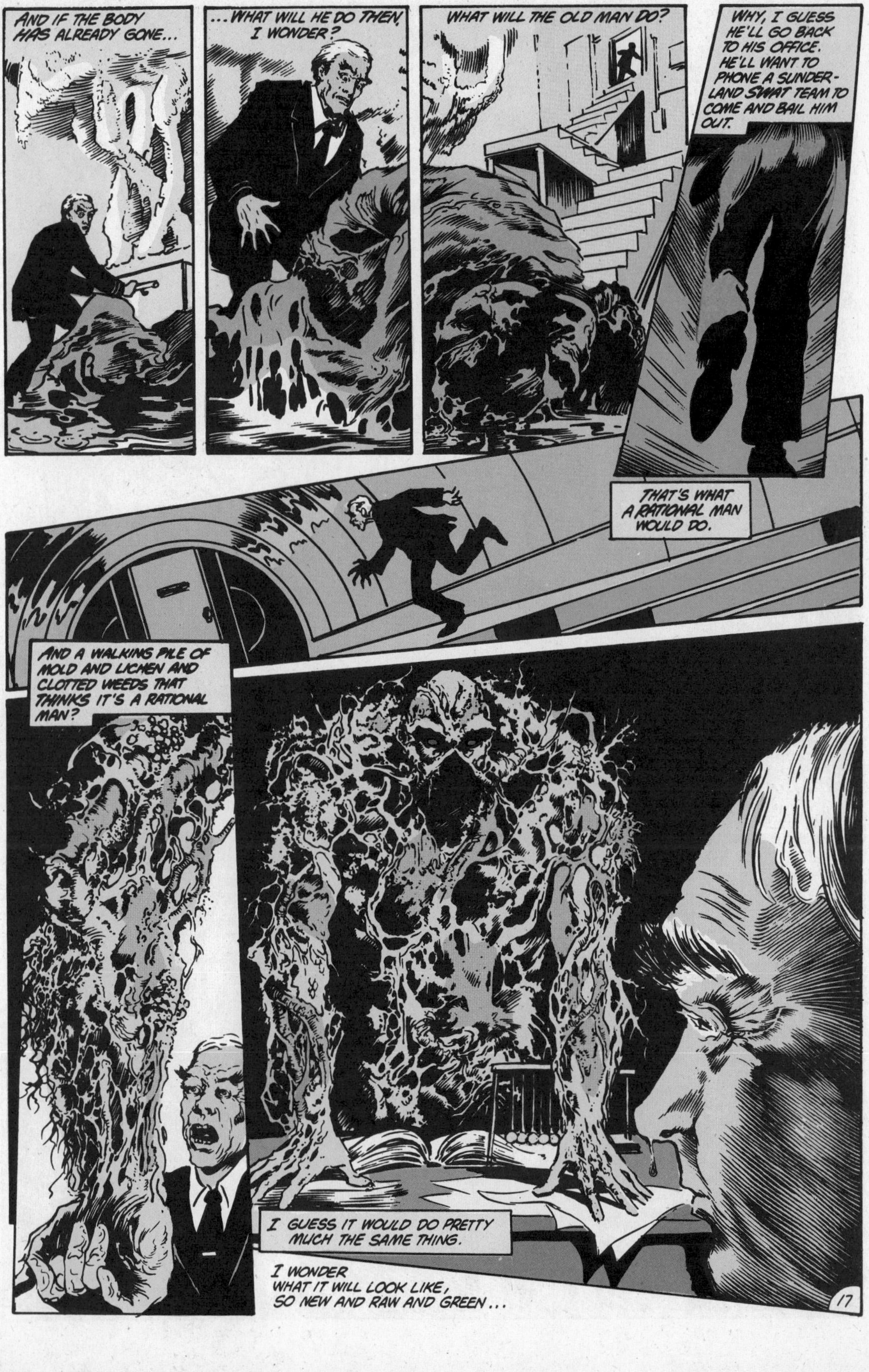
AND IF THE BODY HAS ALREADY GONE...
...WHAT WILL HE DO THEN, I WONDER?
WHAT WILL THE OLD MAN DO?
WHY, I GUESS HE'LL GO BACK TO HIS OFFICE. HE'LL WANT TO PHONE A SUNDER-LAND SWAT TEAM TO COME AND BAIL HIM OUT.
THAT'S WHAT A RATIONAL MAN WOULD DO.
AND A WALKING PILE OF MOLD AND LICHEN AND CLOTTED WEEDS THAT THINKS IT'S A RATIONAL MAN?
I GUESS IT WOULD DO PRETTY MUCH THE SAME THING.
I WONDER WHAT IT WILL LOOK LIKE, SO NEW AND RAW AND GREEN...
17

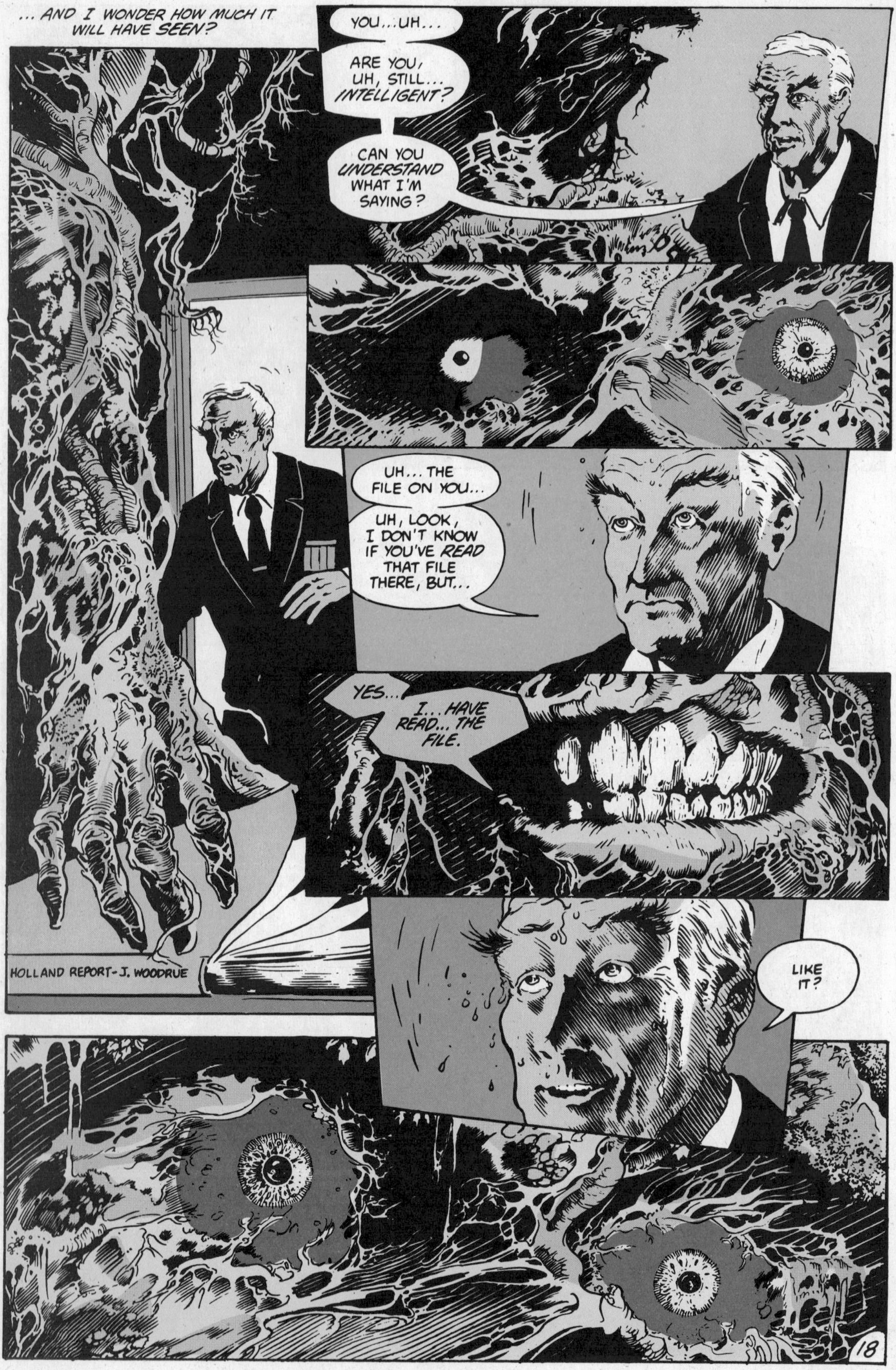
... AND I WONDER HOW MUCH IT WILL HAVE SEEN?
YOU...UH...
ARE YOU, UH, STILL... INTELLIGENT?
CAN YOU UNDERSTAND WHAT I'M SAYING?
UH... THE FILE ON YOU...
UH, LOOK, I DON'T KNOW IF YOU'VE READ THAT FILE THERE, BUT...
YES...
I... HAVE READ... THE FILE.
HOLLAND REPORT - J. WOODRUE
LIKE IT?
18

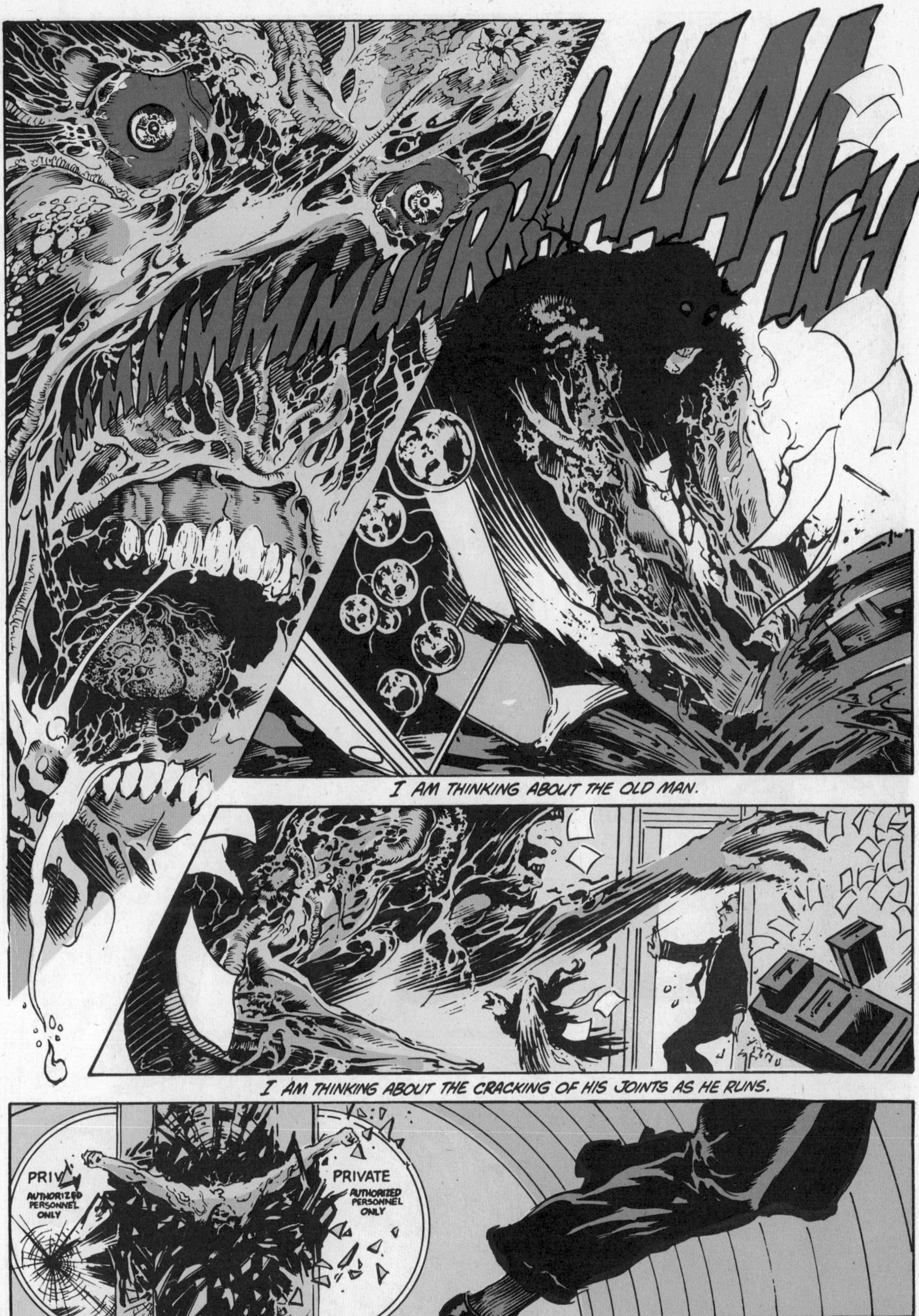
MMMMMMMUHRRAAAAAAAAGH
I AM THINKING ABOUT THE OLD MAN.
I AM THINKING ABOUT THE CRACKING OF HIS JOINTS AS HE RUNS.
PRIV
AUTHORIZED PERSONNEL ONLY
PRIVATE
AUTHORIZED PERSONNEL ONLY
19

I AM THINKING OF THE TERROR IN HIS ANCIENT, ATROPHIED HEART.

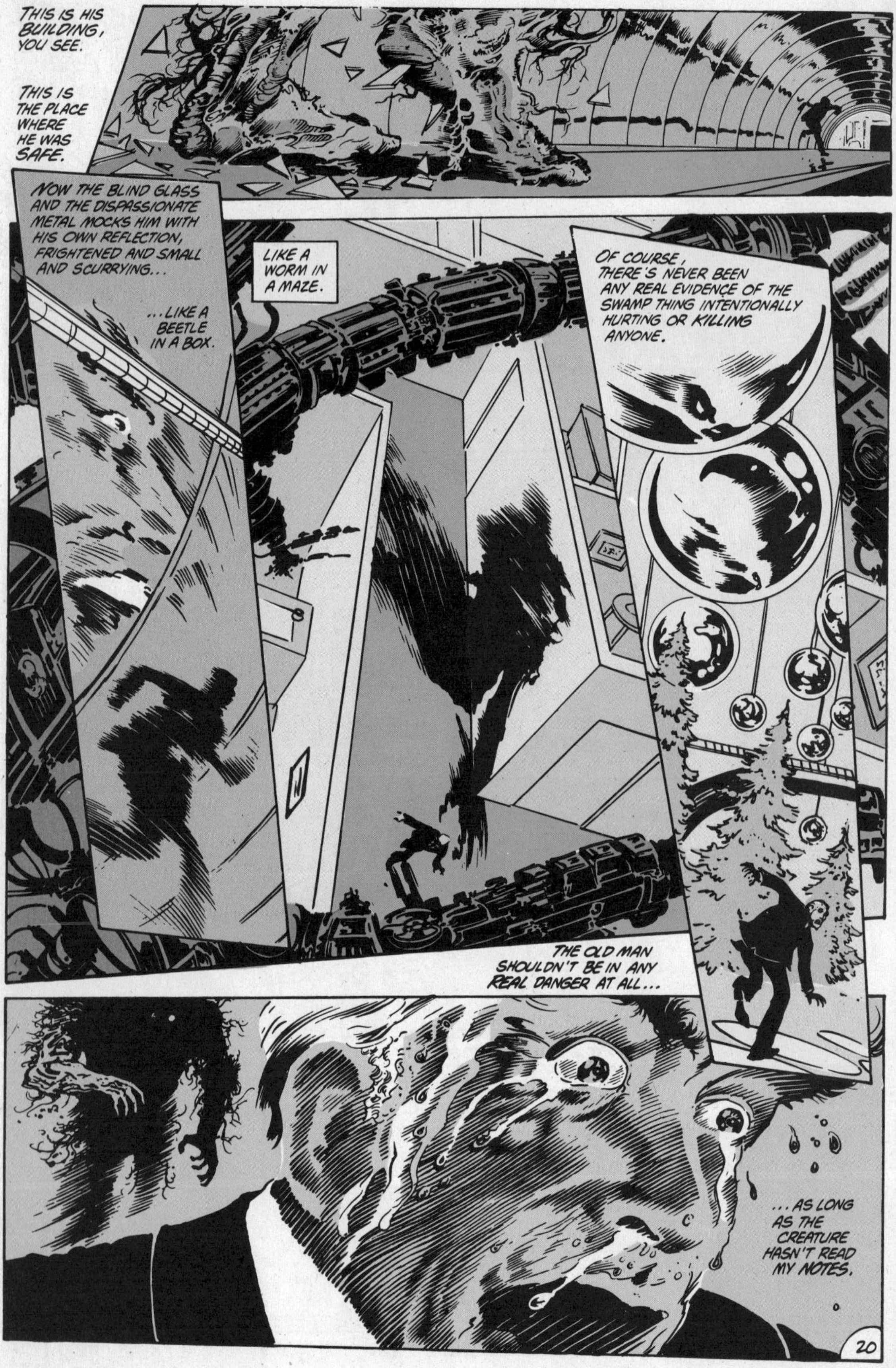
THIS IS HIS BUILDING, YOU SEE.
THIS IS THE PLACE WHERE HE WAS SAFE.
NOW THE BLIND GLASS AND THE DISPASSIONATE METAL MOCKS HIM WITH HIS OWN REFLECTION, FRIGHTENED AND SMALL AND SCURRYING...
...LIKE A BEETLE IN A BOX.
LIKE A WORM IN A MAZE.
OF COURSE, THERE'S NEVER BEEN ANY REAL EVIDENCE OF THE SWAMP THING INTENTIONALLY HURTING OR KILLING ANYONE.
THE OLD MAN SHOULDN'T BE IN ANY REAL DANGER AT ALL...
...AS LONG AS THE CREATURE HASN'T READ MY NOTES.

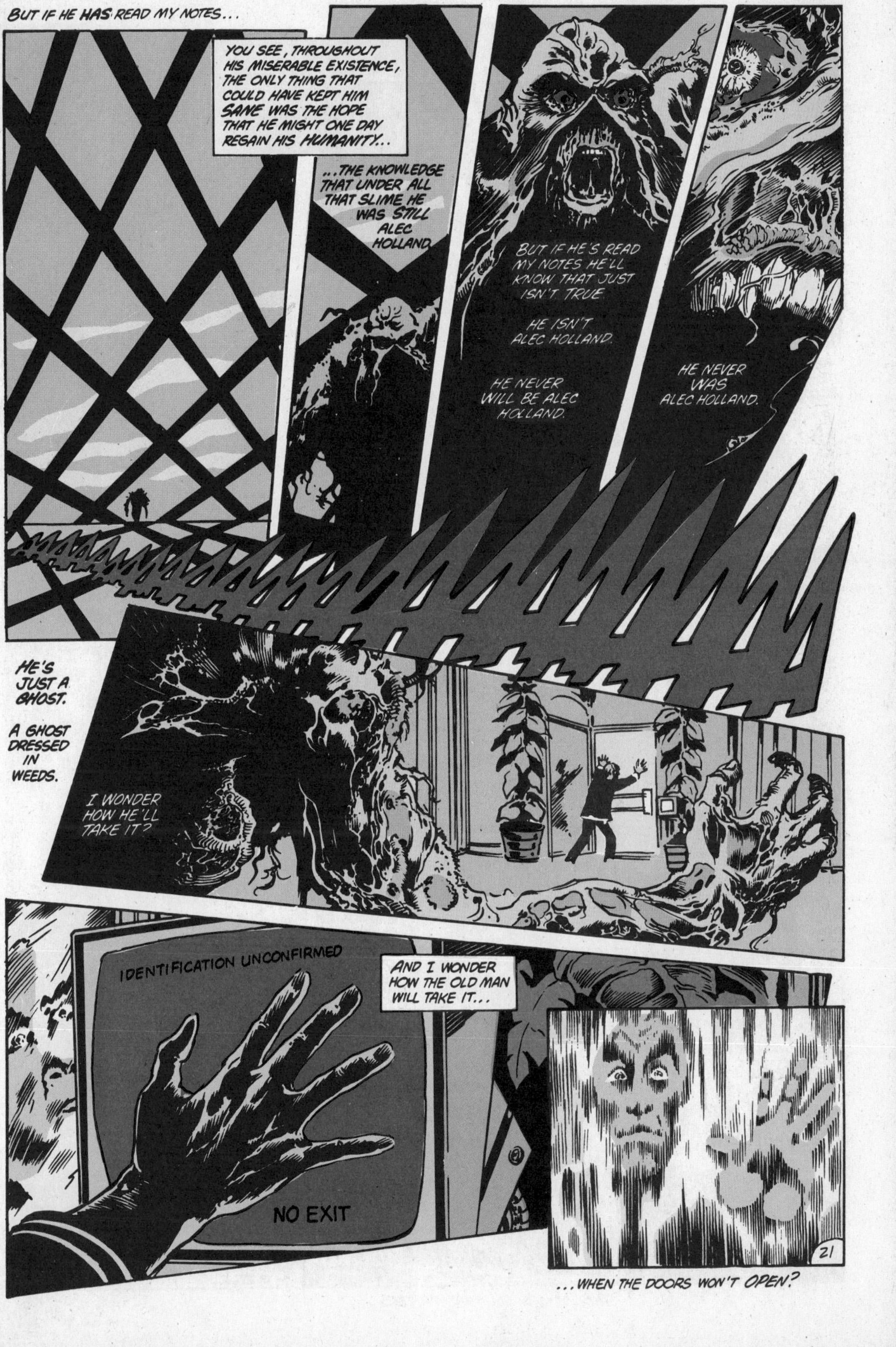
BUT IF HE HAS READ MY NOTES...
YOU SEE, THROUGHOUT HIS MISERABLE EXISTENCE, THE ONLY THING THAT COULD HAVE KEPT HIM SANE WAS THE HOPE THAT HE MIGHT ONE DAY REGAIN HIS HUMANITY...
...THE KNOWLEDGE THAT UNDER ALL THAT SLIME HE WAS STILL ALEC HOLLAND.
BUT IF HE'S READ MY NOTES HE'LL KNOW THAT JUST ISN'T TRUE.
HE ISN'T ALEC HOLLAND.
HE NEVER WILL BE ALEC HOLLAND.
HE NEVER WAS ALEC HOLLAND.
HE'S JUST A GHOST.
A GHOST DRESSED IN WEEDS.
I WONDER HOW HE'LL TAKE IT?
IDENTIFICATION UNCONFIRMED
NO EXIT
AND I WONDER HOW THE OLD MAN WILL TAKE IT...
21
...WHEN THE DOORS WON'T OPEN?

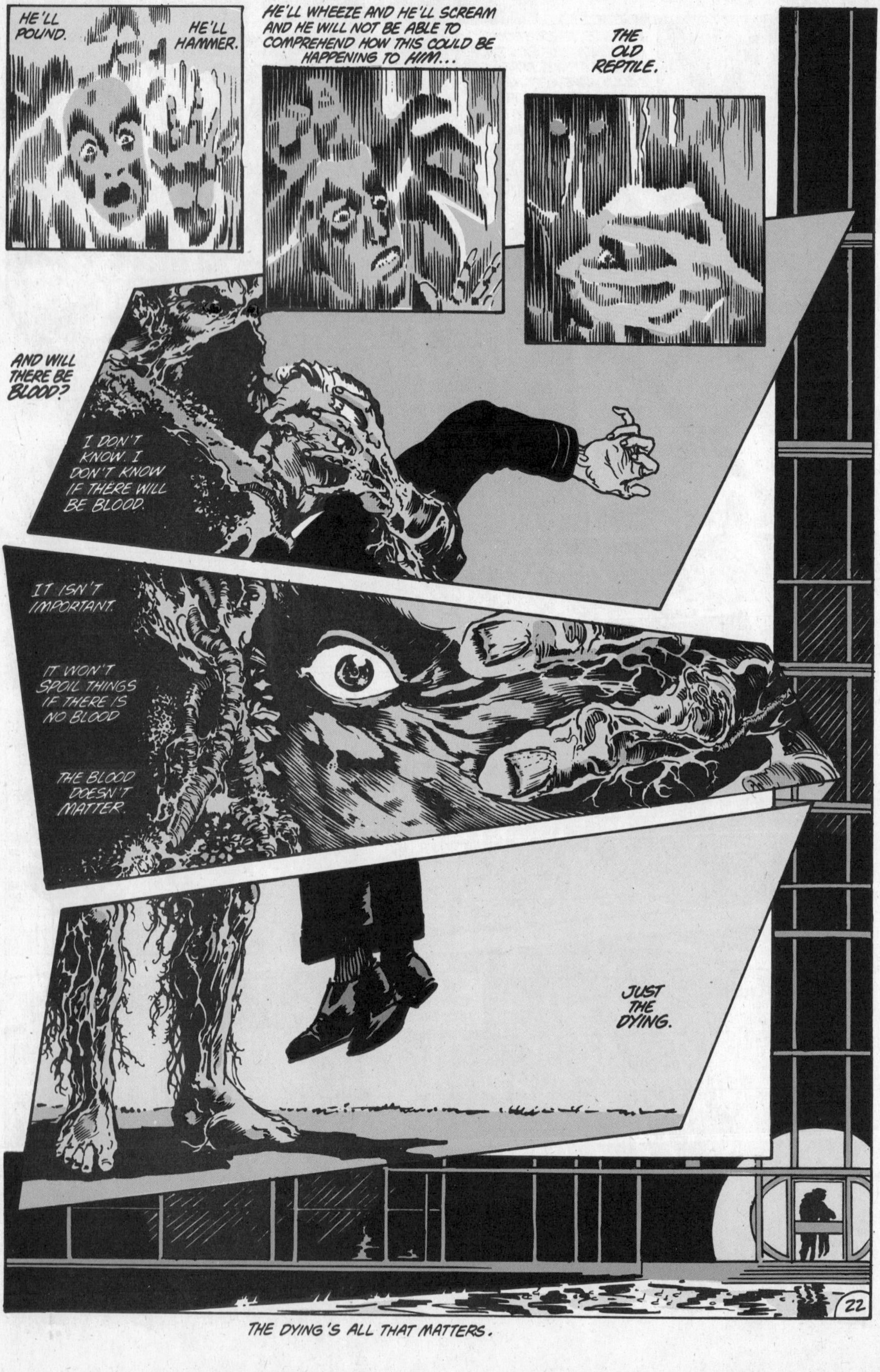
HE'LL POUND.
HE'LL HAMMER.
HE'LL WHEEZE AND HE'LL SCREAM AND HE WILL NOT BE ABLE TO COMPREHEND HOW THIS COULD BE HAPPENING TO HIM...
THE OLD REPTILE.
AND WILL THERE BE BLOOD?
I DON'T KNOW. I DON'T KNOW IF THERE WILL BE BLOOD.
IT ISN'T IMPORTANT.
IT WON'T SPOIL THINGS IF THERE IS NO BLOOD
THE BLOOD DOESN'T MATTER.
JUST THE DYING.
22
THE DYING'S ALL THAT MATTERS.

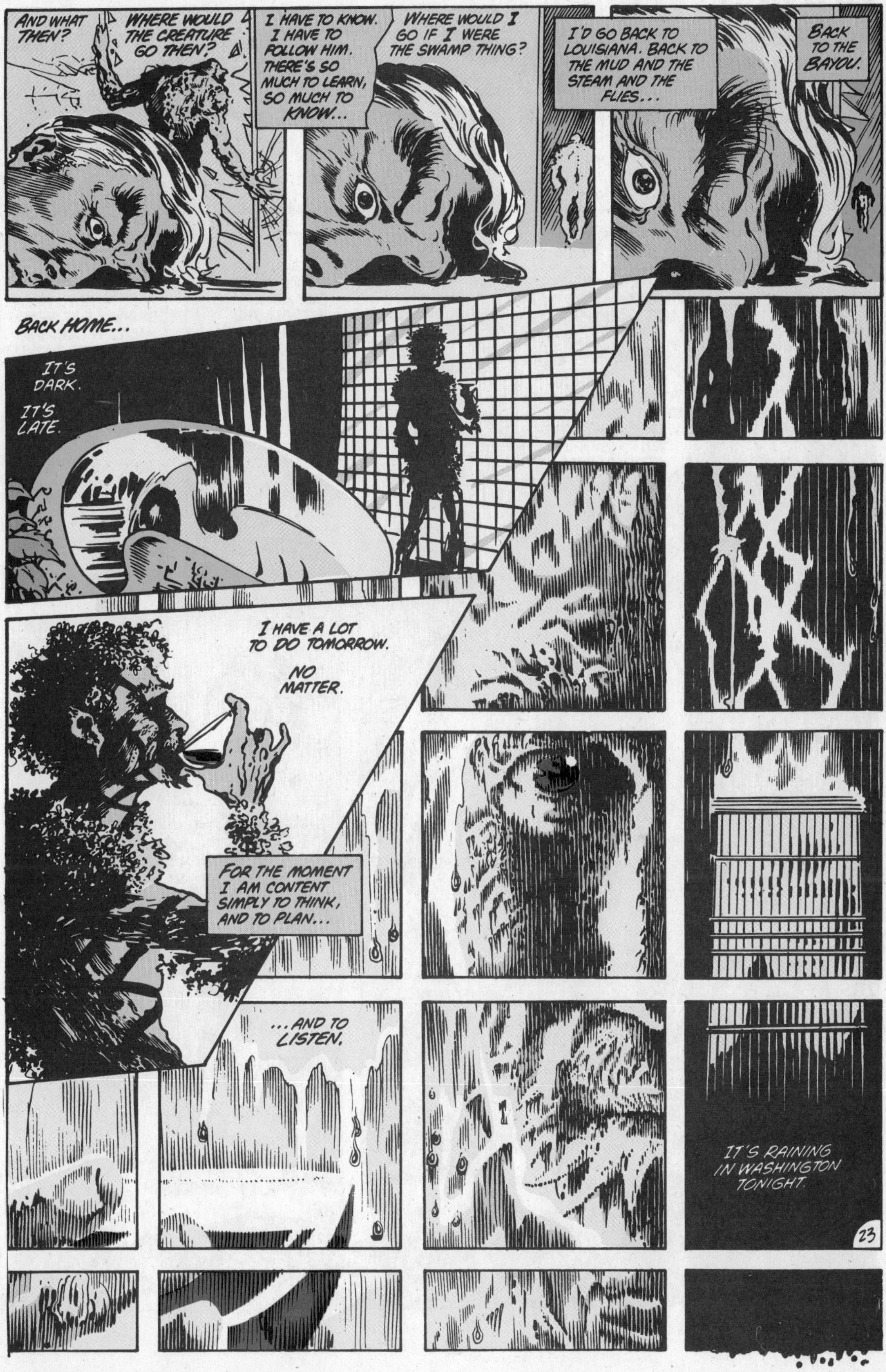
AND WHAT THEN?
WHERE WOULD THE CREATURE GO THEN?
I HAVE TO KNOW. I HAVE TO FOLLOW HIM. THERE'S SO MUCH TO LEARN, SO MUCH TO KNOW...
WHERE WOULD I GO IF I WERE THE SWAMP THING?
I'D GO BACK TO LOUISIANA. BACK TO THE MUD AND THE STEAM AND THE FLIES...
BACK TO THE BAYOU.
BACK HOME...
IT'S DARK.
IT'S LATE.
I HAVE A LOT TO DO TOMORROW.
NO MATTER.
FOR THE MOMENT I AM CONTENT SIMPLY TO THINK, AND TO PLAN...
...AND TO LISTEN.
IT'S RAINING IN WASHINGTON TONIGHT.
23

BOOK TWO

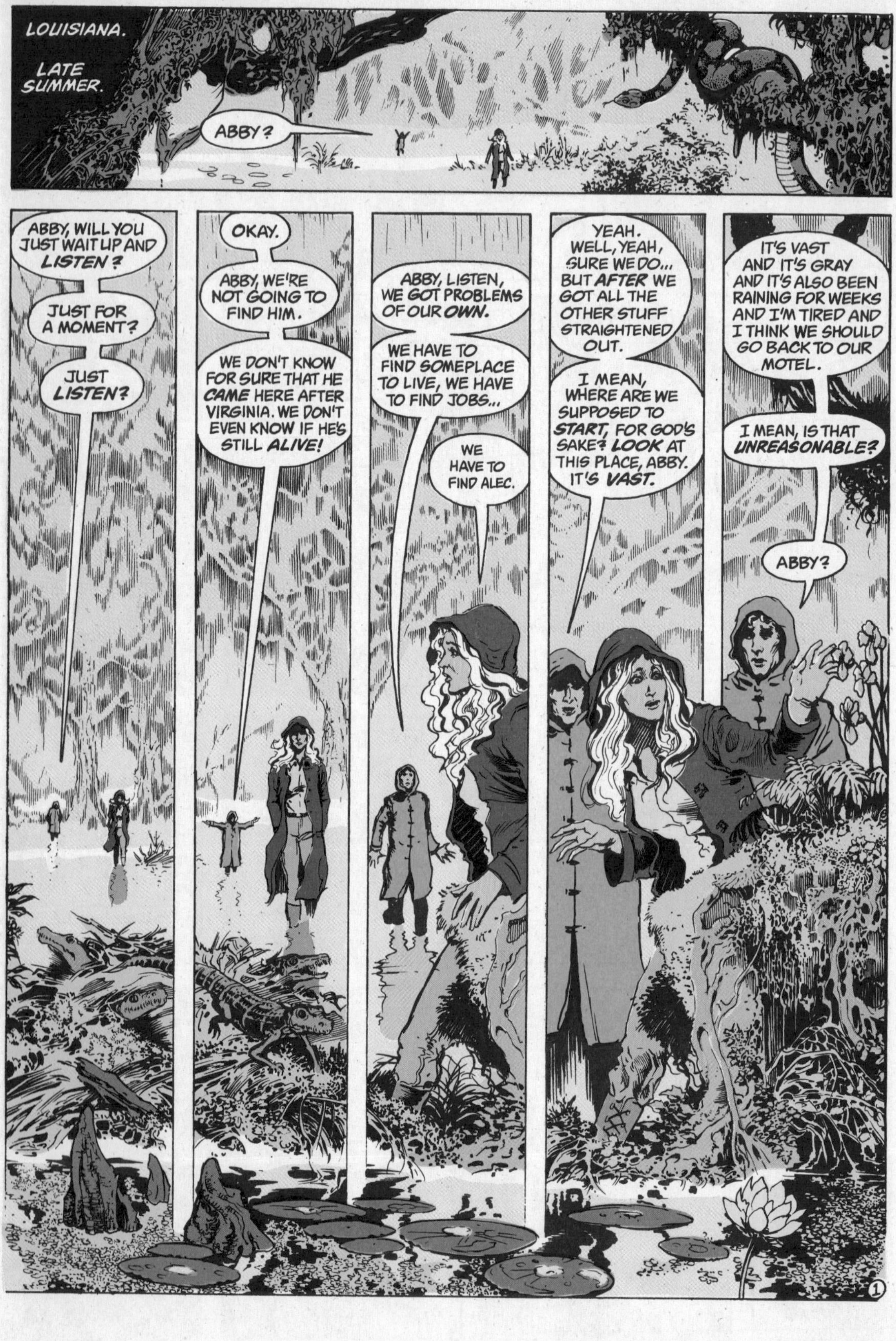
LOUISIANA.
LATE SUMMER.
ABBY?
ABBY, WILL YOU JUST WAIT UP AND LISTEN?
JUST FOR A MOMENT?
JUST LISTEN?
OKAY.
ABBY, WE'RE NOT GOING TO FIND HIM.
WE DON'T KNOW FOR SURE THAT HE CAME HERE AFTER VIRGINIA. WE DON'T EVEN KNOW IF HE'S STILL ALIVE!
ABBY, LISTEN, WE GOT PROBLEMS OF OUR OWN.
WE HAVE TO FIND SOMEPLACE TO LIVE, WE HAVE TO FIND JOBS...
WE HAVE TO FIND ALEC.
YEAH. WELL, YEAH, SURE WE DO... BUT AFTER WE GOT ALL THE OTHER STUFF STRAIGHTENED OUT.
I MEAN, WHERE ARE WE SUPPOSED TO START, FOR GOD'S SAKE? LOOK AT THIS PLACE, ABBY. IT'S VAST.
IT'S VAST AND IT'S GRAY AND IT'S ALSO BEEN RAINING FOR WEEKS AND I'M TIRED AND I THINK WE SHOULD GO BACK TO OUR MOTEL.
I MEAN, IS THAT UNREASONABLE?
ABBY?
1

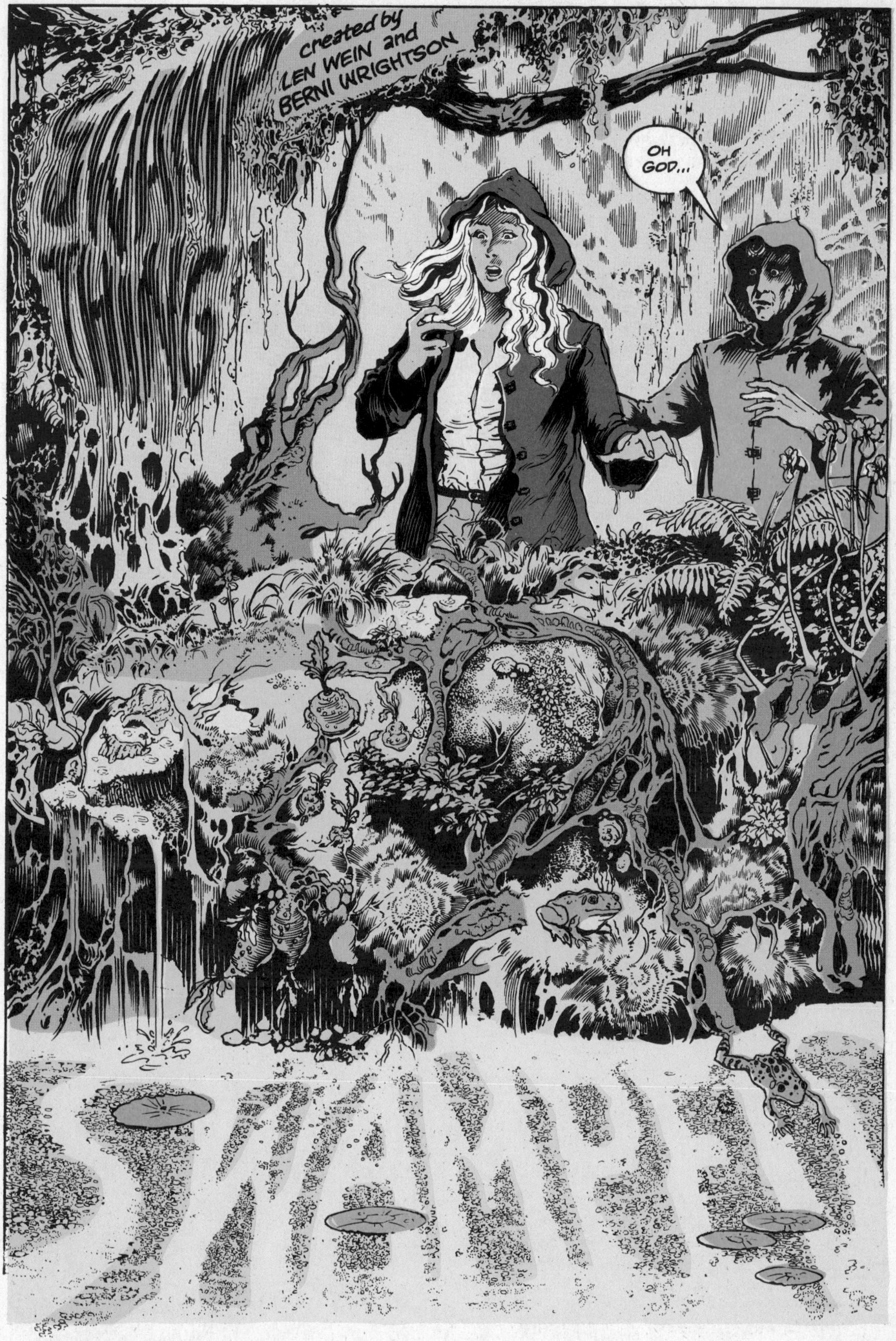
created by
LEN WEIN and
BERNI WRIGHTSON
OH GOD...
SWAMP THING

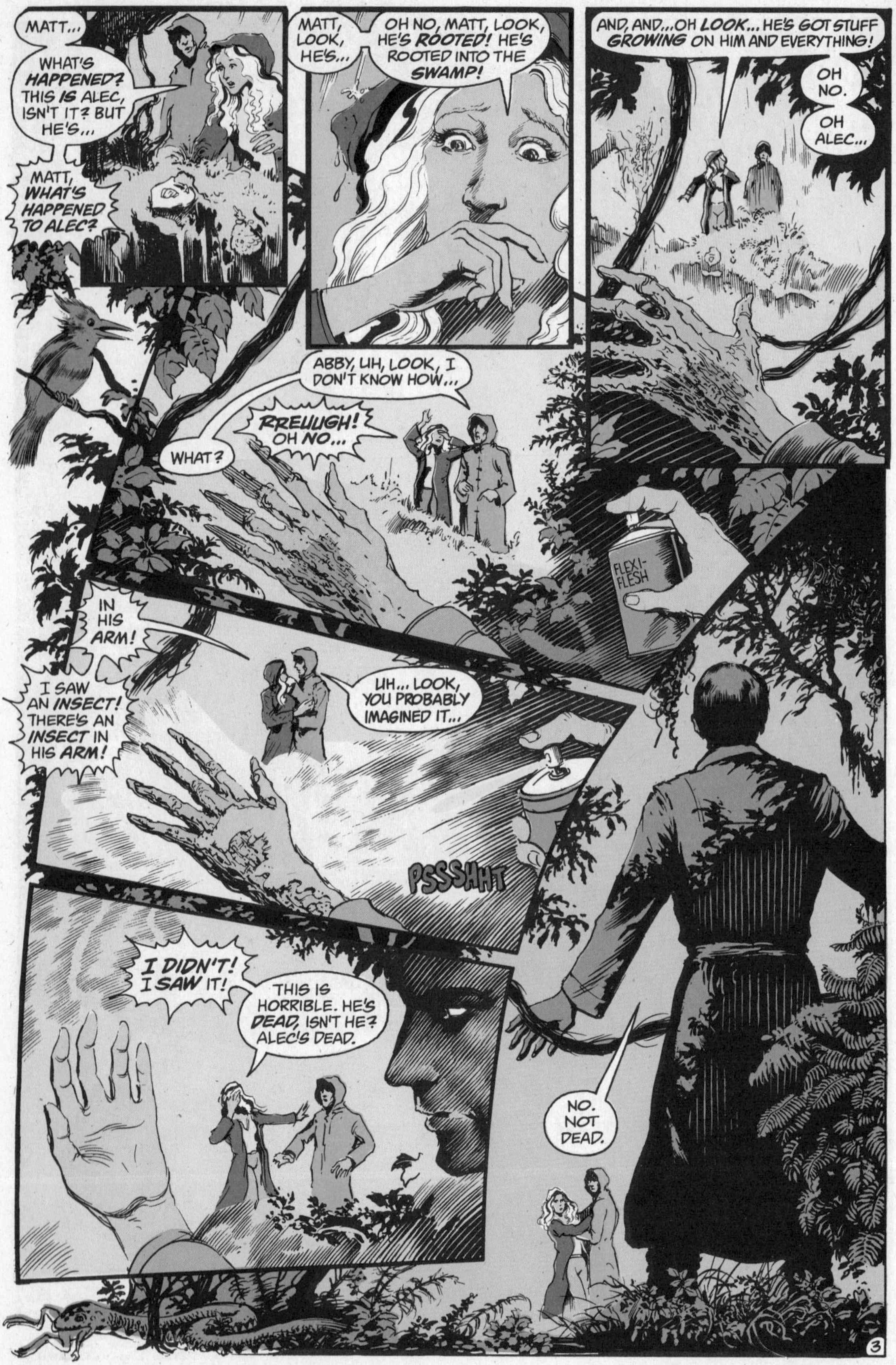
MATT...
WHAT'S HAPPENED? THIS IS ALEC, ISN'T IT? BUT HE'S...
MATT, WHAT'S HAPPENED TO ALEC?
MATT, LOOK, HE'S...
OH NO, MATT, LOOK, HE'S ROOTED! HE'S ROOTED INTO THE SWAMP!
AND, AND,...OH LOOK... HE'S GOT STUFF GROWING ON HIM AND EVERYTHING!
OH NO.
OH ALEC...
ABBY, UH, LOOK, I DON'T KNOW HOW...
RREUUGH! OH NO...
WHAT?
FLEXI-FLESH
IN HIS ARM!
I SAW AN INSECT! THERE'S AN INSECT IN HIS ARM!
UH... LOOK, YOU PROBABLY IMAGINED IT...
PSSSHHT
I DIDN'T! I SAW IT!
THIS IS HORRIBLE. HE'S DEAD, ISN'T HE? ALEC'S DEAD.
NO. NOT DEAD.
3

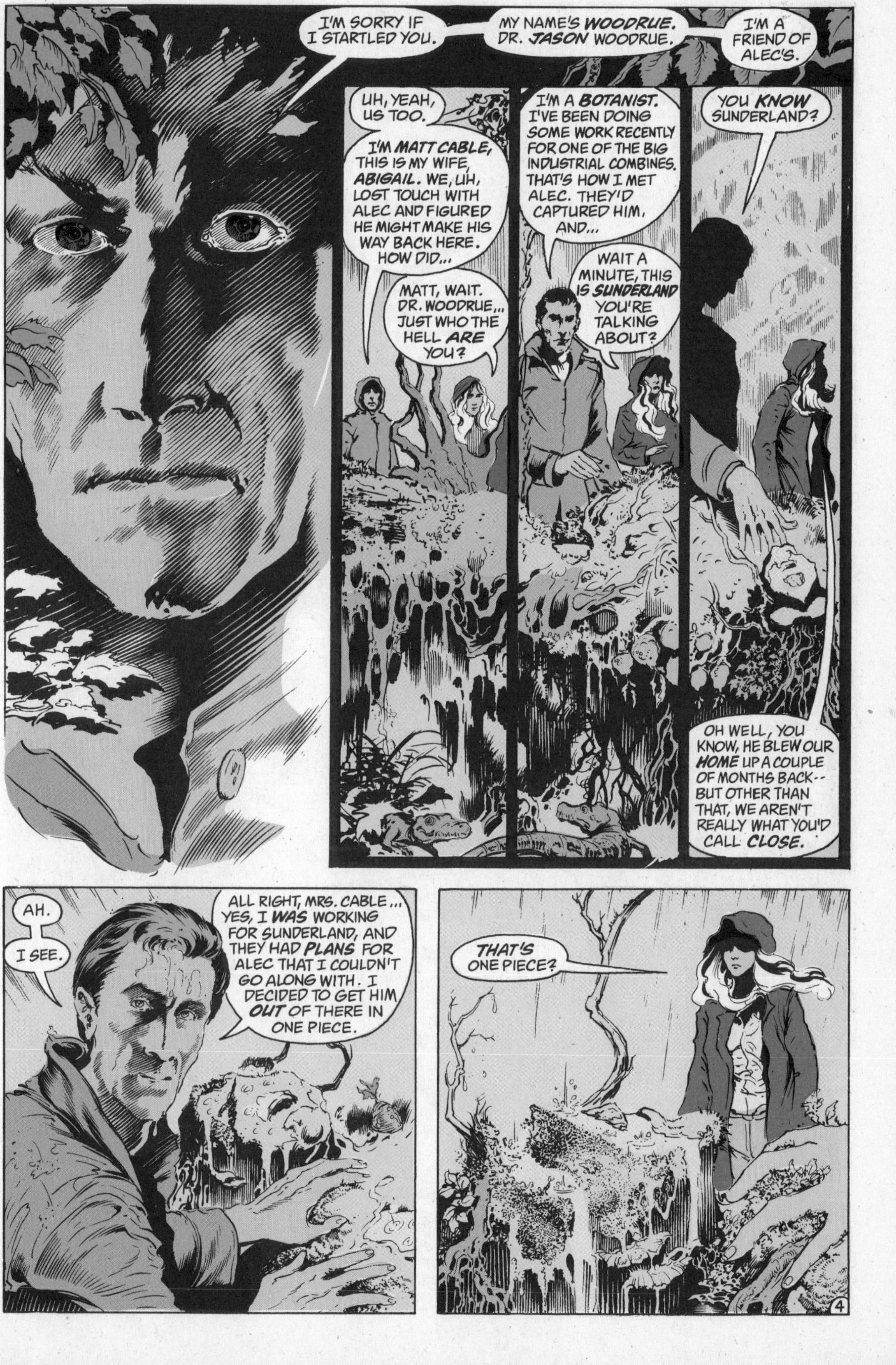
I'M SORRY IF I STARTLED YOU.
MY NAME'S WOODRUE. DR. JASON WOODRUE.
I'M A FRIEND OF ALEC'S.
UH, YEAH, US TOO.
I'M MATT CABLE, THIS IS MY WIFE, ABIGAIL. WE, UH, LOST TOUCH WITH ALEC AND FIGURED HE MIGHT MAKE HIS WAY BACK HERE. HOW DID...
MATT, WAIT. DR. WOODRUE,.. JUST WHO THE HELL ARE YOU?
I'M A BOTANIST. I'VE BEEN DOING SOME WORK RECENTLY FOR ONE OF THE BIG INDUSTRIAL COMBINES. THAT'S HOW I MET ALEC. THEY'D CAPTURED HIM, AND...
WAIT A MINUTE, THIS IS SUNDERLAND YOU'RE TALKING ABOUT?
YOU KNOW SUNDERLAND?
OH WELL, YOU KNOW, HE BLEW OUR HOME UP A COUPLE OF MONTHS BACK-- BUT OTHER THAN THAT, WE AREN'T REALLY WHAT YOU'D CALL CLOSE.
AH.
I SEE.
ALL RIGHT, MRS. CABLE... YES, I WAS WORKING FOR SUNDERLAND, AND THEY HAD PLANS FOR ALEC THAT I COULDN'T GO ALONG WITH. I DECIDED TO GET HIM OUT OF THERE IN ONE PIECE.
THAT'S ONE PIECE?
4

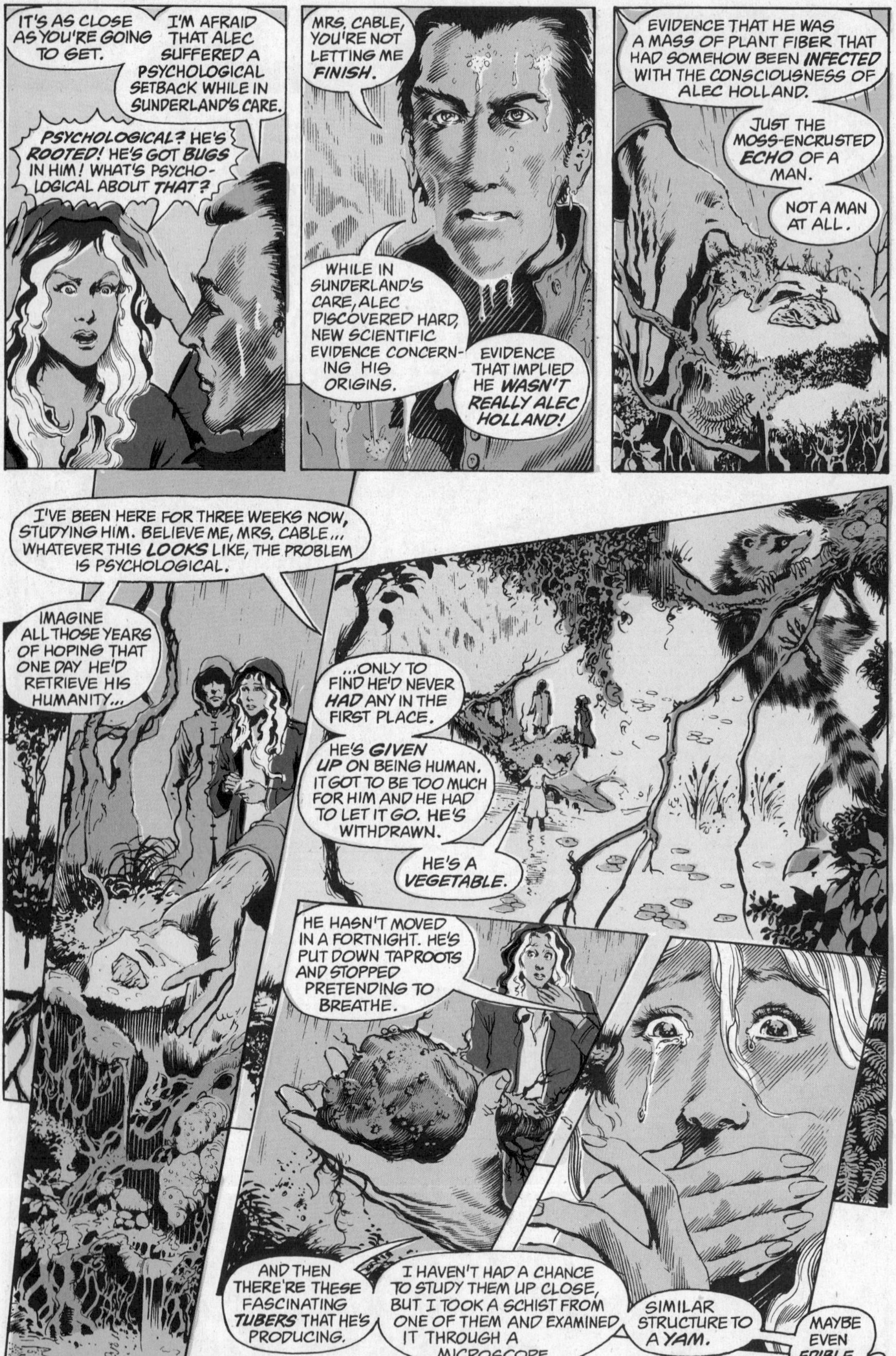
IT'S AS CLOSE AS YOU'RE GOING TO GET.
I'M AFRAID THAT ALEC SUFFERED A PSYCHOLOGICAL SETBACK WHILE IN SUNDERLAND'S CARE.
PSYCHOLOGICAL? HE'S ROOTED! HE'S GOT BUGS IN HIM! WHAT'S PSYCHOLOGICAL ABOUT THAT?
MRS. CABLE, YOU'RE NOT LETTING ME FINISH.
WHILE IN SUNDERLAND'S CARE, ALEC DISCOVERED HARD, NEW SCIENTIFIC EVIDENCE CONCERNING HIS ORIGINS.
EVIDENCE THAT IMPLIED HE WASN'T REALLY ALEC HOLLAND!
EVIDENCE THAT HE WAS A MASS OF PLANT FIBER THAT HAD SOMEHOW BEEN INFECTED WITH THE CONSCIOUSNESS OF ALEC HOLLAND.
JUST THE MOSS-ENCRUSTED ECHO OF A MAN.
NOT A MAN AT ALL.
I'VE BEEN HERE FOR THREE WEEKS NOW, STUDYING HIM. BELIEVE ME, MRS. CABLE... WHATEVER THIS LOOKS LIKE, THE PROBLEM IS PSYCHOLOGICAL.
IMAGINE ALL THOSE YEARS OF HOPING THAT ONE DAY HE'D RETRIEVE HIS HUMANITY...
...ONLY TO FIND HE'D NEVER HAD ANY IN THE FIRST PLACE.
HE'S GIVEN UP ON BEING HUMAN. IT GOT TO BE TOO MUCH FOR HIM AND HE HAD TO LET IT GO. HE'S WITHDRAWN.
HE'S A VEGETABLE.
HE HASN'T MOVED IN A FORTNIGHT. HE'S PUT DOWN TAPROOTS AND STOPPED PRETENDING TO BREATHE.
AND THEN THERE'RE THESE FASCINATING TUBERS THAT HE'S PRODUCING.
I HAVEN'T HAD A CHANCE TO STUDY THEM UP CLOSE, BUT I TOOK A SCHIST FROM ONE OF THEM AND EXAMINED IT THROUGH A MICROSCOPE.
SIMILAR STRUCTURE TO A YAM.
MAYBE EVEN EDIBLE.
5

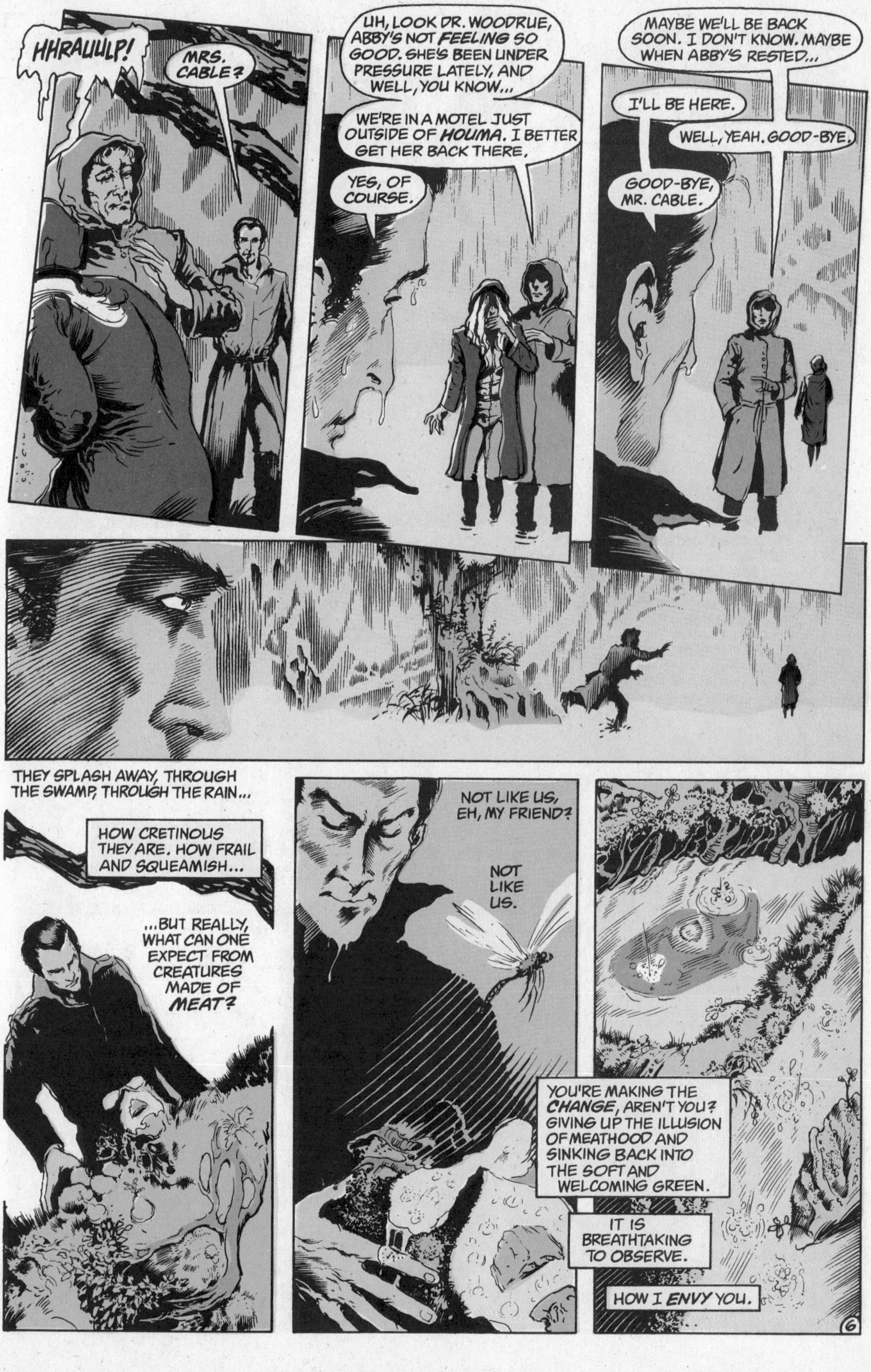
HHRAUULP!
MRS. CABLE?
UH, LOOK DR. WOODRUE, ABBY'S NOT FEELING SO GOOD. SHE'S BEEN UNDER PRESSURE LATELY, AND WELL, YOU KNOW...
WE'RE IN A MOTEL JUST OUTSIDE OF HOUMA. I BETTER GET HER BACK THERE.
YES, OF COURSE.
MAYBE WE'LL BE BACK SOON. I DON'T KNOW. MAYBE WHEN ABBY'S RESTED...
I'LL BE HERE.
WELL, YEAH. GOOD-BYE.
GOOD-BYE, MR. CABLE.
THEY SPLASH AWAY, THROUGH THE SWAMP, THROUGH THE RAIN...
HOW CRETINOUS THEY ARE. HOW FRAIL AND SQUEAMISH...
...BUT REALLY, WHAT CAN ONE EXPECT FROM CREATURES MADE OF MEAT?
NOT LIKE US, EH, MY FRIEND?
NOT LIKE US.
YOU'RE MAKING THE CHANGE, AREN'T YOU? GIVING UP THE ILLUSION OF MEATHOOD AND SINKING BACK INTO THE SOFT AND WELCOMING GREEN.
IT IS BREATHTAKING TO OBSERVE.
HOW I ENVY YOU.
6

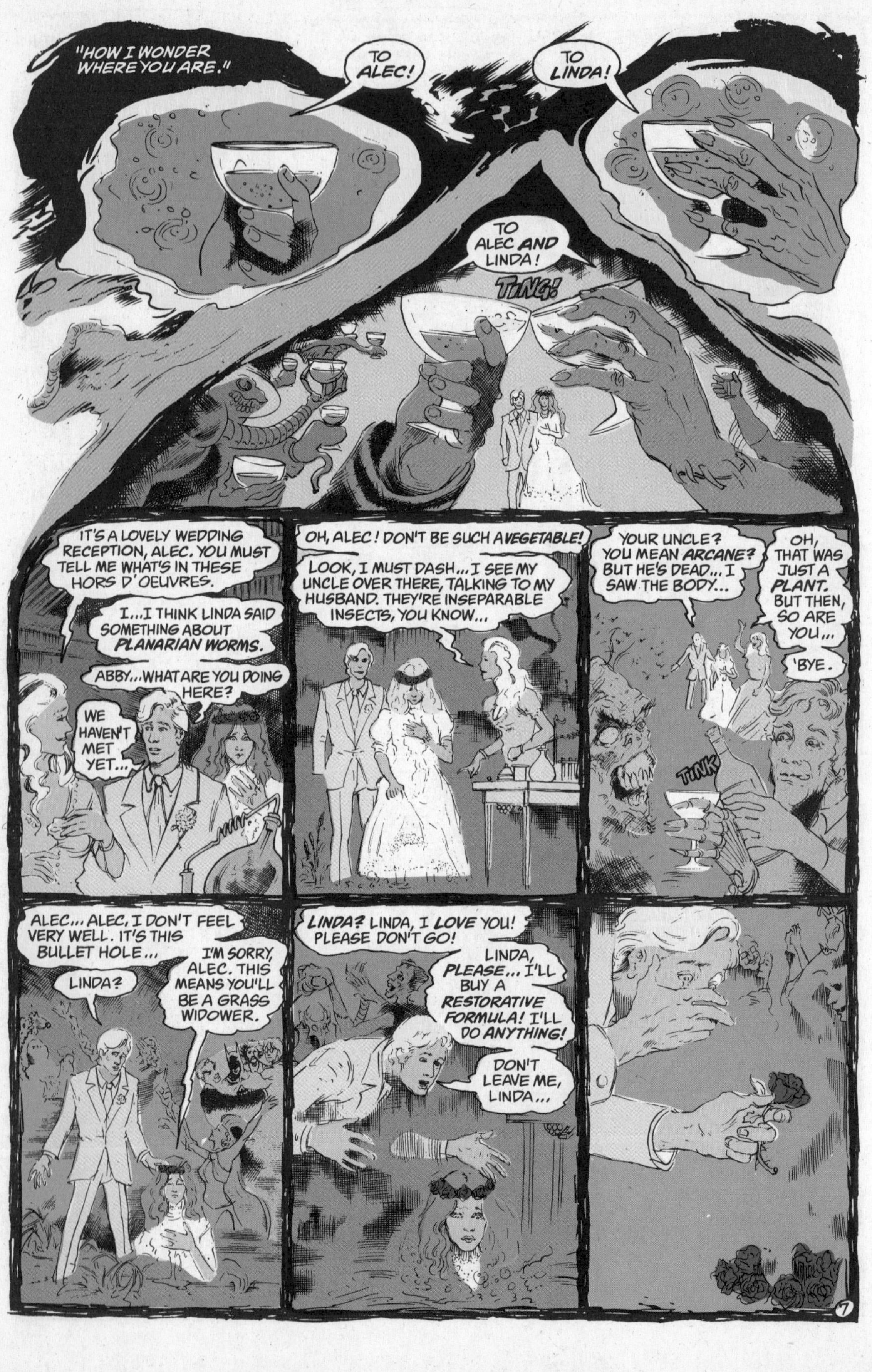
"HOW I WONDER WHERE YOU ARE."
TO ALEC!
TO LINDA!
TO ALEC AND LINDA!
TING!
IT'S A LOVELY WEDDING RECEPTION, ALEC. YOU MUST TELL ME WHAT'S IN THESE HORS D' OEUVRES.
I...I THINK LINDA SAID SOMETHING ABOUT PLANARIAN WORMS.
ABBY...WHAT ARE YOU DOING HERE?
WE HAVEN'T MET YET...
OH, ALEC! DON'T BE SUCH A VEGETABLE!
LOOK, I MUST DASH... I SEE MY UNCLE OVER THERE, TALKING TO MY HUSBAND. THEY'RE INSEPARABLE INSECTS, YOU KNOW...
YOUR UNCLE? YOU MEAN ARCANE? BUT HE'S DEAD... I SAW THE BODY...
OH, THAT WAS JUST A PLANT. BUT THEN, SO ARE YOU...
'BYE.
TINK
ALEC... ALEC, I DON'T FEEL VERY WELL. IT'S THIS BULLET HOLE...
I'M SORRY, ALEC. THIS MEANS YOU'LL BE A GRASS WIDOWER.
LINDA?
LINDA? LINDA, I LOVE YOU! PLEASE DON'T GO!
LINDA, PLEASE... I'LL BUY A RESTORATIVE FORMULA! I'LL DO ANYTHING!
DON'T LEAVE ME, LINDA...
7

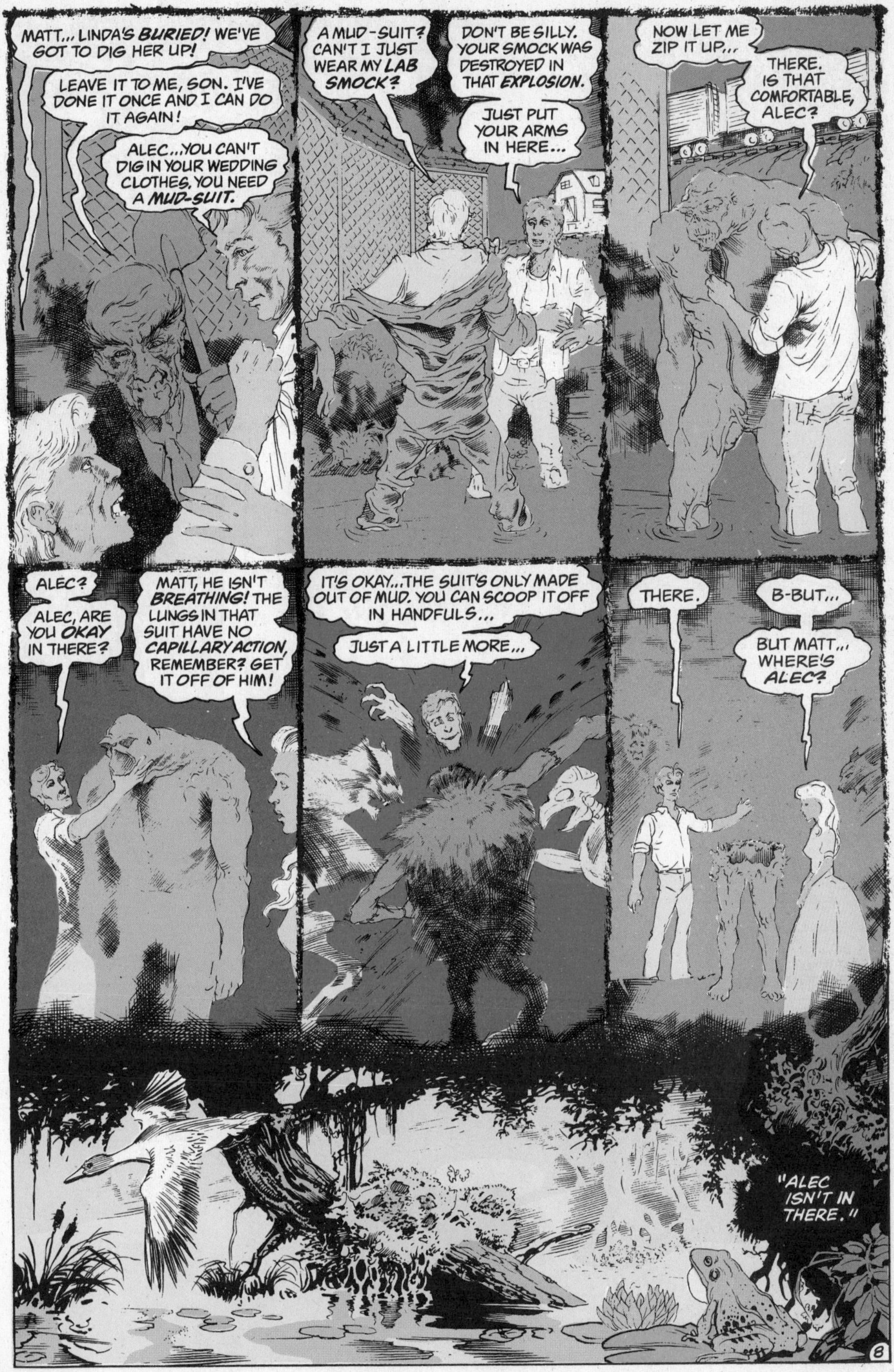
MATT... LINDA'S BURIED! WE'VE GOT TO DIG HER UP!
LEAVE IT TO ME, SON. I'VE DONE IT ONCE AND I CAN DO IT AGAIN!
ALEC...YOU CAN'T DIG IN YOUR WEDDING CLOTHES, YOU NEED A MUD-SUIT.
A MUD-SUIT? CAN'T I JUST WEAR MY LAB SMOCK?
DON'T BE SILLY. YOUR SMOCK WAS DESTROYED IN THAT EXPLOSION.
JUST PUT YOUR ARMS IN HERE...
NOW LET ME ZIP IT UP...
THERE. IS THAT COMFORTABLE, ALEC?
ALEC?
ALEC, ARE YOU OKAY IN THERE?
MATT, HE ISN'T BREATHING! THE LUNGS IN THAT SUIT HAVE NO CAPILLARY ACTION, REMEMBER? GET IT OFF OF HIM!
IT'S OKAY...THE SUIT'S ONLY MADE OUT OF MUD. YOU CAN SCOOP IT OFF IN HANDFULS...
JUST A LITTLE MORE...
THERE.
B-BUT...
BUT MATT... WHERE'S ALEC?
"ALEC ISN'T IN THERE."
8

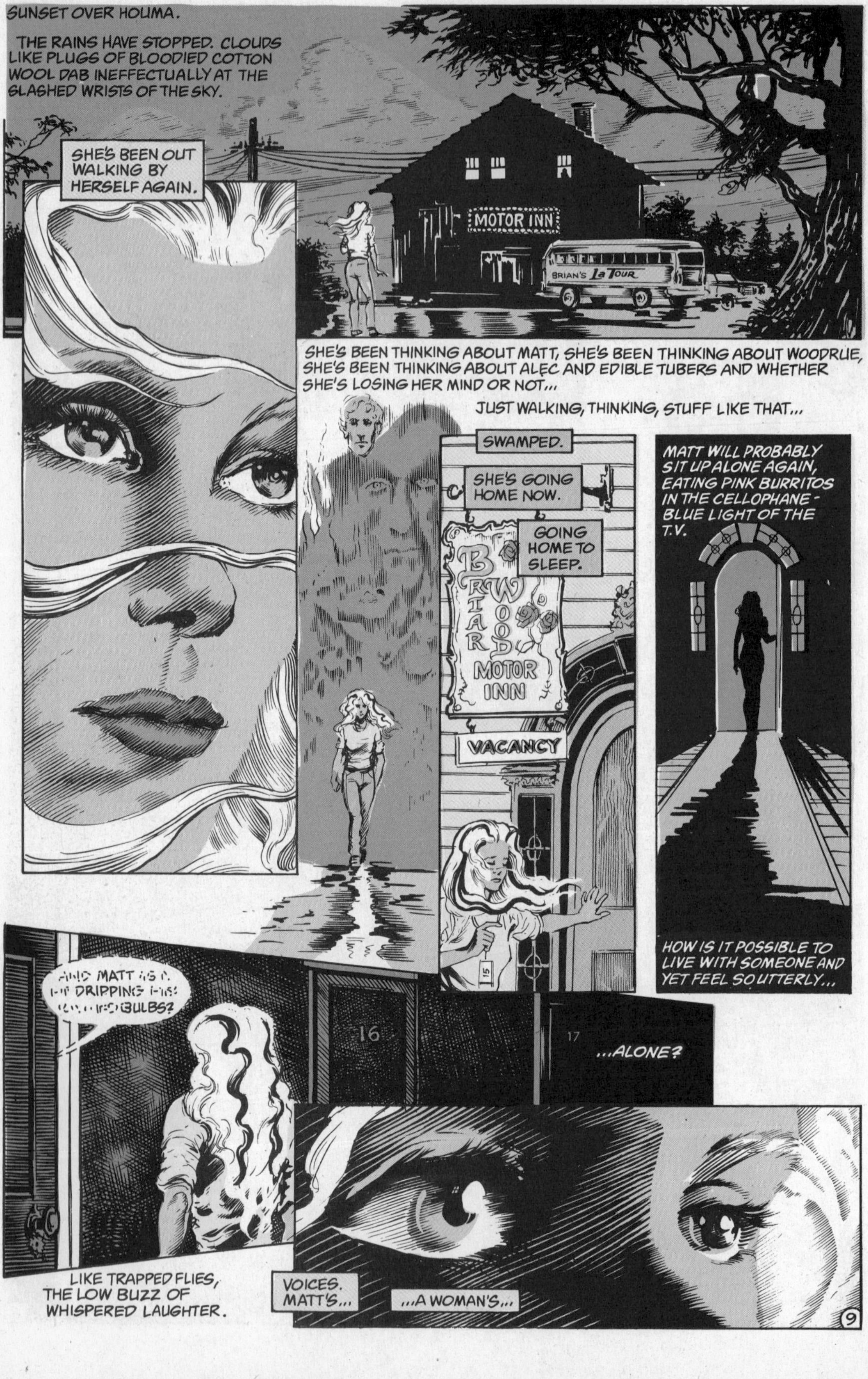
SUNSET OVER HOUMA.
THE RAINS HAVE STOPPED. CLOUDS LIKE PLUGS OF BLOODIED COTTON WOOL DAB INEFFECTUALLY AT THE SLASHED WRISTS OF THE SKY.
SHE'S BEEN OUT WALKING BY HERSELF AGAIN.
MOTOR INN
BRIAN'S La TOUR
SHE'S BEEN THINKING ABOUT MATT, SHE'S BEEN THINKING ABOUT WOODRUE, SHE'S BEEN THINKING ABOUT ALEC AND EDIBLE TUBERS AND WHETHER SHE'S LOSING HER MIND OR NOT...
JUST WALKING, THINKING, STUFF LIKE THAT...
SWAMPED.
SHE'S GOING HOME NOW.
GOING HOME TO SLEEP.
BRIARWOOD MOTOR INN
VACANCY
15
MATT WILL PROBABLY SIT UP ALONE AGAIN, EATING PINK BURRITOS IN THE CELLOPHANE-BLUE LIGHT OF THE T.V.
HOW IS IT POSSIBLE TO LIVE WITH SOMEONE AND YET FEEL SO UTTERLY...
AND MATT
DRIPPING
BULBS?
16
17
...ALONE?
LIKE TRAPPED FLIES, THE LOW BUZZ OF WHISPERED LAUGHTER.
VOICES. MATT'S...
...A WOMAN'S...
9

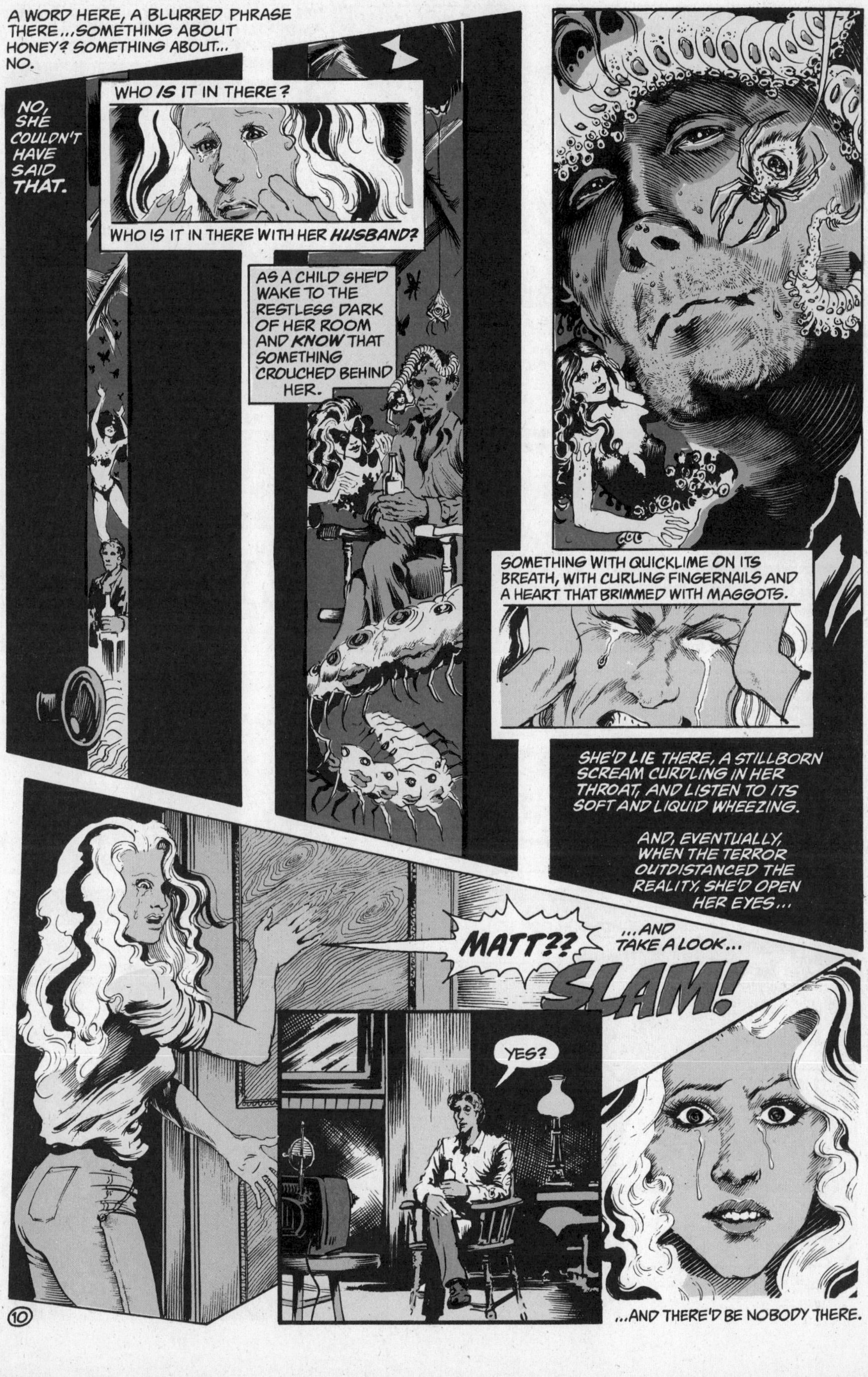
A WORD HERE, A BLURRED PHRASE THERE... SOMETHING ABOUT HONEY? SOMETHING ABOUT... NO.
NO, SHE COULDN'T HAVE SAID THAT.
WHO IS IT IN THERE?
WHO IS IT IN THERE WITH HER HUSBAND?
AS A CHILD SHE'D WAKE TO THE RESTLESS DARK OF HER ROOM AND KNOW THAT SOMETHING CROUCHED BEHIND HER.
SOMETHING WITH QUICKLIME ON ITS BREATH, WITH CURLING FINGERNAILS AND A HEART THAT BRIMMED WITH MAGGOTS.
SHE'D LIE THERE, A STILLBORN SCREAM CURDLING IN HER THROAT, AND LISTEN TO ITS SOFT AND LIQUID WHEEZING.
AND, EVENTUALLY, WHEN THE TERROR OUTDISTANCED THE REALITY, SHE'D OPEN HER EYES...
MATT??
...AND TAKE A LOOK...
SLAM!
YES?
...AND THERE'D BE NOBODY THERE.
10

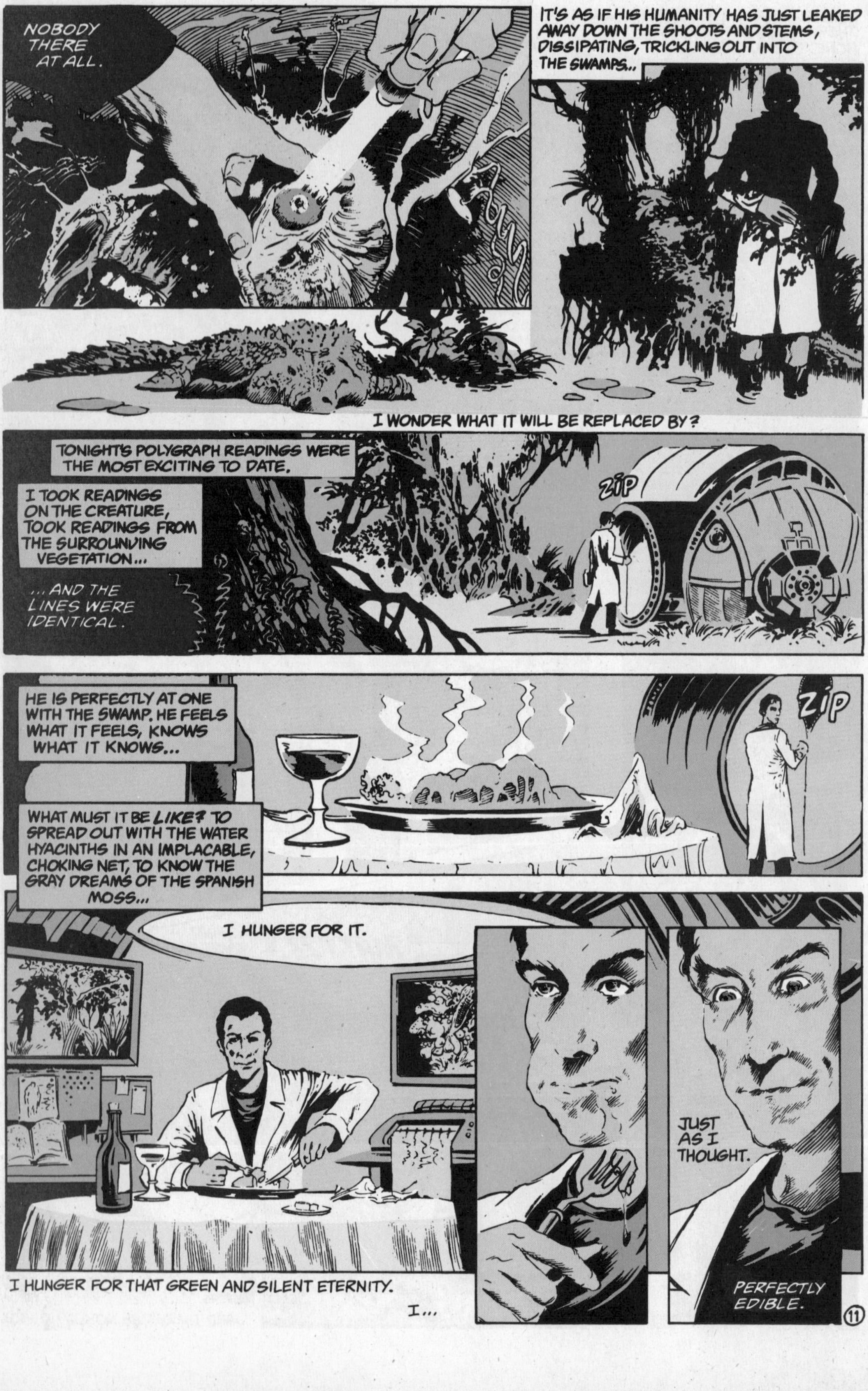
NOBODY THERE AT ALL.
IT'S AS IF HIS HUMANITY HAS JUST LEAKED AWAY DOWN THE SHOOTS AND STEMS, DISSIPATING, TRICKLING OUT INTO THE SWAMPS...
I WONDER WHAT IT WILL BE REPLACED BY?
TONIGHT'S POLYGRAPH READINGS WERE THE MOST EXCITING TO DATE.
I TOOK READINGS ON THE CREATURE, TOOK READINGS FROM THE SURROUNDING VEGETATION...
...AND THE LINES WERE IDENTICAL.
ZIP
HE IS PERFECTLY AT ONE WITH THE SWAMP. HE FEELS WHAT IT FEELS, KNOWS WHAT IT KNOWS...
WHAT MUST IT BE *LIKE*? TO SPREAD OUT WITH THE WATER HYACINTHS IN AN IMPLACABLE, CHOKING NET, TO KNOW THE GRAY DREAMS OF THE SPANISH MOSS...
ZIP
I HUNGER FOR IT.
I HUNGER FOR THAT GREEN AND SILENT ETERNITY.
I...
JUST AS I THOUGHT.
PERFECTLY EDIBLE.
11

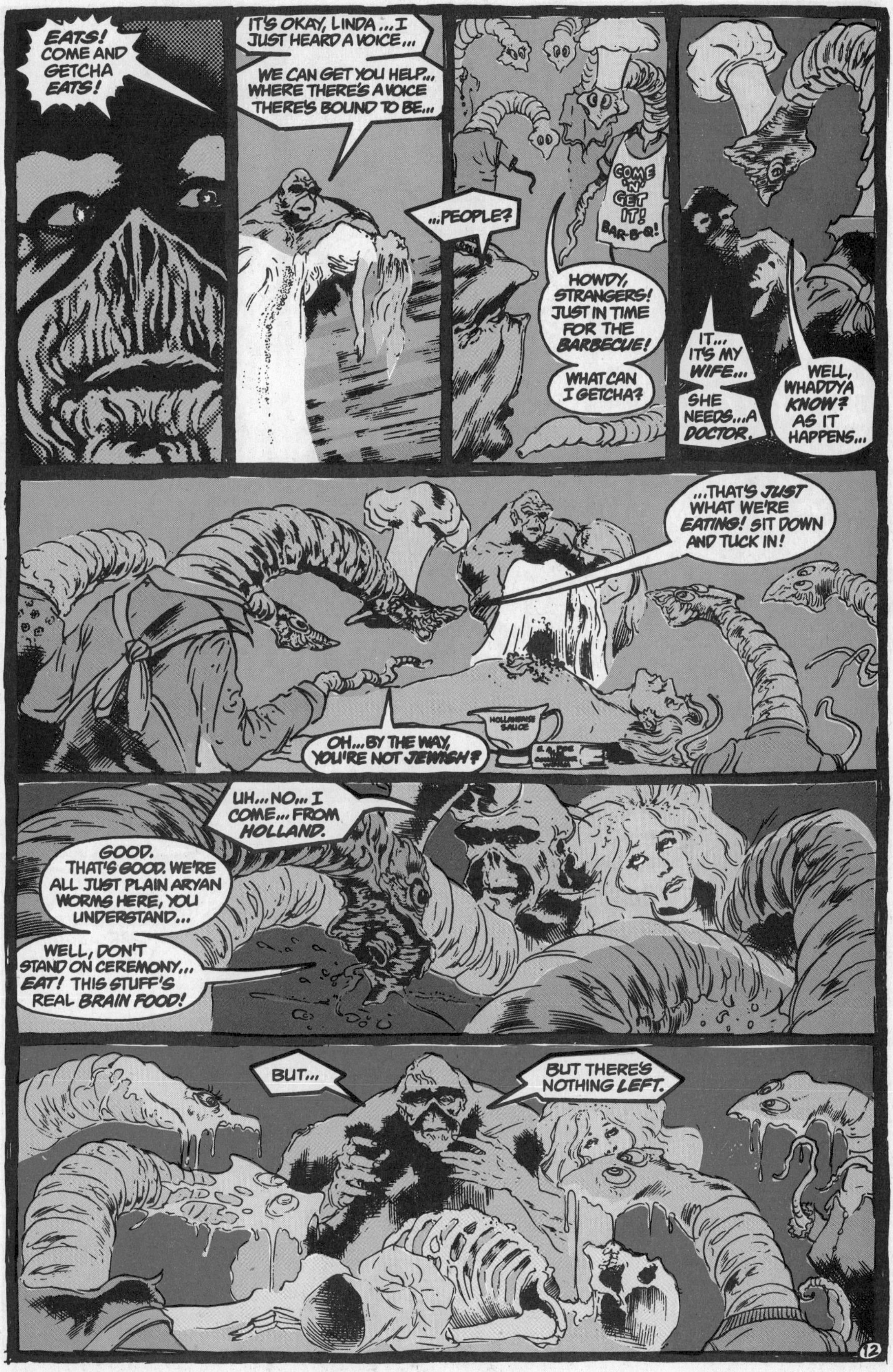
EATS! COME AND GETCHA EATS!
IT'S OKAY, LINDA... I JUST HEARD A VOICE...
WE CAN GET YOU HELP... WHERE THERE'S A VOICE THERE'S BOUND TO BE...
...PEOPLE?
COME 'N' GET IT! BAR-B-Q!
HOWDY, STRANGERS! JUST IN TIME FOR THE BARBECUE!
WHAT CAN I GETCHA?
IT... IT'S MY WIFE...
SHE NEEDS... A DOCTOR.
WELL, WHADDYA KNOW? AS IT HAPPENS...
...THAT'S JUST WHAT WE'RE EATING! SIT DOWN AND TUCK IN!
HOLLANDAISE SAUCE
OH... BY THE WAY, YOU'RE NOT JEWISH?
UH... NO... I COME... FROM HOLLAND.
GOOD. THAT'S GOOD. WE'RE ALL JUST PLAIN ARYAN WORMS HERE, YOU UNDERSTAND...
WELL, DON'T STAND ON CEREMONY... EAT! THIS STUFF'S REAL BRAIN FOOD!
BUT...
BUT THERE'S NOTHING LEFT.
12

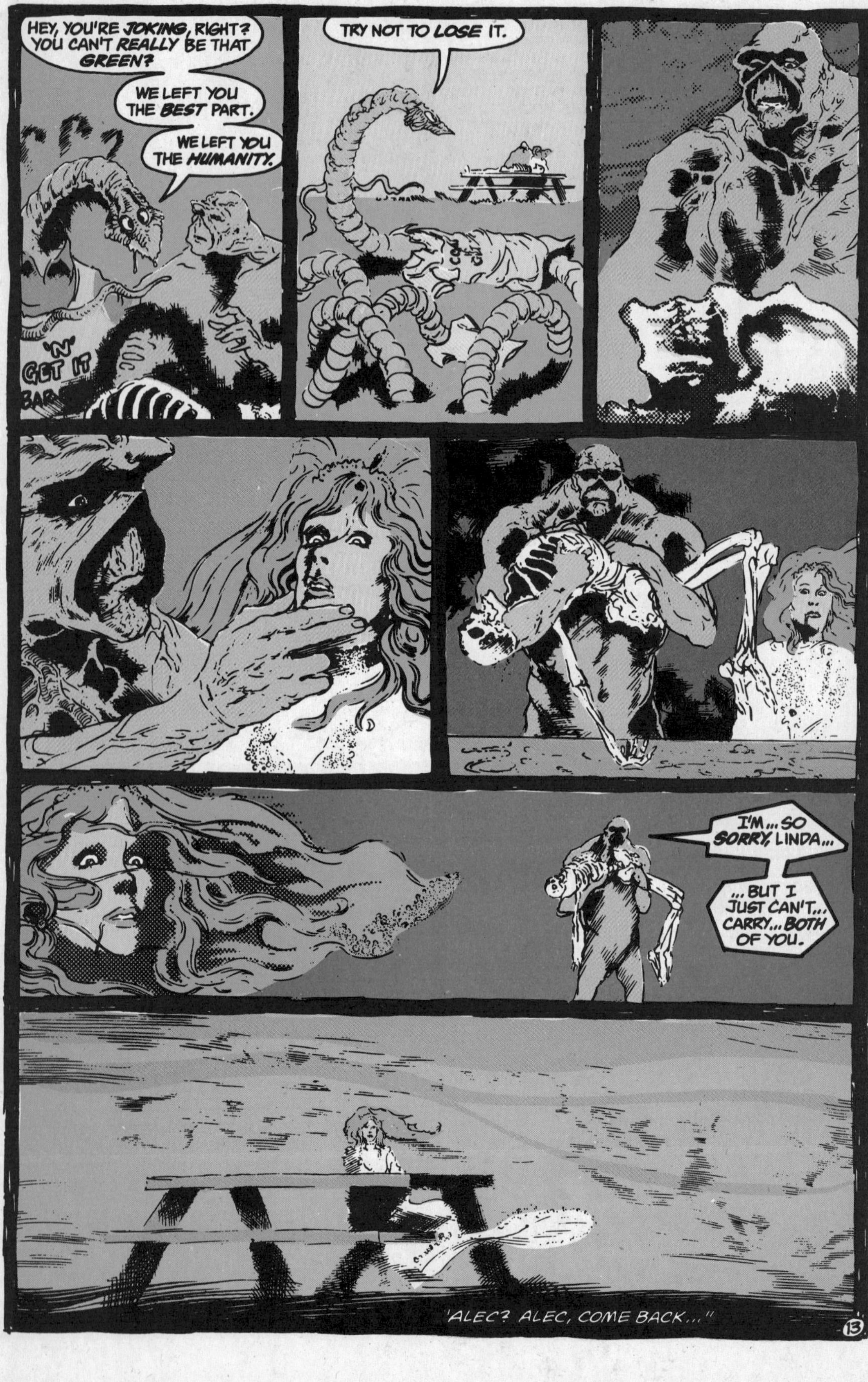
HEY, YOU'RE JOKING, RIGHT? YOU CAN'T REALLY BE THAT GREEN?
WE LEFT YOU THE BEST PART.
WE LEFT YOU THE HUMANITY.
'N' GET IT
TRY NOT TO LOSE IT.
I'M... SO SORRY, LINDA...
...BUT I JUST CAN'T... CARRY... BOTH OF YOU.
"ALEC? ALEC, COME BACK..."
13

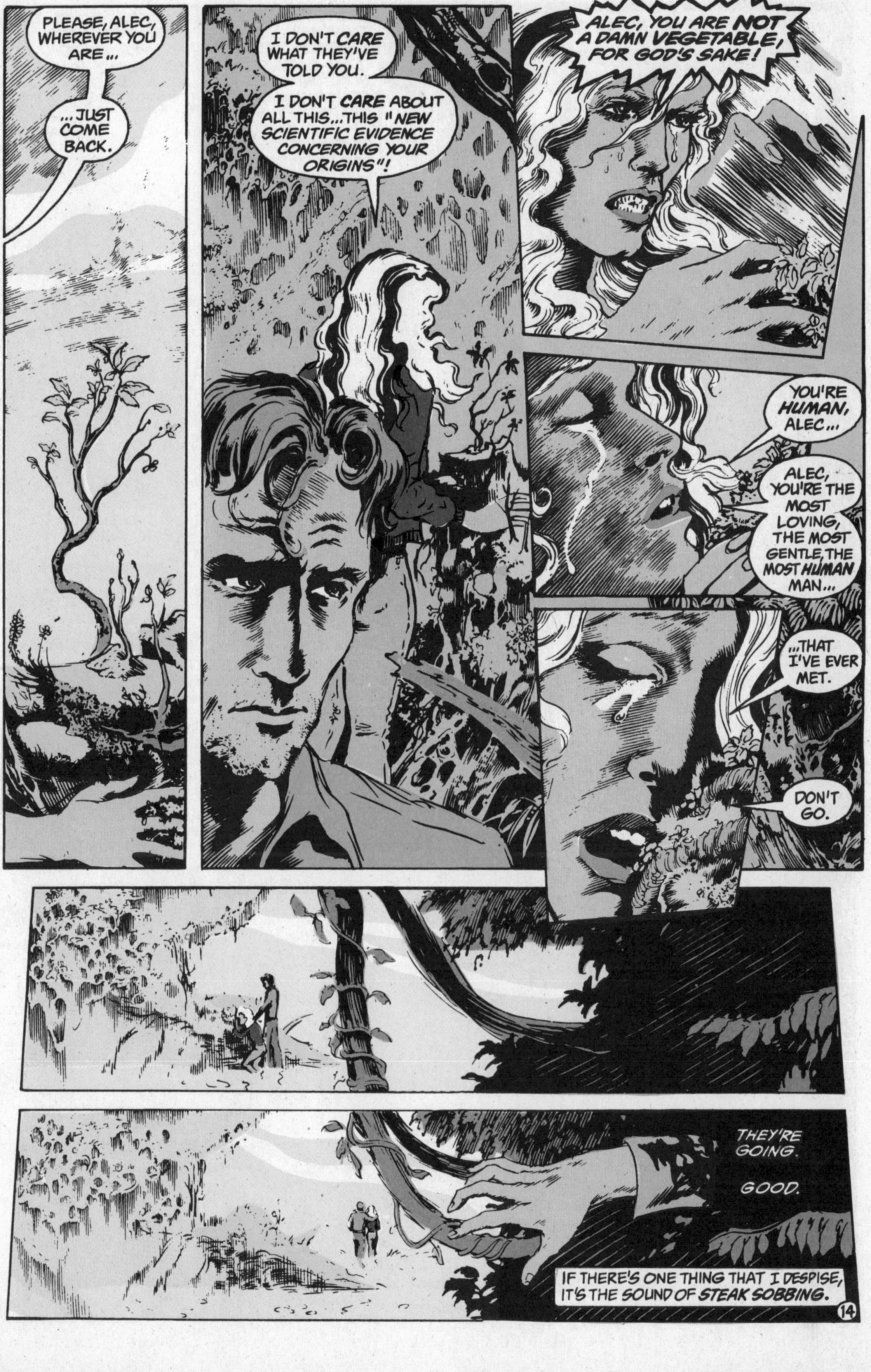
PLEASE, ALEC, WHEREVER YOU ARE...
...JUST COME BACK.
I DON'T CARE WHAT THEY'VE TOLD YOU.
I DON'T CARE ABOUT ALL THIS...THIS "NEW SCIENTIFIC EVIDENCE CONCERNING YOUR ORIGINS"!
ALEC, YOU ARE NOT A DAMN VEGETABLE, FOR GOD'S SAKE!
YOU'RE HUMAN, ALEC...
ALEC, YOU'RE THE MOST LOVING, THE MOST GENTLE, THE MOST HUMAN MAN...
...THAT I'VE EVER MET.
DON'T GO.
THEY'RE GOING.
GOOD.
IF THERE'S ONE THING THAT I DESPISE, IT'S THE SOUND OF STEAK SOBBING.
14

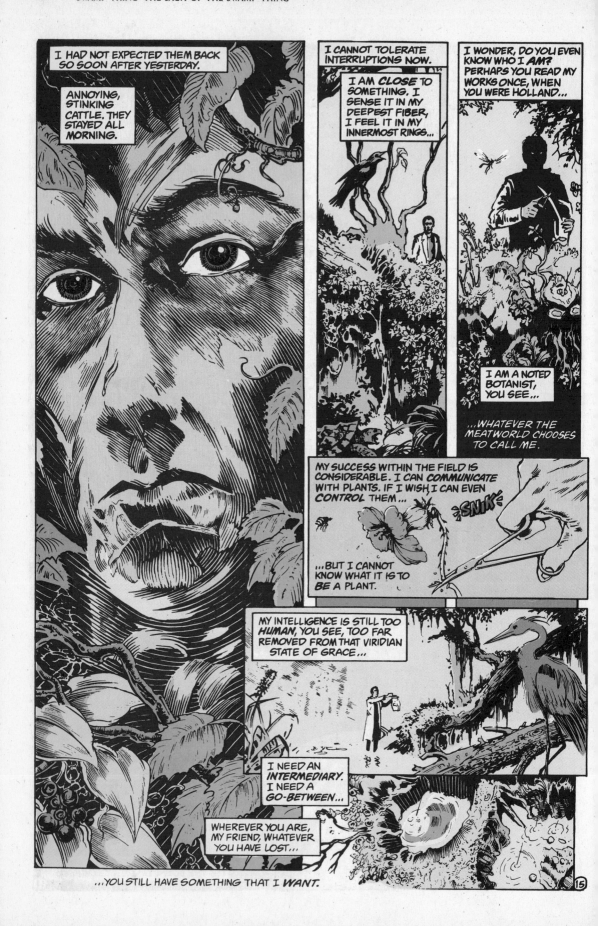

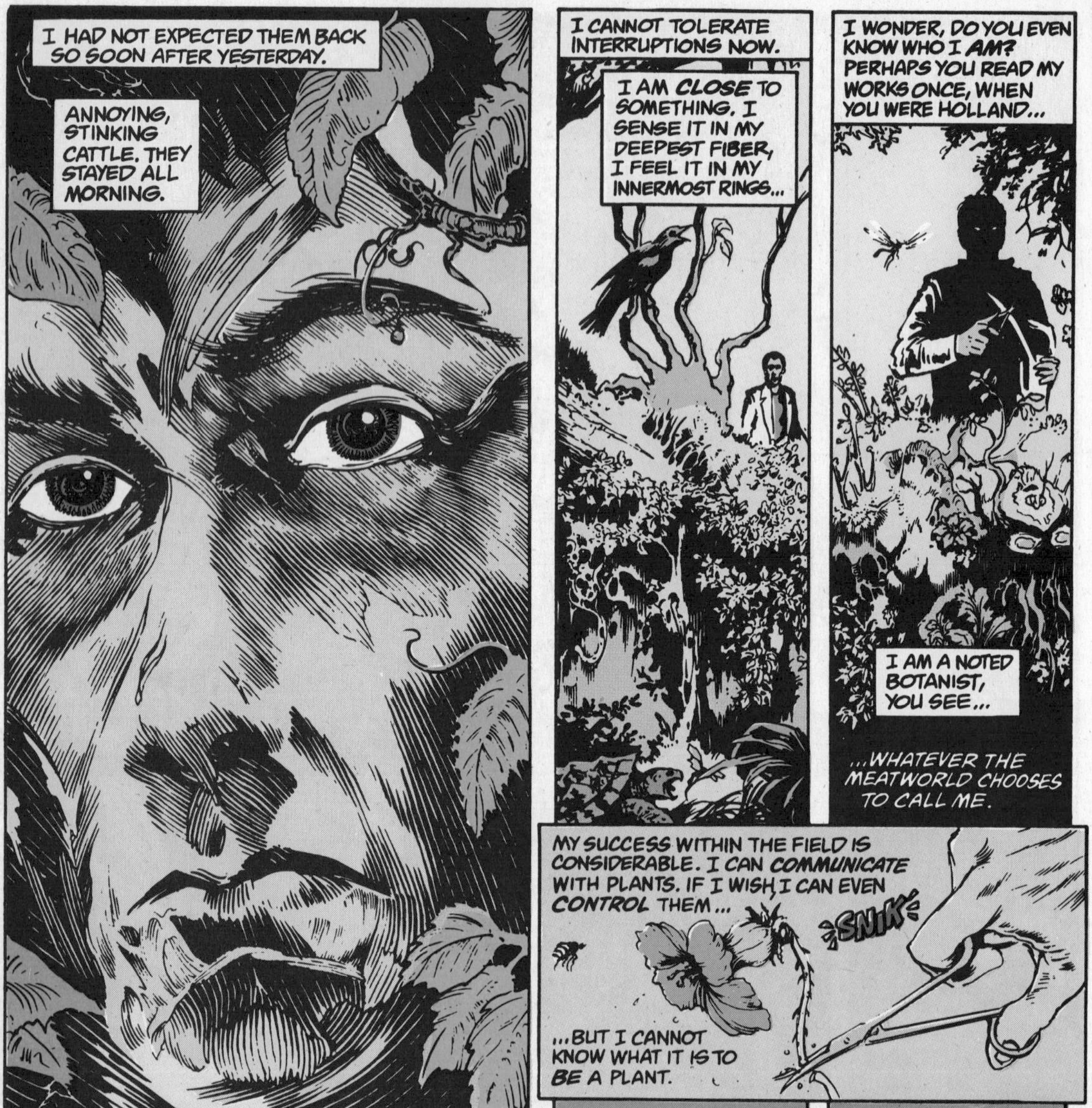
I HAD NOT EXPECTED THEM BACK SO SOON AFTER YESTERDAY.
ANNOYING, STINKING CATTLE. THEY STAYED ALL MORNING.
I CANNOT TOLERATE INTERRUPTIONS NOW.
I AM CLOSE TO SOMETHING. I SENSE IT IN MY DEEPEST FIBER, I FEEL IT IN MY INNERMOST RINGS...
I WONDER, DO YOU EVEN KNOW WHO I AM? PERHAPS YOU READ MY WORKS ONCE, WHEN YOU WERE HOLLAND...
I AM A NOTED BOTANIST, YOU SEE...
...WHATEVER THE MEATWORLD CHOOSES TO CALL ME.
MY SUCCESS WITHIN THE FIELD IS CONSIDERABLE. I CAN COMMUNICATE WITH PLANTS. IF I WISH, I CAN EVEN CONTROL THEM...
SNIK
...BUT I CANNOT KNOW WHAT IT IS TO BE A PLANT.
MY INTELLIGENCE IS STILL TOO HUMAN, YOU SEE, TOO FAR REMOVED FROM THAT VIRIDIAN STATE OF GRACE...
I NEED AN INTERMEDIARY. I NEED A GO-BETWEEN...
WHEREVER YOU ARE, MY FRIEND, WHATEVER YOU HAVE LOST...
...YOU STILL HAVE SOMETHING THAT I WANT.
15

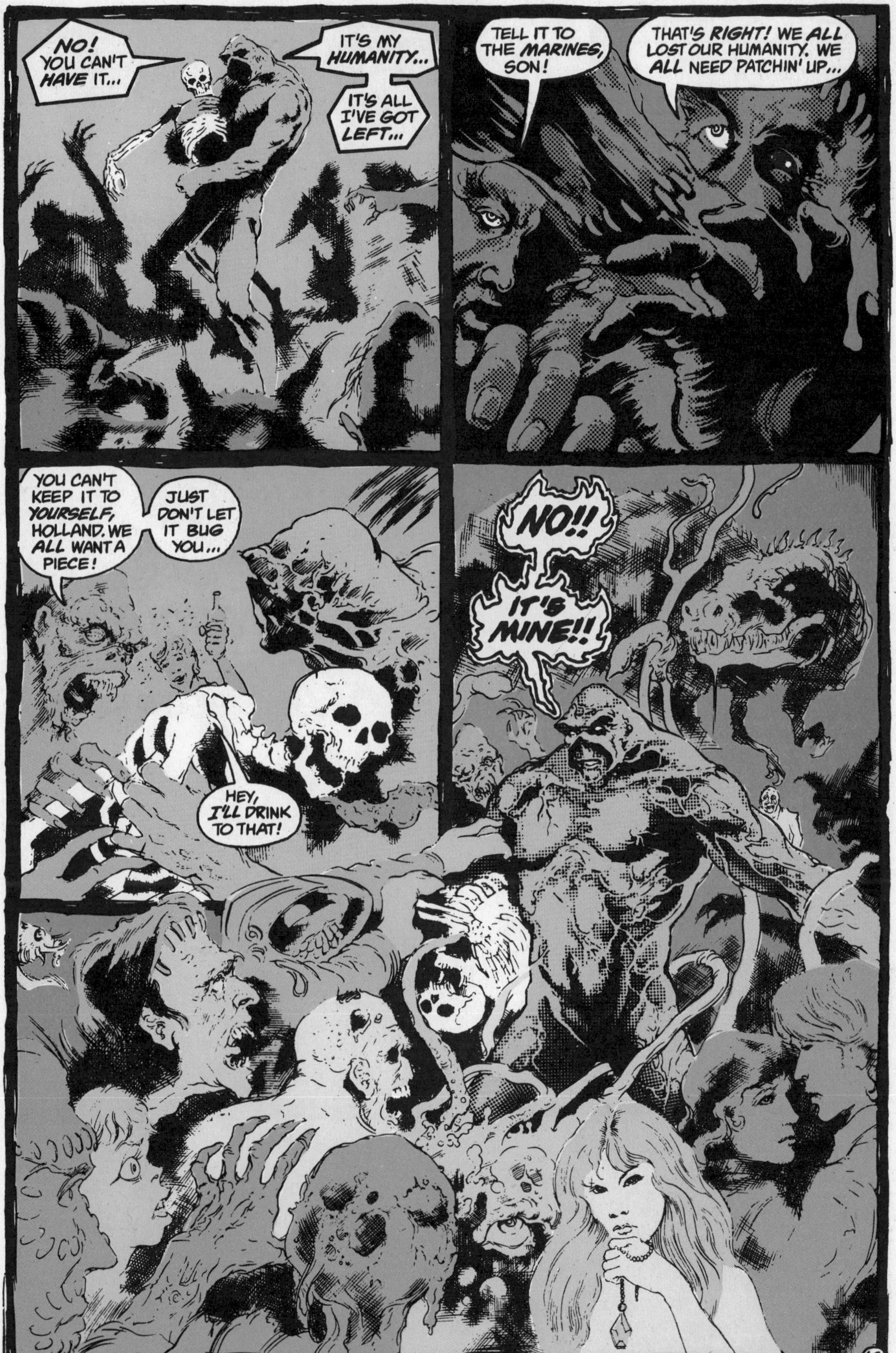
NO! YOU CAN'T HAVE IT...
IT'S MY HUMANITY...
IT'S ALL I'VE GOT LEFT...
TELL IT TO THE MARINES, SON!
THAT'S RIGHT! WE ALL LOST OUR HUMANITY. WE ALL NEED PATCHIN' UP...
YOU CAN'T KEEP IT TO YOURSELF, HOLLAND. WE ALL WANT A PIECE!
JUST DON'T LET IT BUG YOU...
HEY, I'LL DRINK TO THAT!
NO!!
IT'S MINE!!
16

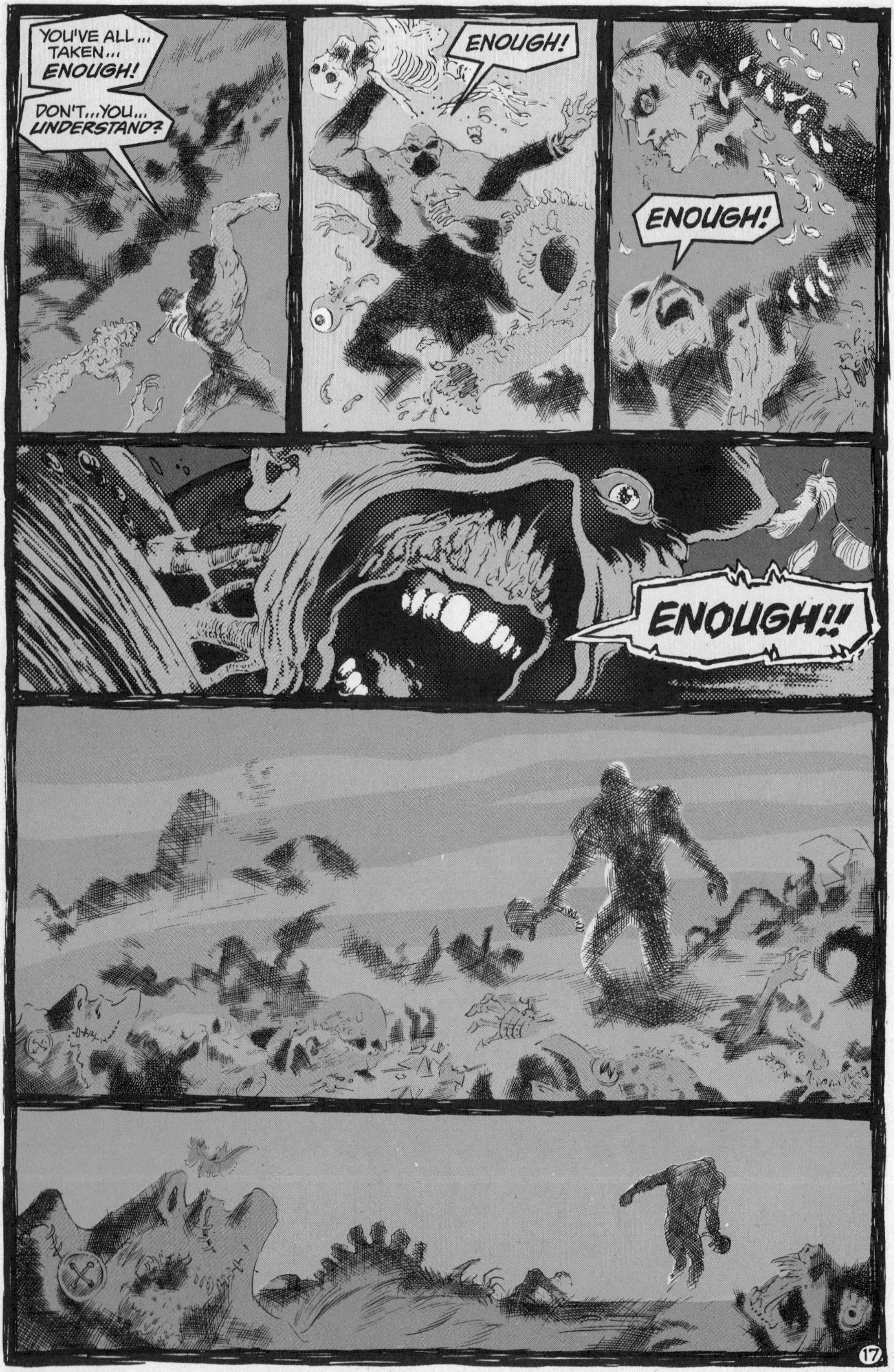
YOU'VE ALL... TAKEN... ENOUGH!
DON'T...YOU... UNDERSTAND?
ENOUGH!
ENOUGH!
ENOUGH!!
17

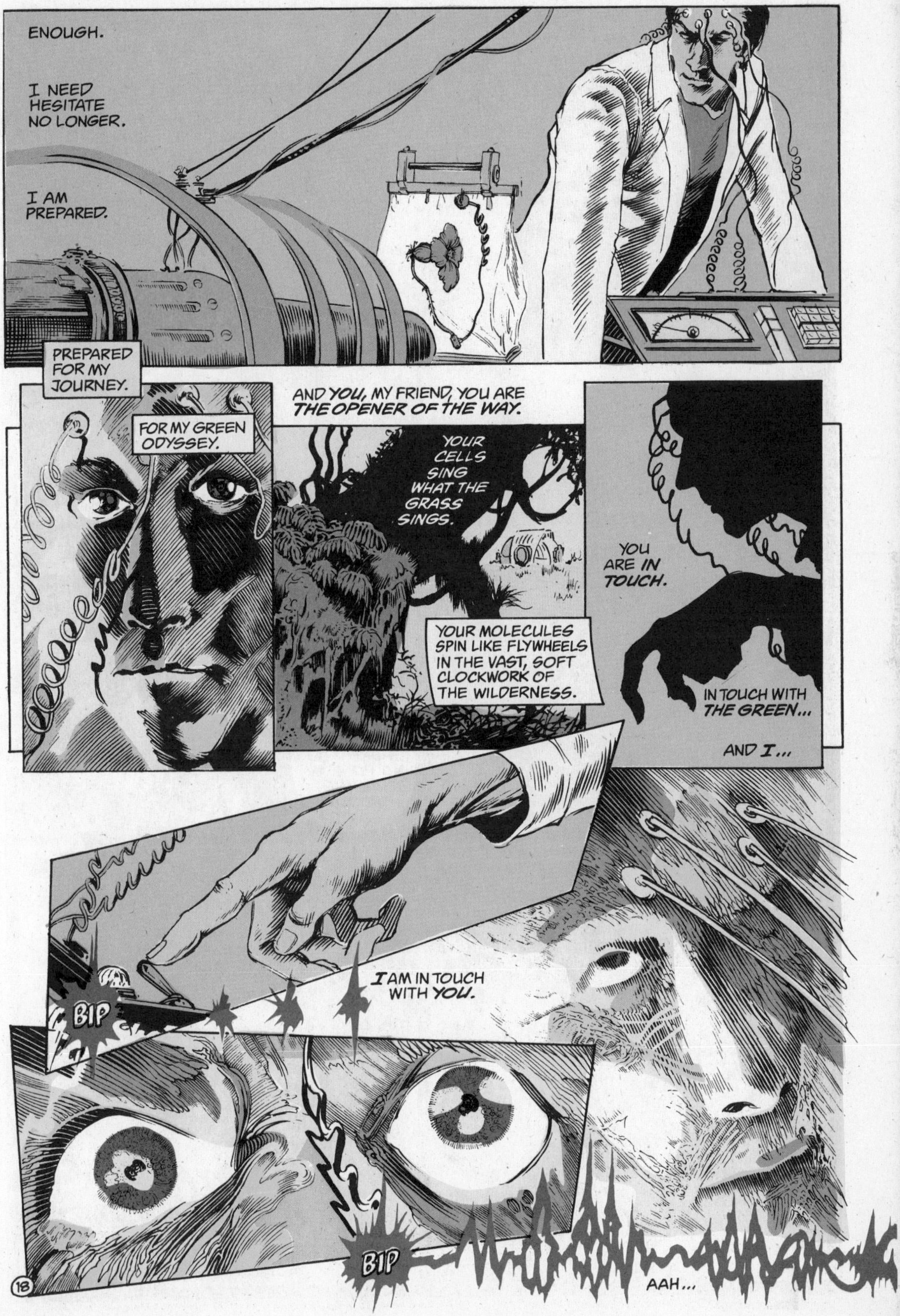
ENOUGH.
I NEED HESITATE NO LONGER.
I AM PREPARED.
PREPARED FOR MY JOURNEY.
FOR MY GREEN ODYSSEY.
AND YOU, MY FRIEND, YOU ARE THE OPENER OF THE WAY.
YOUR CELLS SING WHAT THE GRASS SINGS.
YOUR MOLECULES SPIN LIKE FLYWHEELS IN THE VAST, SOFT CLOCKWORK OF THE WILDERNESS.
YOU ARE IN TOUCH.
IN TOUCH WITH THE GREEN...
AND I...
I AM IN TOUCH WITH YOU.
BIP
BIP
AAH...
18

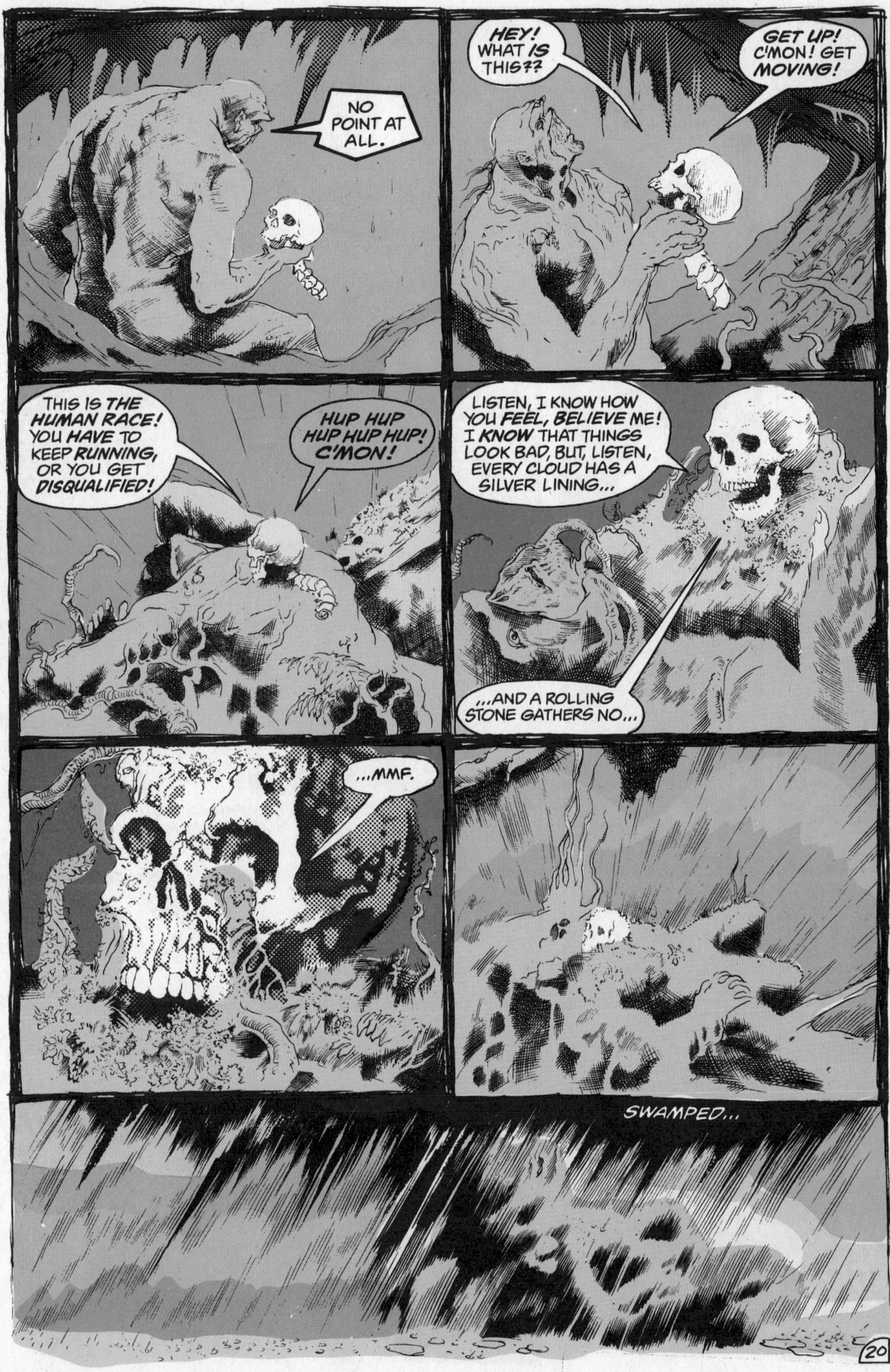
NO POINT AT ALL.
HEY! WHAT IS THIS??
GET UP! C'MON! GET MOVING!
THIS IS THE HUMAN RACE! YOU HAVE TO KEEP RUNNING, OR YOU GET DISQUALIFIED!
HUP HUP HUP HUP HUP! C'MON!
LISTEN, I KNOW HOW YOU FEEL, BELIEVE ME! I KNOW THAT THINGS LOOK BAD, BUT, LISTEN, EVERY CLOUD HAS A SILVER LINING...
...AND A ROLLING STONE GATHERS NO...
...MMF.
SWAMPED...
20

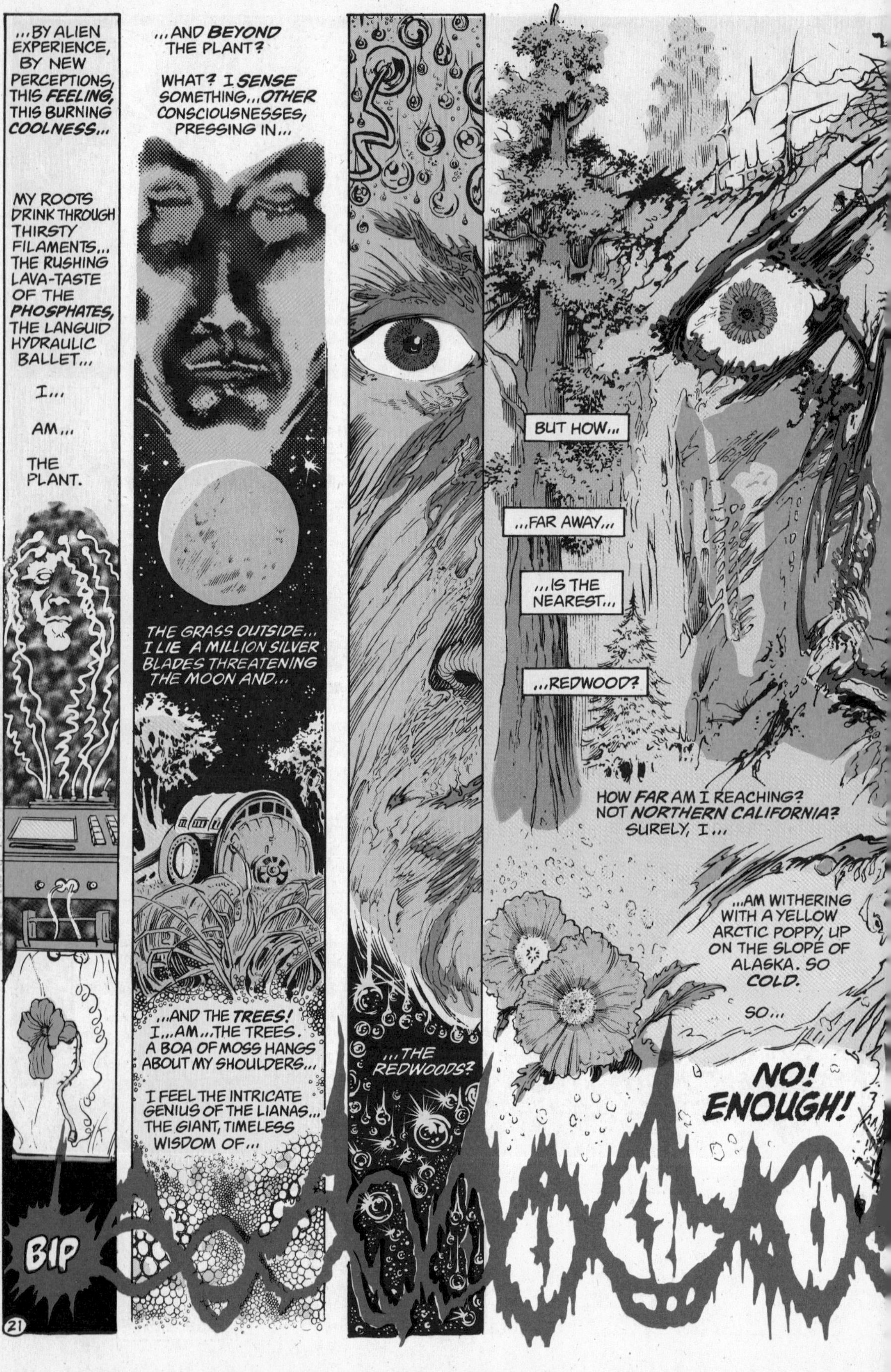
...BY ALIEN EXPERIENCE, BY NEW PERCEPTIONS, THIS FEELING, THIS BURNING COOLNESS...
MY ROOTS DRINK THROUGH THIRSTY FILAMENTS... THE RUSHING LAVA-TASTE OF THE PHOSPHATES, THE LANGUID HYDRAULIC BALLET...
I...
AM...
THE PLANT.
BIP
...AND BEYOND THE PLANT?
WHAT? I SENSE SOMETHING... OTHER CONSCIOUSNESSES, PRESSING IN...
THE GRASS OUTSIDE... I LIE A MILLION SILVER BLADES THREATENING THE MOON AND...
...AND THE TREES! I...AM...THE TREES. A BOA OF MOSS HANGS ABOUT MY SHOULDERS...
I FEEL THE INTRICATE GENIUS OF THE LIANAS... THE GIANT, TIMELESS WISDOM OF...
...THE REDWOODS?
BUT HOW...
...FAR AWAY...
...IS THE NEAREST...
...REDWOOD?
HOW FAR AM I REACHING? NOT NORTHERN CALIFORNIA? SURELY, I...
...AM WITHERING WITH A YELLOW ARCTIC POPPY, UP ON THE SLOPE OF ALASKA. SO COLD.
SO...
NO! ENOUGH!
21

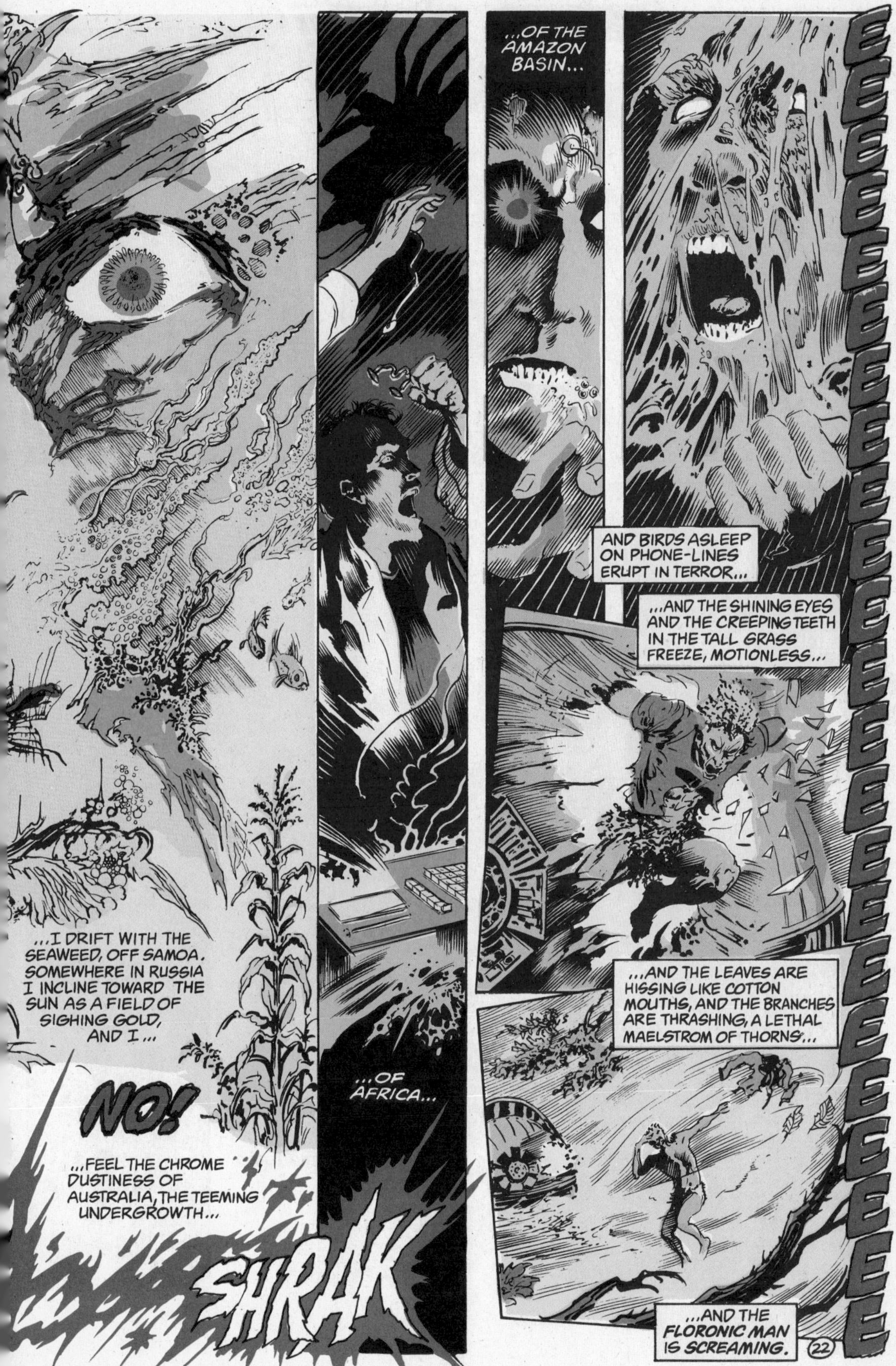
...I DRIFT WITH THE SEAWEED, OFF SAMOA. SOMEWHERE IN RUSSIA I INCLINE TOWARD THE SUN AS A FIELD OF SIGHING GOLD, AND I...
NO!
...FEEL THE CHROME DUSTINESS OF AUSTRALIA, THE TEEMING UNDERGROWTH...
SHRAK
...OF AFRICA...
...OF THE AMAZON BASIN...
AND BIRDS ASLEEP ON PHONE-LINES ERUPT IN TERROR...
...AND THE SHINING EYES AND THE CREEPING TEETH IN THE TALL GRASS FREEZE, MOTIONLESS...
...AND THE LEAVES ARE HISSING LIKE COTTON MOUTHS, AND THE BRANCHES ARE THRASHING, A LETHAL MAELSTROM OF THORNS...
...AND THE FLORONIC MAN IS SCREAMING.
EEEEEEEEEEEEEEEEEEEEEEEEEEEEEEEEE
22

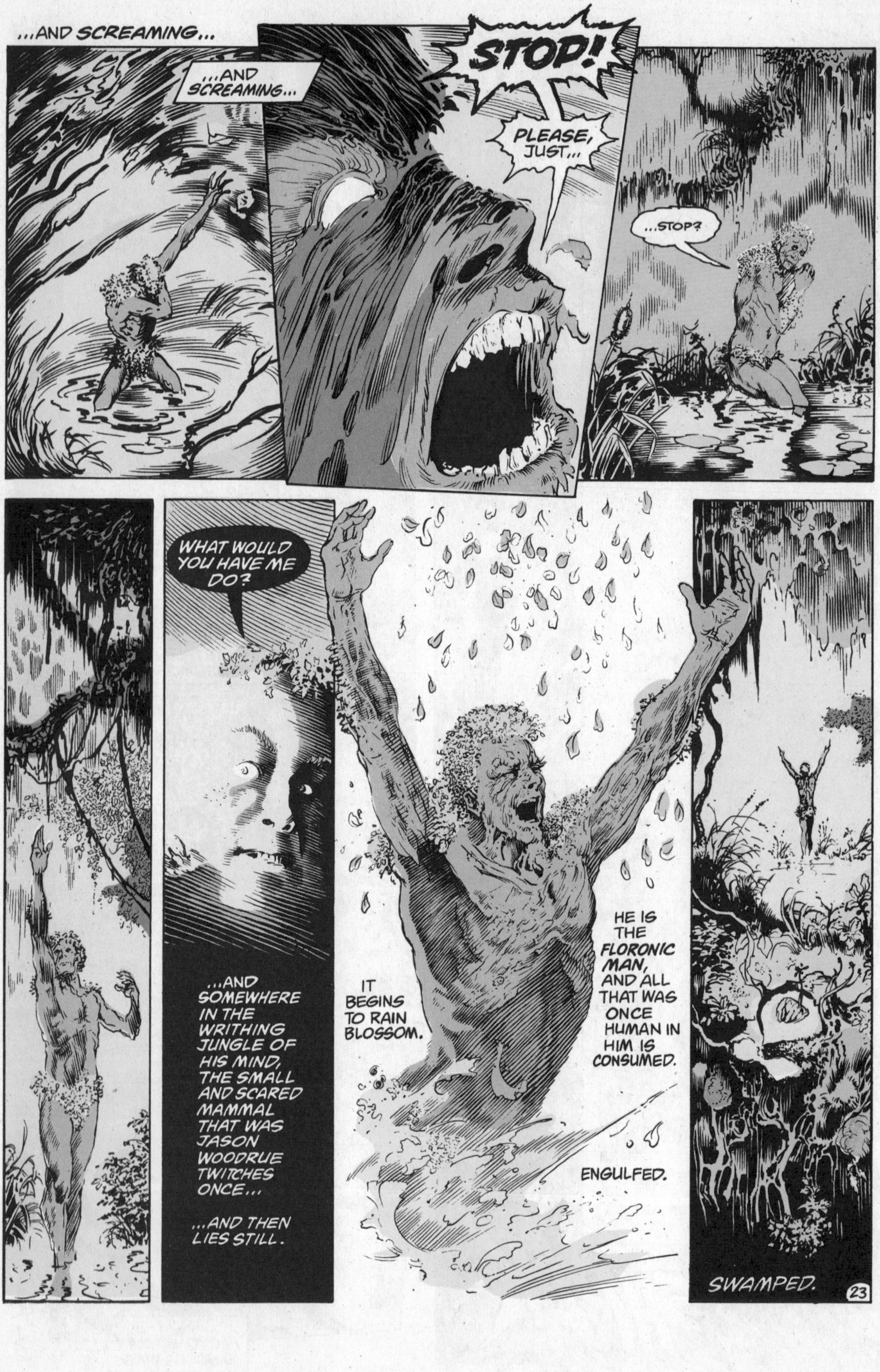
...AND SCREAMING...
...AND SCREAMING...
STOP!
PLEASE, JUST...
...STOP?
WHAT WOULD YOU HAVE ME DO?
...AND SOMEWHERE IN THE WRITHING JUNGLE OF HIS MIND, THE SMALL AND SCARED MAMMAL THAT WAS JASON WOODRUE TWITCHES ONCE...
...AND THEN LIES STILL.
IT BEGINS TO RAIN BLOSSOM.
HE IS THE FLORONIC MAN, AND ALL THAT WAS ONCE HUMAN IN HIM IS CONSUMED.
ENGULFED.
SWAMPED.
23

BOOK THREE

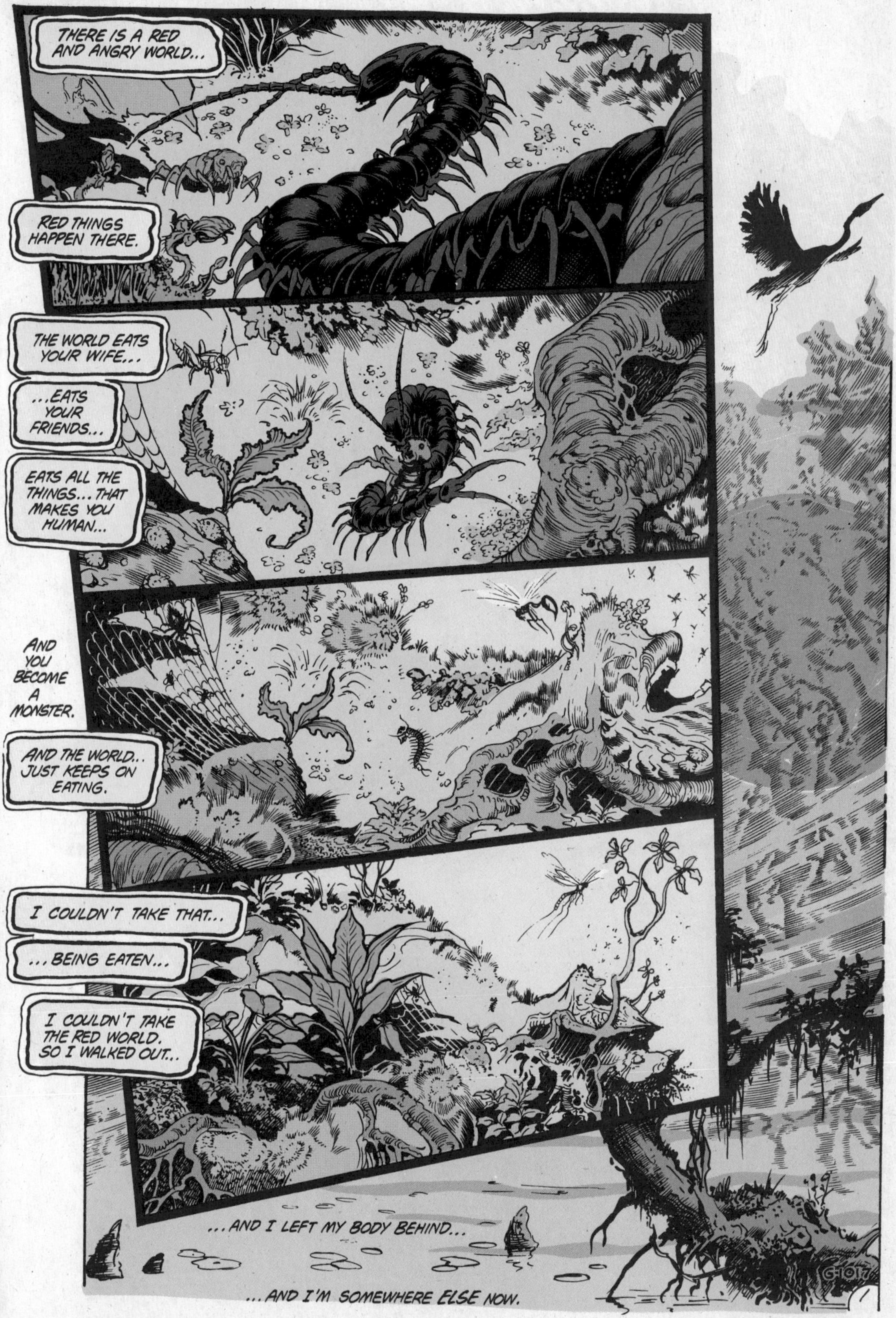
THERE IS A RED AND ANGRY WORLD...
RED THINGS HAPPEN THERE.
THE WORLD EATS YOUR WIFE...
...EATS YOUR FRIENDS...
EATS ALL THE THINGS... THAT MAKES YOU HUMAN...
AND YOU BECOME A MONSTER.
AND THE WORLD.. JUST KEEPS ON EATING.
I COULDN'T TAKE THAT...
...BEING EATEN...
I COULDN'T TAKE THE RED WORLD. SO I WALKED OUT...
...AND I LEFT MY BODY BEHIND...
...AND I'M SOMEWHERE ELSE NOW.

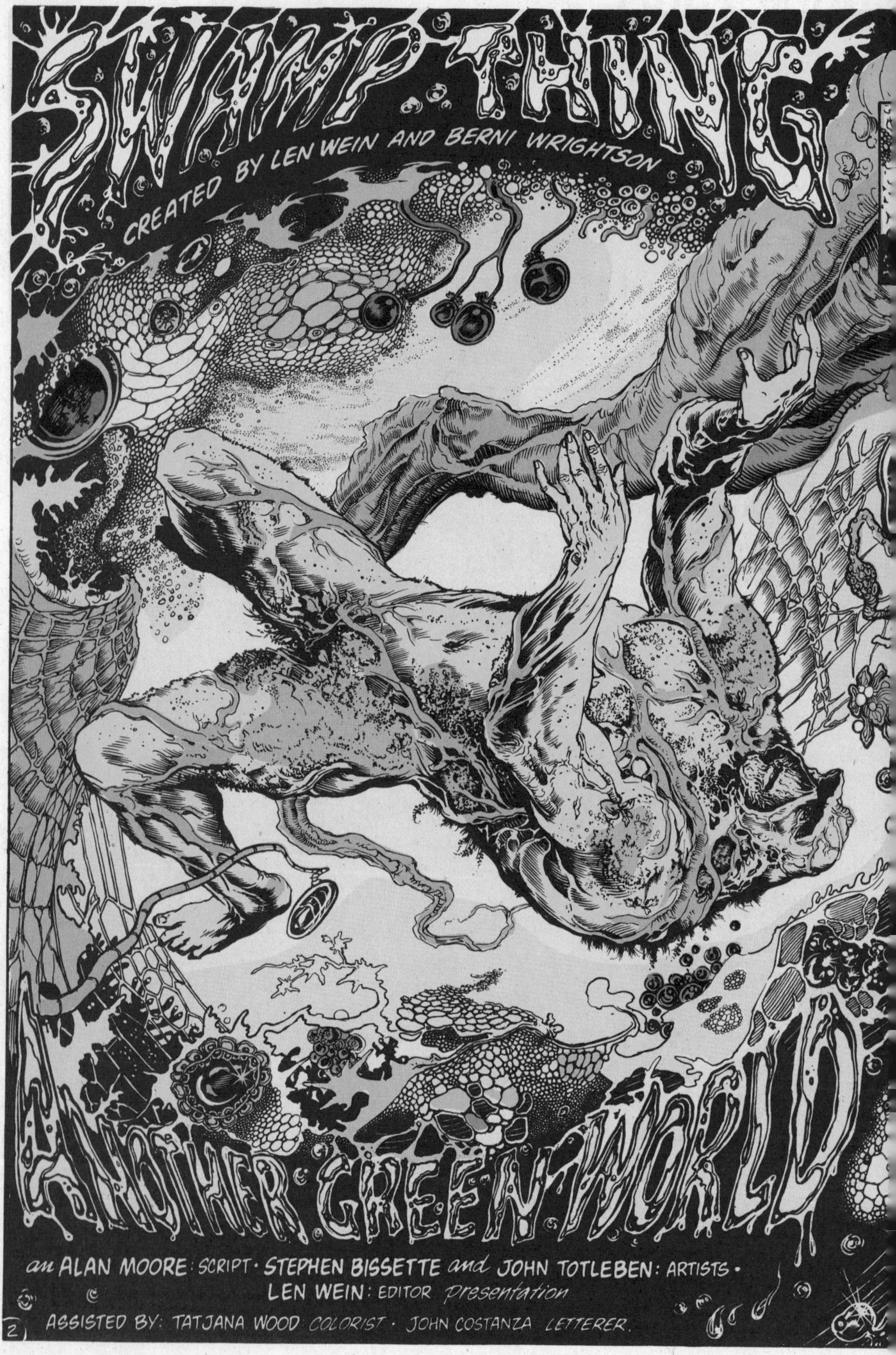
SWAMP THING
CREATED BY LEN WEIN AND BERNI WRIGHTSON
ANOTHER GREEN WORLD
an ALAN MOORE: SCRIPT · STEPHEN BISSETTE and JOHN TOTLEBEN: ARTISTS · LEN WEIN: EDITOR presentation
ASSISTED BY: TATJANA WOOD COLORIST · JOHN COSTANZA LETTERER.
2

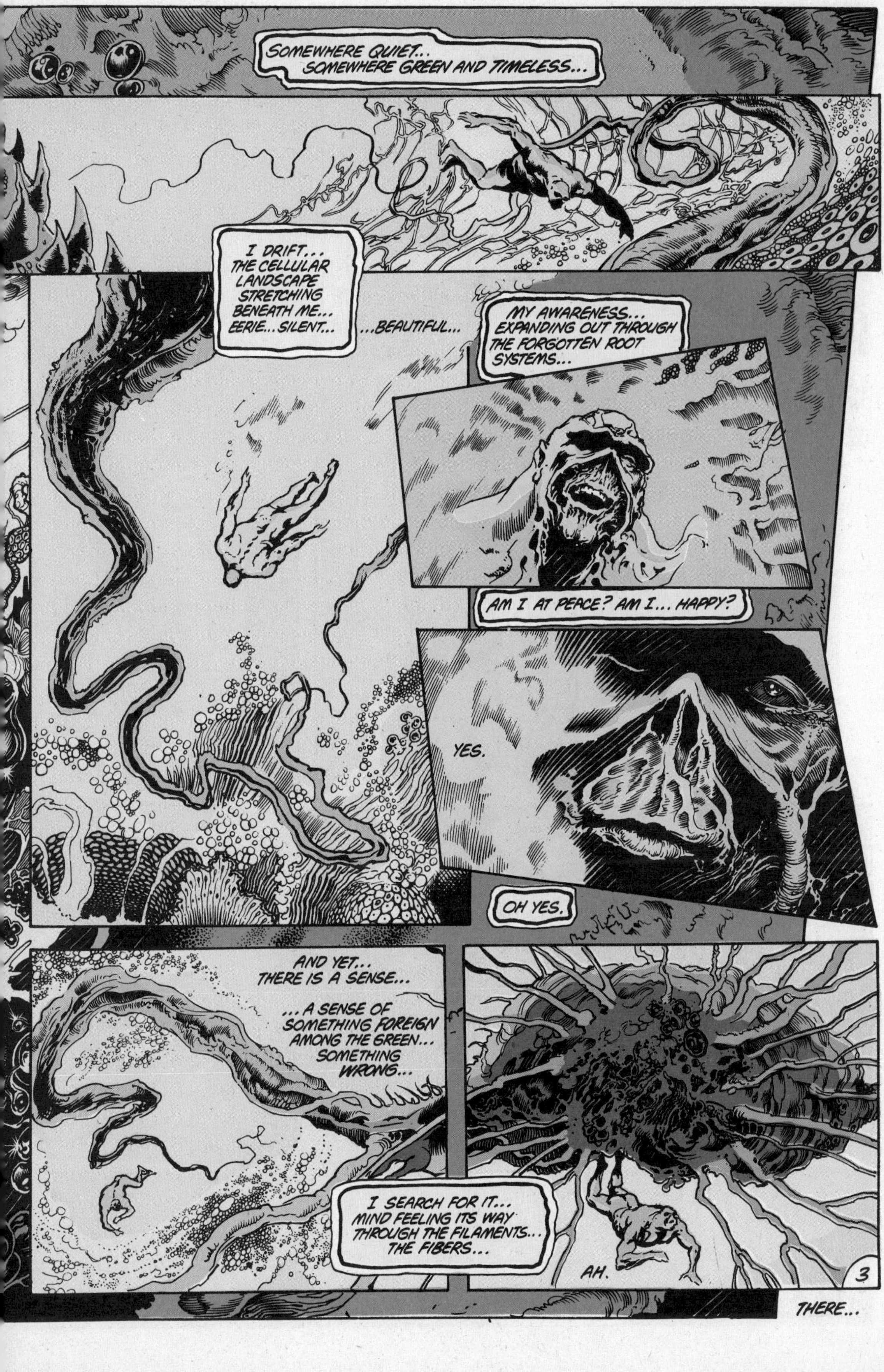
SOMEWHERE QUIET...
SOMEWHERE GREEN AND TIMELESS...
I DRIFT... THE CELLULAR LANDSCAPE STRETCHING BENEATH ME... EERIE... SILENT...
...BEAUTIFUL...
MY AWARENESS... EXPANDING OUT THROUGH THE FORGOTTEN ROOT SYSTEMS...
AM I AT PEACE? AM I... HAPPY?
YES.
OH YES.
AND YET... THERE IS A SENSE...
...A SENSE OF SOMETHING FOREIGN AMONG THE GREEN... SOMETHING WRONG...
I SEARCH FOR IT... MIND FEELING ITS WAY THROUGH THE FILAMENTS... THE FIBERS...
AH.
3
THERE...

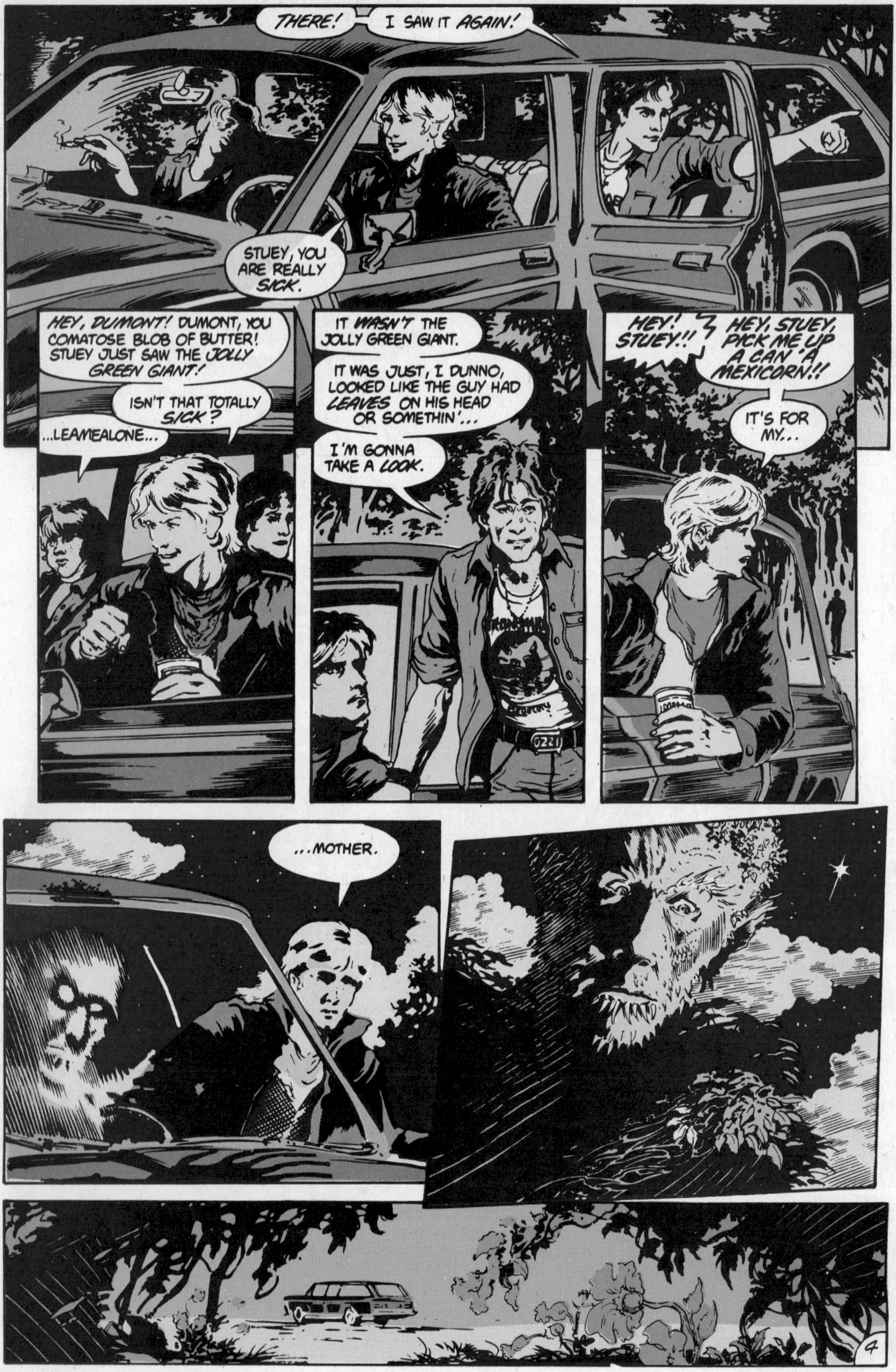
THERE!
I SAW IT AGAIN!
STUEY, YOU ARE REALLY SICK.
HEY, DUMONT! DUMONT, YOU COMATOSE BLOB OF BUTTER! STUEY JUST SAW THE JOLLY GREEN GIANT!
ISN'T THAT TOTALLY SICK?
...LEAMEALONE...
IT WASN'T THE JOLLY GREEN GIANT.
IT WAS JUST, I DUNNO, LOOKED LIKE THE GUY HAD LEAVES ON HIS HEAD OR SOMETHIN'...
I'M GONNA TAKE A LOOK.
HEY! STUEY!!
HEY, STUEY, PICK ME UP A CAN 'A MEXICORN!!
IT'S FOR MY...
...MOTHER.
4

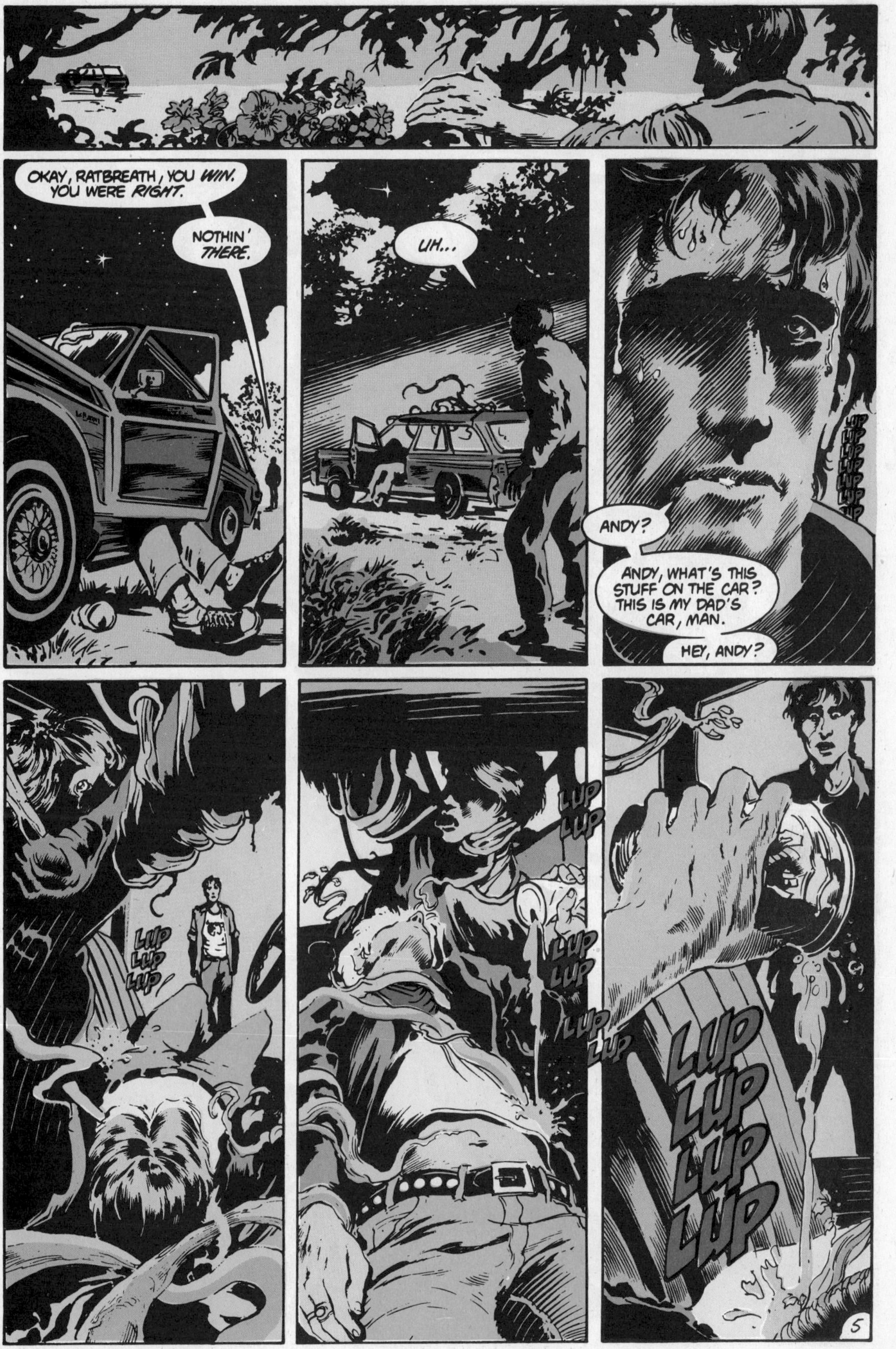
OKAY, RATBREATH, YOU WIN. YOU WERE RIGHT.
NOTHIN' THERE.
UH...
LUP LUP LUP LUP LUP LUP LUP
ANDY?
ANDY, WHAT'S THIS STUFF ON THE CAR? THIS IS MY DAD'S CAR, MAN.
HEY, ANDY?
LUP LUP LUP
LUP LUP
LUP LUP
LUP LUP
LUP LUP LUP LUP
5

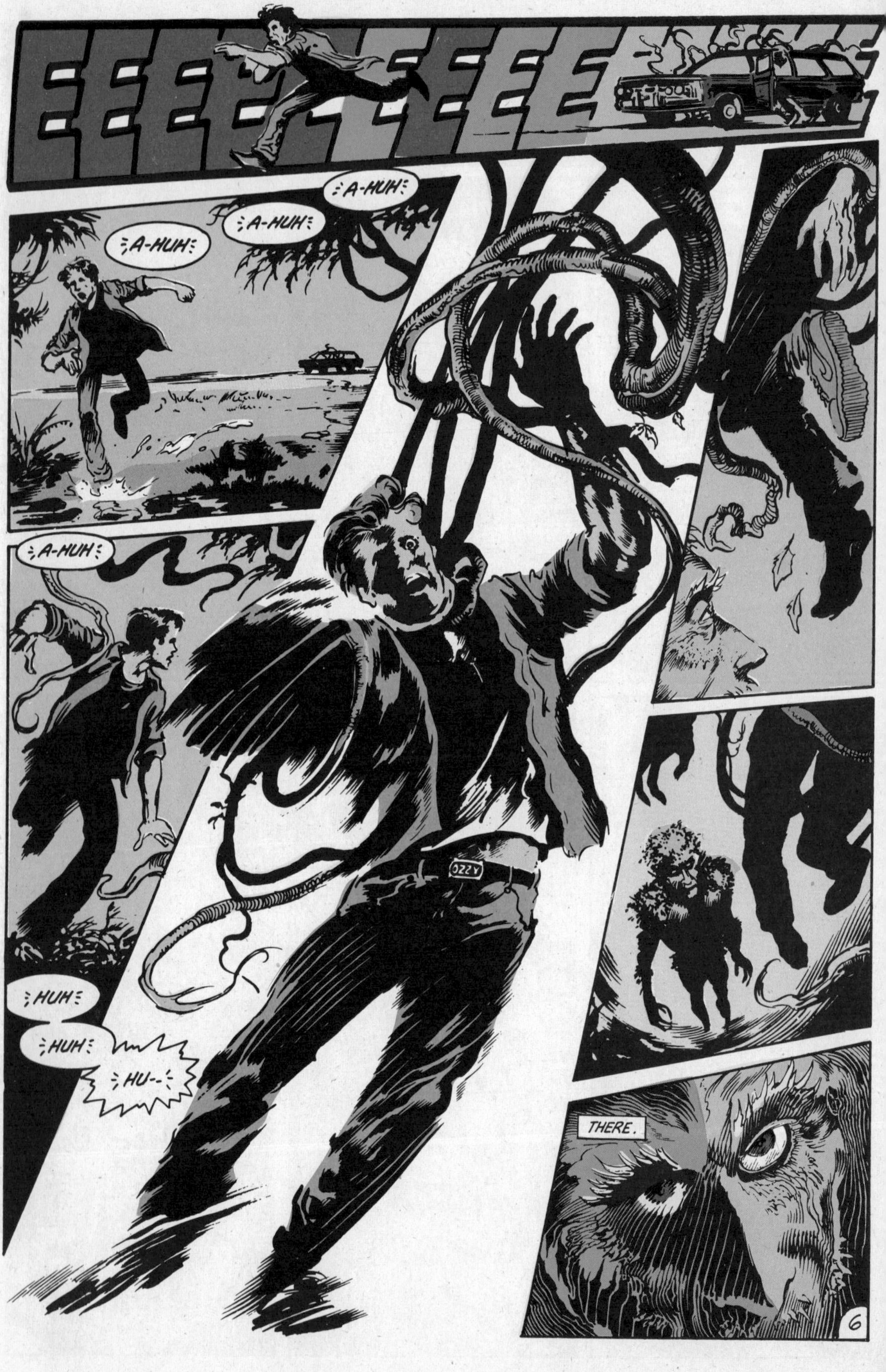
EEEEEEEEEEE
A-HUH
A-HUH
A-HUH
A-HUH
OZZY
HUH
HUH
HU--
THERE.
6

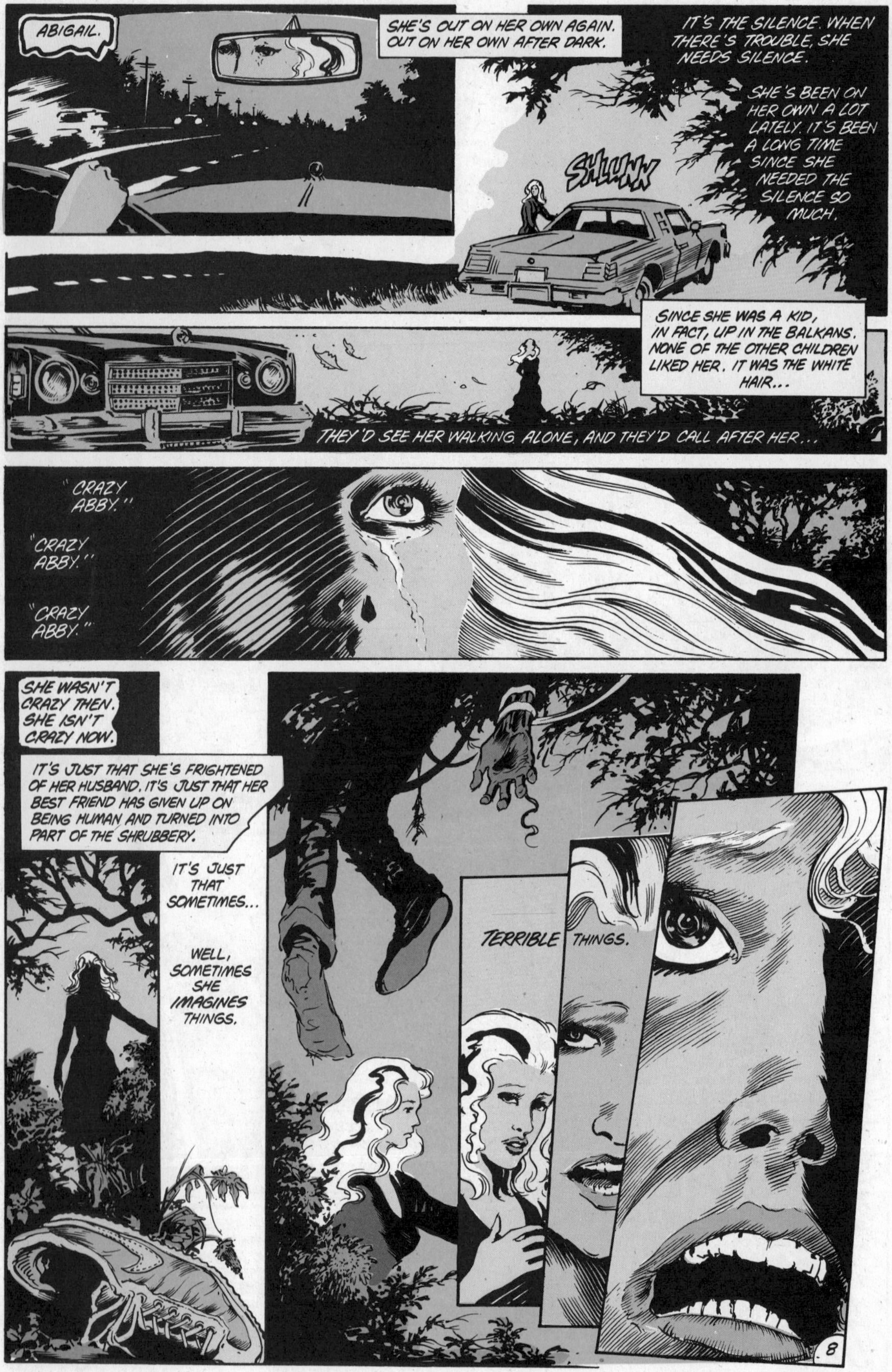
ABIGAIL.
SHE'S OUT ON HER OWN AGAIN. OUT ON HER OWN AFTER DARK.
IT'S THE SILENCE. WHEN THERE'S TROUBLE, SHE NEEDS SILENCE.
SHE'S BEEN ON HER OWN A LOT LATELY. IT'S BEEN A LONG TIME SINCE SHE NEEDED THE SILENCE SO MUCH.
SHLUNK
SINCE SHE WAS A KID, IN FACT, UP IN THE BALKANS. NONE OF THE OTHER CHILDREN LIKED HER. IT WAS THE WHITE HAIR...
THEY'D SEE HER WALKING ALONE, AND THEY'D CALL AFTER HER...
"CRAZY ABBY."
"CRAZY ABBY."
"CRAZY ABBY."
SHE WASN'T CRAZY THEN. SHE ISN'T CRAZY NOW.
IT'S JUST THAT SHE'S FRIGHTENED OF HER HUSBAND. IT'S JUST THAT HER BEST FRIEND HAS GIVEN UP ON BEING HUMAN AND TURNED INTO PART OF THE SHRUBBERY.
IT'S JUST THAT SOMETIMES...
WELL, SOMETIMES SHE IMAGINES THINGS.
TERRIBLE THINGS.
8

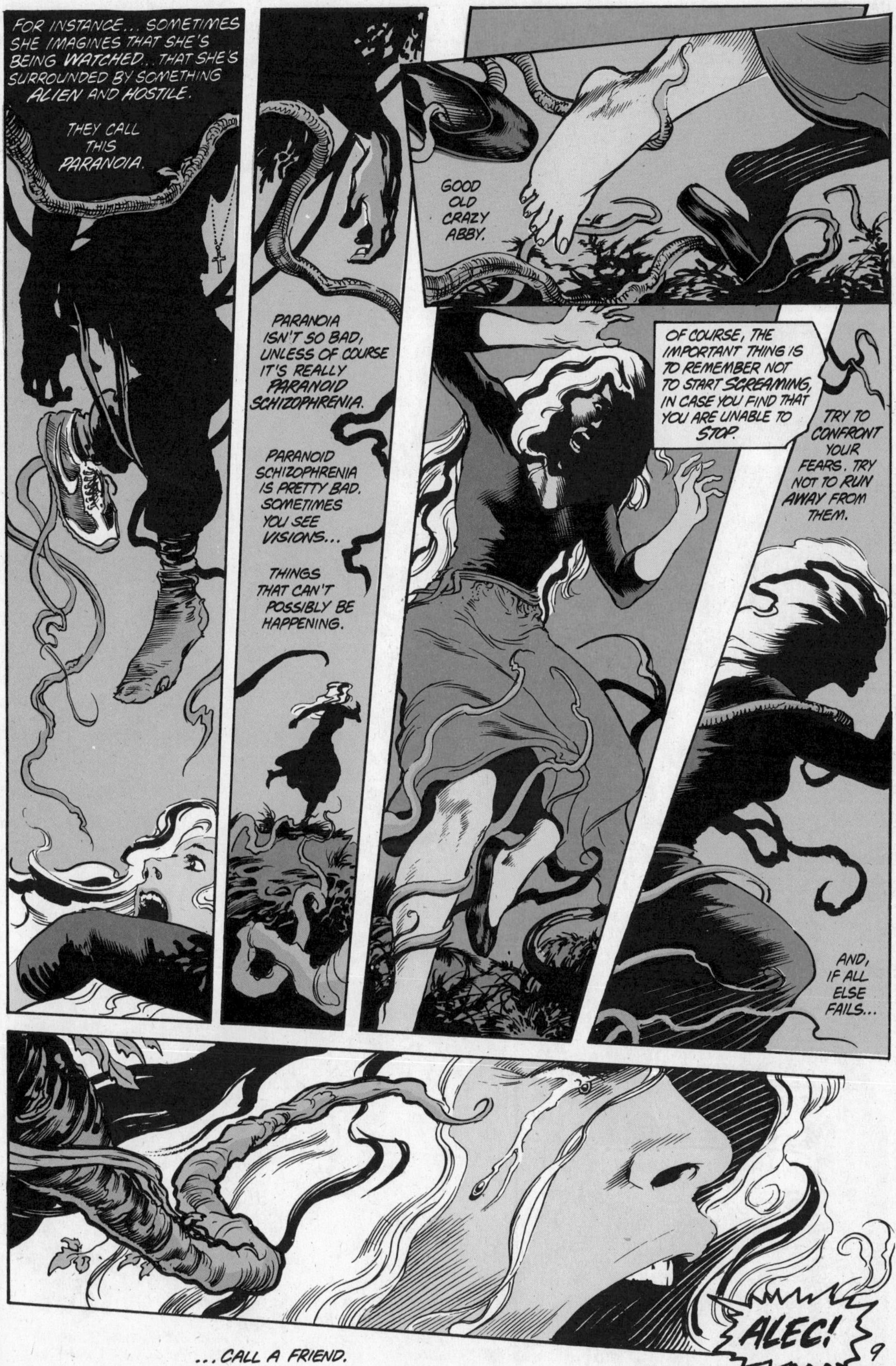
FOR INSTANCE... SOMETIMES SHE IMAGINES THAT SHE'S BEING WATCHED... THAT SHE'S SURROUNDED BY SOMETHING ALIEN AND HOSTILE.
THEY CALL THIS PARANOIA.
GOOD OLD CRAZY ABBY.
PARANOIA ISN'T SO BAD, UNLESS OF COURSE IT'S REALLY PARANOID SCHIZOPHRENIA.
PARANOID SCHIZOPHRENIA IS PRETTY BAD. SOMETIMES YOU SEE VISIONS...
THINGS THAT CAN'T POSSIBLY BE HAPPENING.
OF COURSE, THE IMPORTANT THING IS TO REMEMBER NOT TO START SCREAMING, IN CASE YOU FIND THAT YOU ARE UNABLE TO STOP.
TRY TO CONFRONT YOUR FEARS. TRY NOT TO RUN AWAY FROM THEM.
AND, IF ALL ELSE FAILS...
ALEC!
...CALL A FRIEND.
9

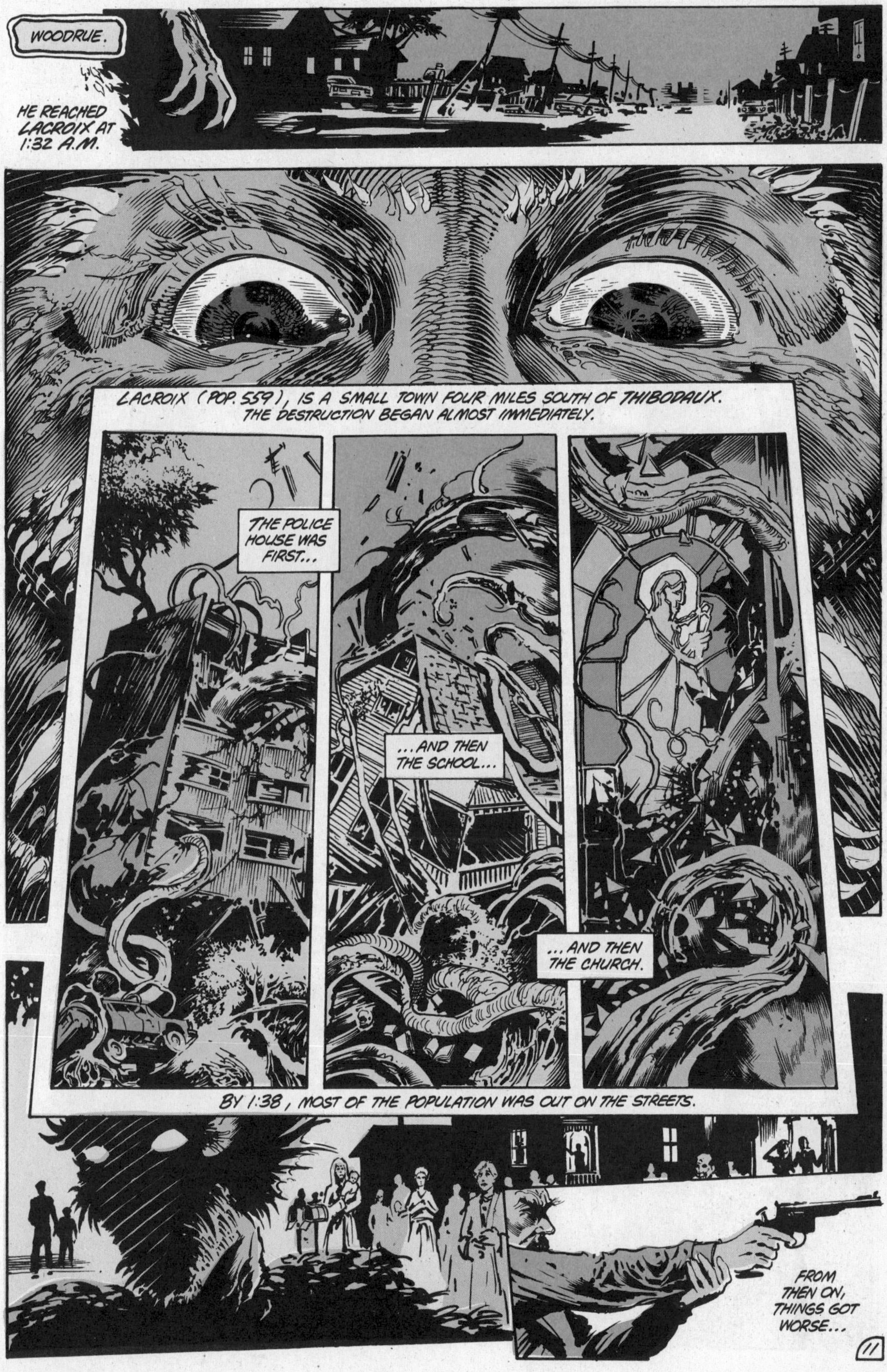
WOODRUE.
HE REACHED LACROIX AT 1:32 A.M.
LACROIX (POP. 559), IS A SMALL TOWN FOUR MILES SOUTH OF THIBODAUX. THE DESTRUCTION BEGAN ALMOST IMMEDIATELY.
THE POLICE HOUSE WAS FIRST...
...AND THEN THE SCHOOL...
...AND THEN THE CHURCH.
BY 1:38, MOST OF THE POPULATION WAS OUT ON THE STREETS.
FROM THEN ON, THINGS GOT WORSE...
11

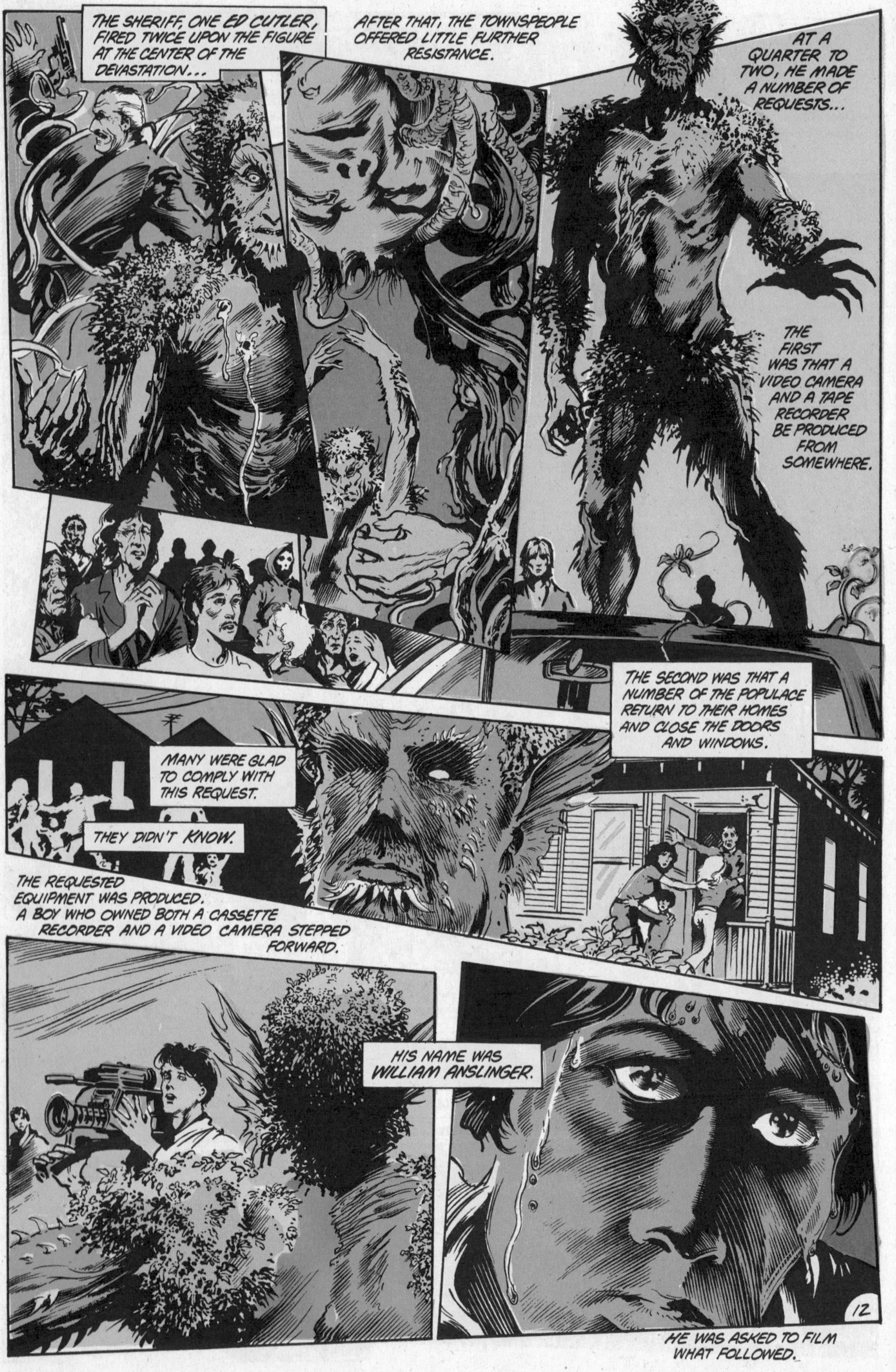
THE SHERIFF, ONE ED CUTLER, FIRED TWICE UPON THE FIGURE AT THE CENTER OF THE DEVASTATION...
AFTER THAT, THE TOWNSPEOPLE OFFERED LITTLE FURTHER RESISTANCE.
AT A QUARTER TO TWO, HE MADE A NUMBER OF REQUESTS...
THE FIRST WAS THAT A VIDEO CAMERA AND A TAPE RECORDER BE PRODUCED FROM SOMEWHERE.
THE SECOND WAS THAT A NUMBER OF THE POPULACE RETURN TO THEIR HOMES AND CLOSE THE DOORS AND WINDOWS.
MANY WERE GLAD TO COMPLY WITH THIS REQUEST.
THEY DIDN'T KNOW.
THE REQUESTED EQUIPMENT WAS PRODUCED. A BOY WHO OWNED BOTH A CASSETTE RECORDER AND A VIDEO CAMERA STEPPED FORWARD.
HIS NAME WAS WILLIAM ANSLINGER.
12
HE WAS ASKED TO FILM WHAT FOLLOWED.

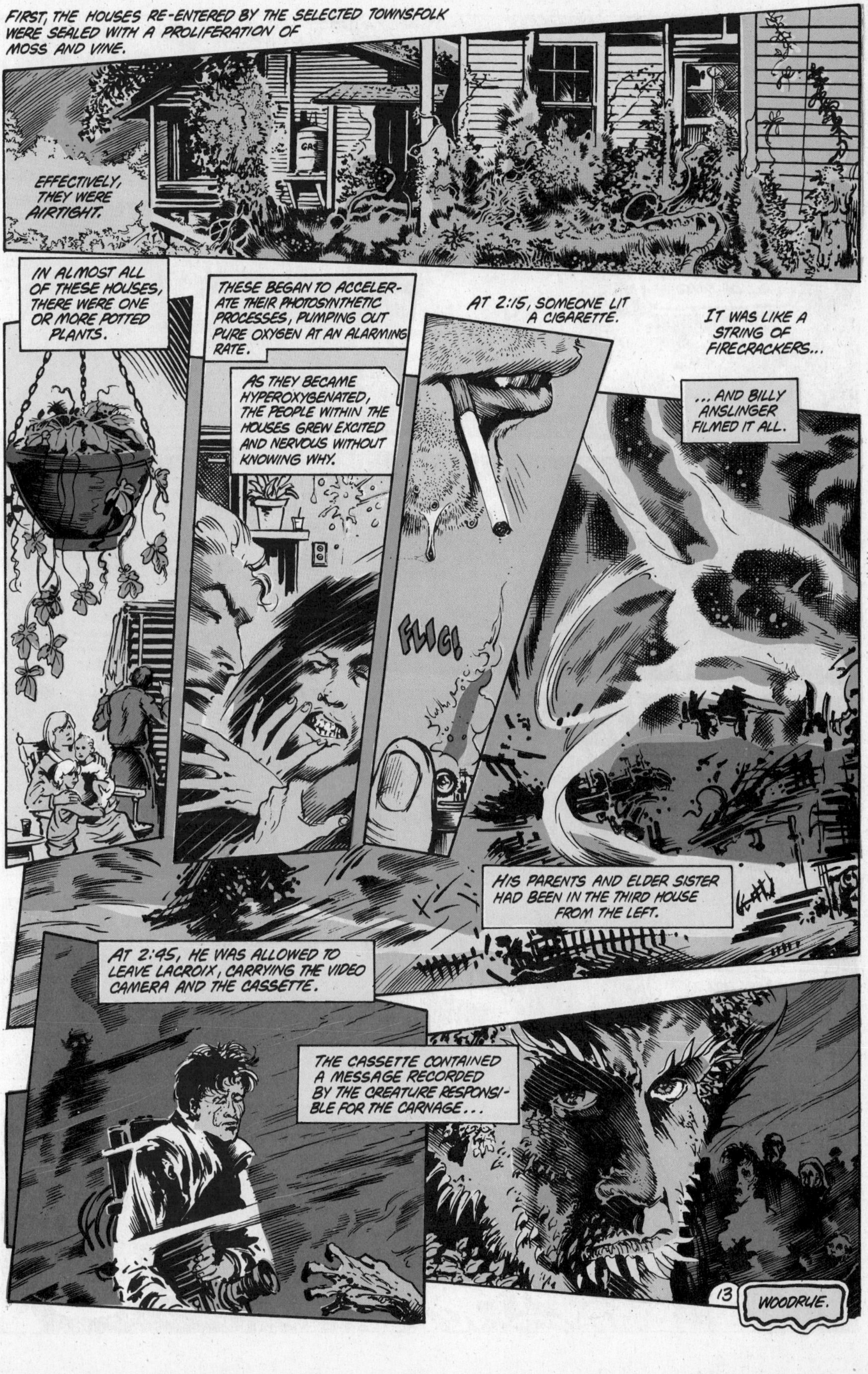
FIRST, THE HOUSES RE-ENTERED BY THE SELECTED TOWNSFOLK WERE SEALED WITH A PROLIFERATION OF MOSS AND VINE.
EFFECTIVELY, THEY WERE AIRTIGHT.
IN ALMOST ALL OF THESE HOUSES, THERE WERE ONE OR MORE POTTED PLANTS.
THESE BEGAN TO ACCELERATE THEIR PHOTOSYNTHETIC PROCESSES, PUMPING OUT PURE OXYGEN AT AN ALARMING RATE.
AS THEY BECAME HYPEROXYGENATED, THE PEOPLE WITHIN THE HOUSES GREW EXCITED AND NERVOUS WITHOUT KNOWING WHY.
AT 2:15, SOMEONE LIT A CIGARETTE.
FLIC!
IT WAS LIKE A STRING OF FIRECRACKERS...
...AND BILLY ANSLINGER FILMED IT ALL.
HIS PARENTS AND ELDER SISTER HAD BEEN IN THE THIRD HOUSE FROM THE LEFT.
AT 2:45, HE WAS ALLOWED TO LEAVE LACROIX, CARRYING THE VIDEO CAMERA AND THE CASSETTE.
THE CASSETTE CONTAINED A MESSAGE RECORDED BY THE CREATURE RESPONSIBLE FOR THE CARNAGE...
13
WOODRUE.

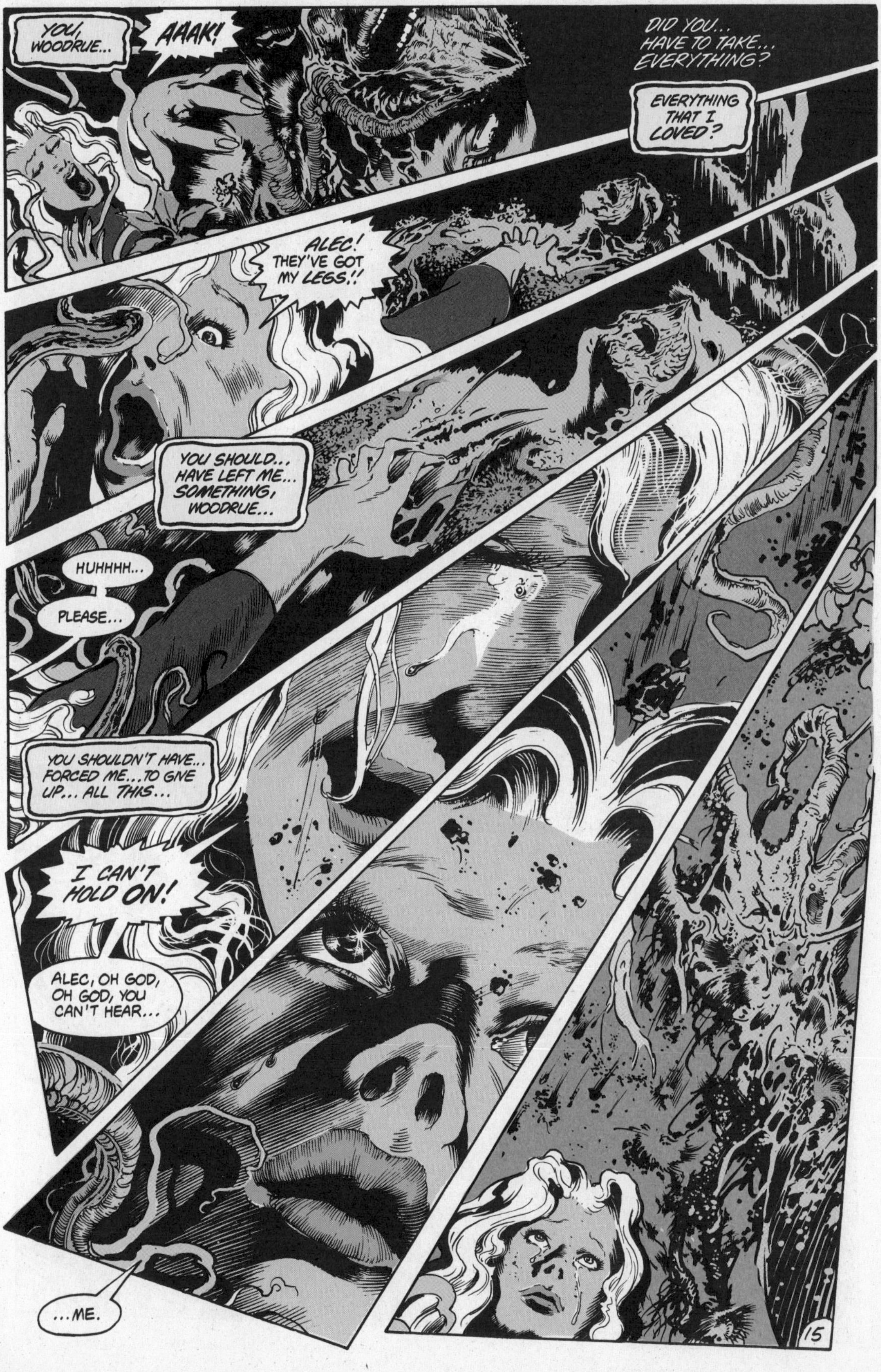
YOU, WOODRUE...
AAAK!
DID YOU... HAVE TO TAKE... EVERYTHING?
EVERYTHING THAT I LOVED?
ALEC! THEY'VE GOT MY LEGS!!
YOU SHOULD... HAVE LEFT ME... SOMETHING, WOODRUE...
HUHHHH...
PLEASE...
YOU SHOULDN'T HAVE... FORCED ME... TO GIVE UP... ALL THIS...
I CAN'T HOLD ON!
ALEC, OH GOD, OH GOD, YOU CAN'T HEAR...
...ME.
15

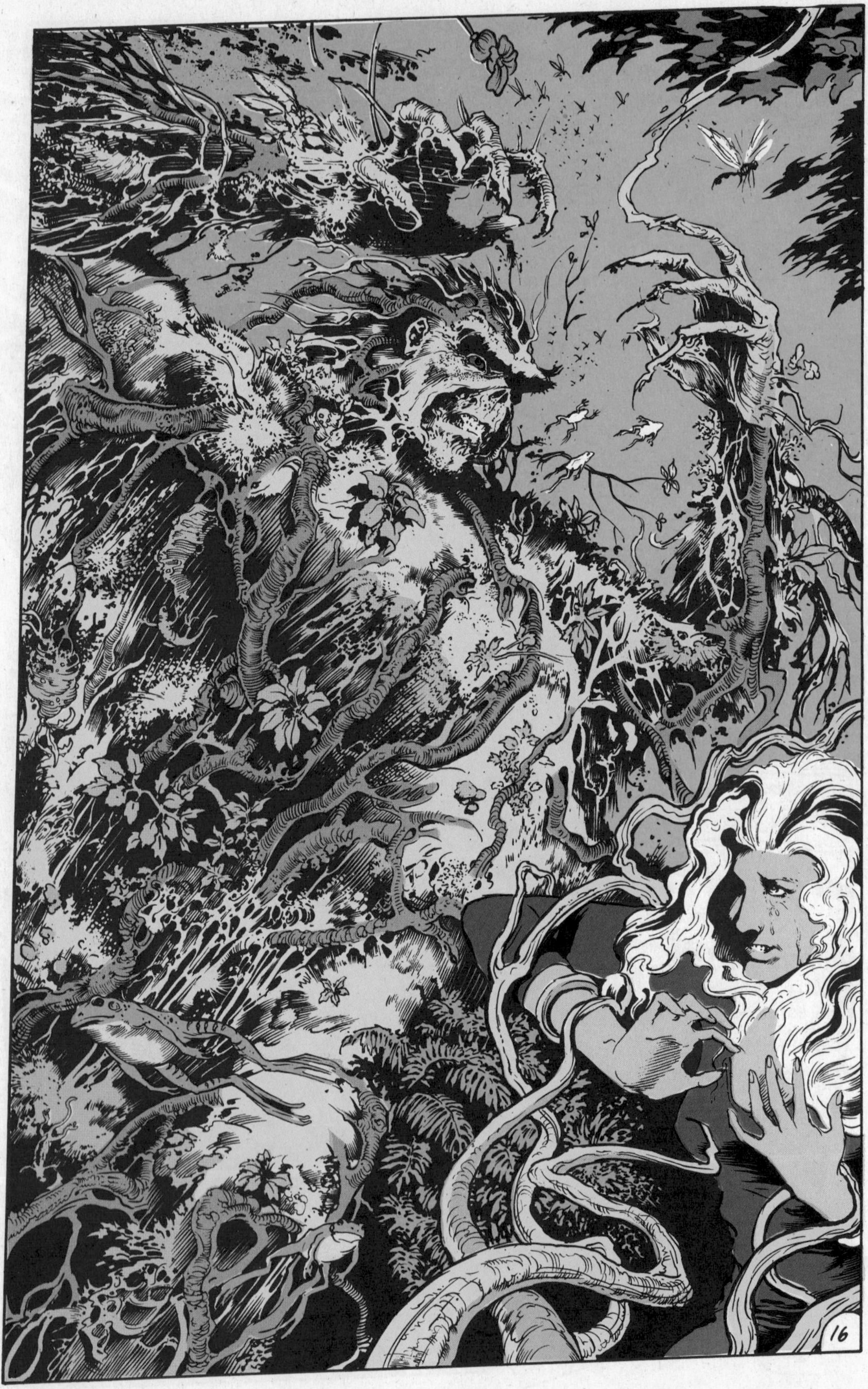
16

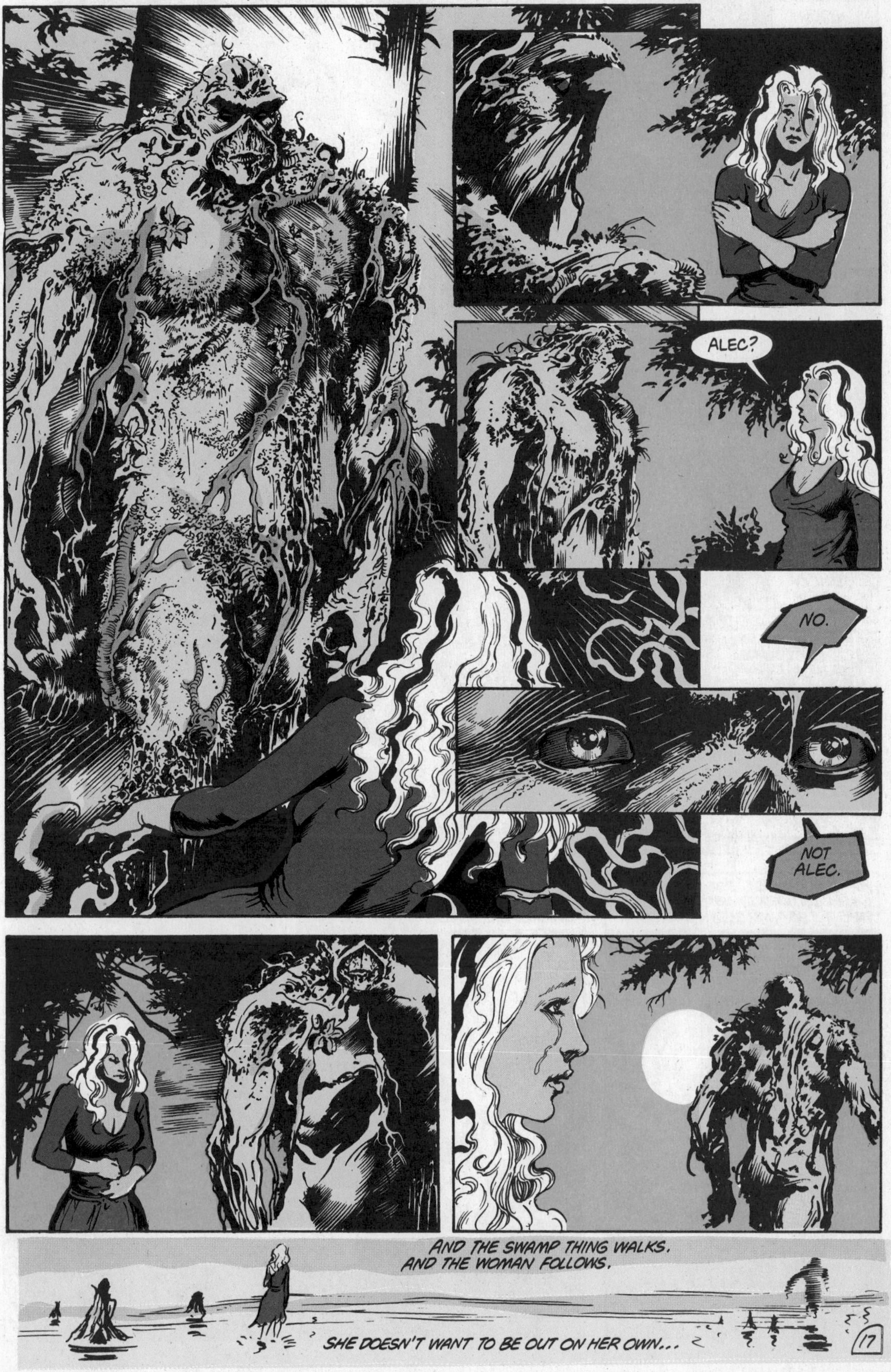
ALEC?
NO.
NOT ALEC.
AND THE SWAMP THING WALKS.
AND THE WOMAN FOLLOWS.
SHE DOESN'T WANT TO BE OUT ON HER OWN...
17

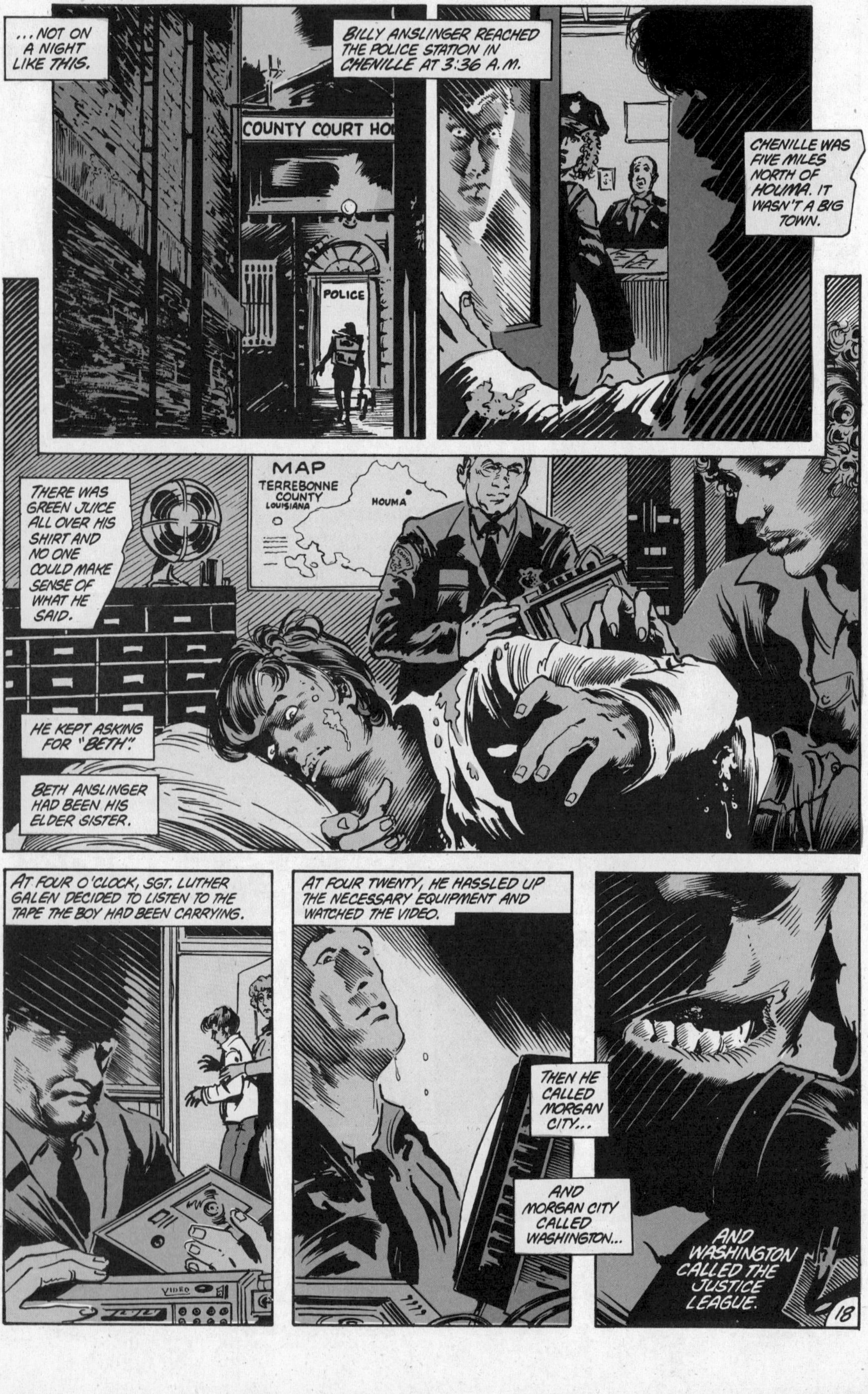

...NOT ON A NIGHT LIKE THIS.
BILLY ANSLINGER REACHED THE POLICE STATION IN CHENILLE AT 3:36 A.M.
COUNTY COURT HO
POLICE
CHENILLE WAS FIVE MILES NORTH OF HOUMA. IT WASN'T A BIG TOWN.
MAP
TERREBONNE COUNTY LOUISIANA
HOUMA
THERE WAS GREEN JUICE ALL OVER HIS SHIRT AND NO ONE COULD MAKE SENSE OF WHAT HE SAID.
HE KEPT ASKING FOR "BETH".
BETH ANSLINGER HAD BEEN HIS ELDER SISTER.
AT FOUR O'CLOCK, SGT. LUTHER GALEN DECIDED TO LISTEN TO THE TAPE THE BOY HAD BEEN CARRYING.
VIDEO
AT FOUR TWENTY, HE HASSLED UP THE NECESSARY EQUIPMENT AND WATCHED THE VIDEO.
THEN HE CALLED MORGAN CITY...
AND MORGAN CITY CALLED WASHINGTON...
AND WASHINGTON CALLED THE JUSTICE LEAGUE.
18

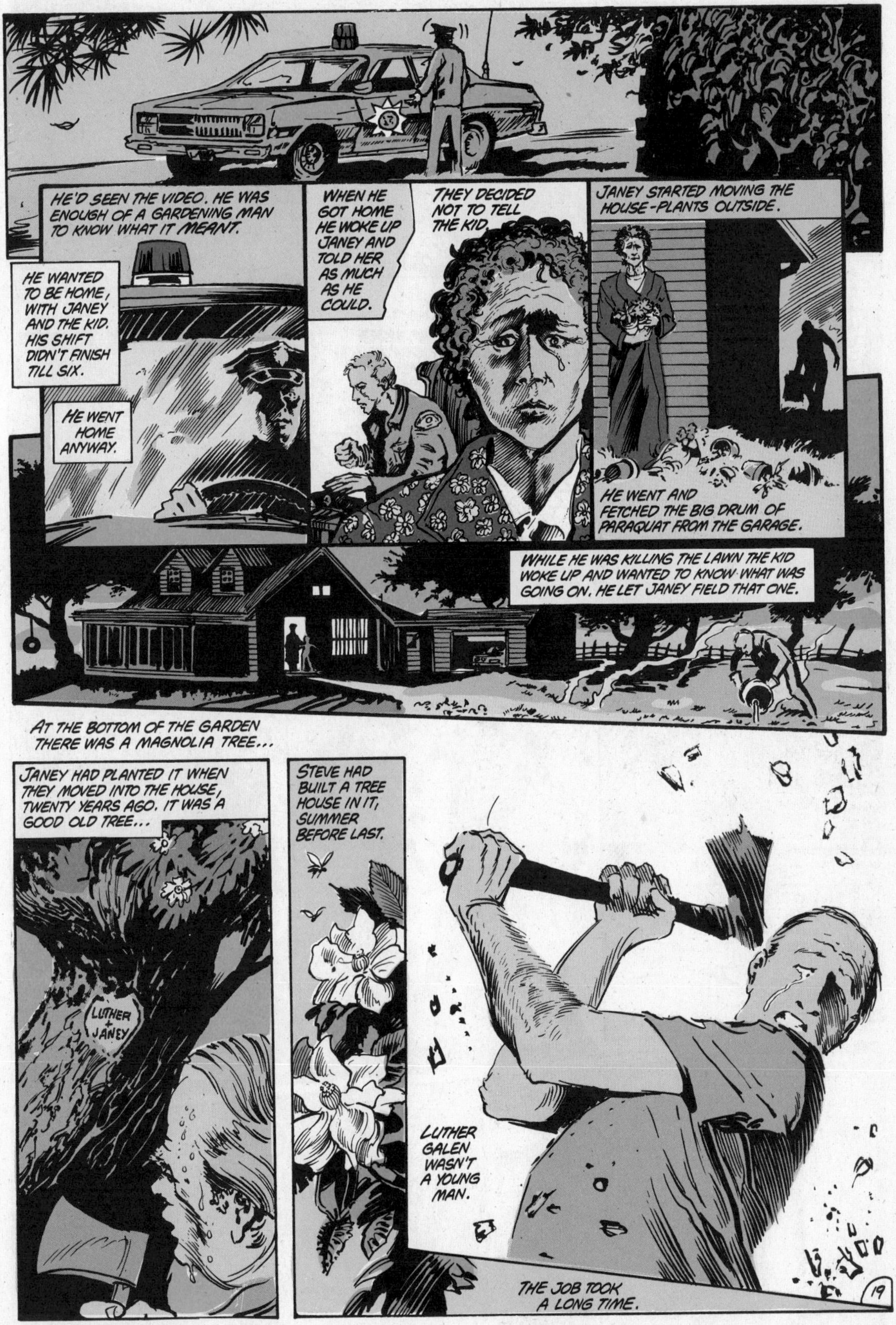
HE'D SEEN THE VIDEO. HE WAS ENOUGH OF A GARDENING MAN TO KNOW WHAT IT MEANT.
HE WANTED TO BE HOME, WITH JANEY AND THE KID. HIS SHIFT DIDN'T FINISH TILL SIX.
HE WENT HOME ANYWAY.
WHEN HE GOT HOME HE WOKE UP JANEY AND TOLD HER AS MUCH AS HE COULD.
THEY DECIDED NOT TO TELL THE KID.
JANEY STARTED MOVING THE HOUSE-PLANTS OUTSIDE.
HE WENT AND FETCHED THE BIG DRUM OF PARAQUAT FROM THE GARAGE.
WHILE HE WAS KILLING THE LAWN THE KID WOKE UP AND WANTED TO KNOW WHAT WAS GOING ON. HE LET JANEY FIELD THAT ONE.
AT THE BOTTOM OF THE GARDEN THERE WAS A MAGNOLIA TREE...
JANEY HAD PLANTED IT WHEN THEY MOVED INTO THE HOUSE, TWENTY YEARS AGO. IT WAS A GOOD OLD TREE...
LUTHER + JANEY
STEVE HAD BUILT A TREE HOUSE IN IT, SUMMER BEFORE LAST.
LUTHER GALEN WASN'T A YOUNG MAN.
THE JOB TOOK A LONG TIME.
19

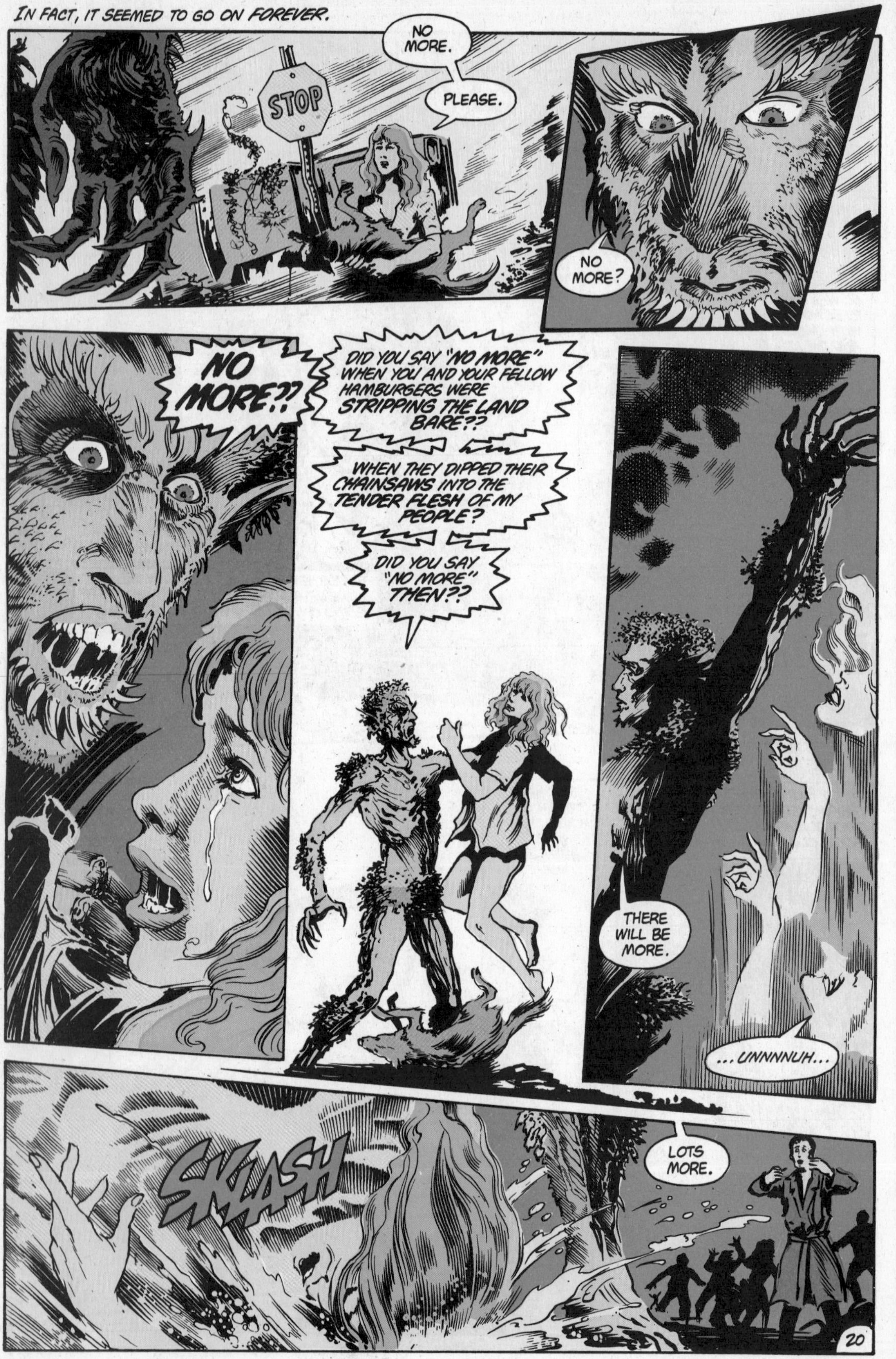
IN FACT, IT SEEMED TO GO ON FOREVER.
NO MORE.
PLEASE.
STOP
NO MORE?
NO MORE??
DID YOU SAY "NO MORE" WHEN YOU AND YOUR FELLOW HAMBURGERS WERE STRIPPING THE LAND BARE??
WHEN THEY DIPPED THEIR CHAINSAWS INTO THE TENDER FLESH OF MY PEOPLE?
DID YOU SAY "NO MORE" THEN??
THERE WILL BE MORE.
...UNNNNUH...
SKLASH
LOTS MORE.
20

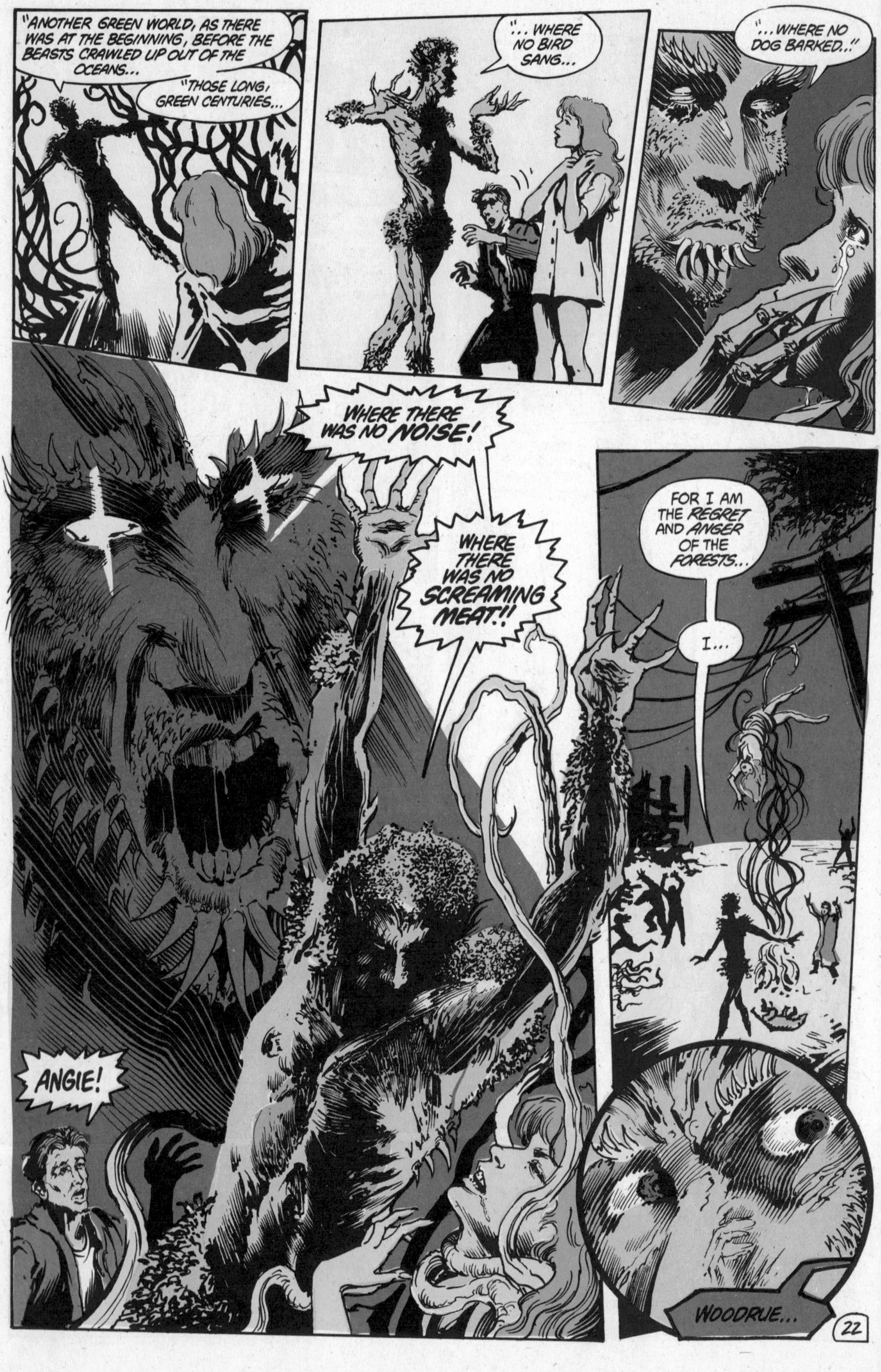
"ANOTHER GREEN WORLD, AS THERE WAS AT THE BEGINNING, BEFORE THE BEASTS CRAWLED UP OUT OF THE OCEANS...
"THOSE LONG, GREEN CENTURIES...
"...WHERE NO BIRD SANG...
"...WHERE NO DOG BARKED..!"
WHERE THERE WAS NO NOISE!
WHERE THERE WAS NO SCREAMING MEAT!!
FOR I AM THE REGRET AND ANGER OF THE FORESTS...
I...
ANGIE!
WOODRUE...
22

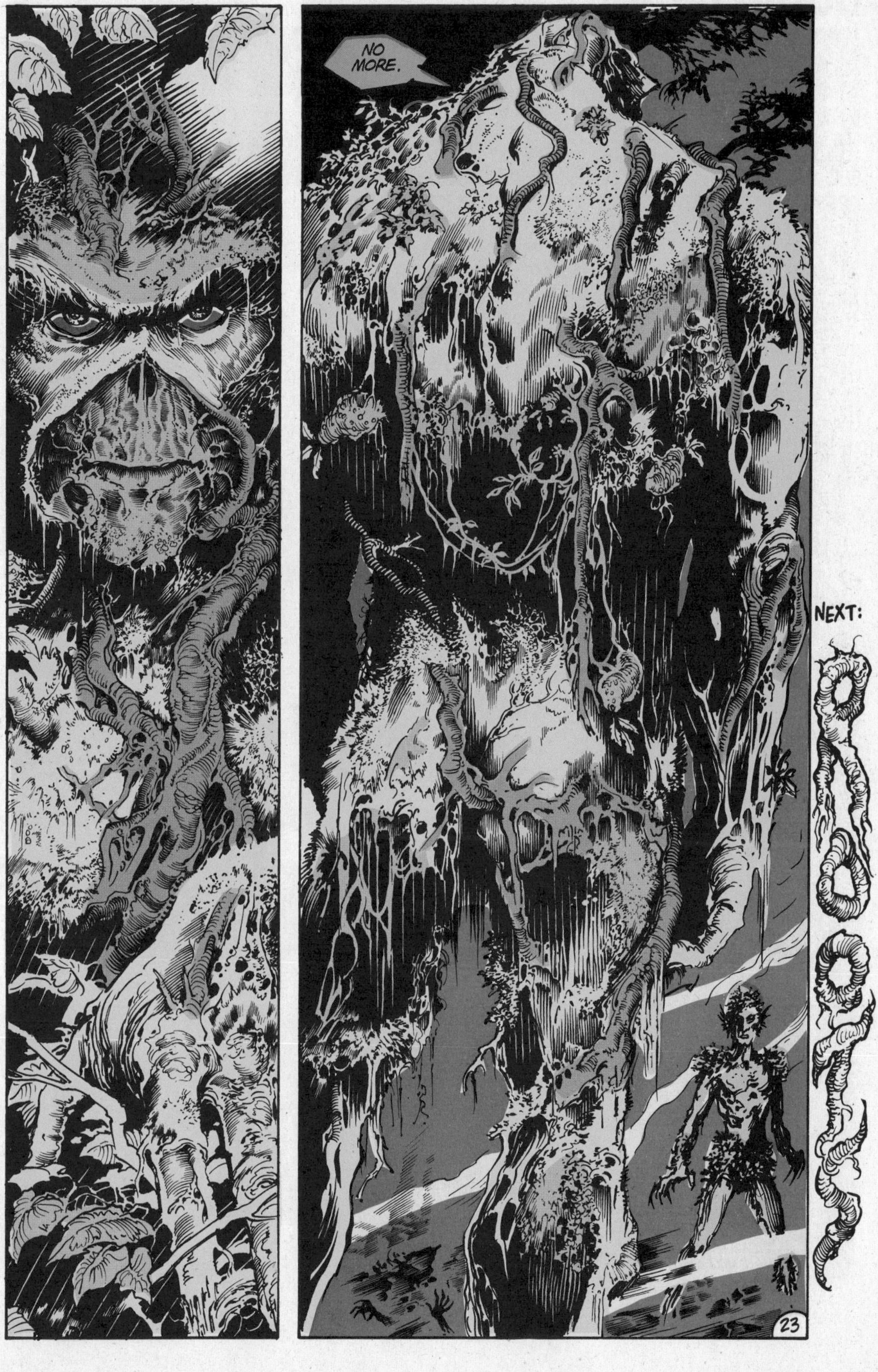
NO MORE.
NEXT:
23

BOOK FOUR

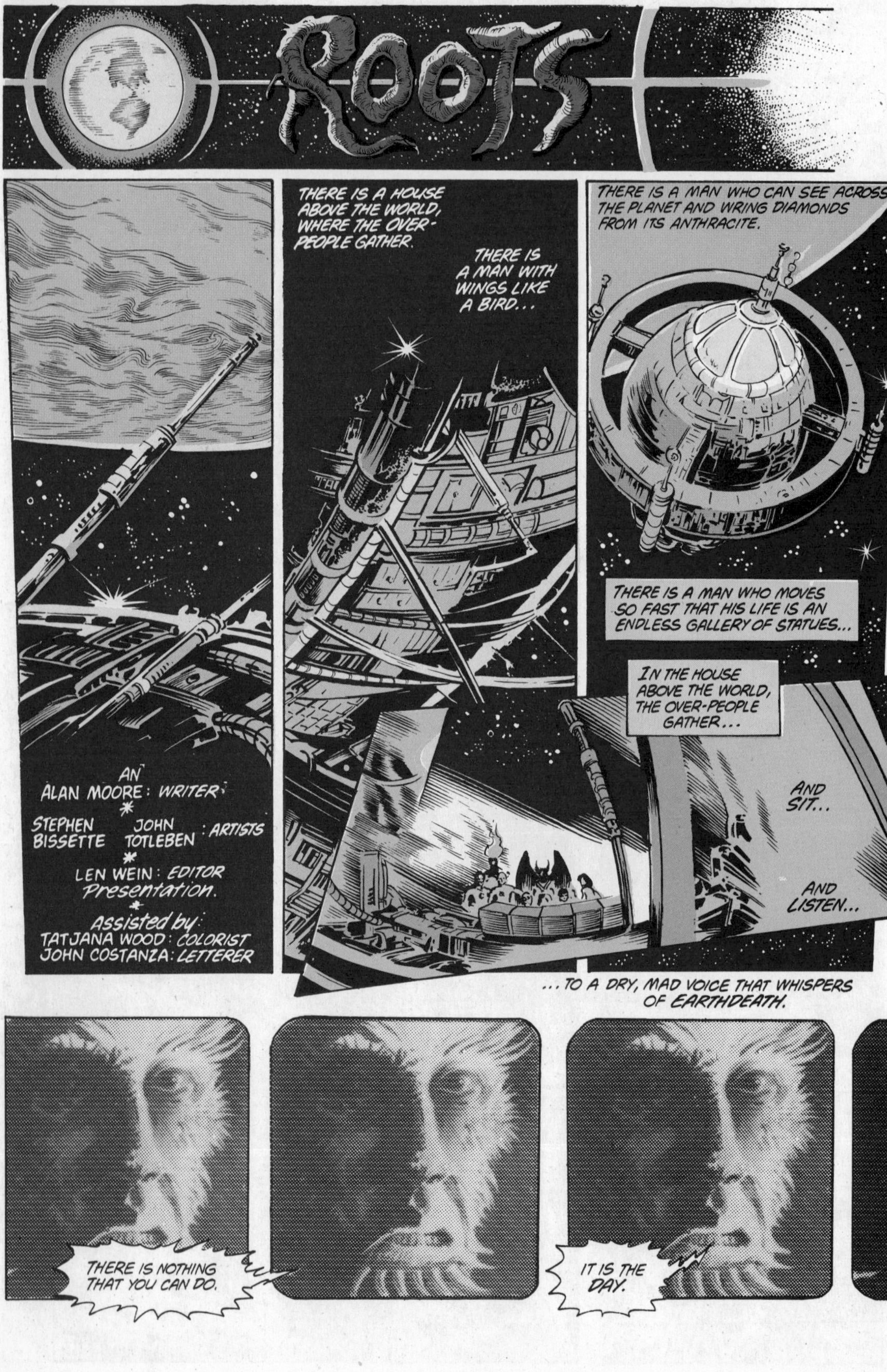
ROOTS
AN ALAN MOORE: WRITER
STEPHEN BISSETTE JOHN TOTLEBEN: ARTISTS
LEN WEIN: EDITOR
Presentation.
Assisted by: TATJANA WOOD: COLORIST
JOHN COSTANZA: LETTERER
THERE IS A HOUSE ABOVE THE WORLD, WHERE THE OVER-PEOPLE GATHER.
THERE IS A MAN WITH WINGS LIKE A BIRD...
THERE IS A MAN WHO CAN SEE ACROSS THE PLANET AND WRING DIAMONDS FROM ITS ANTHRACITE.
THERE IS A MAN WHO MOVES SO FAST THAT HIS LIFE IS AN ENDLESS GALLERY OF STATUES...
IN THE HOUSE ABOVE THE WORLD, THE OVER-PEOPLE GATHER...
AND SIT...
AND LISTEN...
...TO A DRY, MAD VOICE THAT WHISPERS OF EARTHDEATH.
THERE IS NOTHING THAT YOU CAN DO.
IT IS THE DAY.

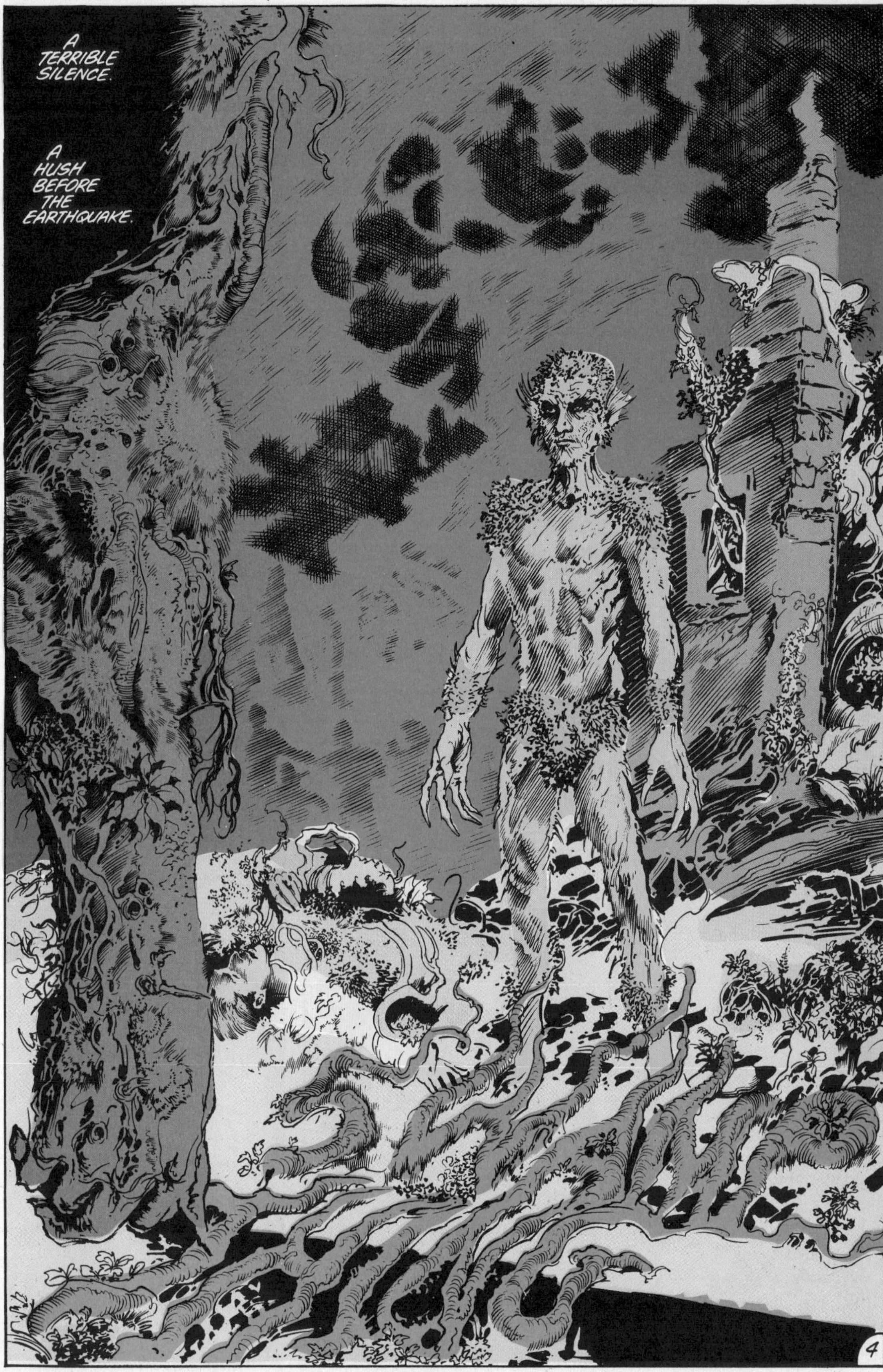
A TERRIBLE SILENCE.
A HUSH BEFORE THE EARTHQUAKE.
4

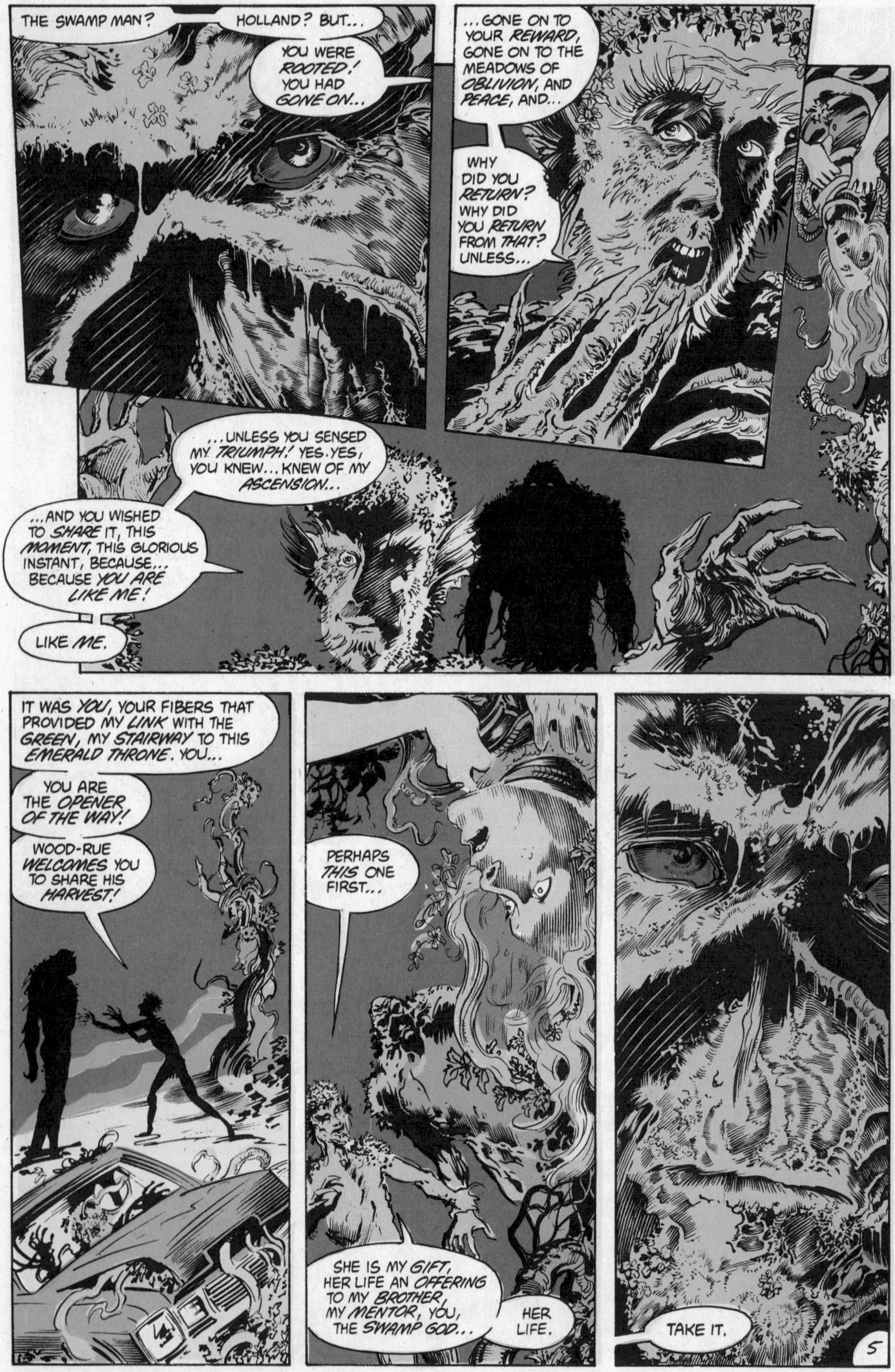
THE SWAMP MAN?
HOLLAND? BUT...
YOU WERE ROOTED! YOU HAD GONE ON...
...GONE ON TO YOUR REWARD, GONE ON TO THE MEADOWS OF OBLIVION, AND PEACE, AND...
WHY DID YOU RETURN? WHY DID YOU RETURN FROM THAT? UNLESS...
...UNLESS YOU SENSED MY TRIUMPH! YES. YES, YOU KNEW... KNEW OF MY ASCENSION...
...AND YOU WISHED TO SHARE IT, THIS MOMENT, THIS GLORIOUS INSTANT, BECAUSE... BECAUSE YOU ARE LIKE ME!
LIKE ME.
IT WAS YOU, YOUR FIBERS THAT PROVIDED MY LINK WITH THE GREEN, MY STAIRWAY TO THIS EMERALD THRONE. YOU...
YOU ARE THE OPENER OF THE WAY!
WOOD-RUE WELCOMES YOU TO SHARE HIS HARVEST!
PERHAPS THIS ONE FIRST...
SHE IS MY GIFT, HER LIFE AN OFFERING TO MY BROTHER, MY MENTOR, YOU, THE SWAMP GOD...
HER LIFE.
TAKE IT.
5

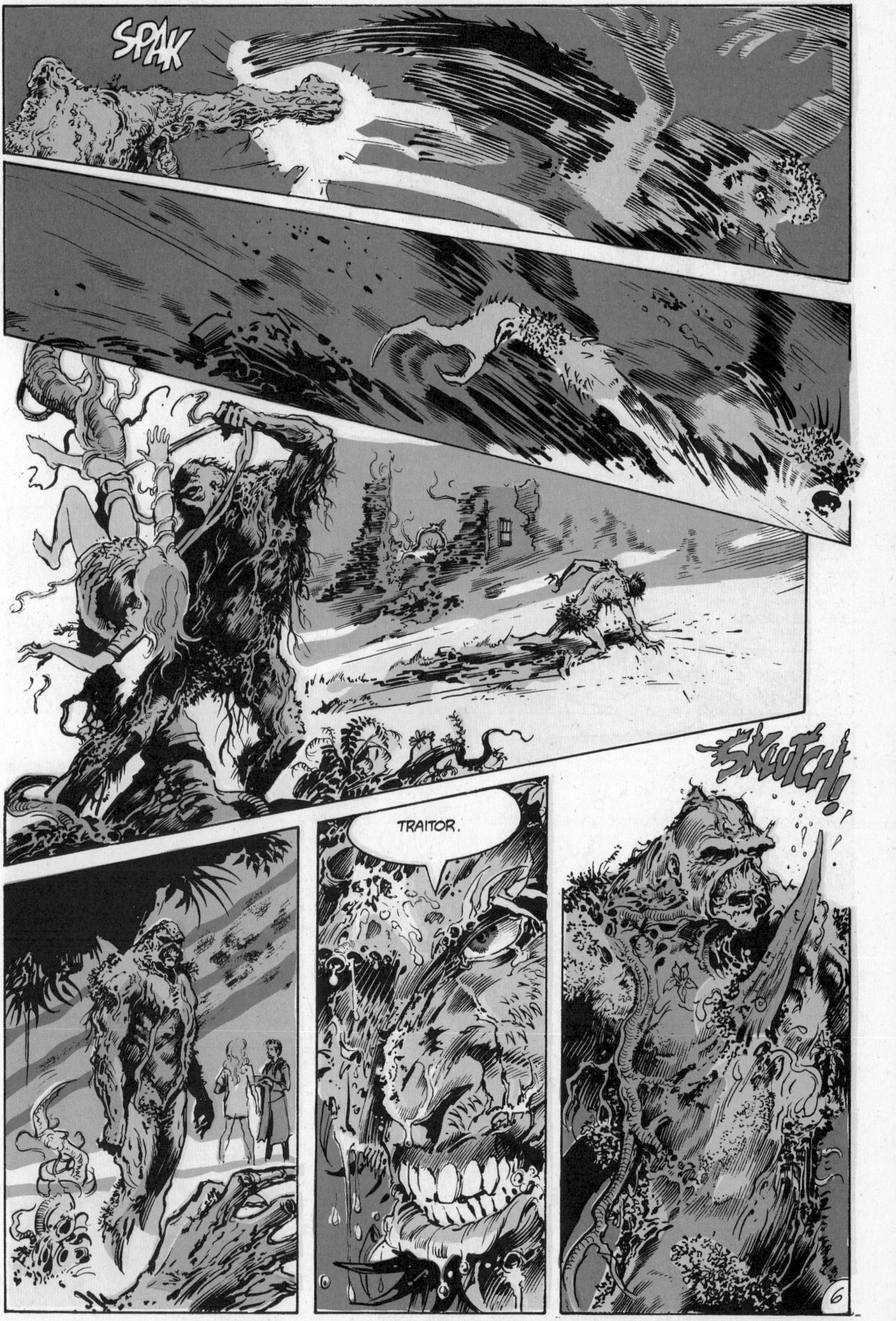
SPAK
SKLUTCH!
TRAITOR.
6

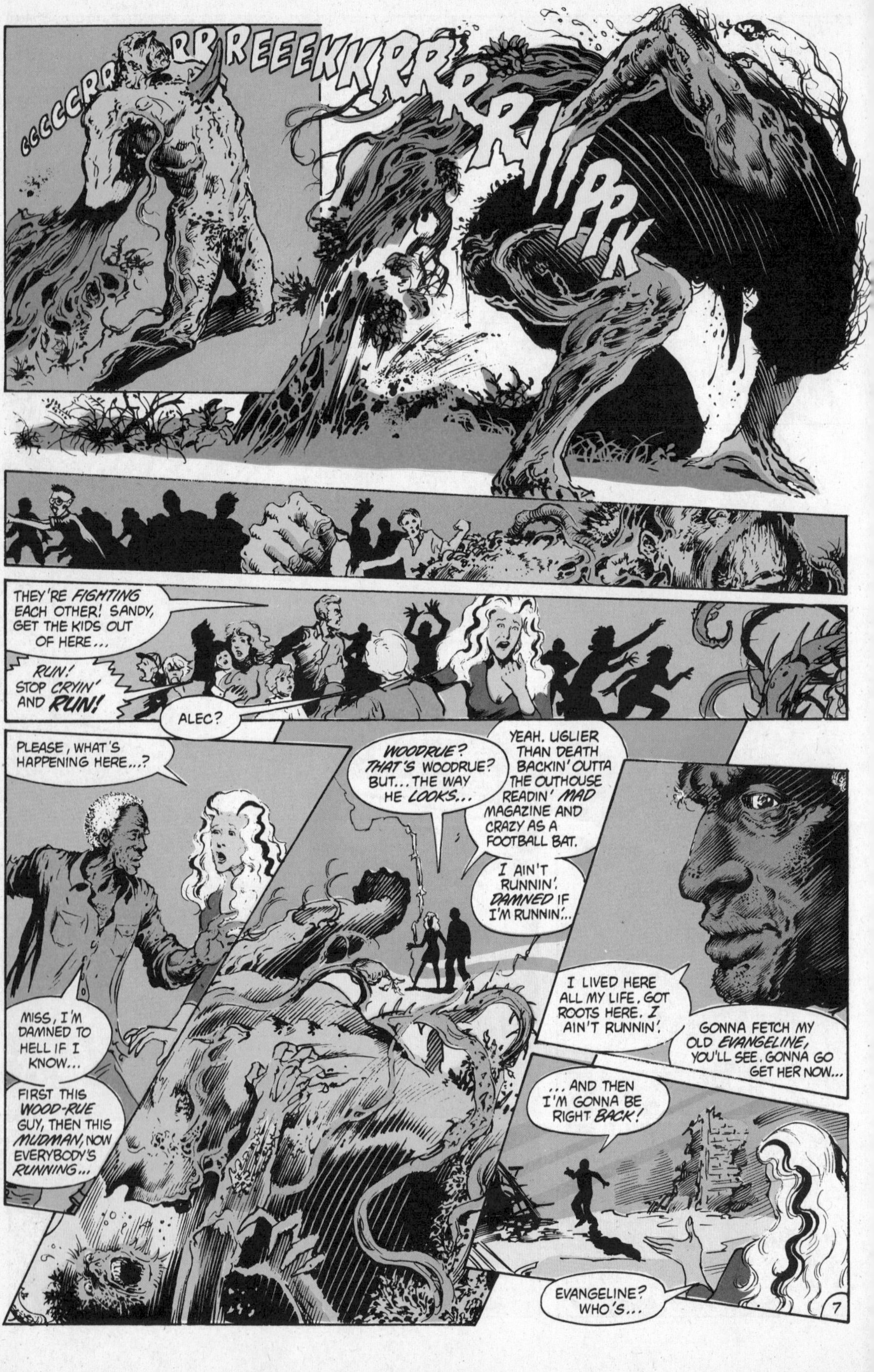
CCCCCRRRRREEEEKKRRRRRIIIPPK
THEY'RE FIGHTING EACH OTHER! SANDY, GET THE KIDS OUT OF HERE...
RUN! STOP CRYIN' AND RUN!
ALEC?
PLEASE, WHAT'S HAPPENING HERE...?
MISS, I'M DAMNED TO HELL IF I KNOW...
FIRST THIS WOOD-RUE GUY, THEN THIS MUDMAN, NOW EVERYBODY'S RUNNING...
WOODRUE? THAT'S WOODRUE? BUT... THE WAY HE LOOKS...
YEAH. UGLIER THAN DEATH BACKIN' OUTTA THE OUTHOUSE READIN' MAD MAGAZINE AND CRAZY AS A FOOTBALL BAT.
I AIN'T RUNNIN'. DAMNED IF I'M RUNNIN'...
I LIVED HERE ALL MY LIFE. GOT ROOTS HERE. I AIN'T RUNNIN'.
GONNA FETCH MY OLD EVANGELINE, YOU'LL SEE. GONNA GO GET HER NOW...
... AND THEN I'M GONNA BE RIGHT BACK!
EVANGELINE? WHO'S...
7

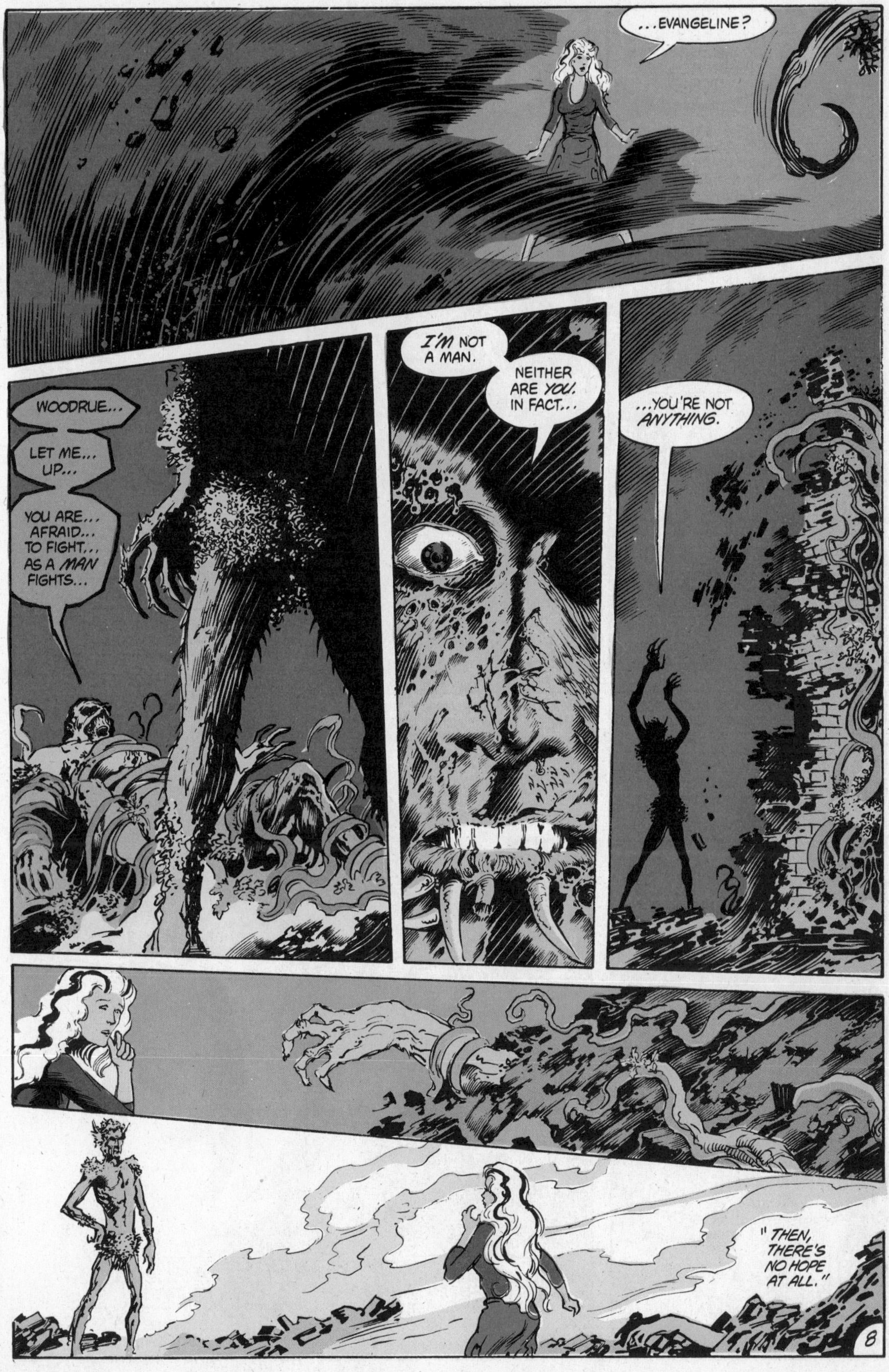
...EVANGELINE?
WOODRUE...
LET ME... UP...
YOU ARE... AFRAID... TO FIGHT... AS A *MAN* FIGHTS...
I'M NOT A MAN.
NEITHER ARE *YOU*. IN FACT...
...YOU'RE NOT *ANYTHING*.
"*THEN, THERE'S NO HOPE AT ALL.*"
8

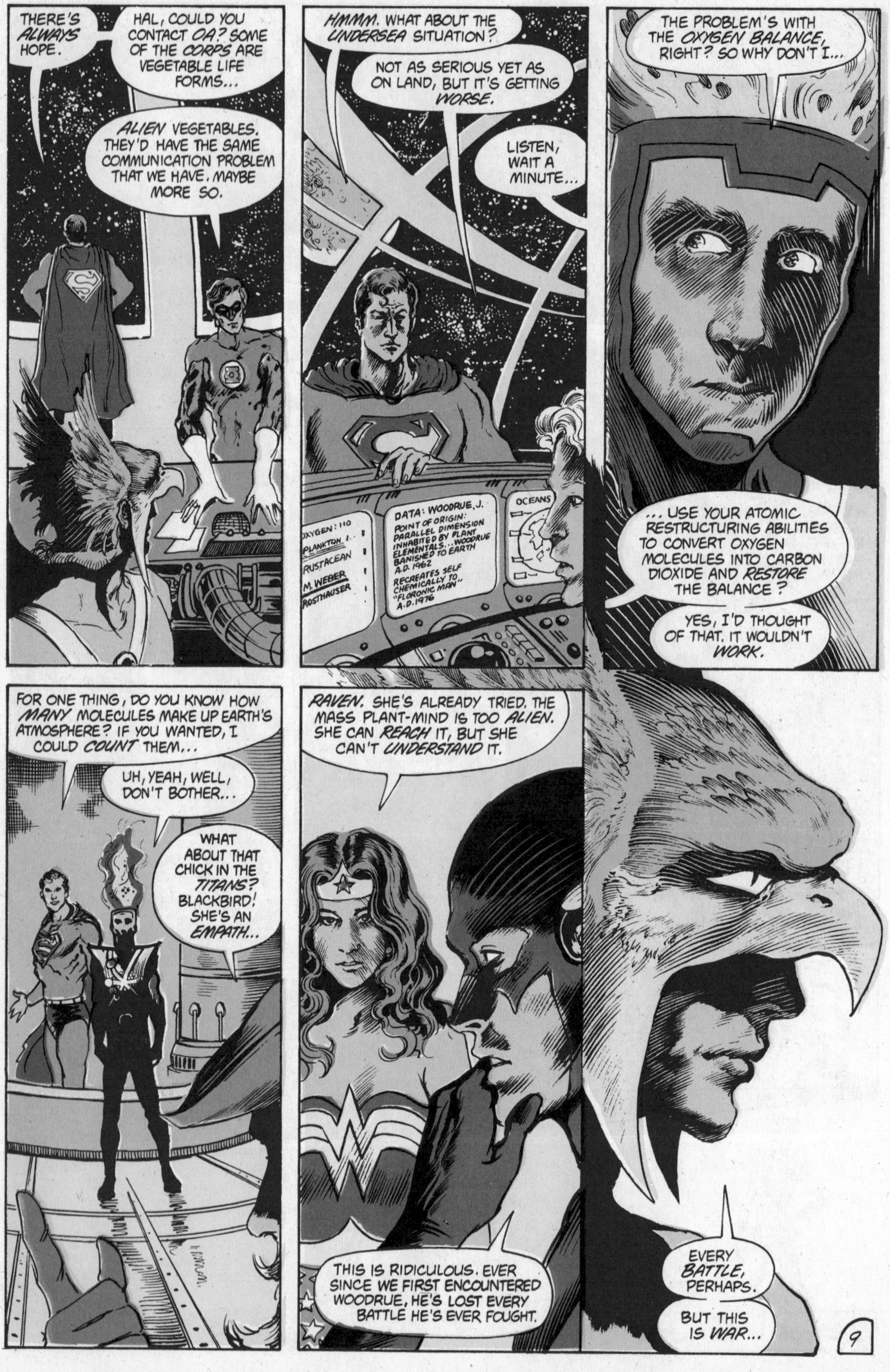
THERE'S *ALWAYS* HOPE.
HAL, COULD YOU CONTACT *OA?* SOME OF THE *CORPS* ARE VEGETABLE LIFE FORMS...
ALIEN VEGETABLES. THEY'D HAVE THE SAME COMMUNICATION PROBLEM THAT WE HAVE. MAYBE MORE SO.
HMMM. WHAT ABOUT THE *UNDERSEA* SITUATION?
NOT AS SERIOUS YET AS ON LAND, BUT IT'S GETTING *WORSE.*
LISTEN, WAIT A MINUTE...
OXYGEN: 110
PLANKTON
RUSTACEAN
M. WEBER
ROSTHAUSER
DATA: WOODRUE, J.
POINT OF ORIGIN: PARALLEL DIMENSION INHABITED BY PLANT ELEMENTALS... WOODRUE BANISHED TO EARTH A.D. 1962
RECREATES SELF CHEMICALLY TO "FLORONIC MAN" A.D. 1976
OCEANS
THE PROBLEM'S WITH THE *OXYGEN BALANCE,* RIGHT? SO WHY DON'T I...
... USE YOUR ATOMIC RESTRUCTURING ABILITIES TO CONVERT OXYGEN MOLECULES INTO CARBON DIOXIDE AND *RESTORE* THE BALANCE?
YES, I'D THOUGHT OF THAT. IT WOULDN'T *WORK.*
FOR ONE THING, DO YOU KNOW HOW *MANY* MOLECULES MAKE UP EARTH'S ATMOSPHERE? IF YOU WANTED, I COULD *COUNT* THEM...
UH, YEAH, WELL, DON'T BOTHER...
WHAT ABOUT THAT CHICK IN THE *TITANS?* BLACKBIRD! SHE'S AN *EMPATH...*
RAVEN. SHE'S ALREADY TRIED. THE MASS PLANT-MIND IS TOO *ALIEN.* SHE CAN *REACH* IT, BUT SHE CAN'T *UNDERSTAND* IT.
THIS IS RIDICULOUS. EVER SINCE WE FIRST ENCOUNTERED WOODRUE, HE'S LOST EVERY BATTLE HE'S EVER FOUGHT.
EVERY *BATTLE,* PERHAPS.
BUT THIS IS *WAR...*
9

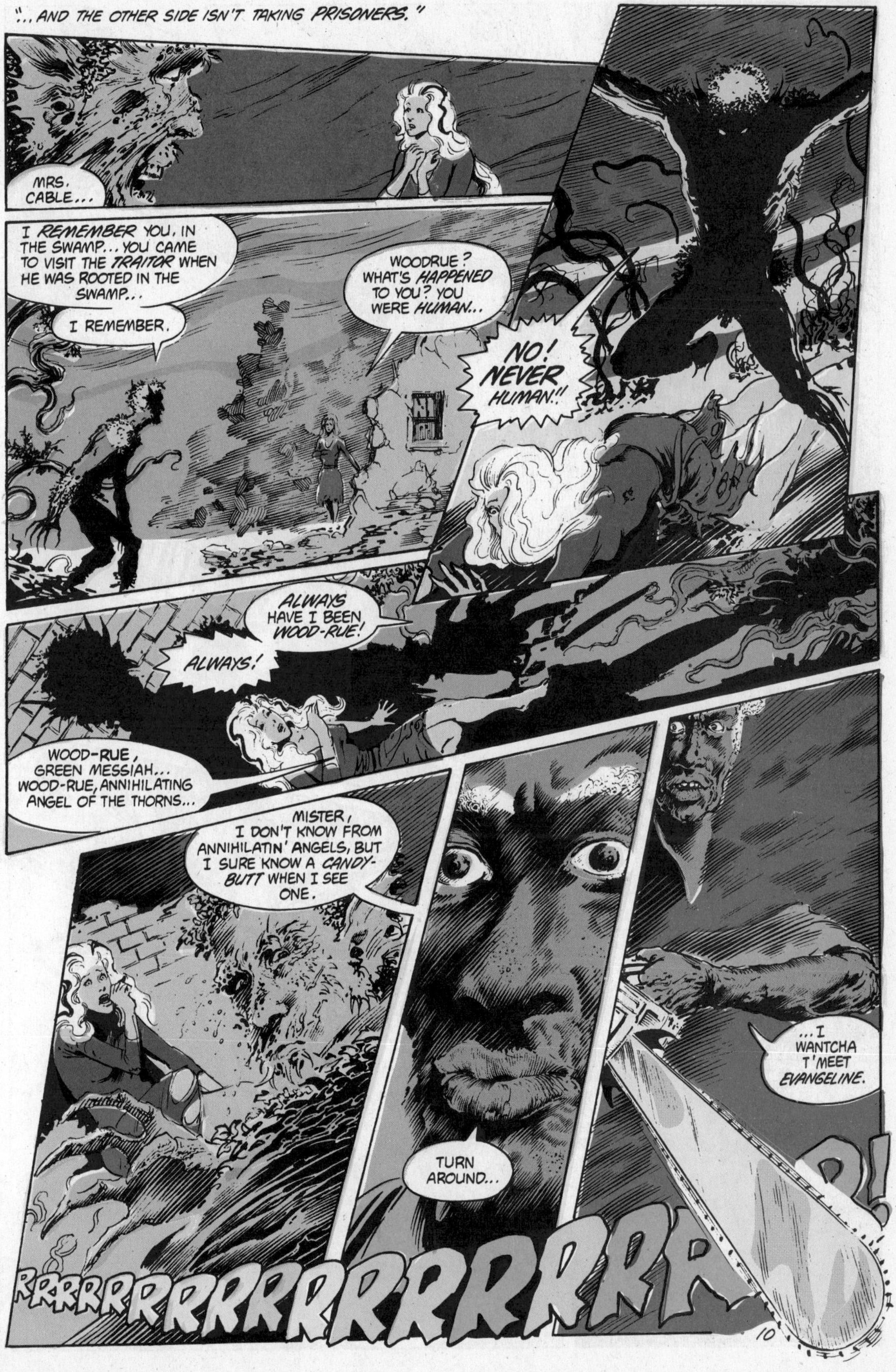
"...AND THE OTHER SIDE ISN'T TAKING PRISONERS."
MRS. CABLE...
I REMEMBER YOU, IN THE SWAMP... YOU CAME TO VISIT THE TRAITOR WHEN HE WAS ROOTED IN THE SWAMP...
I REMEMBER.
WOODRUE? WHAT'S HAPPENED TO YOU? YOU WERE HUMAN...
NO! NEVER HUMAN!!
ALWAYS HAVE I BEEN WOOD-RUE!
ALWAYS!
WOOD-RUE, GREEN MESSIAH... WOOD-RUE, ANNIHILATING ANGEL OF THE THORNS...
MISTER, I DON'T KNOW FROM ANNIHILATIN' ANGELS, BUT I SURE KNOW A CANDY-BUTT WHEN I SEE ONE.
TURN AROUND...
...I WANTCHA T'MEET EVANGELINE.
RRRRRRRRRRRRRRR
10

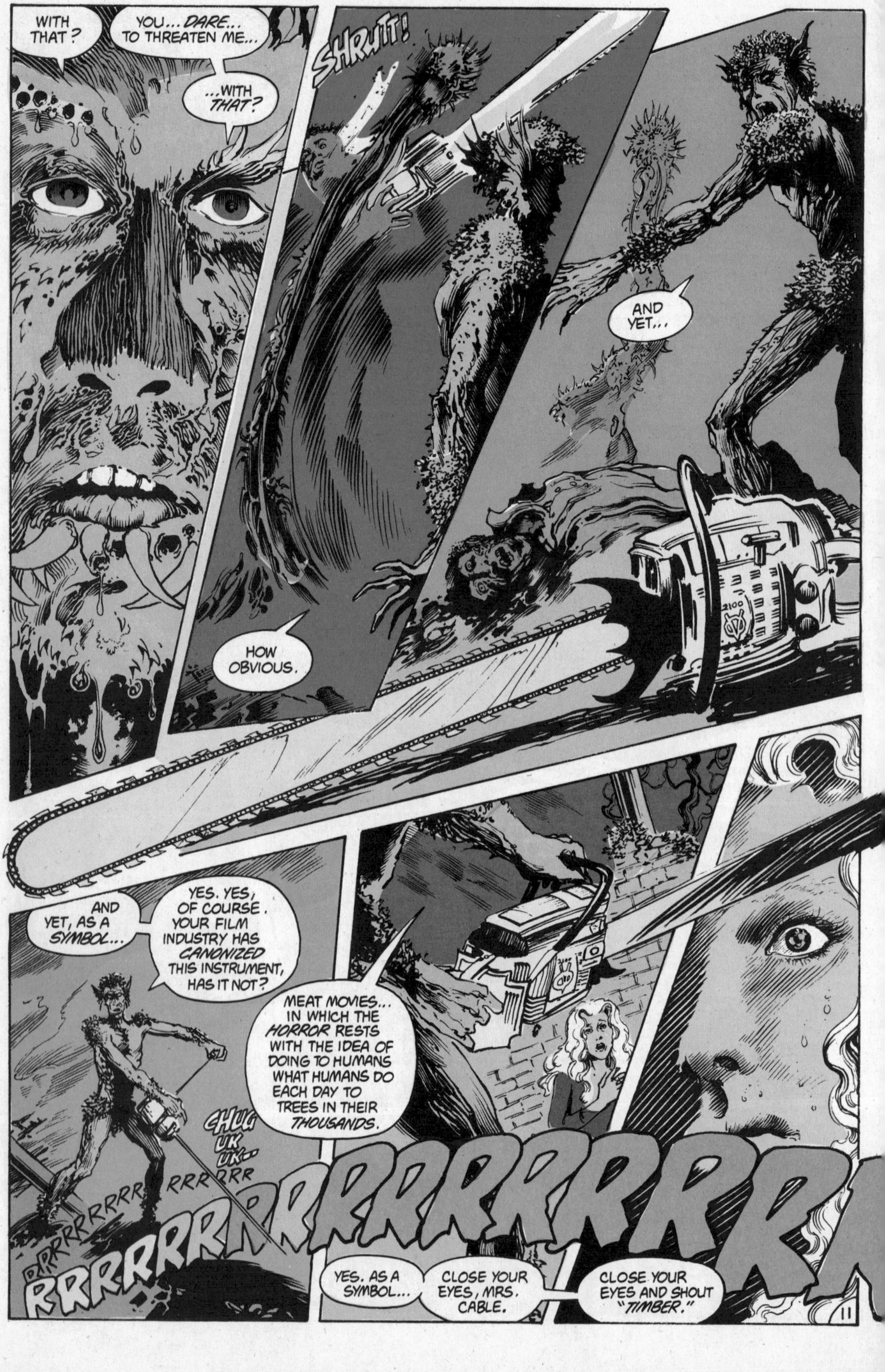
WITH THAT?
YOU... DARE... TO THREATEN ME...
...WITH THAT?
SHRUTT!
HOW OBVIOUS.
AND YET...
AND YET, AS A SYMBOL...
YES. YES, OF COURSE. YOUR FILM INDUSTRY HAS CANONIZED THIS INSTRUMENT, HAS IT NOT?
MEAT MOVIES... IN WHICH THE HORROR RESTS WITH THE IDEA OF DOING TO HUMANS WHAT HUMANS DO EACH DAY TO TREES IN THEIR THOUSANDS.
CHUG UK UK... DRR
RRRRRRRRRRRRRRRRRRR
YES. AS A SYMBOL...
CLOSE YOUR EYES, MRS. CABLE.
CLOSE YOUR EYES AND SHOUT "TIMBER."
11

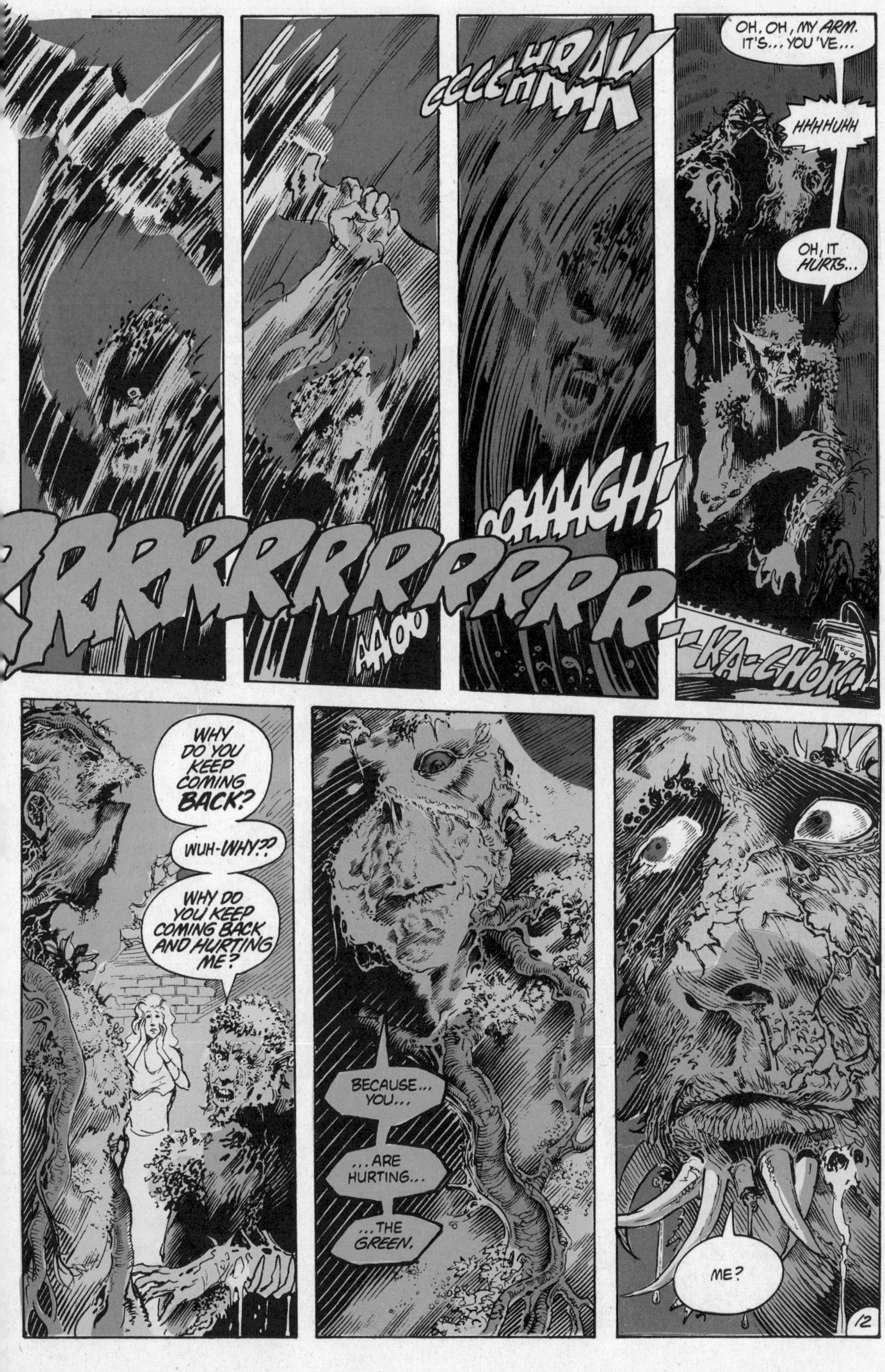
GCCCHRAAK
OH, OH, MY ARM. IT'S... YOU'VE...
HHHHUHH
OH, IT HURTS...
RRRRRRRRRRRRRR--KA-CHOK!
OOHAAAGH!
AA OO
WHY DO YOU KEEP COMING BACK?
WUH-WHY??
WHY DO YOU KEEP COMING BACK AND HURTING ME?
BECAUSE... YOU...
...ARE HURTING...
...THE GREEN.
ME?
12

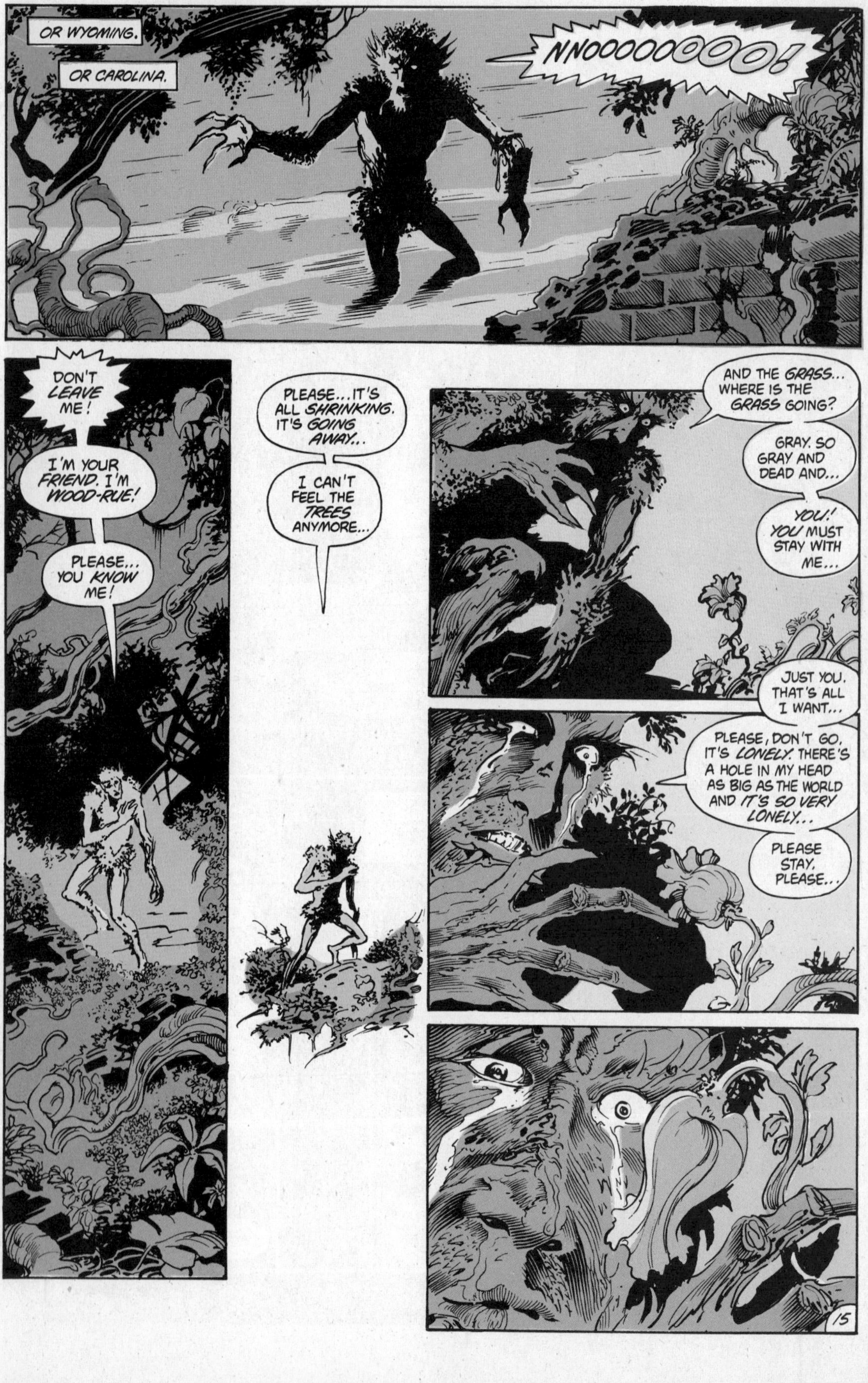
OR WYOMING.
OR CAROLINA.
NNOOOOOOOOO!
DON'T LEAVE ME!
I'M YOUR FRIEND. I'M WOOD-RUE!
PLEASE... YOU KNOW ME!
PLEASE...IT'S ALL SHRINKING. IT'S GOING AWAY...
I CAN'T FEEL THE TREES ANYMORE...
AND THE GRASS... WHERE IS THE GRASS GOING?
GRAY. SO GRAY AND DEAD AND...
YOU! YOU MUST STAY WITH ME...
JUST YOU. THAT'S ALL I WANT...
PLEASE, DON'T GO. IT'S LONELY. THERE'S A HOLE IN MY HEAD AS BIG AS THE WORLD AND IT'S SO VERY LONELY...
PLEASE STAY. PLEASE...
15

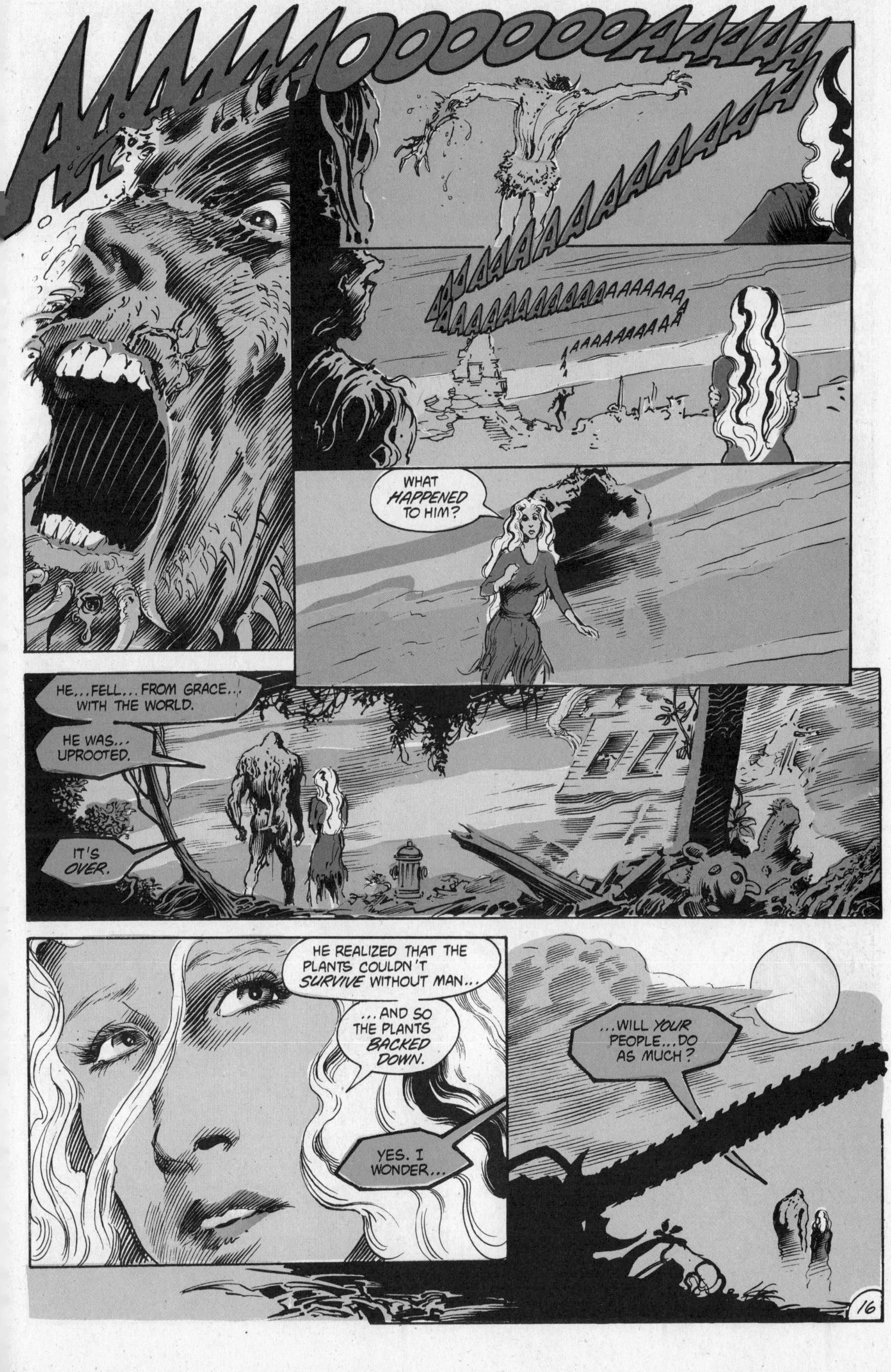
AAAAAOOOOOOOAAAAAA
AAAAAAAAAAAAAAAAA
AAAAAAAAAAAAAAAAAAAA
AAAAAAAAAAAAAAAAAAA
AAAAAAAAAA
WHAT HAPPENED TO HIM?
HE...FELL...FROM GRACE... WITH THE WORLD.
HE WAS... UPROOTED.
IT'S OVER.
HE REALIZED THAT THE PLANTS COULDN'T SURVIVE WITHOUT MAN...
...AND SO THE PLANTS BACKED DOWN.
...WILL YOUR PEOPLE...DO AS MUCH?
YES. I WONDER...
16

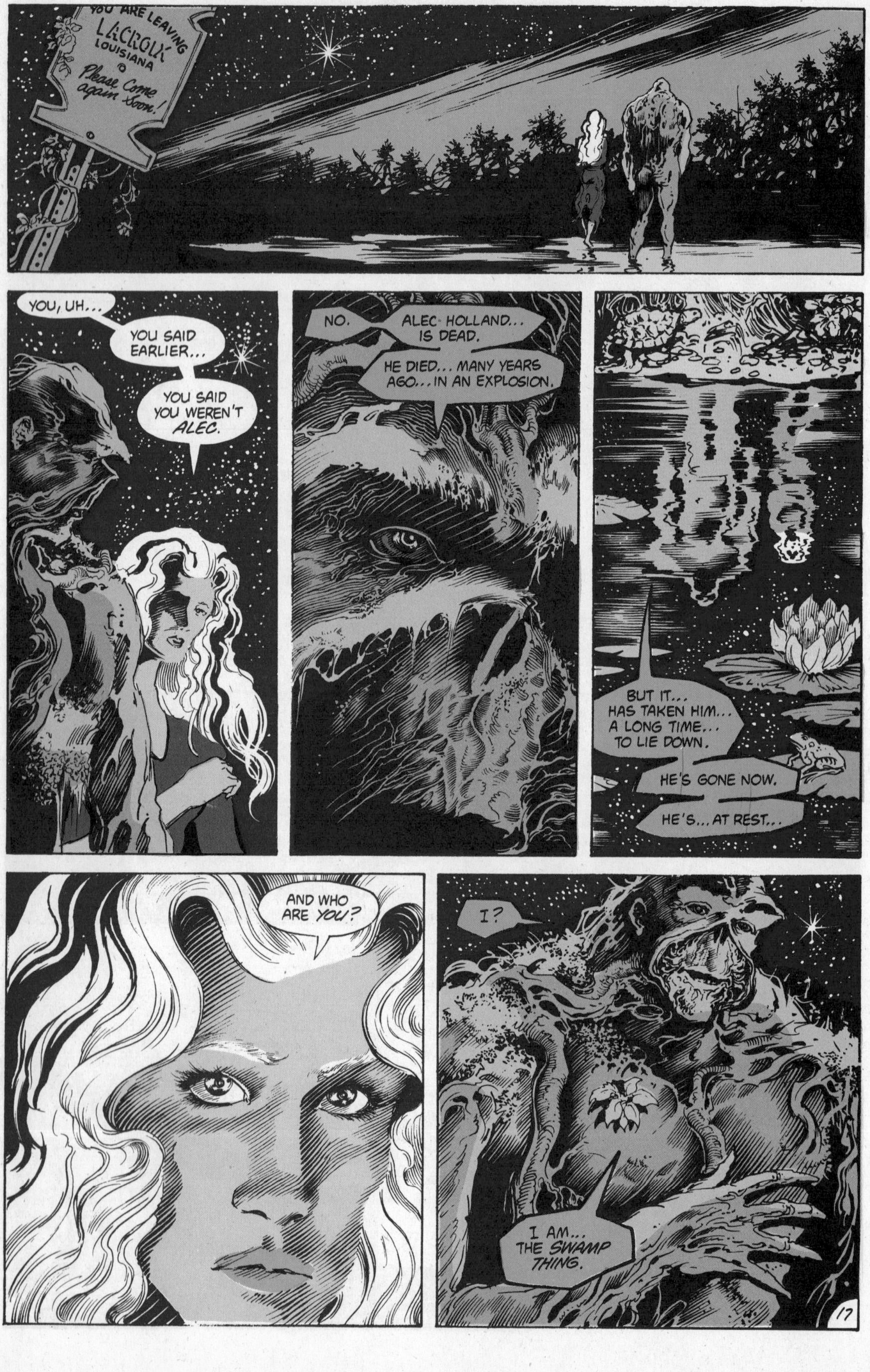
YOU ARE LEAVING
LACROIX
LOUISIANA
Please Come again Soon!
YOU, UH...
YOU SAID EARLIER...
YOU SAID YOU WEREN'T ALEC.
NO.
ALEC HOLLAND... IS DEAD.
HE DIED... MANY YEARS AGO... IN AN EXPLOSION.
BUT IT... HAS TAKEN HIM... A LONG TIME... TO LIE DOWN.
HE'S GONE NOW.
HE'S... AT REST...
AND WHO ARE YOU?
I?
I AM... THE SWAMP THING.
17

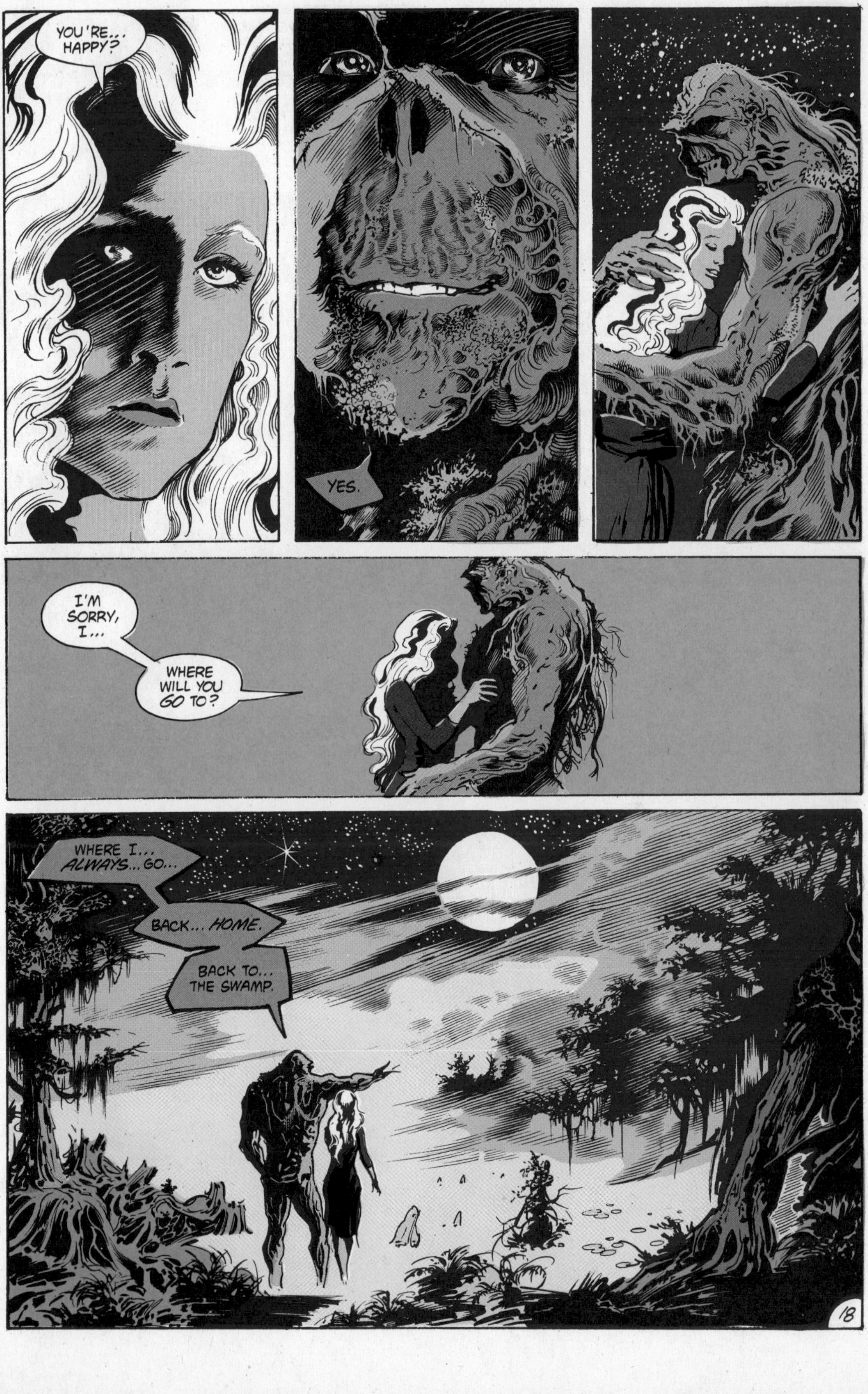
YOU'RE... HAPPY?
YES.
I'M SORRY, I...
WHERE WILL YOU GO TO?
WHERE I... ALWAYS... GO...
BACK... HOME.
BACK TO... THE SWAMP.
18

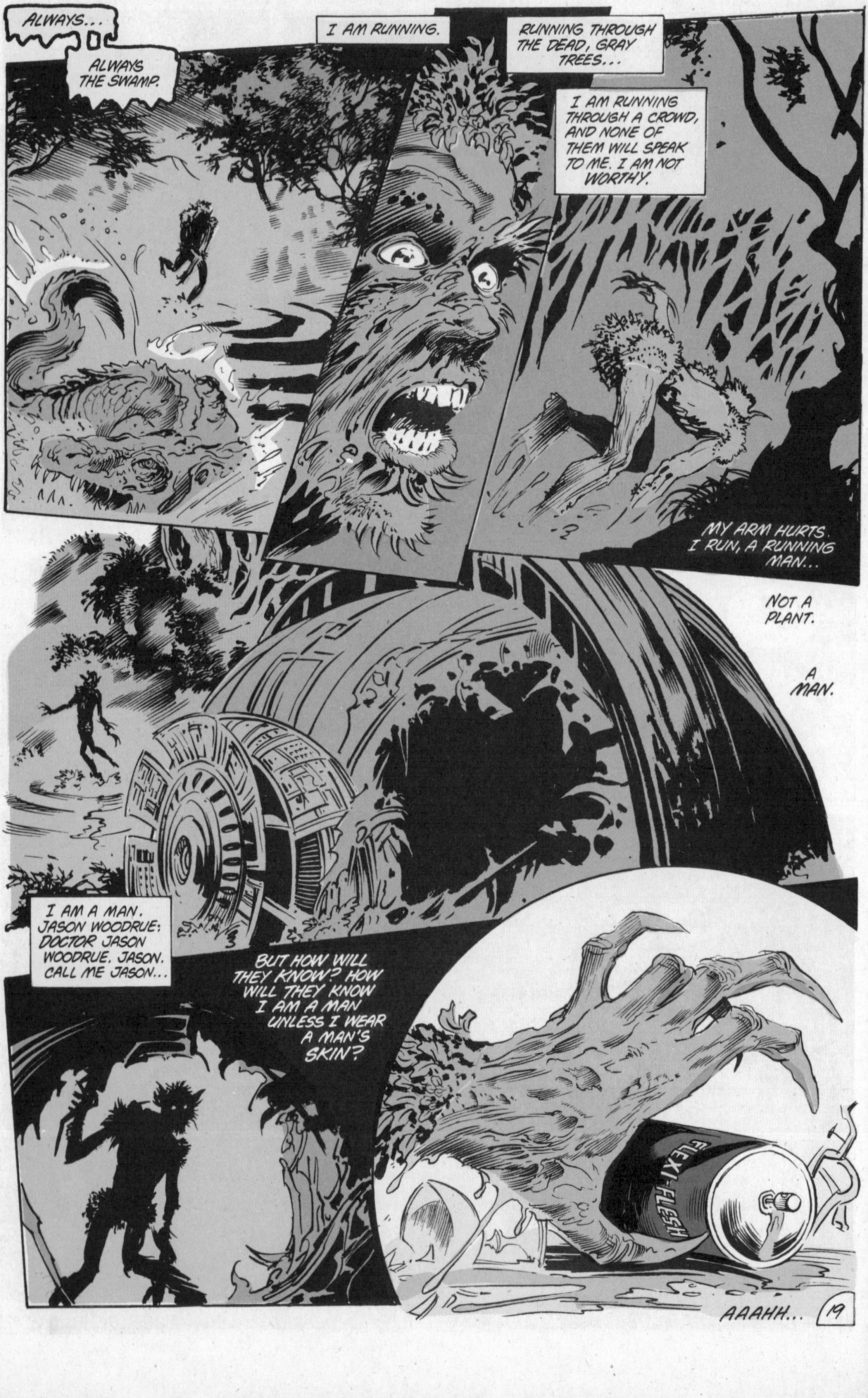
ALWAYS...
ALWAYS THE SWAMP.
I AM RUNNING.
RUNNING THROUGH THE DEAD, GRAY TREES...
I AM RUNNING THROUGH A CROWD, AND NONE OF THEM WILL SPEAK TO ME. I AM NOT WORTHY.
MY ARM HURTS. I RUN, A RUNNING MAN...
NOT A PLANT.
A MAN.
I AM A MAN. JASON WOODRUE: DOCTOR JASON WOODRUE. JASON. CALL ME JASON...
BUT HOW WILL THEY KNOW? HOW WILL THEY KNOW I AM A MAN UNLESS I WEAR A MAN'S SKIN?
FLEXI-FLESH
AAAHH...
19

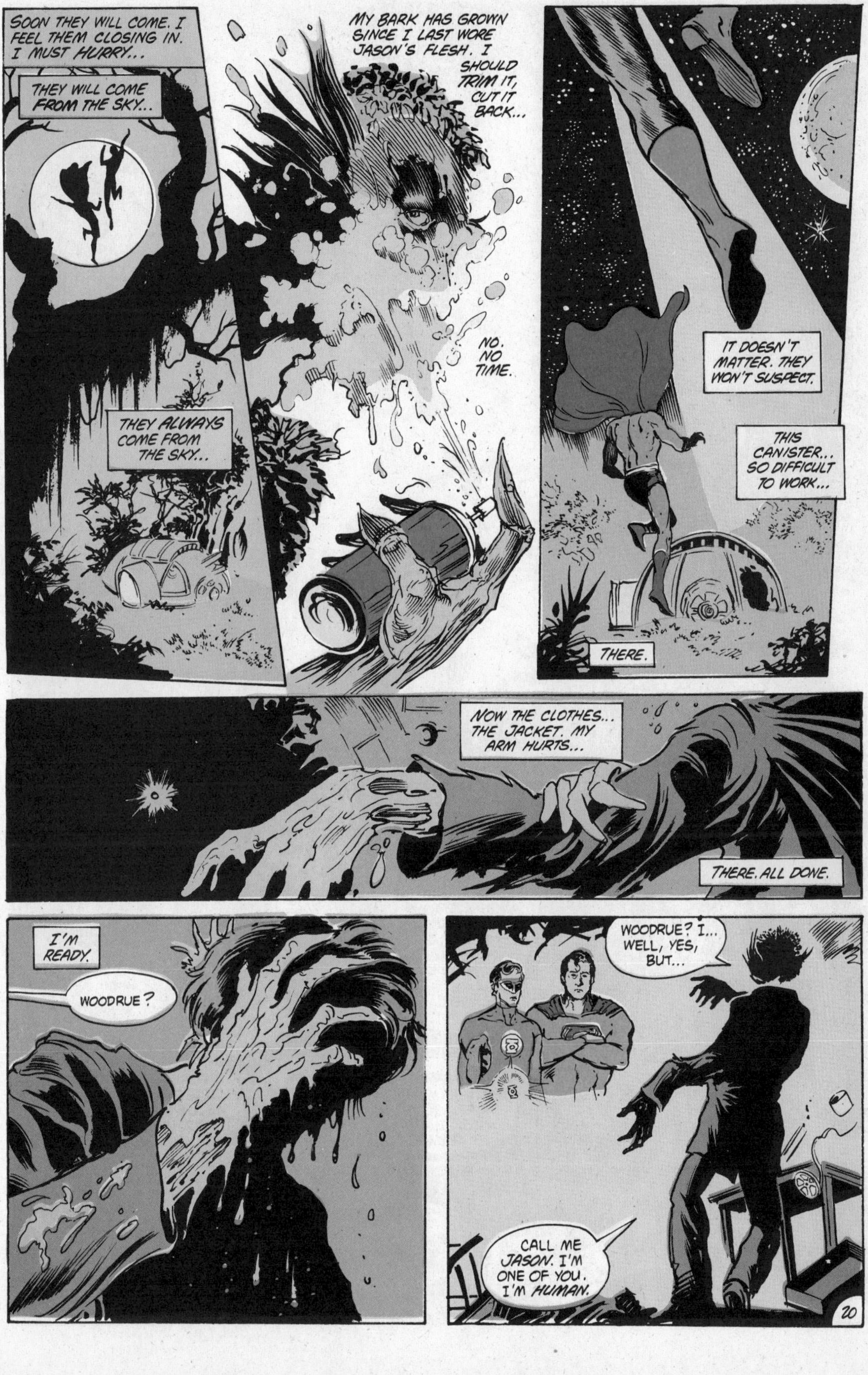
SOON THEY WILL COME. I FEEL THEM CLOSING IN. I MUST HURRY...
THEY WILL COME FROM THE SKY...
THEY ALWAYS COME FROM THE SKY...
MY BARK HAS GROWN SINCE I LAST WORE JASON'S FLESH. I SHOULD TRIM IT, CUT IT BACK...
NO. NO TIME.
IT DOESN'T MATTER. THEY WON'T SUSPECT.
THIS CANISTER... SO DIFFICULT TO WORK...
THERE.
NOW THE CLOTHES... THE JACKET. MY ARM HURTS...
THERE. ALL DONE.
I'M READY.
WOODRUE?
WOODRUE? I... WELL, YES, BUT...
CALL ME JASON. I'M ONE OF YOU. I'M HUMAN.
20

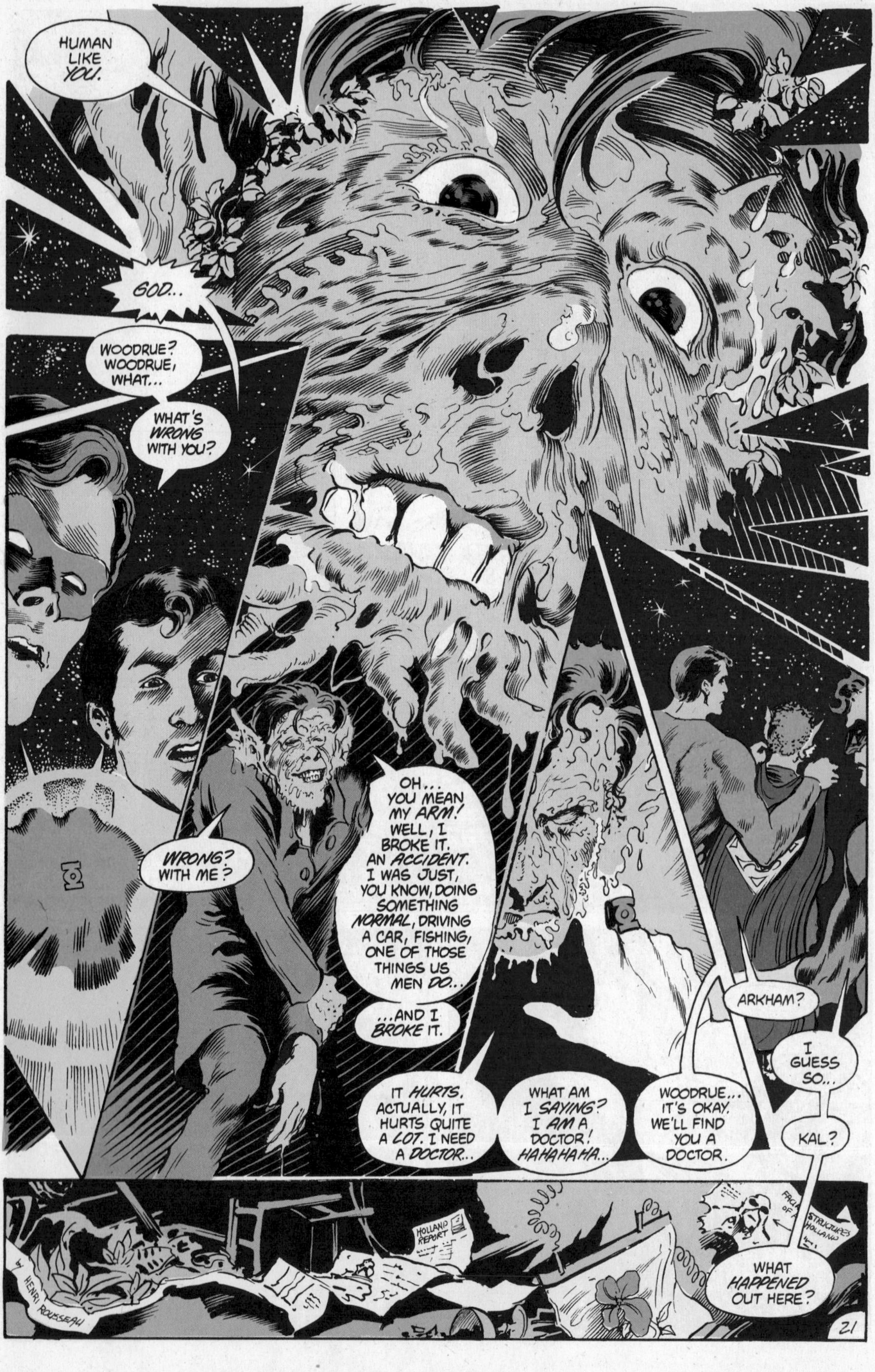
HUMAN LIKE YOU.
GOD...
WOODRUE? WOODRUE, WHAT...
WHAT'S WRONG WITH YOU?
WRONG? WITH ME?
OH... YOU MEAN MY ARM! WELL, I BROKE IT. AN ACCIDENT. I WAS JUST, YOU KNOW, DOING SOMETHING NORMAL, DRIVING A CAR, FISHING, ONE OF THOSE THINGS US MEN DO...
...AND I BROKE IT.
IT HURTS. ACTUALLY, IT HURTS QUITE A LOT. I NEED A DOCTOR...
WHAT AM I SAYING? I AM A DOCTOR! HAHAHAHA...
WOODRUE... IT'S OKAY. WE'LL FIND YOU A DOCTOR.
ARKHAM?
I GUESS SO...
KAL?
HOLLAND REPORT
FACIAL STRUCTURES OF A. HOLLAND
by HENRI ROUSSEAU
WHAT HAPPENED OUT HERE?
21

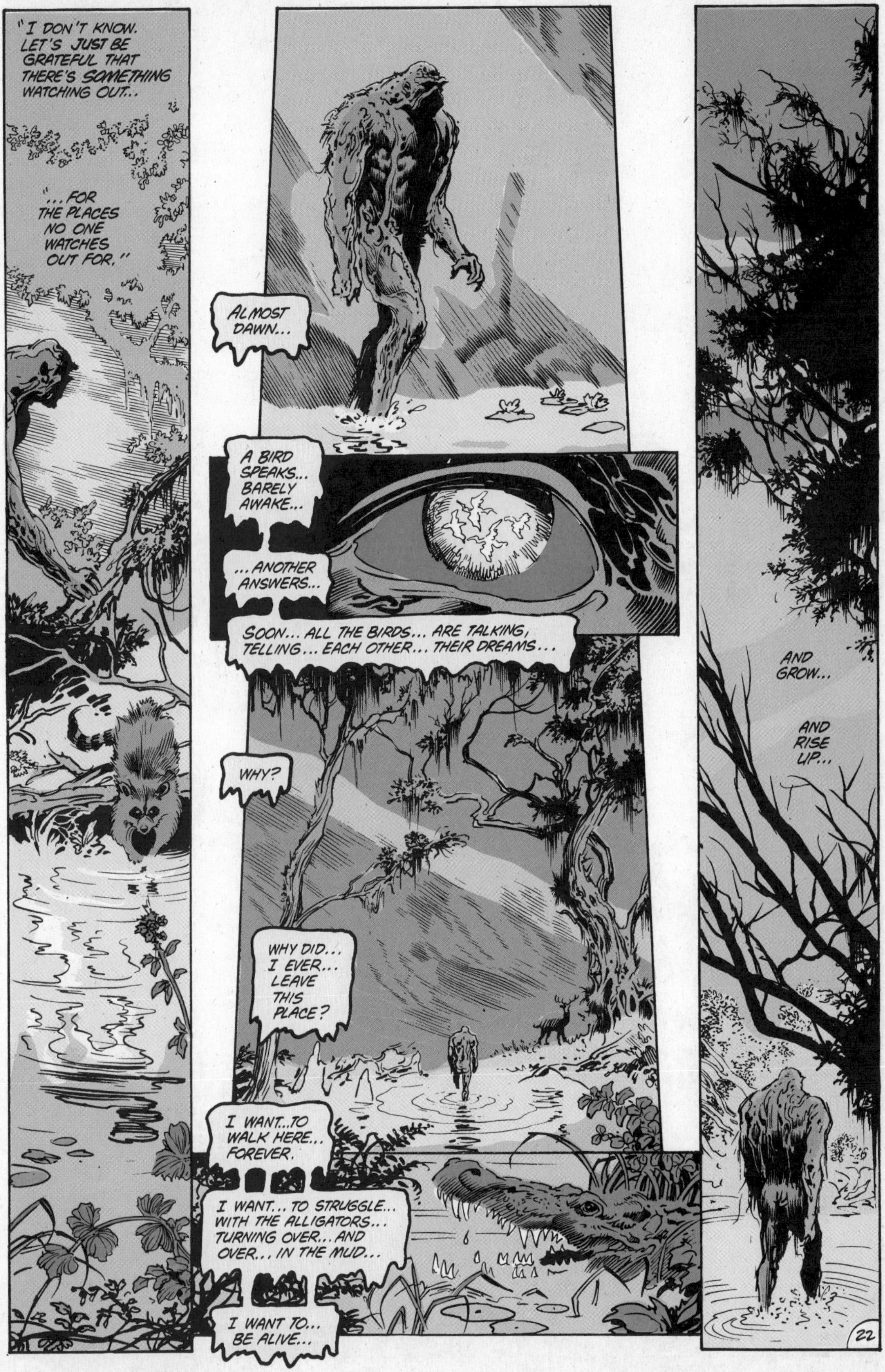
"I DON'T KNOW. LET'S JUST BE GRATEFUL THAT THERE'S SOMETHING WATCHING OUT...
"...FOR THE PLACES NO ONE WATCHES OUT FOR."
ALMOST DAWN...
A BIRD SPEAKS... BARELY AWAKE...
...ANOTHER ANSWERS...
SOON... ALL THE BIRDS... ARE TALKING, TELLING... EACH OTHER... THEIR DREAMS...
WHY?
WHY DID... I EVER... LEAVE THIS PLACE?
I WANT...TO WALK HERE... FOREVER.
I WANT... TO STRUGGLE... WITH THE ALLIGATORS... TURNING OVER... AND OVER... IN THE MUD...
I WANT TO... BE ALIVE...
AND GROW...
AND RISE UP...
22

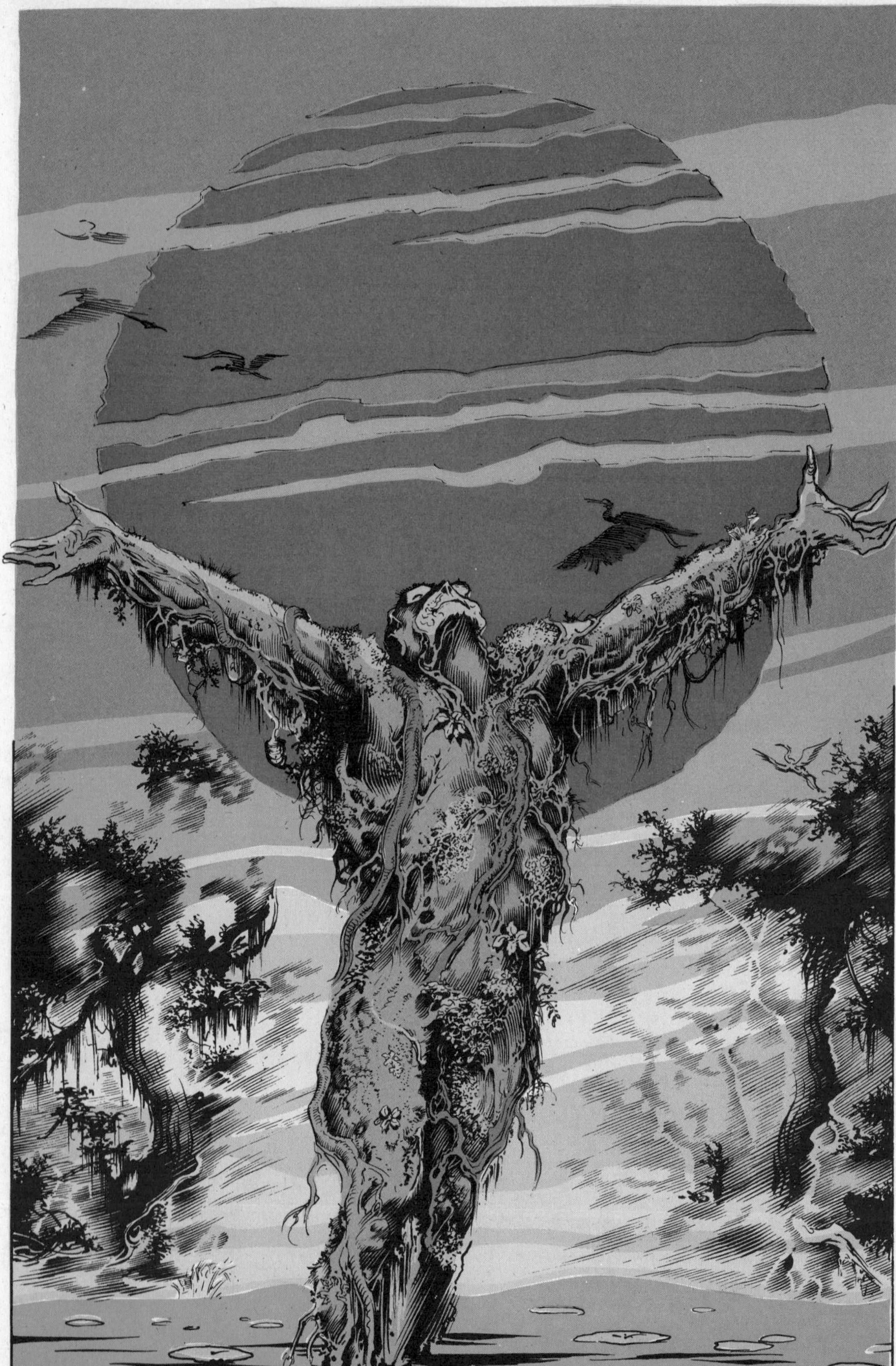
next: The Sleep of Reason...
23

BOOK FIVE

ON HIS WAY TO HIS HOTEL, HE CALLED AT "THIRD EYE BOOKS AND PARAPHERNALIA" AND PURCHASED SOME AMBER INCENSE.

EXCUSE ME...

YHUH?

NEW SINISTER DUCKS 45 ON SALE HERE

"BUY BONGS CHEAP!"

COMIX

GET YOUR GRIS GRIS HERE

SALE ON TAROT DECKS

BEANO PILLS. HEY KIDS... TURN YOUR FRIENDS INTO ZOMBIES! BE THE LIFE OF THE PARTY!

ASAFOETIDA

COBRA BRAND

DO YOU SELL MANY OF THESE?

NAH, AT THE MOMENT, I'M DOING A LOT OF AURA GOGGLES AN' STUFF LIKE THAT, BUT OUIJA BOARDS...

I THINK I SOLD ONE SIX MONTHS AGO. YOU WANT ONE?

POSTER 607

POSTER 361

DRINK TREEFROG BEER

NICE DAY FOR SOMETHIN'

CDEFGHIJKLM. PQRSTUVWXYZ

YES   NO

NO...NO, I DON'T THINK SO.

AHH, BUT THIS... THIS IS GOYA, ISN'T IT?

UH, IS THAT L-402? GOYA. YEAH, I THINK SO. "THE SLEEP OF REASON..."

POSTER 2264

XV

XII

"...BRINGS FORTH MONSTERS." YES, HE SHOWED ME THE ORIGINAL SKETCHES, BUT I LOST TOUCH WITH HIM AND SOMEHOW NEVER GOT TO SEE THE FINISHED WORK.

A MOST APPROPRIATE PIECE, I'LL TAKE IT.

UH, RIGHT...

AT ELEVEN THIRTY-EIGHT HE GAVE THIRTEEN DOLLARS TO A PRIEST COLLECTING FOR THE MISSION FUND, AND THEN LAUGHED FOR A FULL MINUTE.

THE HOTEL WAS NOT THE BEST, BUT IT WAS THE MOST ATMOSPHERIC.

THE DEVIL CHECKED IN AT NOON.

2

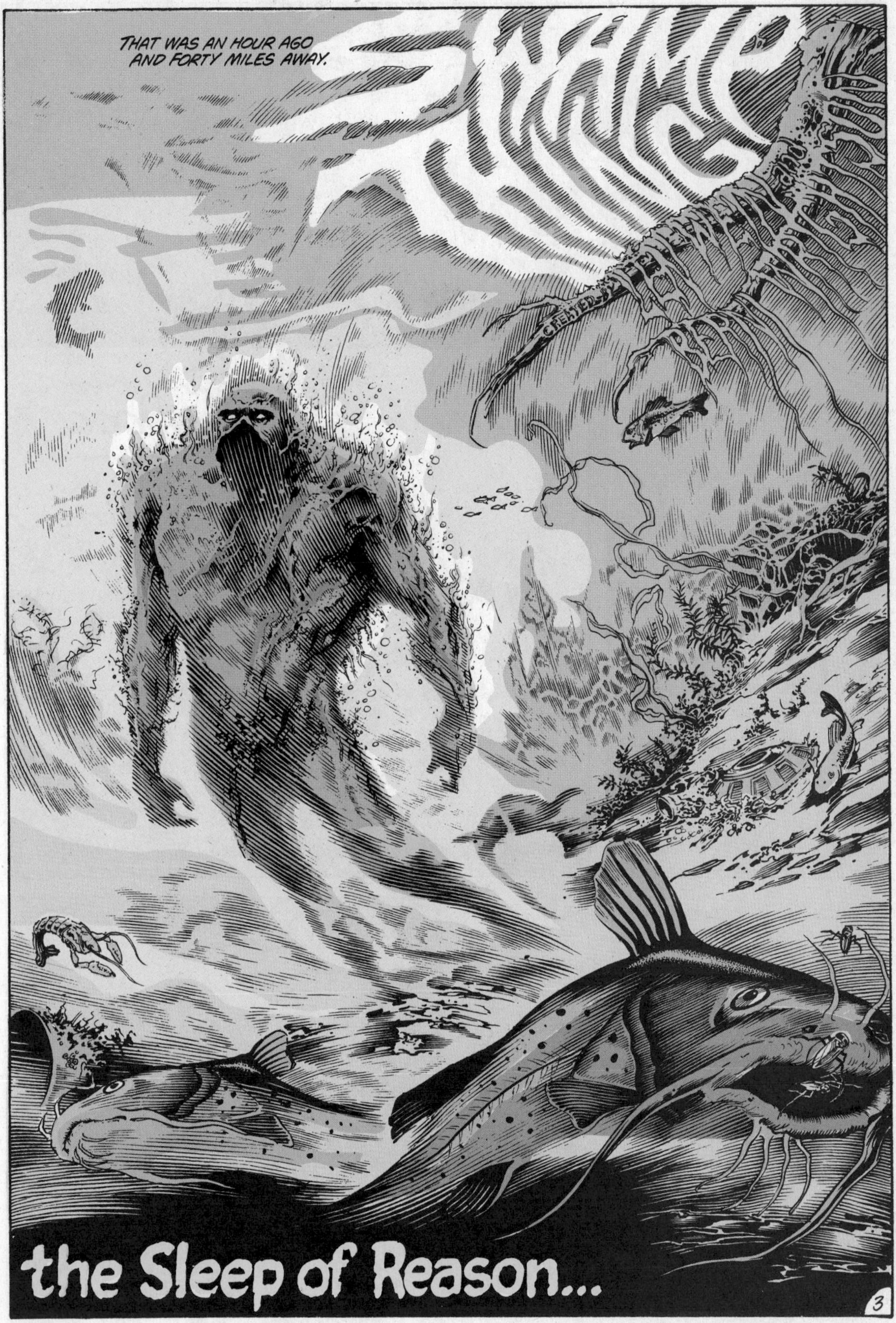
THAT WAS AN HOUR AGO AND FORTY MILES AWAY.
SWAMP THING
the Sleep of Reason...
3

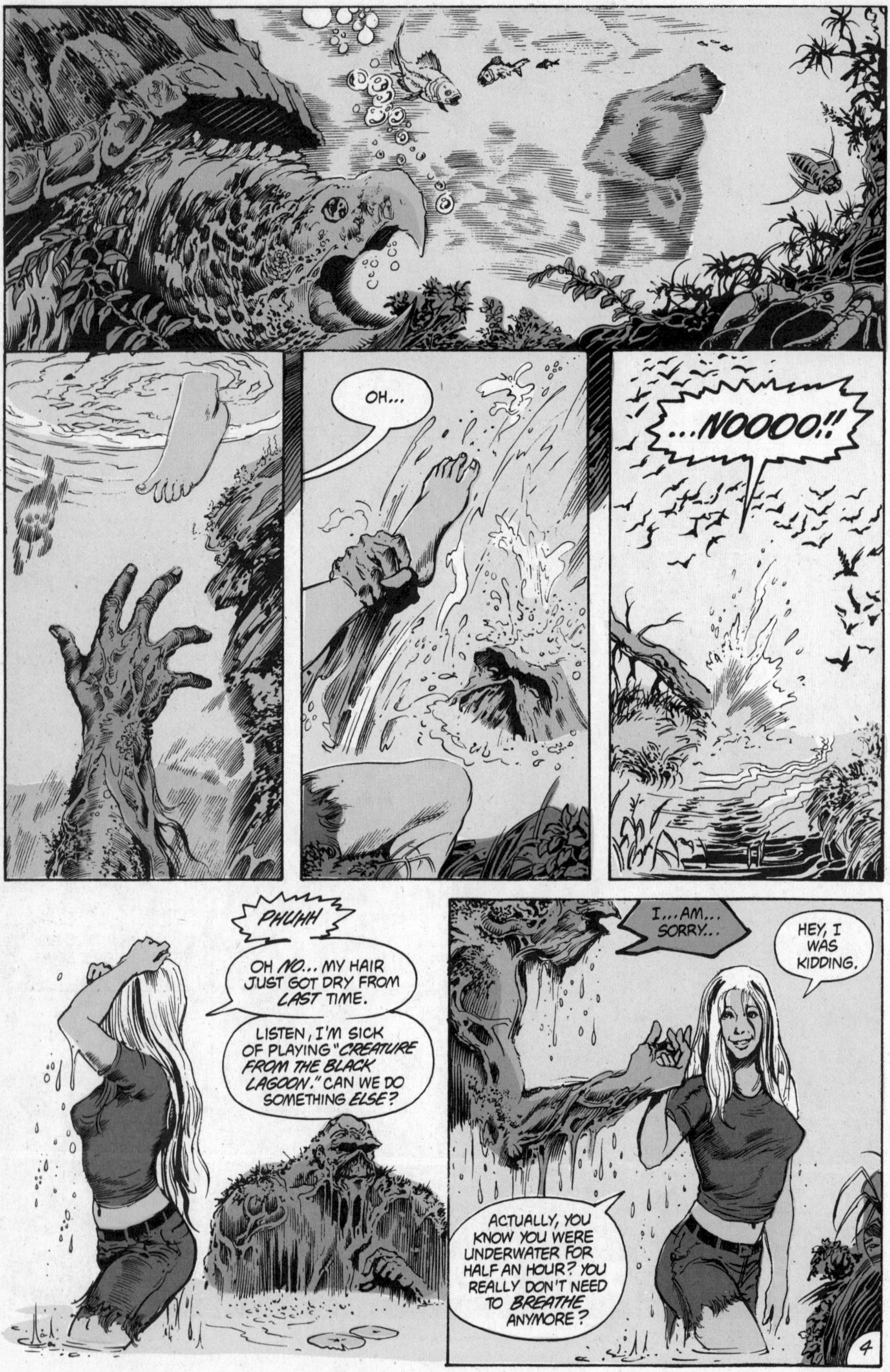
OH...
...NOOOO!!
PHUHH
OH NO... MY HAIR JUST GOT DRY FROM LAST TIME.
LISTEN, I'M SICK OF PLAYING "CREATURE FROM THE BLACK LAGOON." CAN WE DO SOMETHING ELSE?
I... AM... SORRY...
HEY, I WAS KIDDING.
ACTUALLY, YOU KNOW YOU WERE UNDERWATER FOR HALF AN HOUR? YOU REALLY DON'T NEED TO BREATHE ANYMORE?
4

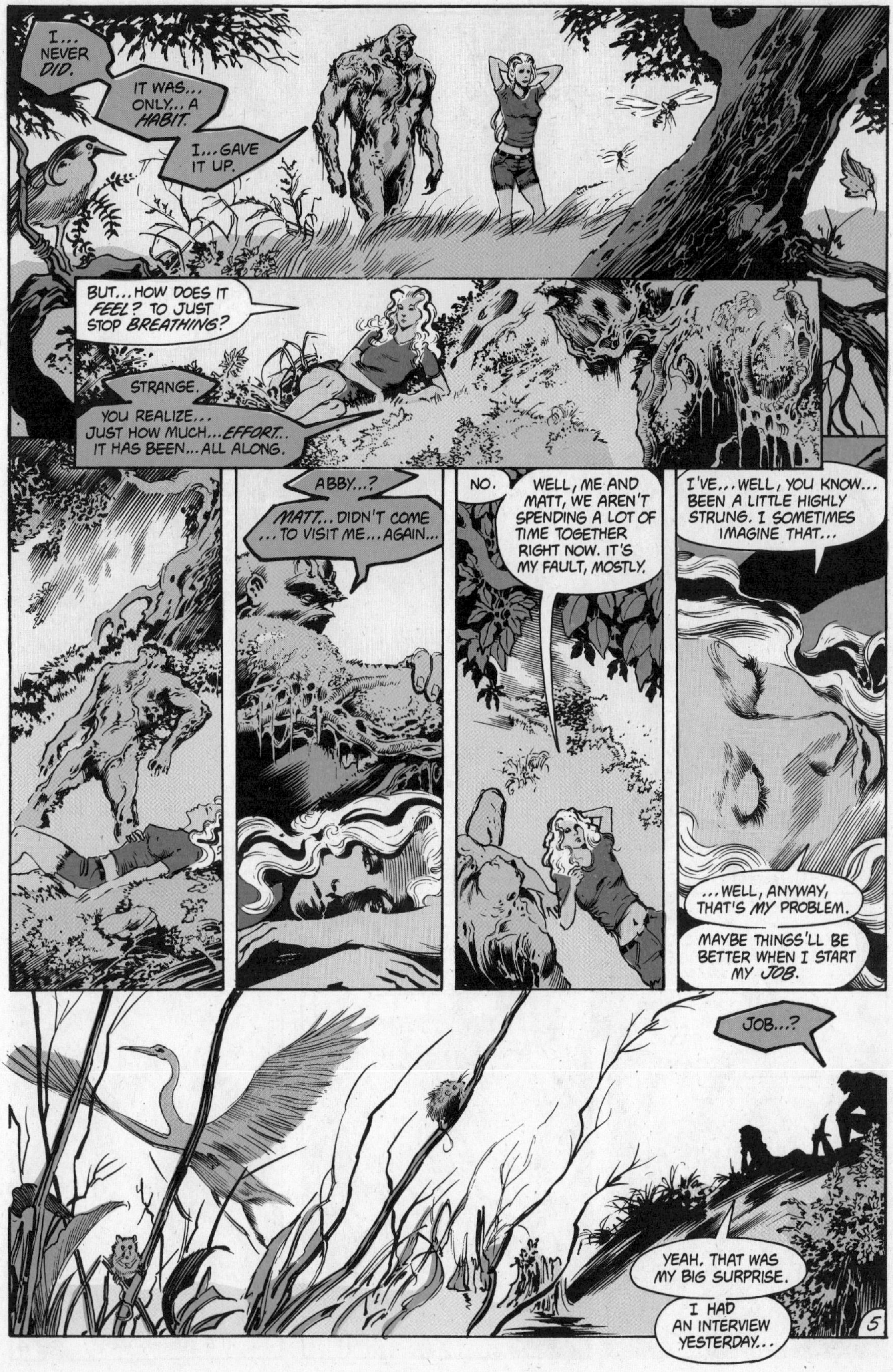
I... NEVER DID.
IT WAS... ONLY... A HABIT.
I... GAVE IT UP.
BUT... HOW DOES IT FEEL? TO JUST STOP BREATHING?
STRANGE.
YOU REALIZE... JUST HOW MUCH... EFFORT... IT HAS BEEN... ALL ALONG.
ABBY...?
MATT... DIDN'T COME ...TO VISIT ME... AGAIN...
NO.
WELL, ME AND MATT, WE AREN'T SPENDING A LOT OF TIME TOGETHER RIGHT NOW. IT'S MY FAULT, MOSTLY.
I'VE... WELL, YOU KNOW... BEEN A LITTLE HIGHLY STRUNG. I SOMETIMES IMAGINE THAT...
...WELL, ANYWAY, THAT'S MY PROBLEM.
MAYBE THINGS'LL BE BETTER WHEN I START MY JOB.
JOB...?
YEAH. THAT WAS MY BIG SURPRISE.
I HAD AN INTERVIEW YESTERDAY...
5

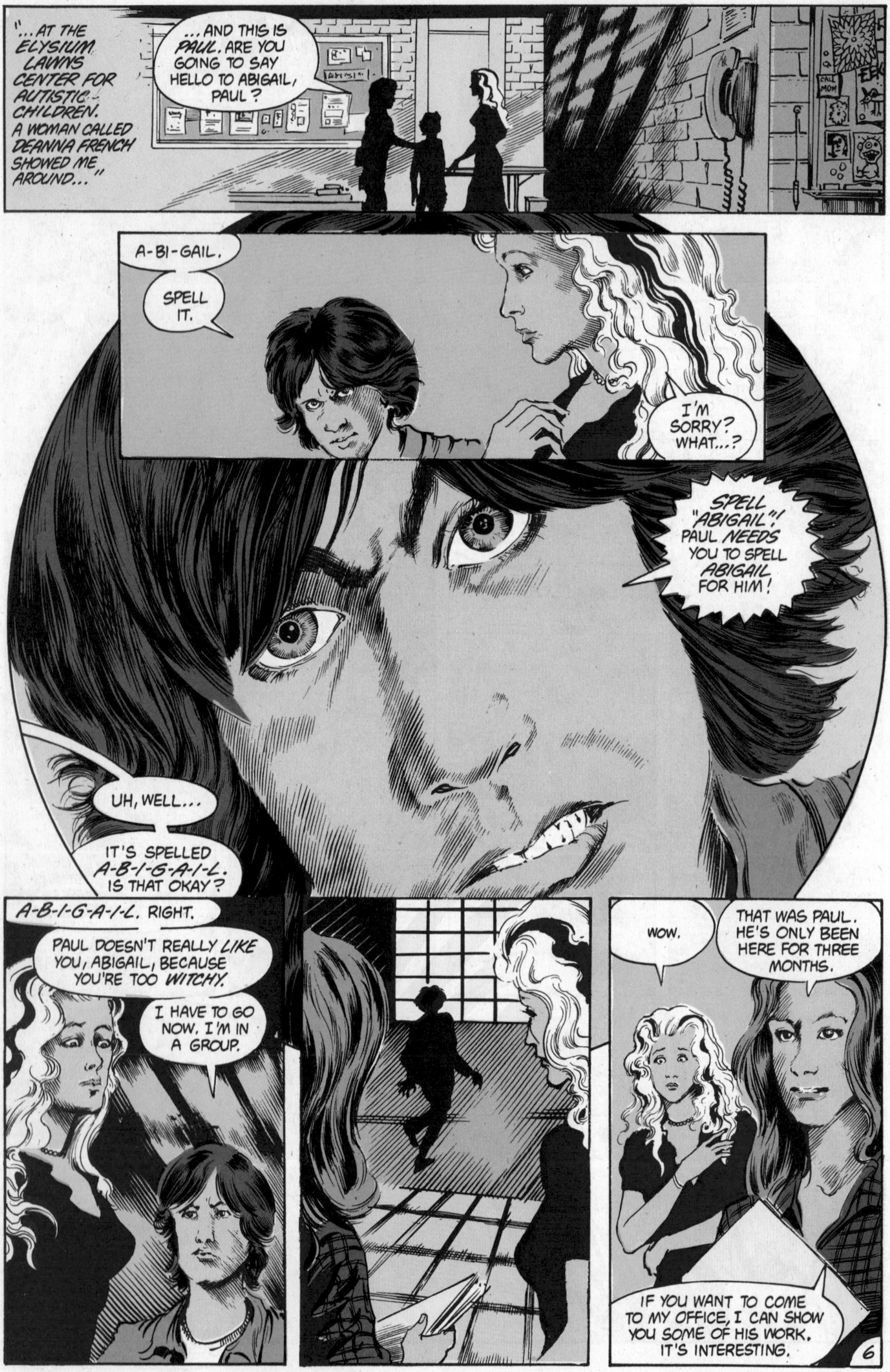
"...AT THE ELYSIUM LAWNS CENTER FOR AUTISTIC CHILDREN. A WOMAN CALLED DEANNA FRENCH SHOWED ME AROUND..."
...AND THIS IS PAUL. ARE YOU GOING TO SAY HELLO TO ABIGAIL, PAUL?
A-BI-GAIL.
SPELL IT.
I'M SORRY? WHAT...?
SPELL "ABIGAIL"! PAUL NEEDS YOU TO SPELL ABIGAIL FOR HIM!
UH, WELL...
IT'S SPELLED A-B-I-G-A-I-L. IS THAT OKAY?
A-B-I-G-A-I-L. RIGHT.
PAUL DOESN'T REALLY LIKE YOU, ABIGAIL, BECAUSE YOU'RE TOO WITCHY.
I HAVE TO GO NOW. I'M IN A GROUP.
WOW.
THAT WAS PAUL. HE'S ONLY BEEN HERE FOR THREE MONTHS.
IF YOU WANT TO COME TO MY OFFICE, I CAN SHOW YOU SOME OF HIS WORK. IT'S INTERESTING.
6

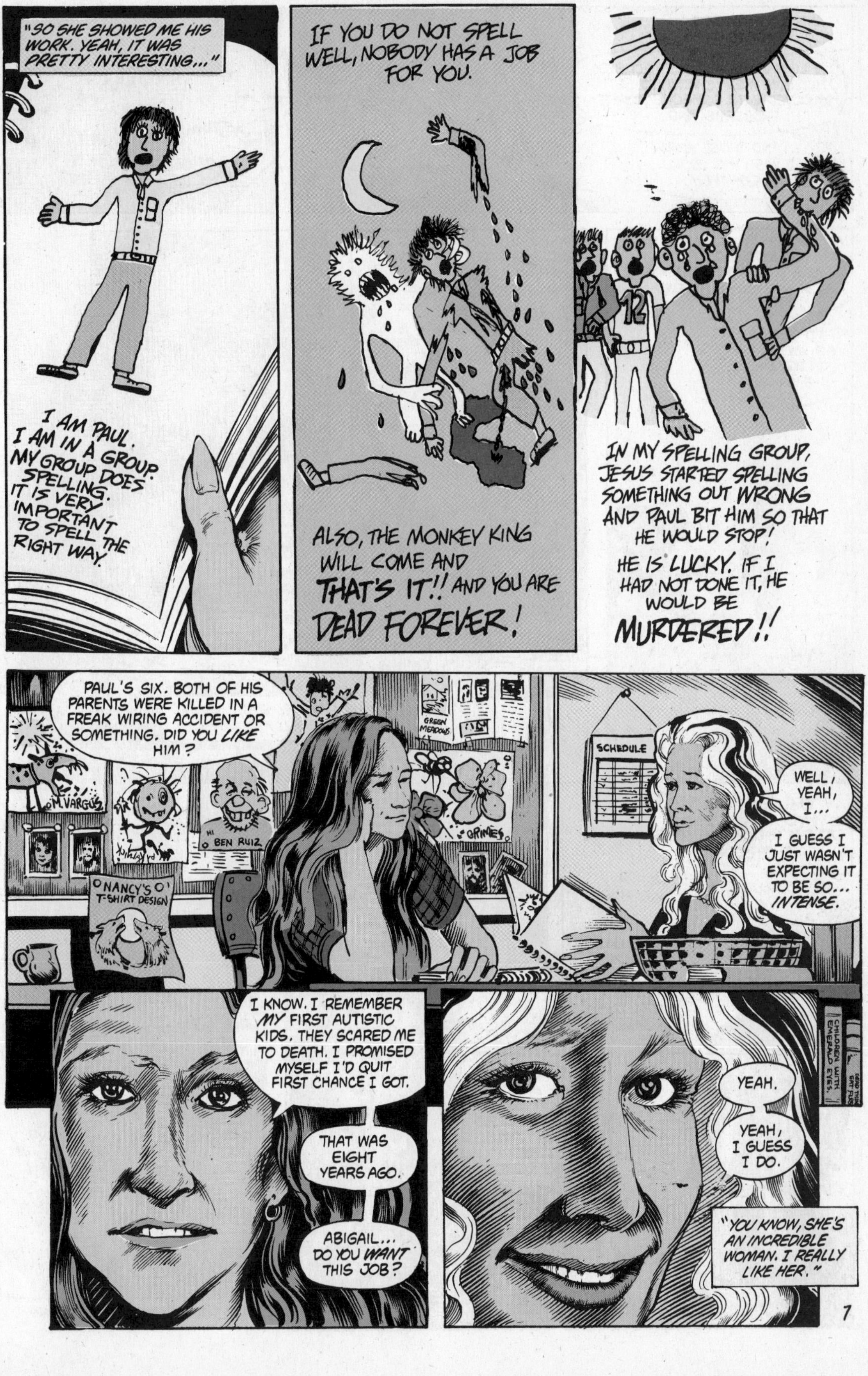
"SO SHE SHOWED ME HIS WORK. YEAH, IT WAS PRETTY INTERESTING..."
I AM PAUL. I AM IN A GROUP. MY GROUP DOES SPELLING. IT IS VERY IMPORTANT TO SPELL THE RIGHT WAY.
IF YOU DO NOT SPELL WELL, NOBODY HAS A JOB FOR YOU.
ALSO, THE MONKEY KING WILL COME AND THAT'S IT!! AND YOU ARE DEAD FOREVER!
IN MY SPELLING GROUP, JESUS STARTED SPELLING SOMETHING OUT WRONG AND PAUL BIT HIM SO THAT HE WOULD STOP!
HE IS LUCKY. IF I HAD NOT DONE IT, HE WOULD BE MURDERED!!
PAUL'S SIX. BOTH OF HIS PARENTS WERE KILLED IN A FREAK WIRING ACCIDENT OR SOMETHING. DID YOU LIKE HIM?
M. VARGUS
BEN RUIZ
GREEN MEADOWS
SCHEDULE
GRIMES
NANCY'S T-SHIRT DESIGN
WELL, YEAH, I...
I GUESS I JUST WASN'T EXPECTING IT TO BE SO... INTENSE.
I KNOW. I REMEMBER MY FIRST AUTISTIC KIDS. THEY SCARED ME TO DEATH. I PROMISED MYSELF I'D QUIT FIRST CHANCE I GOT.
THAT WAS EIGHT YEARS AGO.
ABIGAIL... DO YOU WANT THIS JOB?
CHILDREN WITH EMERALD EYES.
YEAH.
YEAH, I GUESS I DO.
"YOU KNOW, SHE'S AN INCREDIBLE WOMAN. I REALLY LIKE HER."
7

9

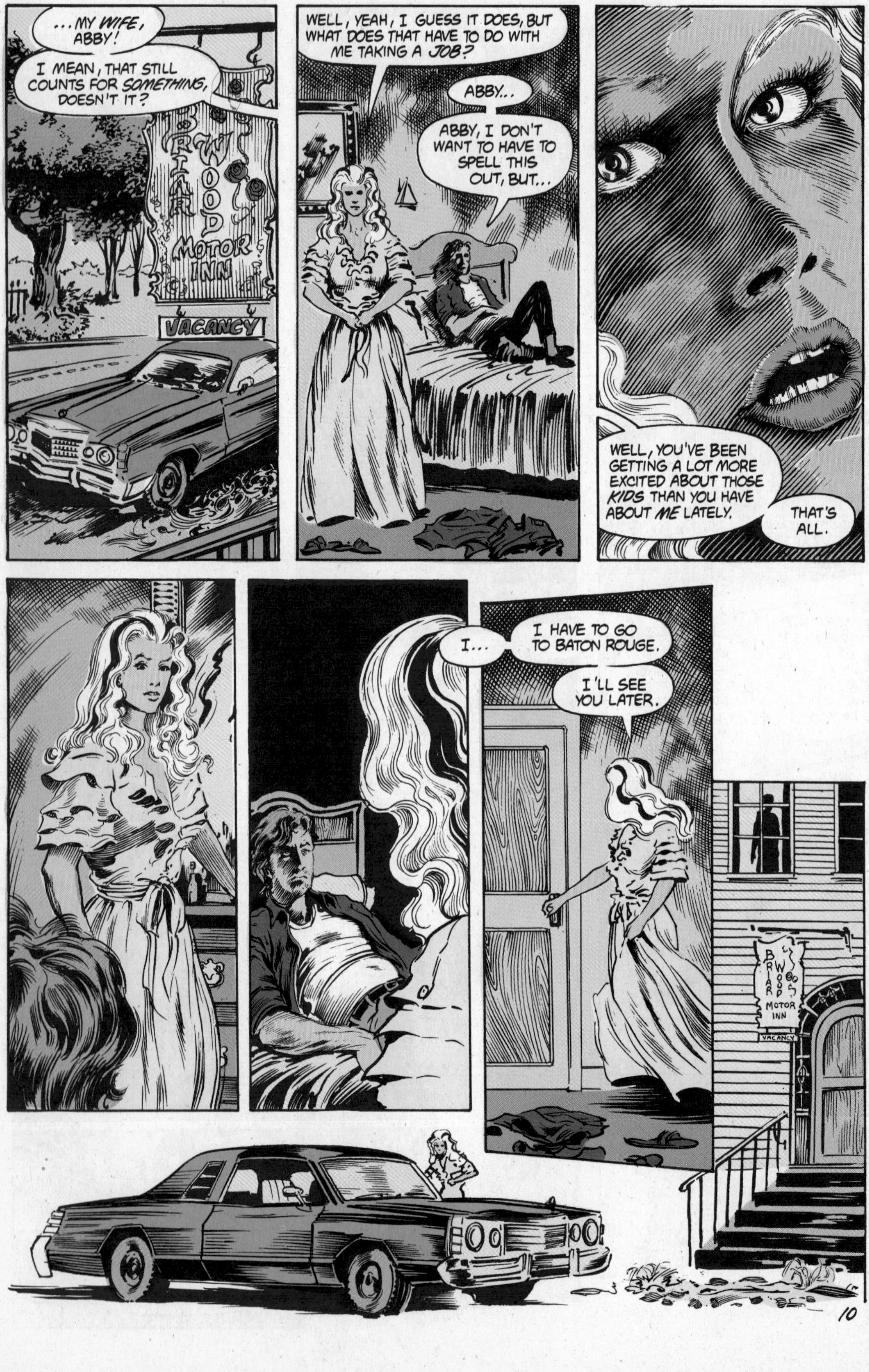
...MY WIFE, ABBY!
I MEAN, THAT STILL COUNTS FOR SOMETHING, DOESN'T IT?
BRIAR WOOD MOTOR INN
VACANCY
WELL, YEAH, I GUESS IT DOES, BUT WHAT DOES THAT HAVE TO DO WITH ME TAKING A JOB?
ABBY...
ABBY, I DON'T WANT TO HAVE TO SPELL THIS OUT, BUT...
WELL, YOU'VE BEEN GETTING A LOT MORE EXCITED ABOUT THOSE KIDS THAN YOU HAVE ABOUT ME LATELY.
THAT'S ALL.
I...
I HAVE TO GO TO BATON ROUGE.
I'LL SEE YOU LATER.
BRIAR WOOD MOTOR INN
VACANCY
10

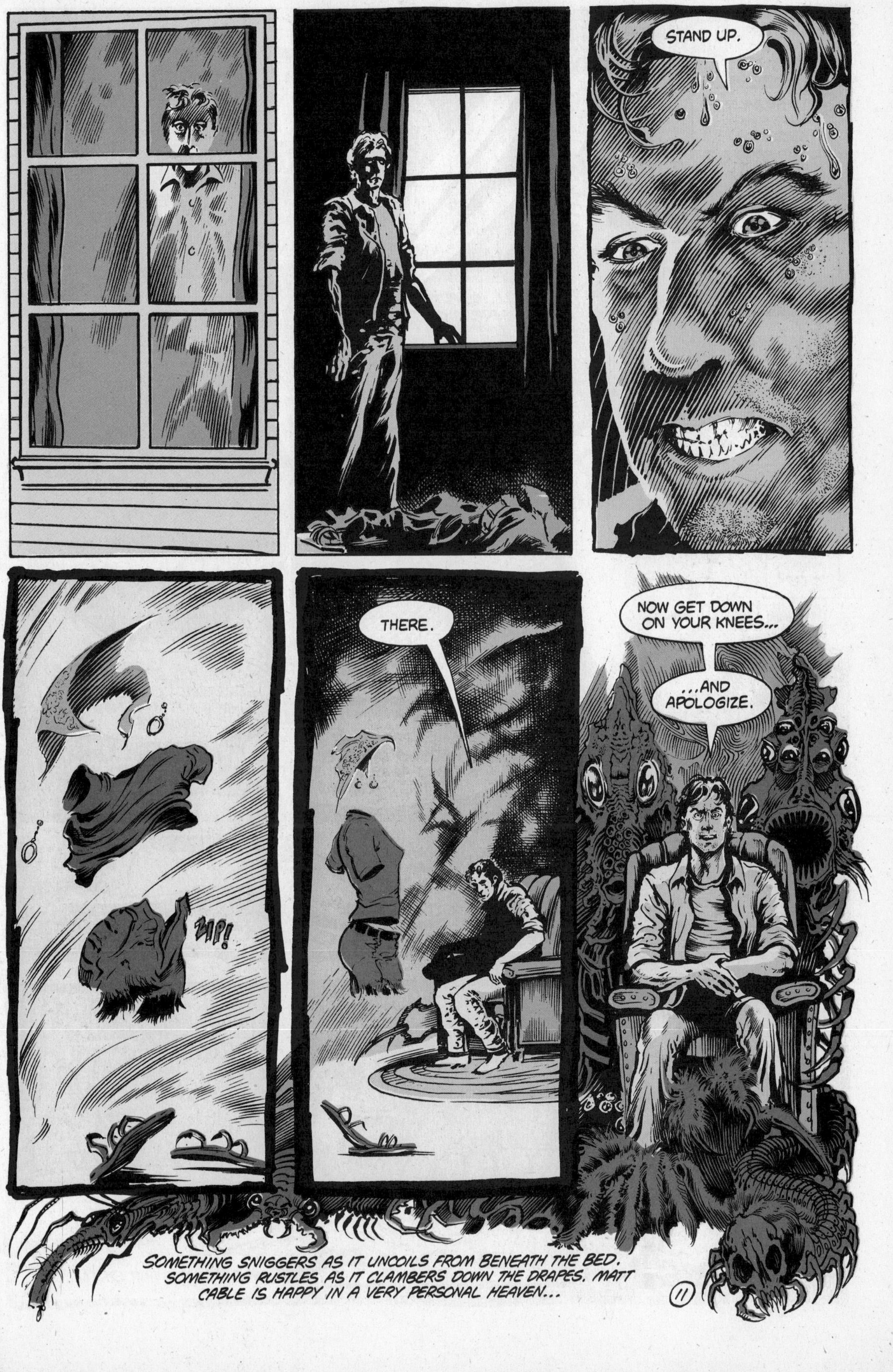
STAND UP.
ZIP!
THERE.
NOW GET DOWN ON YOUR KNEES...
...AND APOLOGIZE.
SOMETHING SNIGGERS AS IT UNCOILS FROM BENEATH THE BED. SOMETHING RUSTLES AS IT CLAMBERS DOWN THE DRAPES. MATT CABLE IS HAPPY IN A VERY PERSONAL HEAVEN...
11

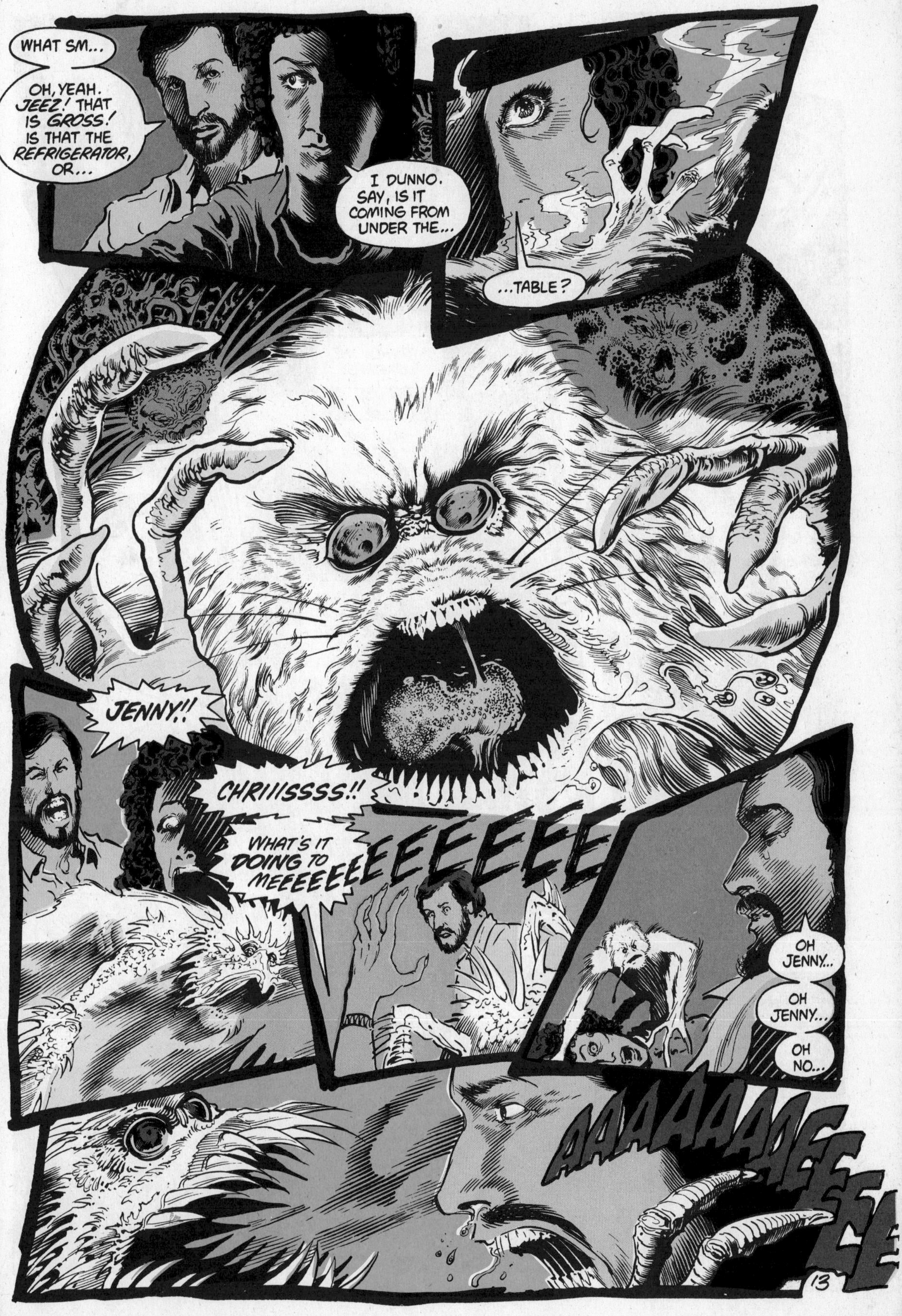
WHAT SM...
OH, YEAH. JEEZ! THAT IS GROSS! IS THAT THE REFRIGERATOR, OR...
I DUNNO. SAY, IS IT COMING FROM UNDER THE...
...TABLE?
JENNY!!
CHRIIISSSS!!
WHAT'S IT DOING TO MEEEEEEEEEEEEEE
OH JENNY...
OH JENNY...
OH NO...
AAAAAAAEEEEEE
13

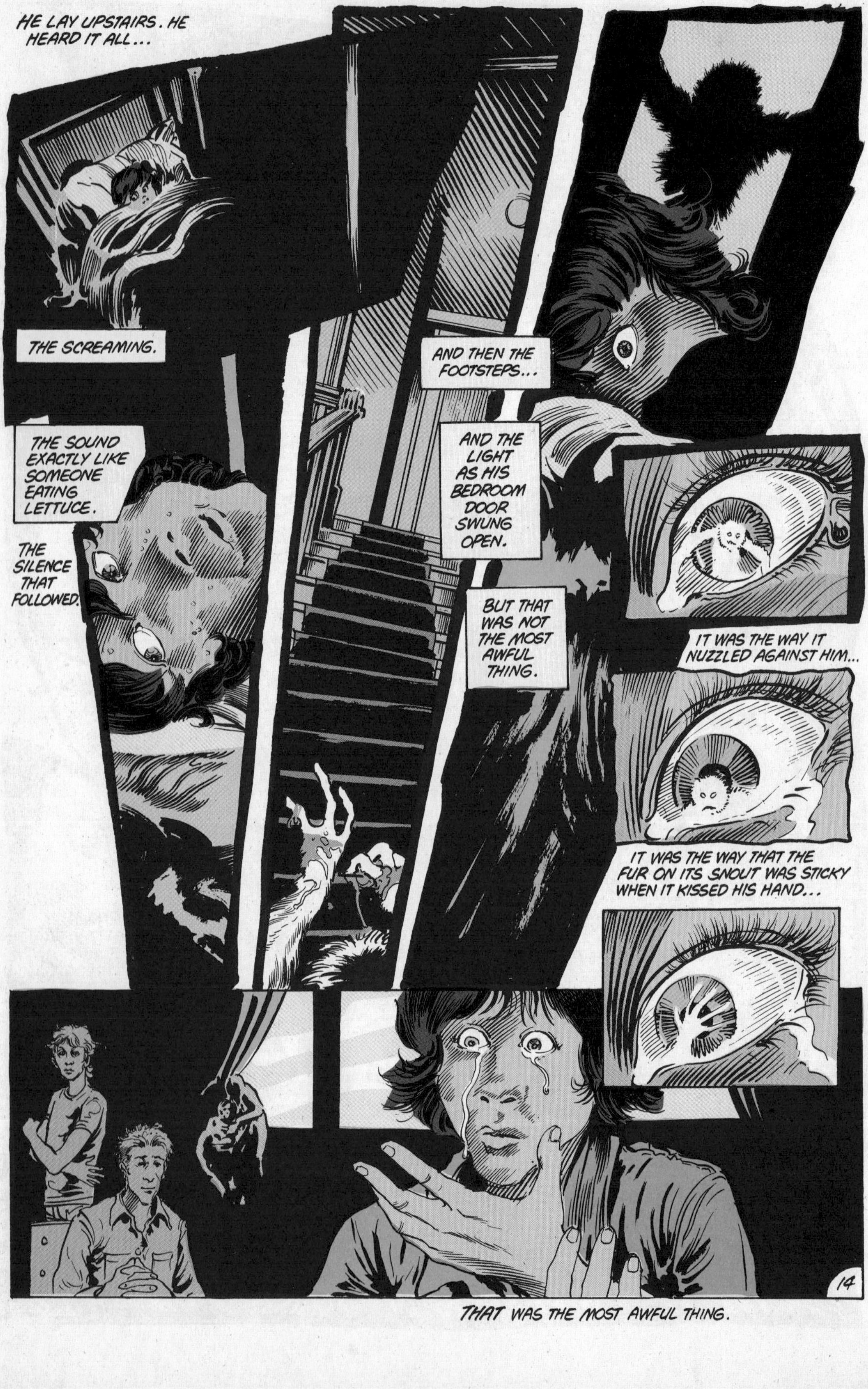
HE LAY UPSTAIRS. HE HEARD IT ALL...
THE SCREAMING.
THE SOUND EXACTLY LIKE SOMEONE EATING LETTUCE.
THE SILENCE THAT FOLLOWED.
AND THEN THE FOOTSTEPS...
AND THE LIGHT AS HIS BEDROOM DOOR SWUNG OPEN.
BUT THAT WAS NOT THE MOST AWFUL THING.
IT WAS THE WAY IT NUZZLED AGAINST HIM...
IT WAS THE WAY THAT THE FUR ON ITS SNOUT WAS STICKY WHEN IT KISSED HIS HAND...
14
THAT WAS THE MOST AWFUL THING.

SELENA, THAT IS THE MOST *AWFUL* THING I HAVE EVER SEEN! WHERE ARE WE GONNA PUT IT?

BOBBY, *SHUT UP* AND TIE IT ONNA ROOF.

SELENA, I DON'T EVEN KNOW IF IT'S *LEGAL* DRIVING WITH STUFF ON THE ROOF!

WHY THE HELL DIDN'T YOU BUY THE *LAWN CHAIRS?*

BECAUSE I DIDN'T *LIKE* THE LAWN CHAIRS AND IT'S *MY* MONEY. NOW *SHUT UP!*

OH, RIGHT, SURE. I SUPPOSE THAT'S WHAT YOU TOLD YOUR *PSYCHO BOYFRIEND* THAT YOU MET IN THE *AUCTION?*

I DIDN'T MEET *ANYONE* AT THE AUCTION. I WISH TO GOD I HAD, BELIEVE ME.

NOW GET IN THE CAR, BOBBY, AND *DRIVE!*

YOU KNOW! THE RED-HAIRED GUY WHO BOUGHT THE *WEEJEE* BOARD...

OH, YOU FEEBLE, SUSPICIOUS-MINDED LITTLE...

AND I SUPPOSE *HE* WAS THE ONE WHO PUT YOU UP TO BUYING THAT PIECE OF JUNK ON THE ROOF?

DRIVE, BOBBY...

JEEZ, NO *WONDER* THOSE PEOPLE GOT KILLED! ANYBODY WHO'D ALLOW AN EYESORE LIKE *THAT* INTO THEIR HOME *DESERVES...*

BO·BEE...

YEAH, YEAH, I KNOW...

KOFF! KAF!

IT'S TEN MINUTES AFTER FIVE... 15

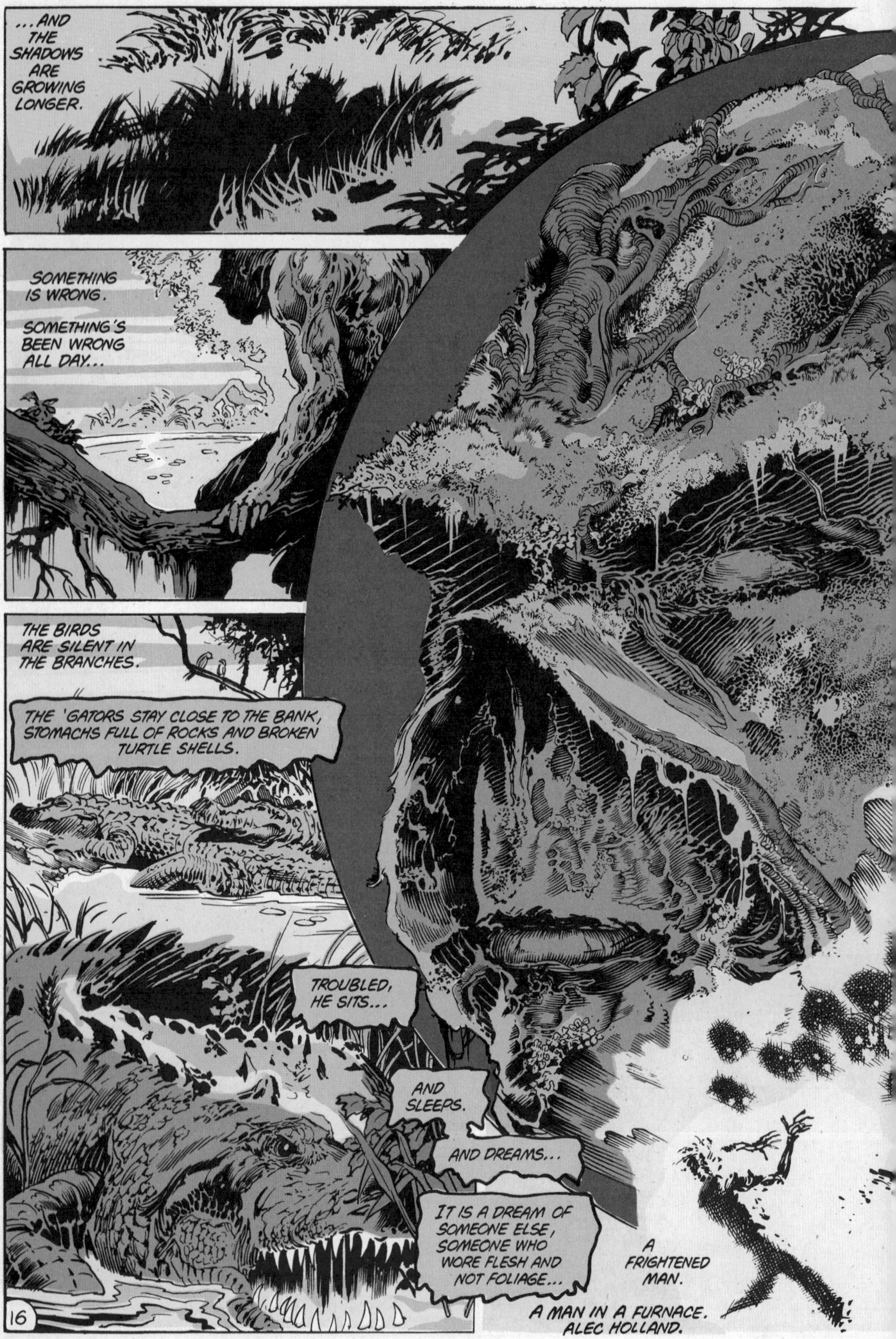
...AND THE SHADOWS ARE GROWING LONGER.
SOMETHING IS WRONG.
SOMETHING'S BEEN WRONG ALL DAY...
THE BIRDS ARE SILENT IN THE BRANCHES.
THE 'GATORS STAY CLOSE TO THE BANK, STOMACHS FULL OF ROCKS AND BROKEN TURTLE SHELLS.
TROUBLED, HE SITS...
AND SLEEPS.
AND DREAMS...
IT IS A DREAM OF SOMEONE ELSE, SOMEONE WHO WORE FLESH AND NOT FOLIAGE...
A FRIGHTENED MAN.
A MAN IN A FURNACE. ALEC HOLLAND.
16

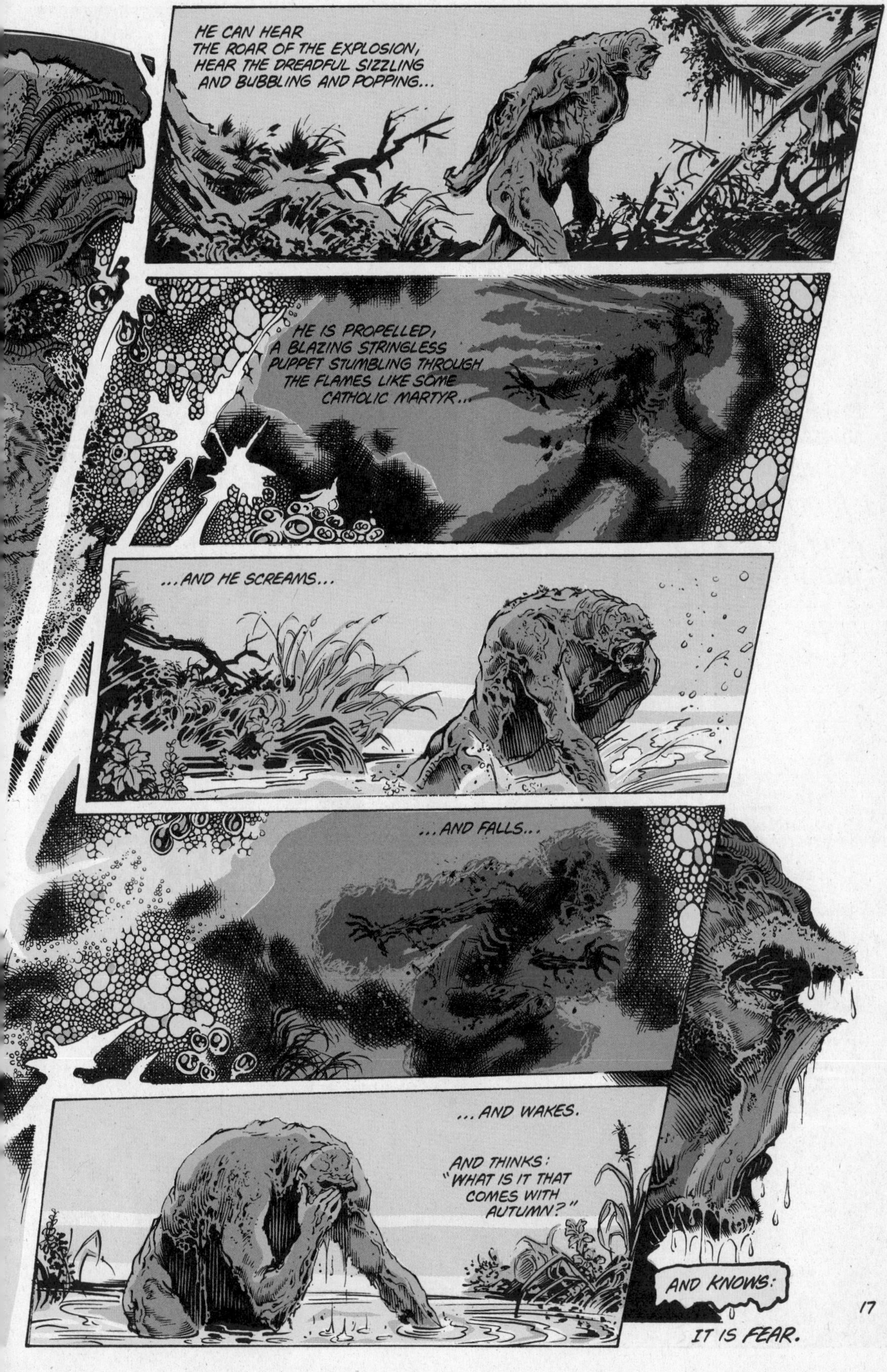
HE CAN HEAR THE ROAR OF THE EXPLOSION, HEAR THE DREADFUL SIZZLING AND BUBBLING AND POPPING...
HE IS PROPELLED, A BLAZING STRINGLESS PUPPET STUMBLING THROUGH THE FLAMES LIKE SOME CATHOLIC MARTYR...
...AND HE SCREAMS...
...AND FALLS...
...AND WAKES.
AND THINKS: "WHAT IS IT THAT COMES WITH AUTUMN?"
AND KNOWS:
IT IS FEAR.
17

IT IS FEAR THAT COMES WITH THE AUTUMN.

HE FEELS IT...

El sueño de la razon produce monstruos

IT THRUMS BENEATH HIS THICK, POWERFUL FINGERS, AND ITS BOUQUET OF SOURED SWEAT IS NOT MASKED BY THE INCENSE.

WITHIN THE DARK POOL OF HIS MIND IMAGES UNFOLD, OPENING LIKE ANEMONES IN BRINE...

THE MAN, THE WOMAN, THE BOY AWAKE UPSTAIRS...

THE PLANCHETTE MOVING...

...OMMOX...

...HODAEL...

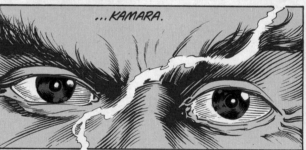

...KAMARA.

THE PENULTIMATE FRAGMENT OF THE CRYPTOGRAM TUMBLES INTO PLACE... AN *INVOCATION*, SPELLED OUT BY A OUIJA BOARD.

THAT WAS HOW THE DAMNED THING HAD CLAWED ITS WAY THROUGH INTO THE WORLD OF SANITY AND REASON.

THERE IS MUCH TO BE DONE.

IT IS ALREADY HALF PAST FIVE... 18

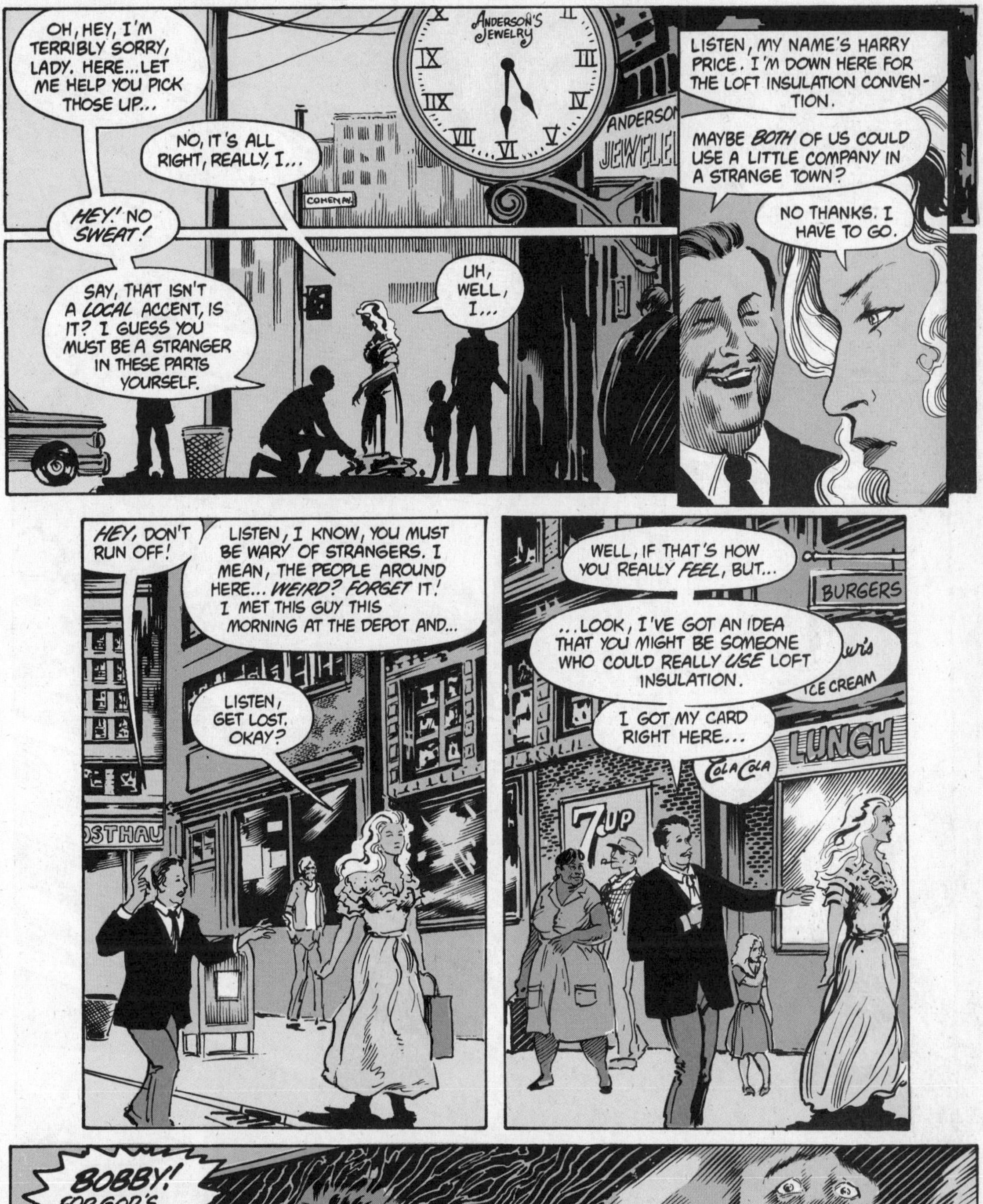
ANDERSON'S JEWELRY
OH, HEY, I'M TERRIBLY SORRY, LADY. HERE...LET ME HELP YOU PICK THOSE UP...
NO, IT'S ALL RIGHT, REALLY, I...
HEY! NO SWEAT!
SAY, THAT ISN'T A LOCAL ACCENT, IS IT? I GUESS YOU MUST BE A STRANGER IN THESE PARTS YOURSELF.
UH, WELL, I...
ANDERSON JEWELER
LISTEN, MY NAME'S HARRY PRICE. I'M DOWN HERE FOR THE LOFT INSULATION CONVENTION.
MAYBE BOTH OF US COULD USE A LITTLE COMPANY IN A STRANGE TOWN?
NO THANKS. I HAVE TO GO.
HEY, DON'T RUN OFF!
LISTEN, I KNOW, YOU MUST BE WARY OF STRANGERS. I MEAN, THE PEOPLE AROUND HERE... WEIRD? FORGET IT! I MET THIS GUY THIS MORNING AT THE DEPOT AND...
LISTEN, GET LOST. OKAY?
WELL, IF THAT'S HOW YOU REALLY FEEL, BUT...
BURGERS
...LOOK, I'VE GOT AN IDEA THAT YOU MIGHT BE SOMEONE WHO COULD REALLY USE LOFT INSULATION.
ICE CREAM
I GOT MY CARD RIGHT HERE...
LUNCH
7UP
BOBBY! FOR GOD'S SAKE LOOK OUT!!
19

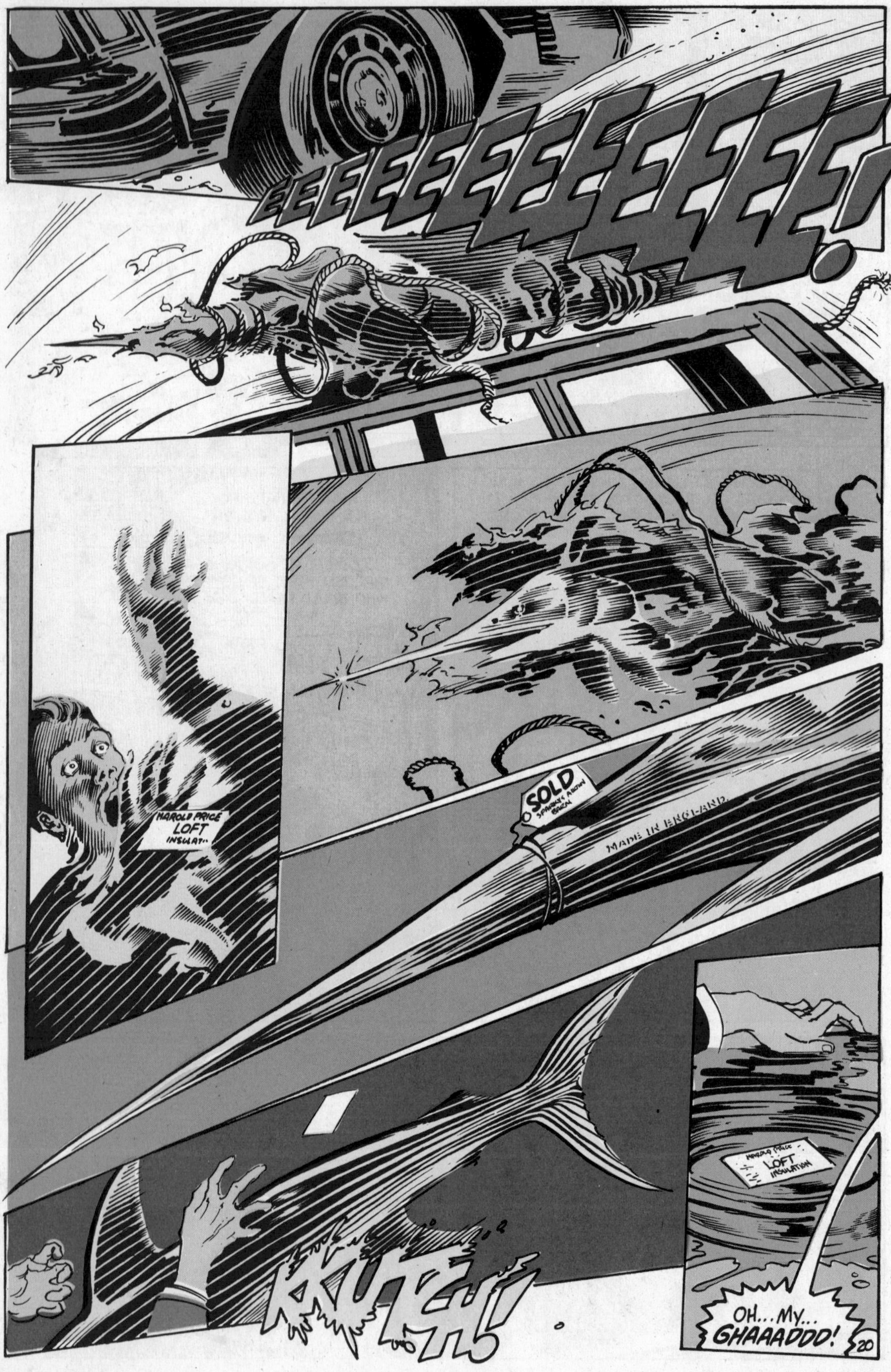
EEEEEEEEEEEE!
HAROLD PRICE LOFT INSULAT...
SOLD
SPARKY'S AUCTION BARN
MADE IN ENGLAND
KUTCH!
HAROLD PRICE LOFT INSULATION
OH... MY... GHAAADDD!
20

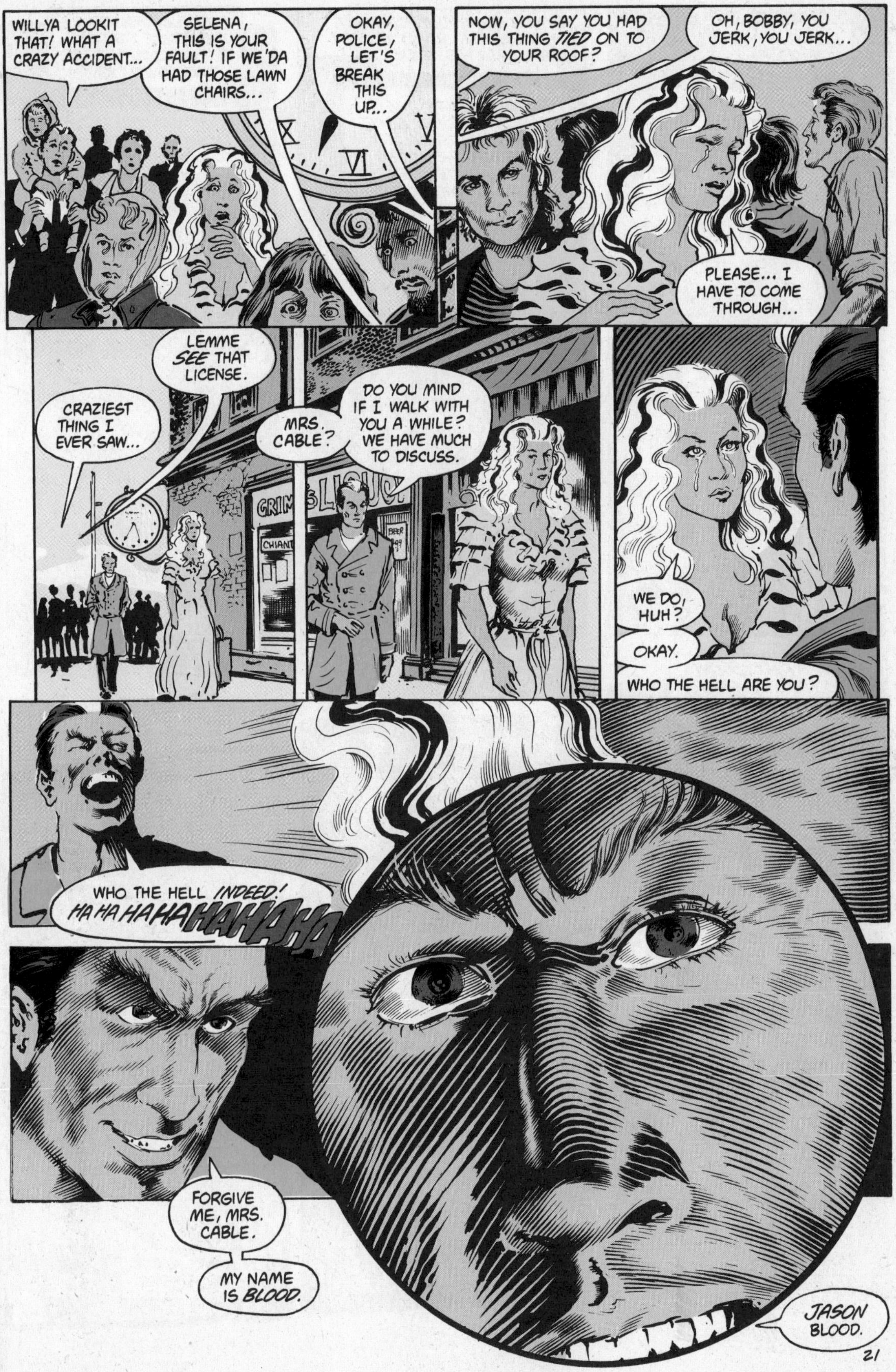
WILLYA LOOKIT THAT! WHAT A CRAZY ACCIDENT...
SELENA, THIS IS YOUR FAULT! IF WE'DA HAD THOSE LAWN CHAIRS...
OKAY, POLICE, LET'S BREAK THIS UP...
NOW, YOU SAY YOU HAD THIS THING TIED ON TO YOUR ROOF?
OH, BOBBY, YOU JERK, YOU JERK...
PLEASE... I HAVE TO COME THROUGH...
LEMME SEE THAT LICENSE.
CRAZIEST THING I EVER SAW...
MRS. CABLE?
DO YOU MIND IF I WALK WITH YOU A WHILE? WE HAVE MUCH TO DISCUSS.
GRIM'S LIQUOR
CHIANTI
BEER
WE DO, HUH?
OKAY.
WHO THE HELL ARE YOU?
WHO THE HELL INDEED! HA HA HA HA HA HA HA HA HA
FORGIVE ME, MRS. CABLE.
MY NAME IS BLOOD.
JASON BLOOD.

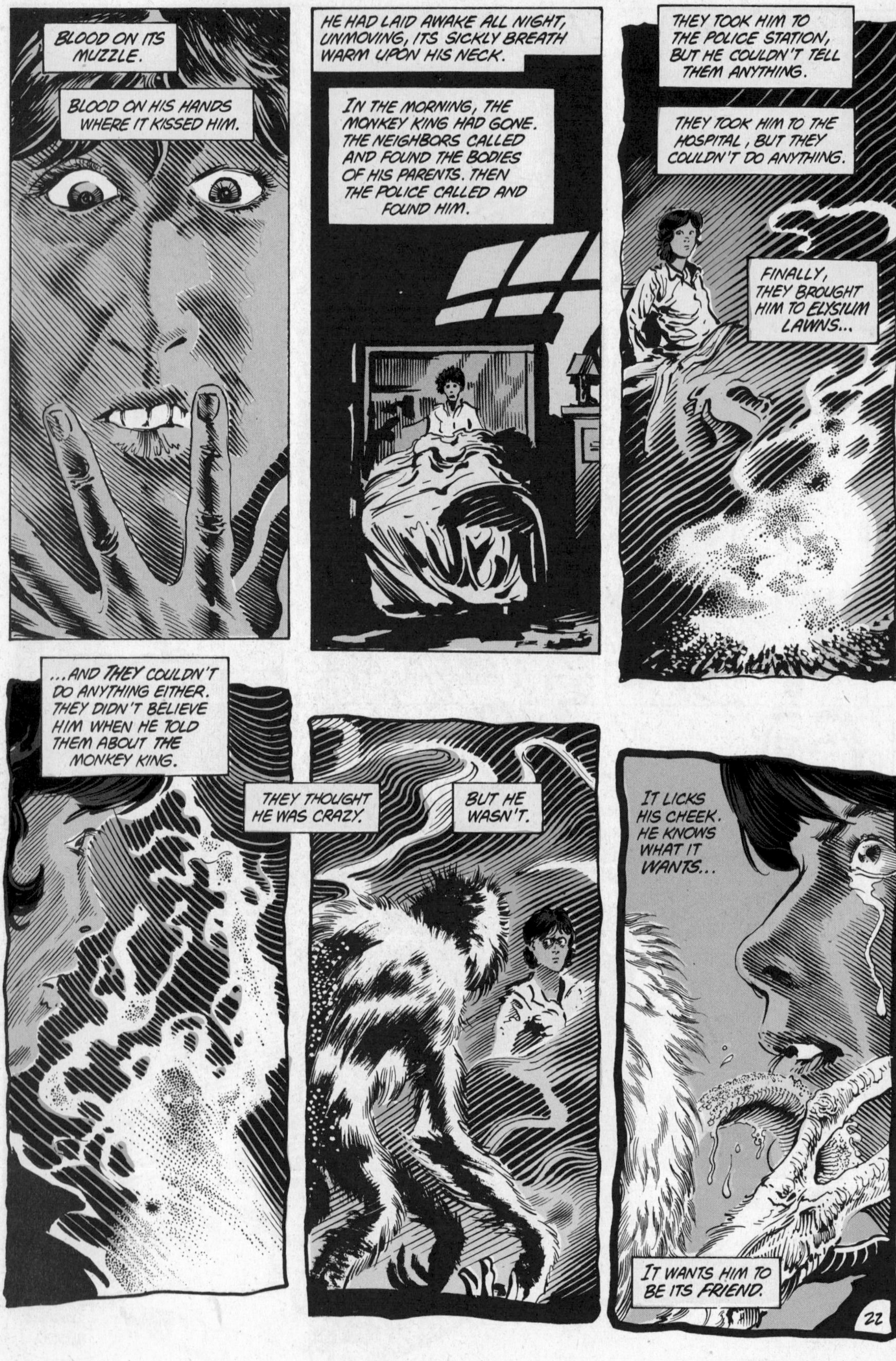
BLOOD ON ITS MUZZLE.
BLOOD ON HIS HANDS WHERE IT KISSED HIM.
HE HAD LAID AWAKE ALL NIGHT, UNMOVING, ITS SICKLY BREATH WARM UPON HIS NECK.
IN THE MORNING, THE MONKEY KING HAD GONE. THE NEIGHBORS CALLED AND FOUND THE BODIES OF HIS PARENTS. THEN THE POLICE CALLED AND FOUND HIM.
THEY TOOK HIM TO THE POLICE STATION, BUT HE COULDN'T TELL THEM ANYTHING.
THEY TOOK HIM TO THE HOSPITAL, BUT THEY COULDN'T DO ANYTHING.
FINALLY, THEY BROUGHT HIM TO ELYSIUM LAWNS...
...AND THEY COULDN'T DO ANYTHING EITHER. THEY DIDN'T BELIEVE HIM WHEN HE TOLD THEM ABOUT THE MONKEY KING.
THEY THOUGHT HE WAS CRAZY.
BUT HE WASN'T.
IT LICKS HIS CHEEK. HE KNOWS WHAT IT WANTS...
IT WANTS HIM TO BE ITS FRIEND.
22

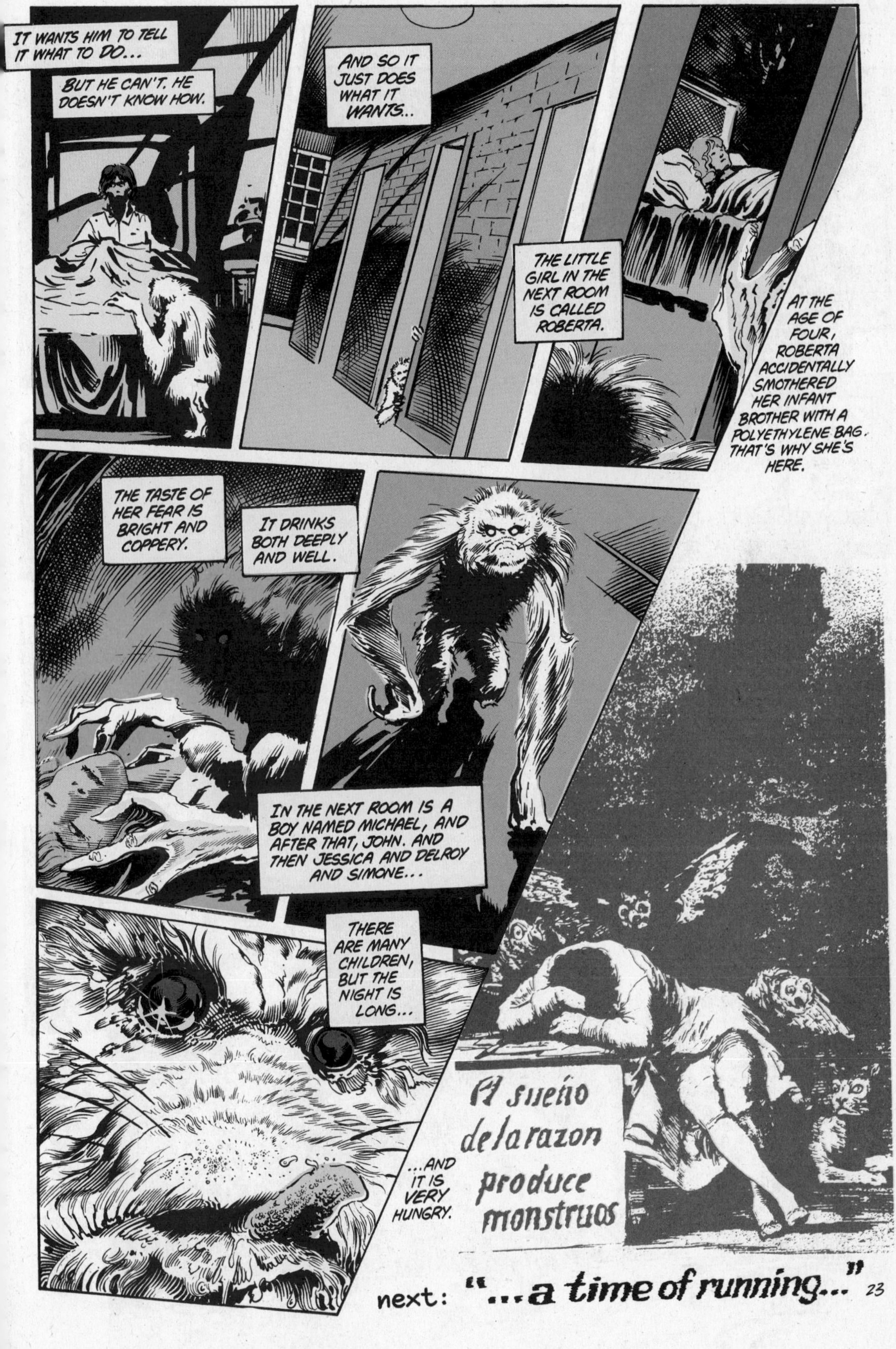
IT WANTS HIM TO TELL IT WHAT TO DO...
BUT HE CAN'T. HE DOESN'T KNOW HOW.
AND SO IT JUST DOES WHAT IT WANTS...
THE LITTLE GIRL IN THE NEXT ROOM IS CALLED ROBERTA.
AT THE AGE OF FOUR, ROBERTA ACCIDENTALLY SMOTHERED HER INFANT BROTHER WITH A POLYETHYLENE BAG. THAT'S WHY SHE'S HERE.
THE TASTE OF HER FEAR IS BRIGHT AND COPPERY.
IT DRINKS BOTH DEEPLY AND WELL.
IN THE NEXT ROOM IS A BOY NAMED MICHAEL, AND AFTER THAT, JOHN. AND THEN JESSICA AND DELROY AND SIMONE...
THERE ARE MANY CHILDREN, BUT THE NIGHT IS LONG...
...AND IT IS VERY HUNGRY.
El sueño de la razon produce monstruos
next: "...a time of running..."
23

BOOK SIX

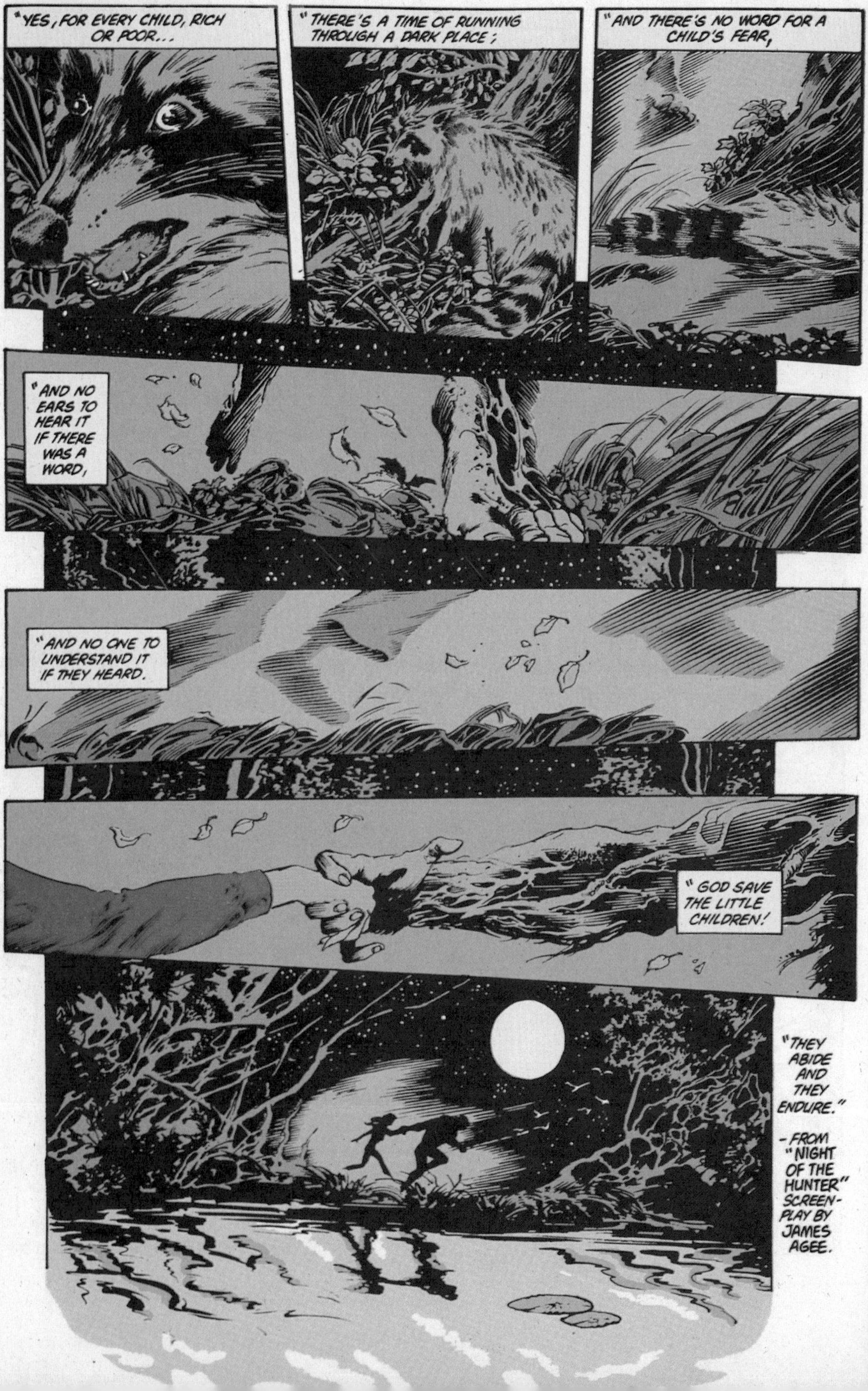
"YES, FOR EVERY CHILD, RICH OR POOR...
"THERE'S A TIME OF RUNNING THROUGH A DARK PLACE;
"AND THERE'S NO WORD FOR A CHILD'S FEAR,
"AND NO EARS TO HEAR IT IF THERE WAS A WORD,
"AND NO ONE TO UNDERSTAND IT IF THEY HEARD.
"GOD SAVE THE LITTLE CHILDREN!
"THEY ABIDE AND THEY ENDURE."
-FROM "NIGHT OF THE HUNTER" SCREEN-PLAY BY JAMES AGEE.

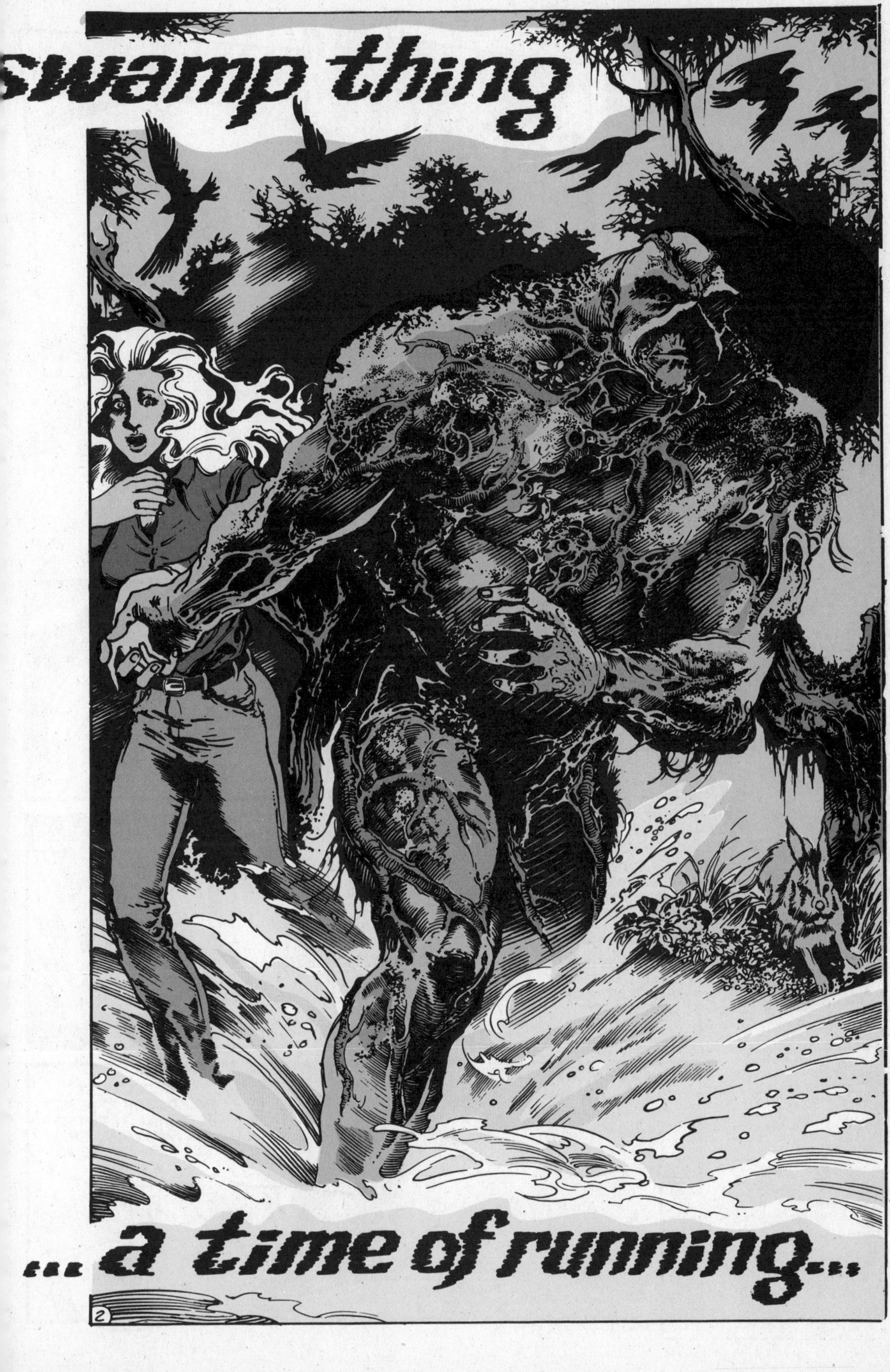
swamp thing
...a time of running...
2

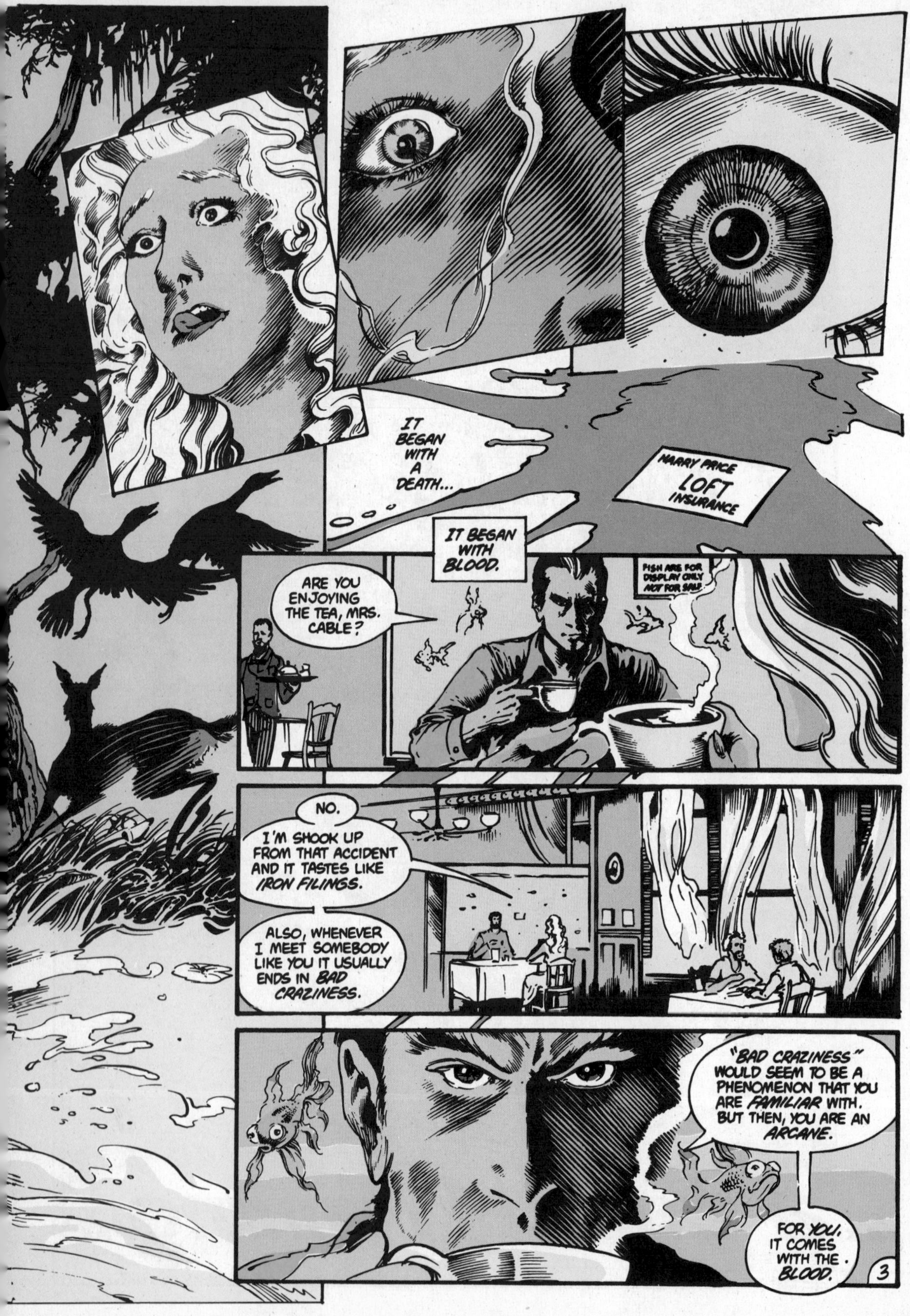
IT BEGAN WITH A DEATH...
HARRY PRICE
LOFT INSURANCE
IT BEGAN WITH BLOOD.
ARE YOU ENJOYING THE TEA, MRS. CABLE?
FISH ARE FOR DISPLAY ONLY NOT FOR SALE
NO.
I'M SHOOK UP FROM THAT ACCIDENT AND IT TASTES LIKE IRON FILINGS.
ALSO, WHENEVER I MEET SOMEBODY LIKE YOU IT USUALLY ENDS IN BAD CRAZINESS.
"BAD CRAZINESS" WOULD SEEM TO BE A PHENOMENON THAT YOU ARE FAMILIAR WITH. BUT THEN, YOU ARE AN ARCANE.
FOR YOU, IT COMES WITH THE BLOOD.
3

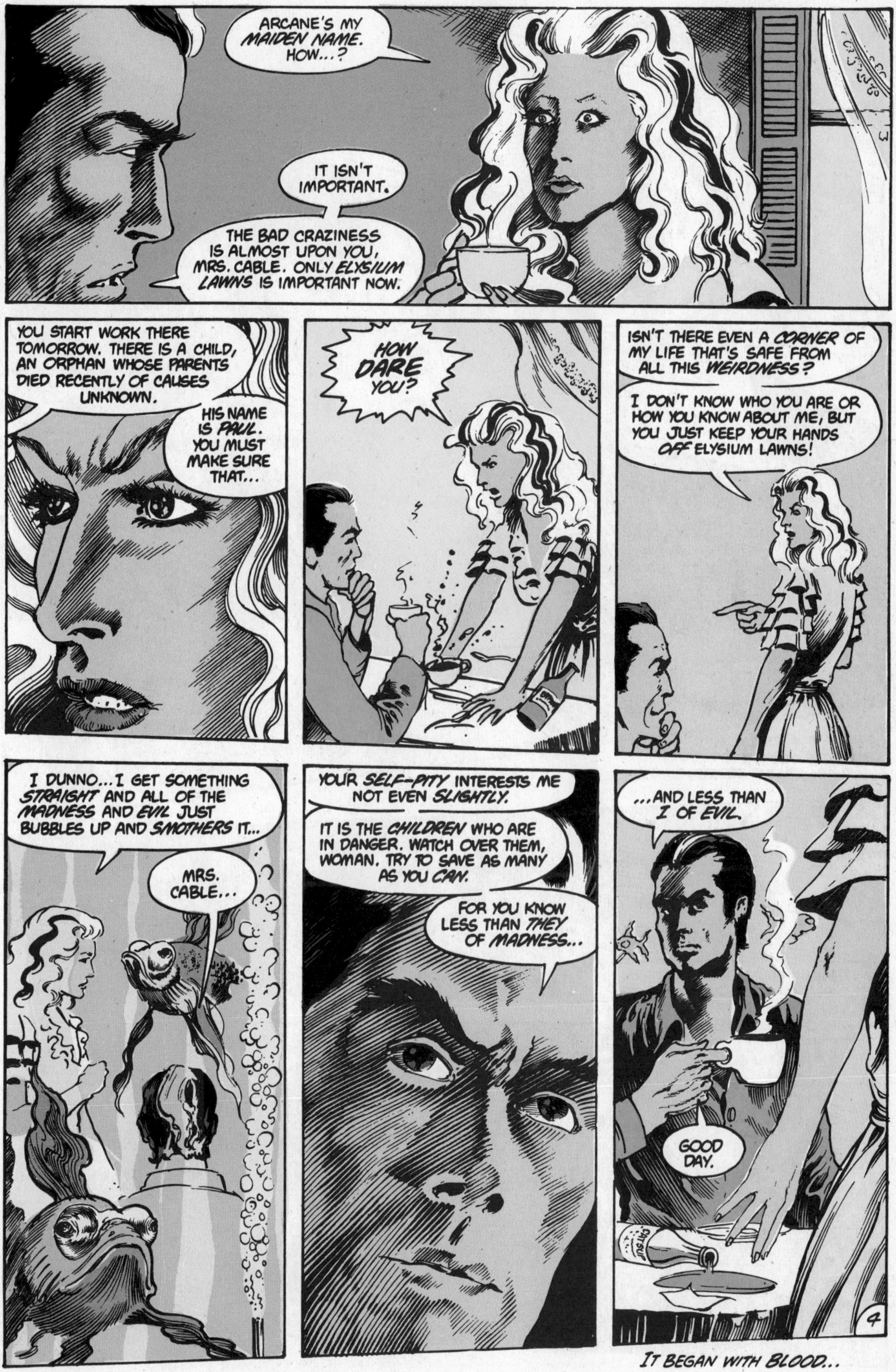
ARCANE'S MY MAIDEN NAME. HOW...?
IT ISN'T IMPORTANT.
THE BAD CRAZINESS IS ALMOST UPON YOU, MRS. CABLE. ONLY ELYSIUM LAWNS IS IMPORTANT NOW.
YOU START WORK THERE TOMORROW. THERE IS A CHILD, AN ORPHAN WHOSE PARENTS DIED RECENTLY OF CAUSES UNKNOWN.
HIS NAME IS PAUL. YOU MUST MAKE SURE THAT...
HOW DARE YOU?
ISN'T THERE EVEN A CORNER OF MY LIFE THAT'S SAFE FROM ALL THIS WEIRDNESS?
I DON'T KNOW WHO YOU ARE OR HOW YOU KNOW ABOUT ME, BUT YOU JUST KEEP YOUR HANDS OFF ELYSIUM LAWNS!
I DUNNO...I GET SOMETHING STRAIGHT AND ALL OF THE MADNESS AND EVIL JUST BUBBLES UP AND SMOTHERS IT...
MRS. CABLE...
YOUR SELF-PITY INTERESTS ME NOT EVEN SLIGHTLY.
IT IS THE CHILDREN WHO ARE IN DANGER. WATCH OVER THEM, WOMAN. TRY TO SAVE AS MANY AS YOU CAN.
FOR YOU KNOW LESS THAN THEY OF MADNESS...
...AND LESS THAN I OF EVIL.
GOOD DAY.
4

IT BEGAN WITH BLOOD...

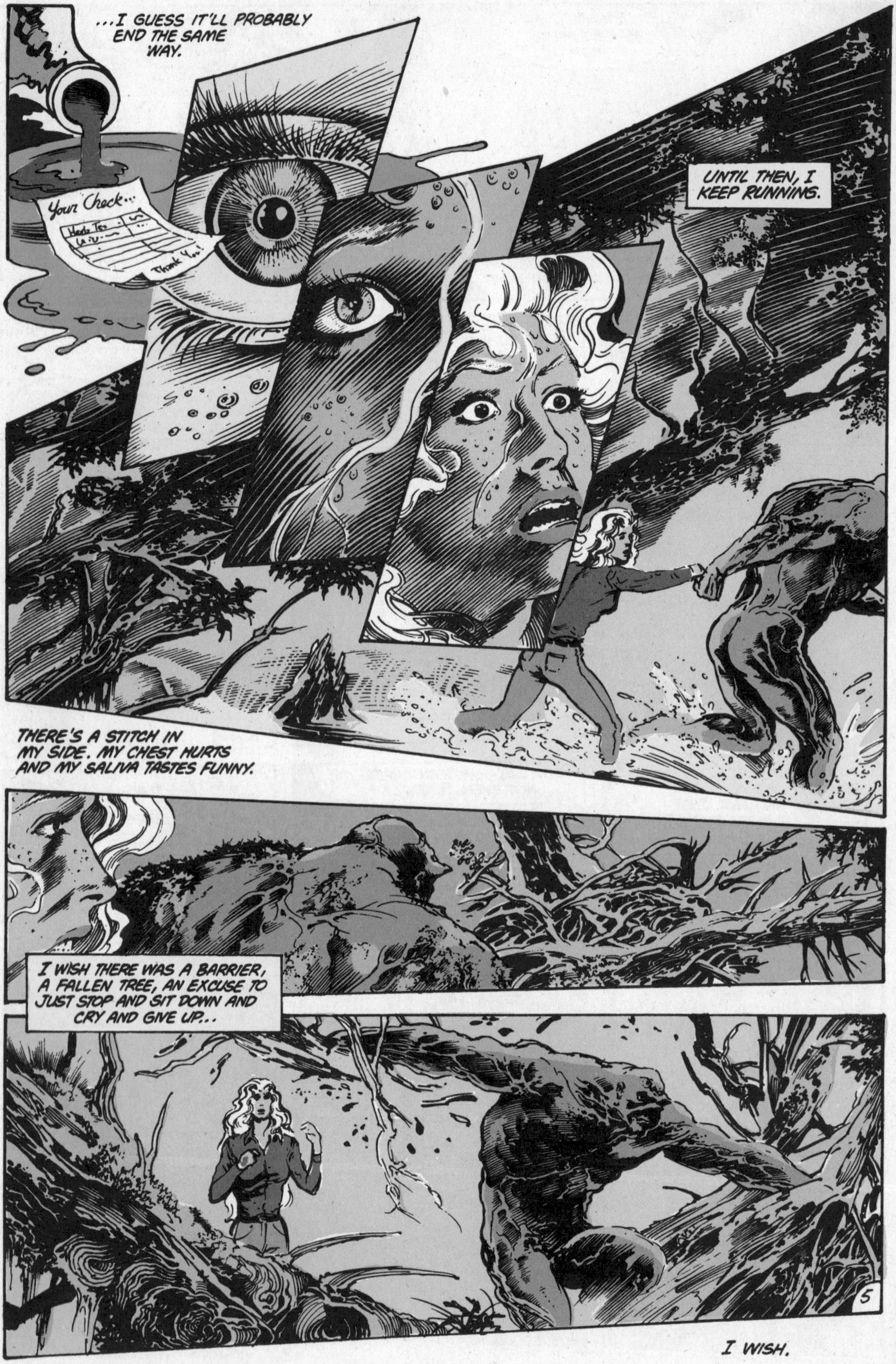
...I GUESS IT'LL PROBABLY END THE SAME WAY.
Your Check...
Thank You!
UNTIL THEN, I KEEP RUNNING.
THERE'S A STITCH IN MY SIDE. MY CHEST HURTS AND MY SALIVA TASTES FUNNY.
I WISH THERE WAS A BARRIER, A FALLEN TREE, AN EXCUSE TO JUST STOP AND SIT DOWN AND CRY AND GIVE UP...
5
I WISH.

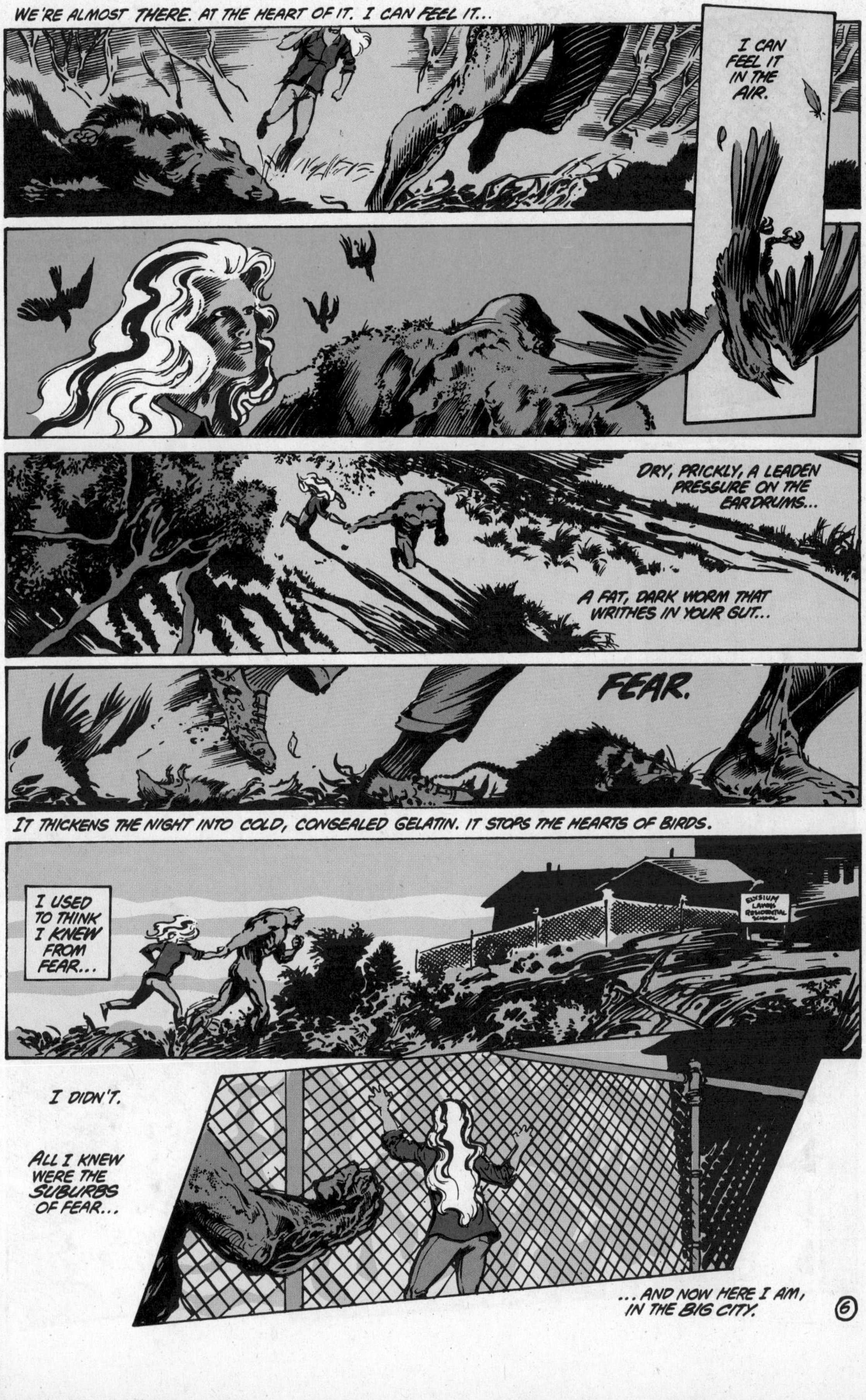
WE'RE ALMOST THERE. AT THE HEART OF IT. I CAN FEEL IT...
I CAN FEEL IT IN THE AIR.
DRY, PRICKLY, A LEADEN PRESSURE ON THE EARDRUMS...
A FAT, DARK WORM THAT WRITHES IN YOUR GUT...
FEAR.
IT THICKENS THE NIGHT INTO COLD, CONGEALED GELATIN. IT STOPS THE HEARTS OF BIRDS.
I USED TO THINK I KNEW FROM FEAR...
ELYSIUM LAWNS RESIDENTIAL SCHOOL
I DIDN'T.
ALL I KNEW WERE THE SUBURBS OF FEAR...
...AND NOW HERE I AM, IN THE BIG CITY.
6

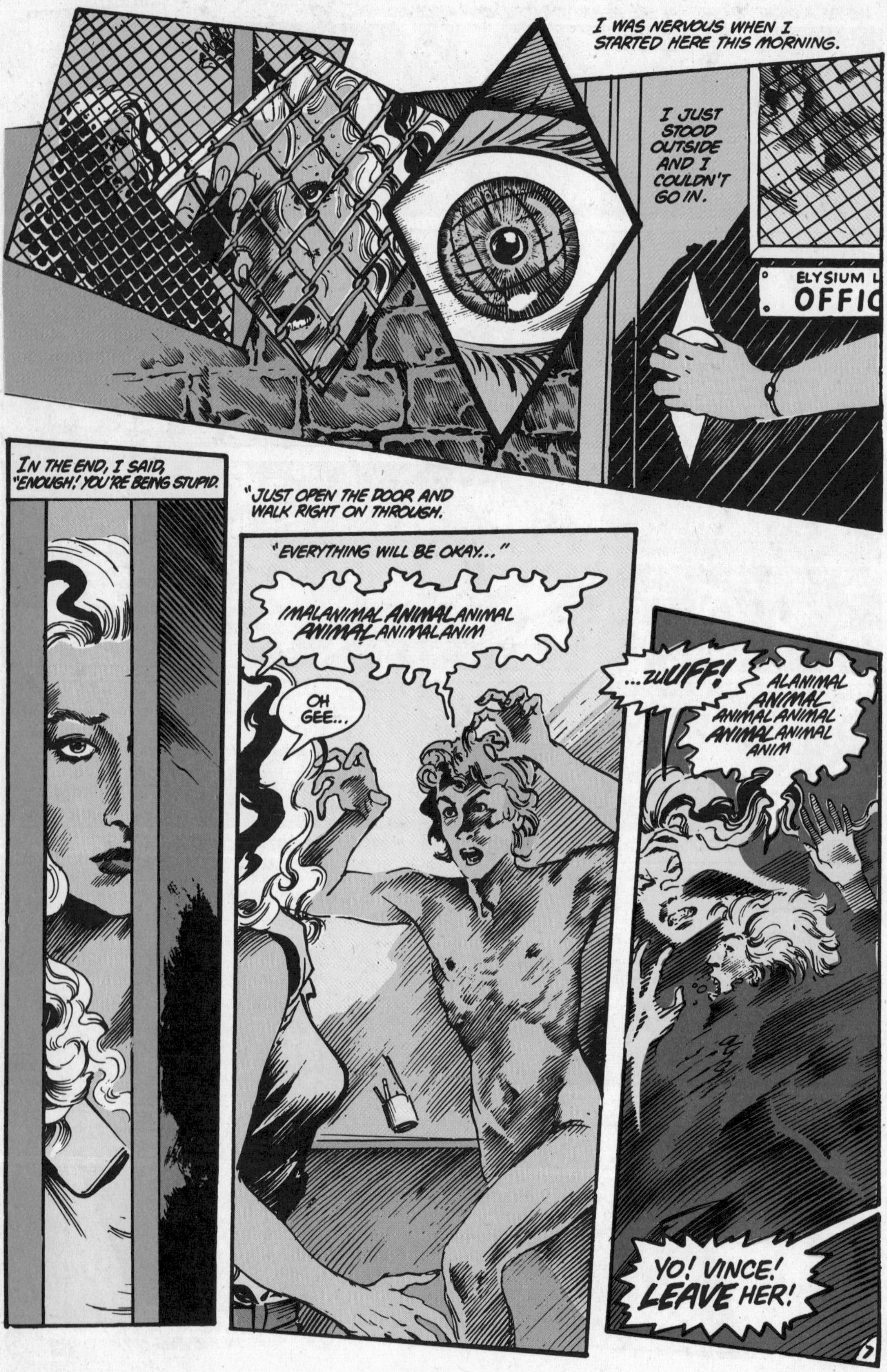
I WAS NERVOUS WHEN I STARTED HERE THIS MORNING.
I JUST STOOD OUTSIDE AND I COULDN'T GO IN.
ELYSIUM L
OFFIC
IN THE END, I SAID, "ENOUGH! YOU'RE BEING STUPID.
"JUST OPEN THE DOOR AND WALK RIGHT ON THROUGH.
"EVERYTHING WILL BE OKAY..."
IMALANIMAL ANIMALANIMAL ANIMALANIMALANIM
OH GEE...
...zuUFF!
ALANIMAL ANIMAL ANIMALANIMAL ANIMALANIMAL ANIM
YO! VINCE! LEAVE HER!
7

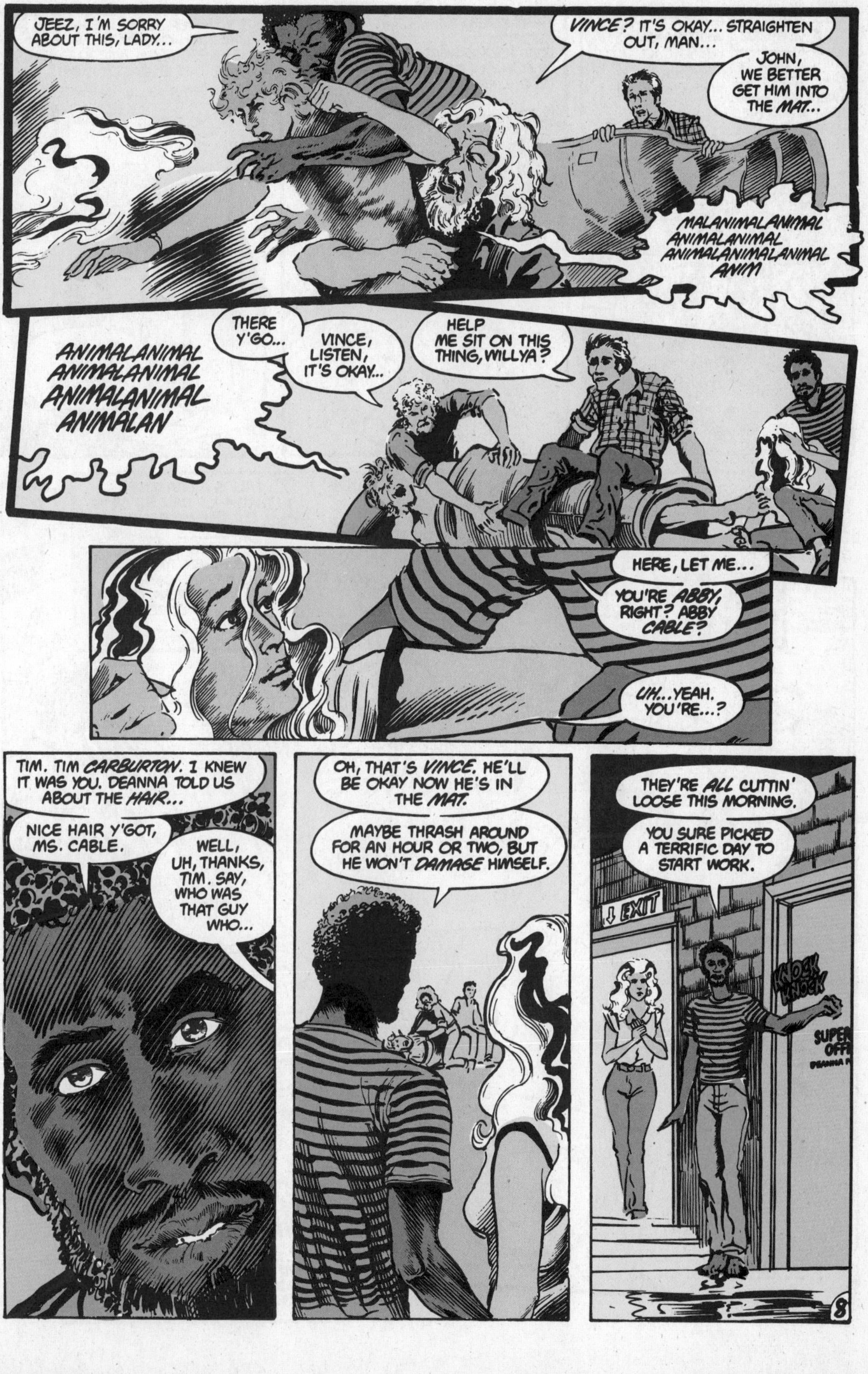
JEEZ, I'M SORRY ABOUT THIS, LADY...
VINCE? IT'S OKAY... STRAIGHTEN OUT, MAN...
JOHN, WE BETTER GET HIM INTO THE MAT...
MALANIMALANIMAL ANIMALANIMAL ANIMALANIMALANIMAL ANIM
ANIMALANIMAL ANIMALANIMAL ANIMALANIMAL ANIMALAN
THERE Y'GO...
VINCE, LISTEN, IT'S OKAY...
HELP ME SIT ON THIS THING, WILLYA?
HERE, LET ME...
YOU'RE ABBY, RIGHT? ABBY CABLE?
UH...YEAH. YOU'RE...?
TIM. TIM CARBURTON. I KNEW IT WAS YOU. DEANNA TOLD US ABOUT THE HAIR...
NICE HAIR Y'GOT, MS. CABLE.
WELL, UH, THANKS, TIM. SAY, WHO WAS THAT GUY WHO...
OH, THAT'S VINCE. HE'LL BE OKAY NOW HE'S IN THE MAT.
MAYBE THRASH AROUND FOR AN HOUR OR TWO, BUT HE WON'T DAMAGE HIMSELF.
THEY'RE ALL CUTTIN' LOOSE THIS MORNING.
YOU SURE PICKED A TERRIFIC DAY TO START WORK.
EXIT
KNOCK KNOCK
8

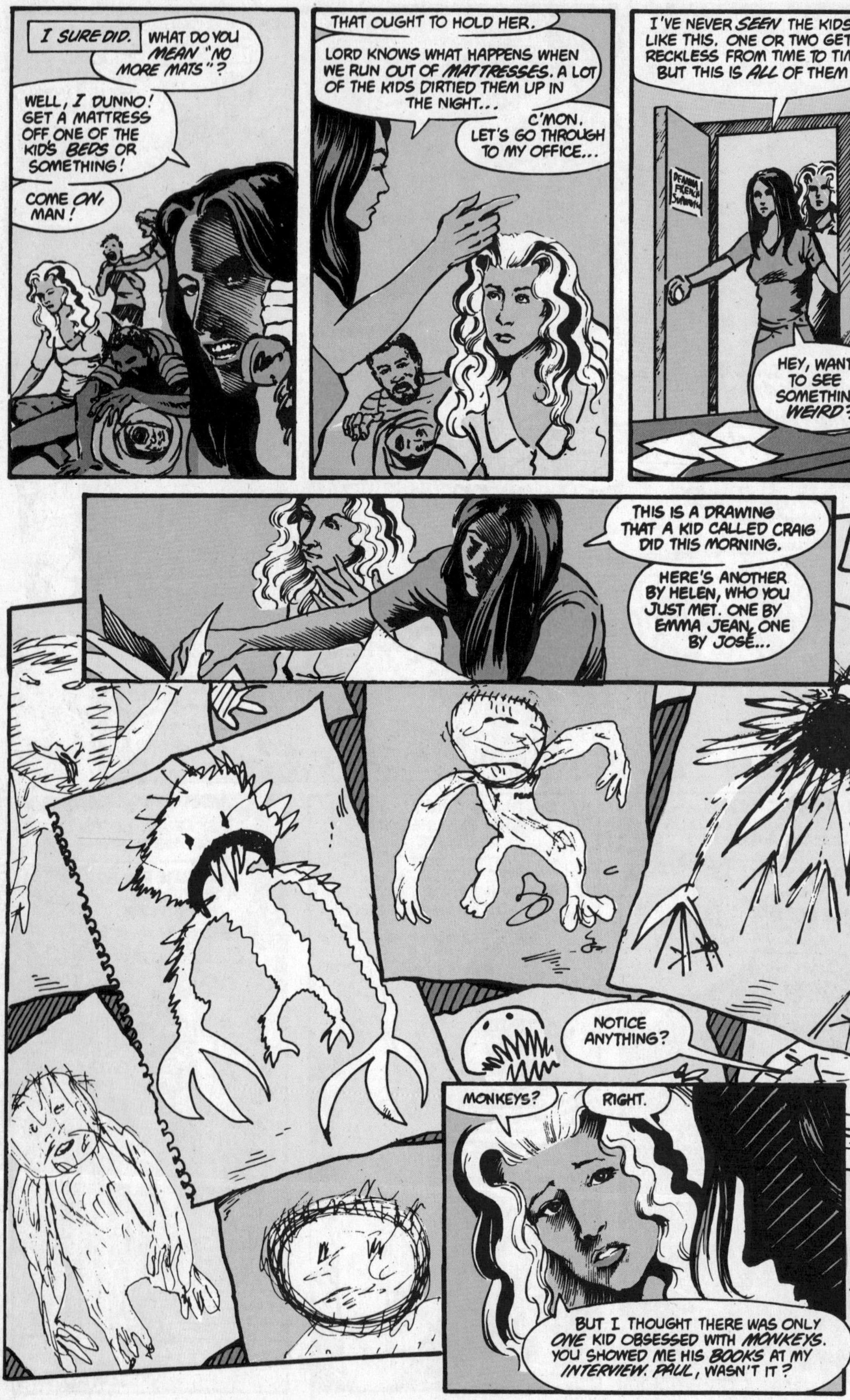
I SURE DID.
WHAT DO YOU MEAN "NO MORE MATS"?
WELL, I DUNNO! GET A MATTRESS OFF ONE OF THE KID'S BEDS OR SOMETHING!
COME ON, MAN!
THAT OUGHT TO HOLD HER.
LORD KNOWS WHAT HAPPENS WHEN WE RUN OUT OF MATTRESSES. A LOT OF THE KIDS DIRTIED THEM UP IN THE NIGHT...
C'MON, LET'S GO THROUGH TO MY OFFICE...
I'VE NEVER SEEN THE KIDS LIKE THIS. ONE OR TWO GET RECKLESS FROM TIME TO TIME, BUT THIS IS ALL OF THEM!
HEY, WANT TO SEE SOMETHING WEIRD?
THIS IS A DRAWING THAT A KID CALLED CRAIG DID THIS MORNING.
HERE'S ANOTHER BY HELEN, WHO YOU JUST MET. ONE BY EMMA JEAN, ONE BY JOSÉ...
NOTICE ANYTHING?
MONKEYS?
RIGHT.
BUT I THOUGHT THERE WAS ONLY ONE KID OBSESSED WITH MONKEYS. YOU SHOWED ME HIS BOOKS AT MY INTERVIEW. PAUL, WASN'T IT?

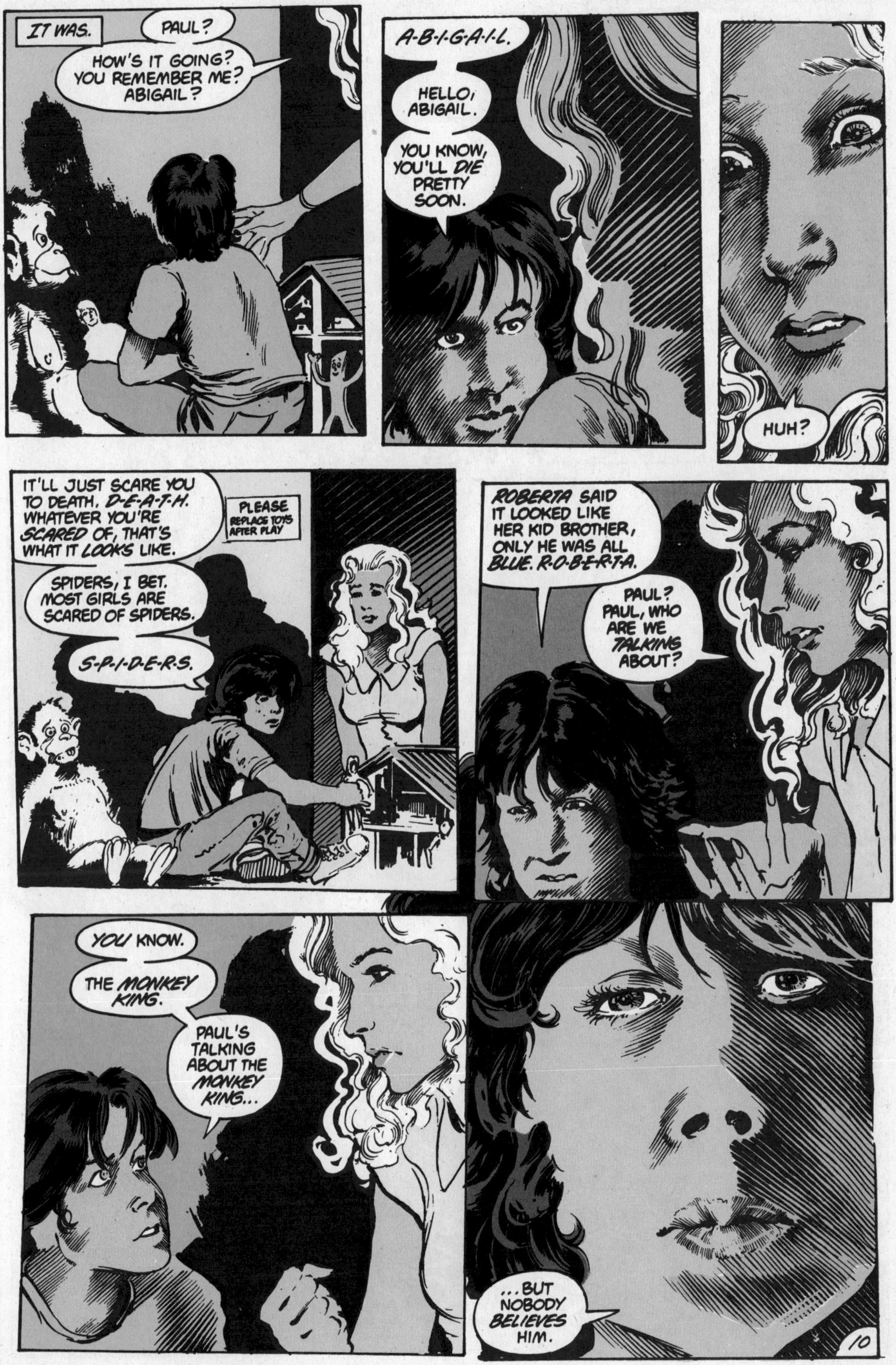
IT WAS.
PAUL?
HOW'S IT GOING? YOU REMEMBER ME? ABIGAIL?
A-B-I-G-A-I-L.
HELLO, ABIGAIL.
YOU KNOW, YOU'LL DIE PRETTY SOON.
HUH?
IT'LL JUST SCARE YOU TO DEATH. D-E-A-T-H. WHATEVER YOU'RE SCARED OF, THAT'S WHAT IT LOOKS LIKE.
PLEASE REPLACE TOYS AFTER PLAY
SPIDERS, I BET. MOST GIRLS ARE SCARED OF SPIDERS.
S-P-I-D-E-R-S.
ROBERTA SAID IT LOOKED LIKE HER KID BROTHER, ONLY HE WAS ALL BLUE. R-O-B-E-R-T-A.
PAUL? PAUL, WHO ARE WE TALKING ABOUT?
YOU KNOW.
THE MONKEY KING.
PAUL'S TALKING ABOUT THE MONKEY KING...
...BUT NOBODY BELIEVES HIM.
10

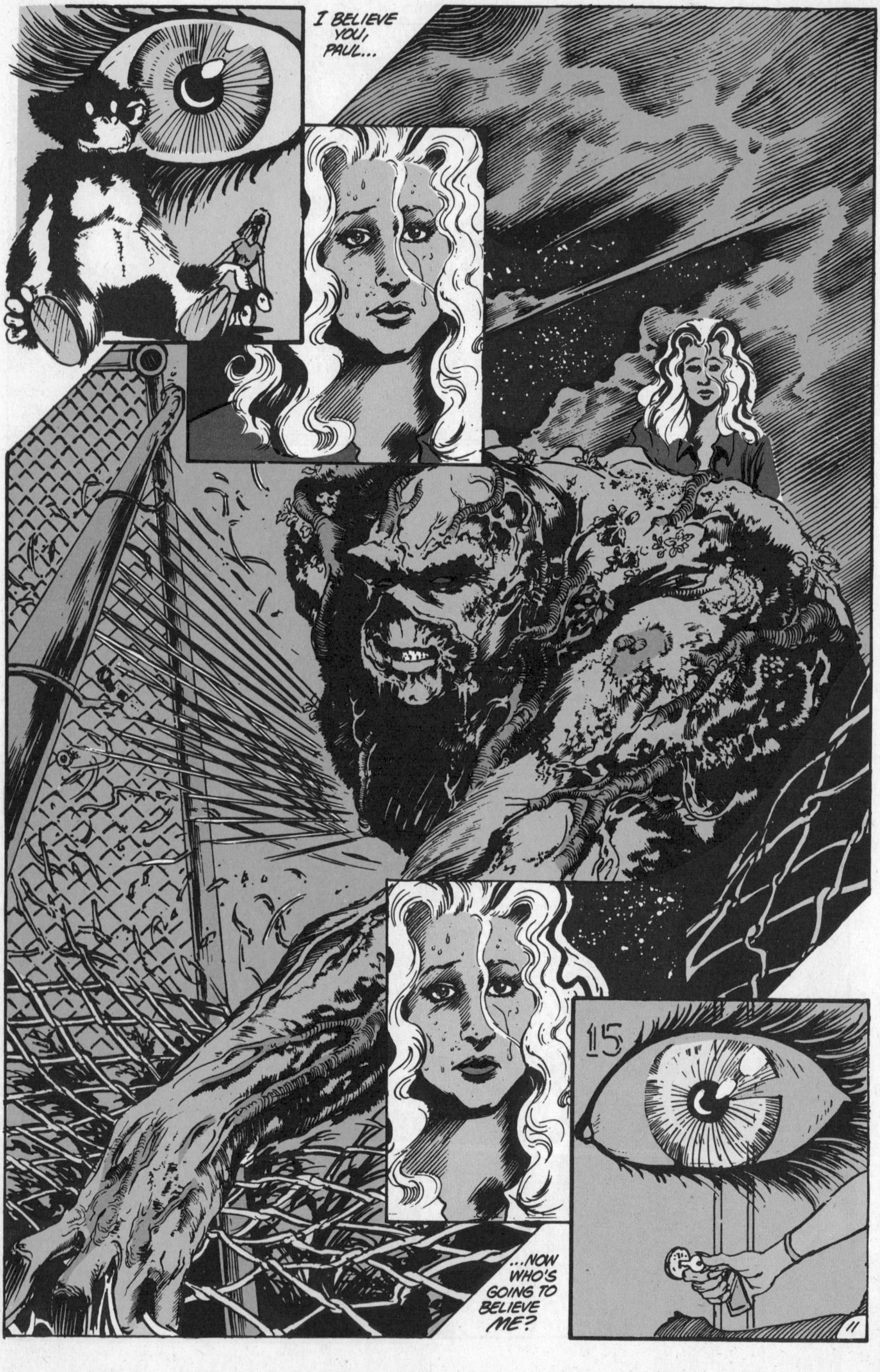
I BELIEVE YOU, PAUL...
15
...NOW WHO'S GOING TO BELIEVE ME?
11

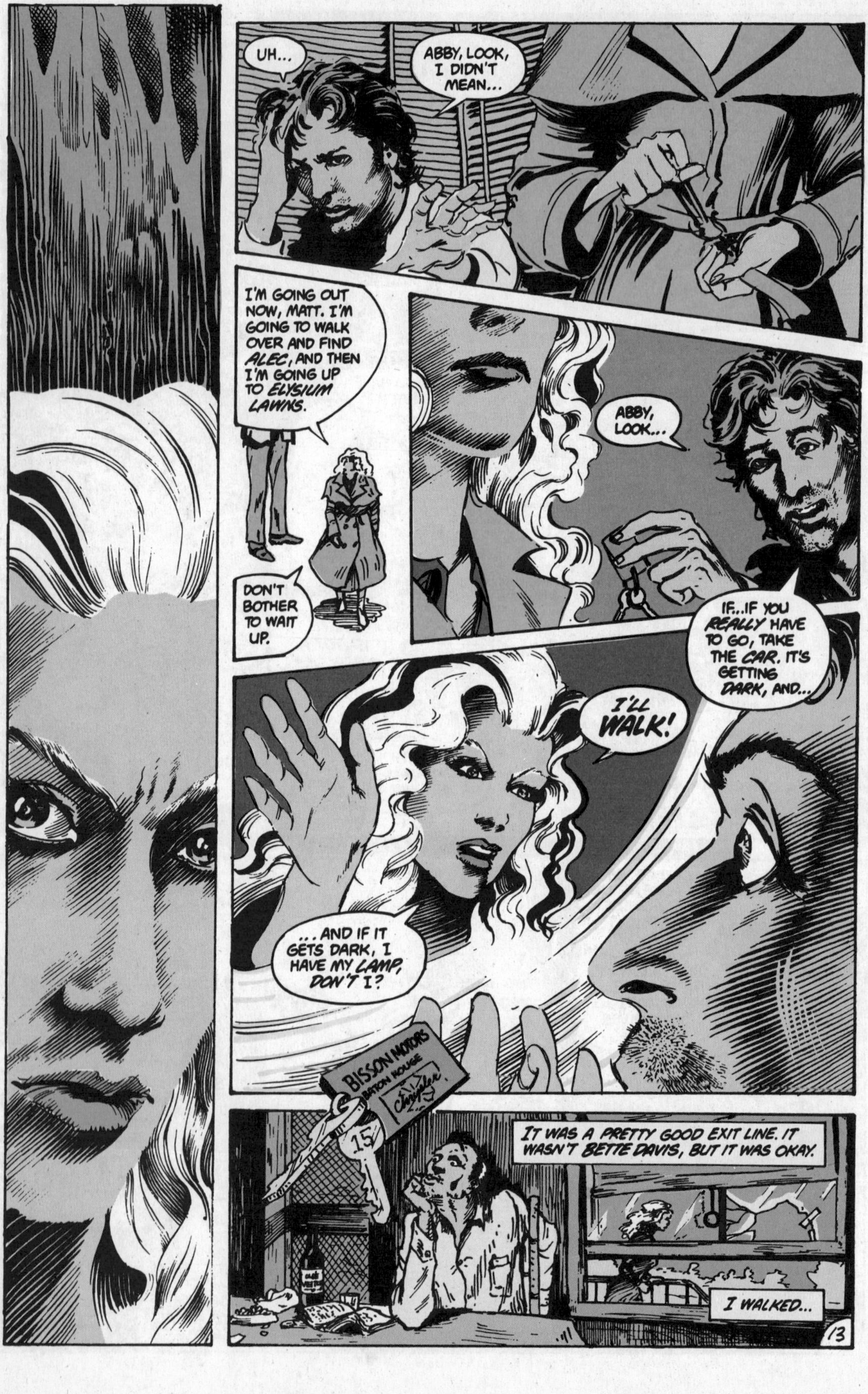
UH...
ABBY, LOOK, I DIDN'T MEAN...
I'M GOING OUT NOW, MATT. I'M GOING TO WALK OVER AND FIND ALEC, AND THEN I'M GOING UP TO ELYSIUM LAWNS.
DON'T BOTHER TO WAIT UP.
ABBY, LOOK...
IF...IF YOU REALLY HAVE TO GO, TAKE THE CAR. IT'S GETTING DARK, AND...
I'LL WALK!
...AND IF IT GETS DARK, I HAVE MY LAMP, DON'T I?
BISSON MOTORS
BATON ROUGE
15
IT WAS A PRETTY GOOD EXIT LINE. IT WASN'T BETTE DAVIS, BUT IT WAS OKAY.
I WALKED...
13

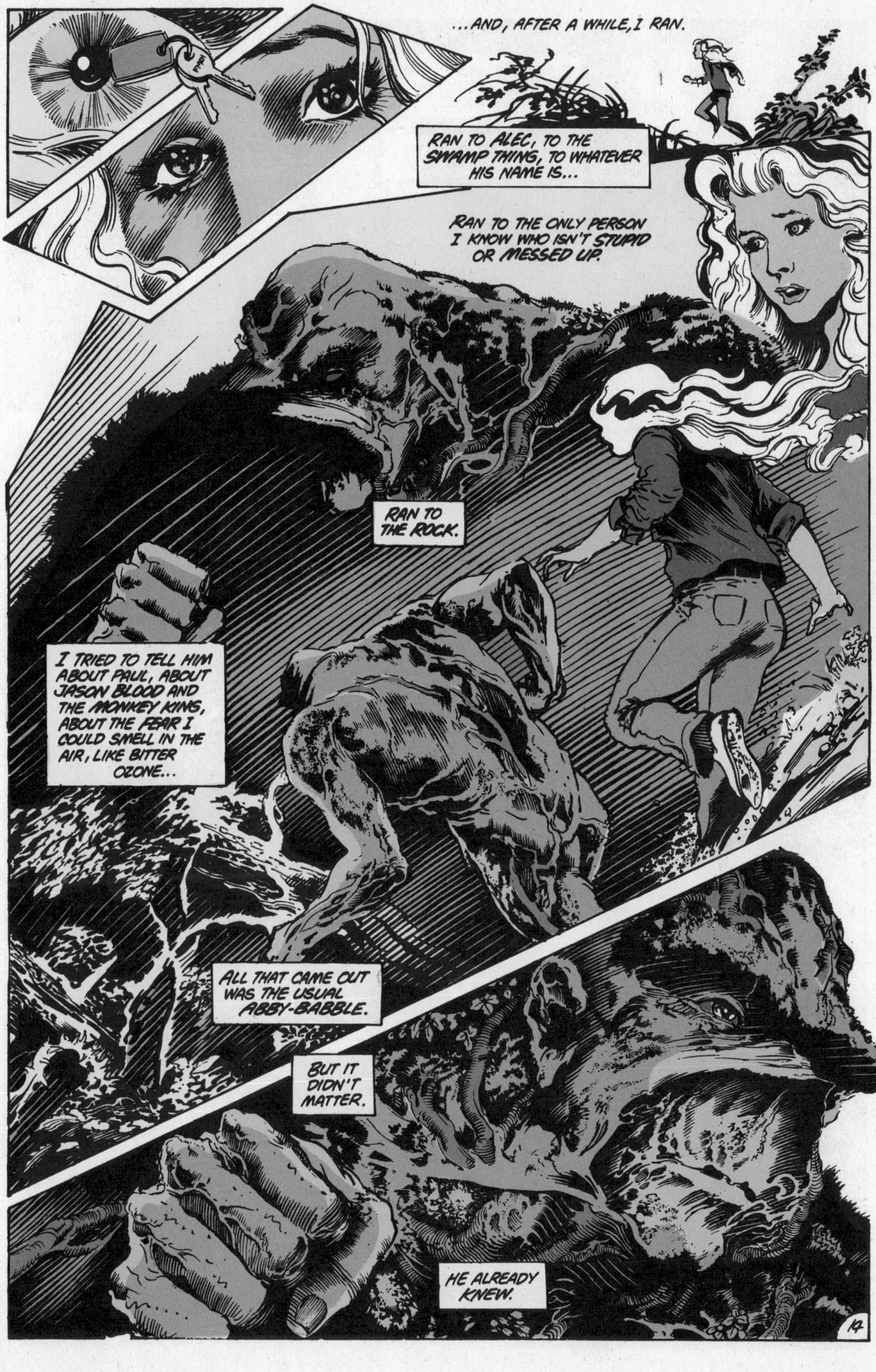
...AND, AFTER A WHILE, I RAN.
RAN TO ALEC, TO THE SWAMP THING, TO WHATEVER HIS NAME IS...
RAN TO THE ONLY PERSON I KNOW WHO ISN'T STUPID OR MESSED UP.
RAN TO THE ROCK.
I TRIED TO TELL HIM ABOUT PAUL, ABOUT JASON BLOOD AND THE MONKEY KING, ABOUT THE FEAR I COULD SMELL IN THE AIR, LIKE BITTER OZONE...
ALL THAT CAME OUT WAS THE USUAL ABBY-BABBLE.
BUT IT DIDN'T MATTER.
HE ALREADY KNEW.
14

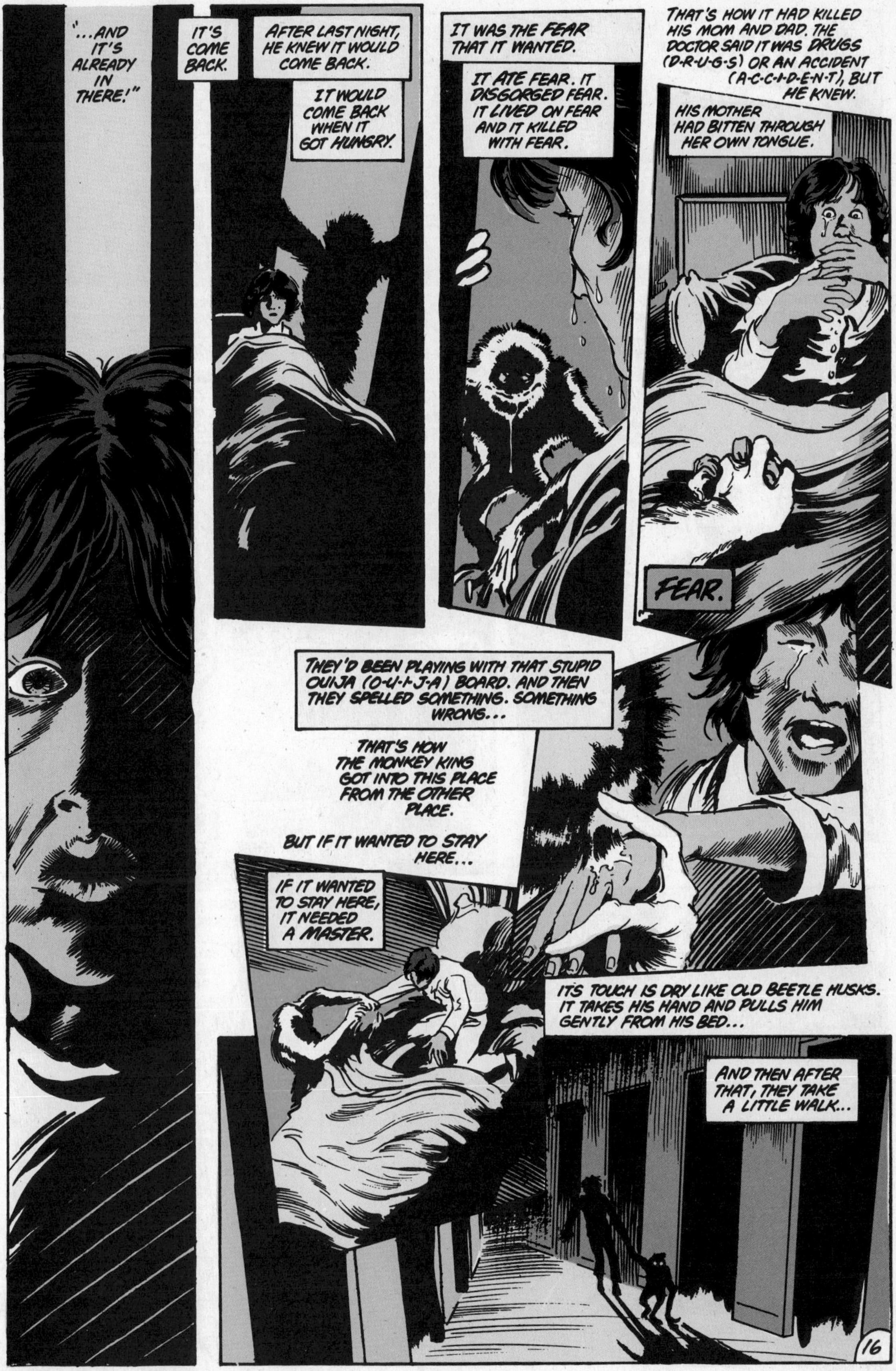
"...AND IT'S ALREADY IN THERE!"
IT'S COME BACK.
AFTER LAST NIGHT, HE KNEW IT WOULD COME BACK.
IT WOULD COME BACK WHEN IT GOT HUNGRY.
IT WAS THE FEAR THAT IT WANTED.
IT ATE FEAR. IT DISGORGED FEAR. IT LIVED ON FEAR AND IT KILLED WITH FEAR.
THAT'S HOW IT HAD KILLED HIS MOM AND DAD. THE DOCTOR SAID IT WAS DRUGS (D-R-U-G-S) OR AN ACCIDENT (A-C-C-I-D-E-N-T), BUT HE KNEW.
HIS MOTHER HAD BITTEN THROUGH HER OWN TONGUE.
FEAR.
THEY'D BEEN PLAYING WITH THAT STUPID OUIJA (O-U-I-J-A) BOARD. AND THEN THEY SPELLED SOMETHING. SOMETHING WRONG...
THAT'S HOW THE MONKEY KING GOT INTO THIS PLACE FROM THE OTHER PLACE.
BUT IF IT WANTED TO STAY HERE...
IF IT WANTED TO STAY HERE, IT NEEDED A MASTER.
ITS TOUCH IS DRY LIKE OLD BEETLE HUSKS. IT TAKES HIS HAND AND PULLS HIM GENTLY FROM HIS BED...
AND THEN AFTER THAT, THEY TAKE A LITTLE WALK...
16

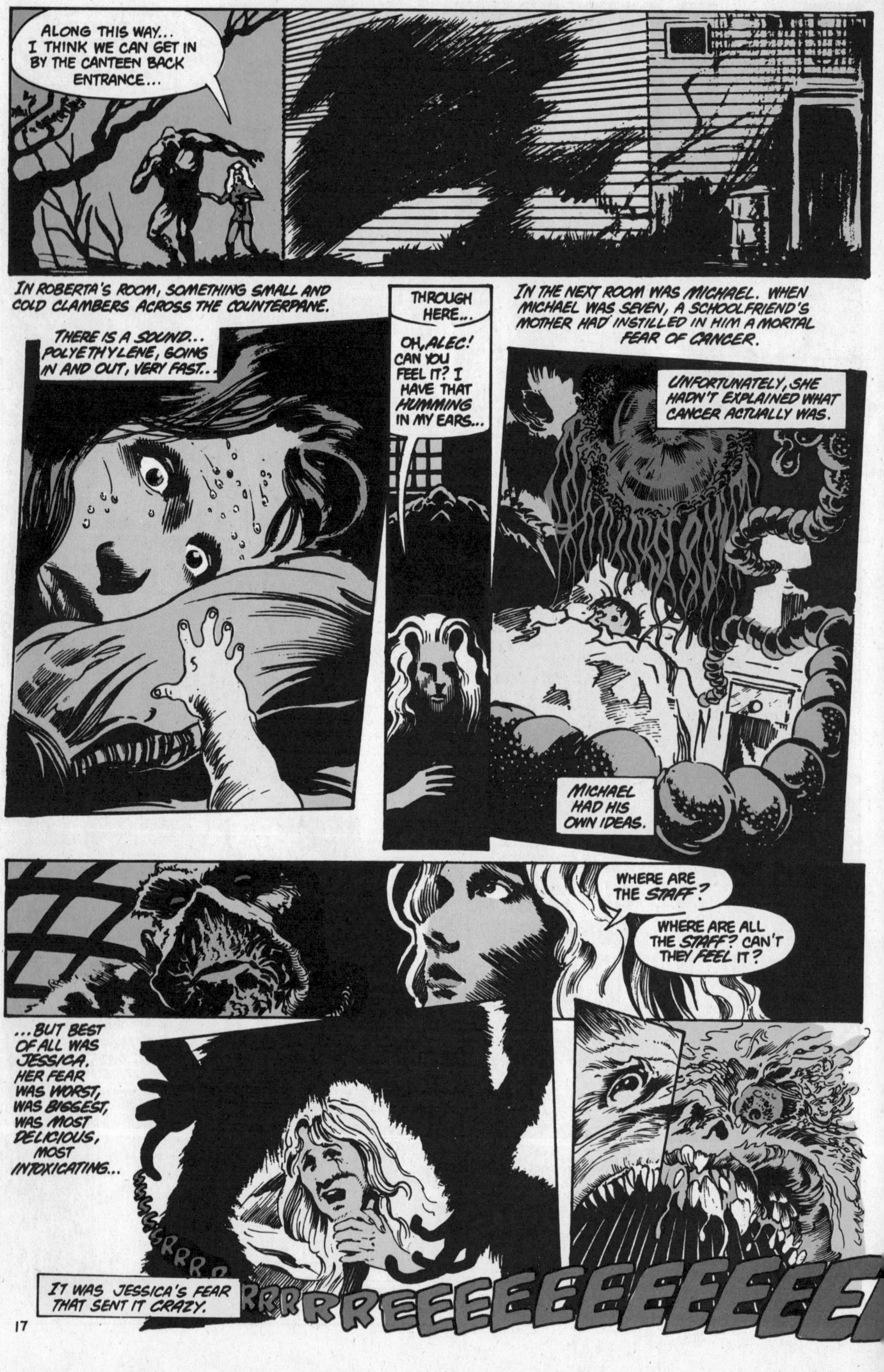
ALONG THIS WAY... I THINK WE CAN GET IN BY THE CANTEEN BACK ENTRANCE...
IN ROBERTA'S ROOM, SOMETHING SMALL AND COLD CLAMBERS ACROSS THE COUNTERPANE.
THERE IS A SOUND... POLYETHYLENE, GOING IN AND OUT, VERY FAST...
THROUGH HERE...
OH, ALEC! CAN YOU FEEL IT? I HAVE THAT HUMMING IN MY EARS...
IN THE NEXT ROOM WAS MICHAEL. WHEN MICHAEL WAS SEVEN, A SCHOOLFRIEND'S MOTHER HAD INSTILLED IN HIM A MORTAL FEAR OF CANCER.
UNFORTUNATELY, SHE HADN'T EXPLAINED WHAT CANCER ACTUALLY WAS.
MICHAEL HAD HIS OWN IDEAS.
WHERE ARE THE STAFF?
WHERE ARE ALL THE STAFF? CAN'T THEY FEEL IT?
...BUT BEST OF ALL WAS JESSICA. HER FEAR WAS WORST, WAS BIGGEST, WAS MOST DELICIOUS, MOST INTOXICATING...
SSSSRRRRRRRRREEEEEEEEEEEEEEE
IT WAS JESSICA'S FEAR THAT SENT IT CRAZY.

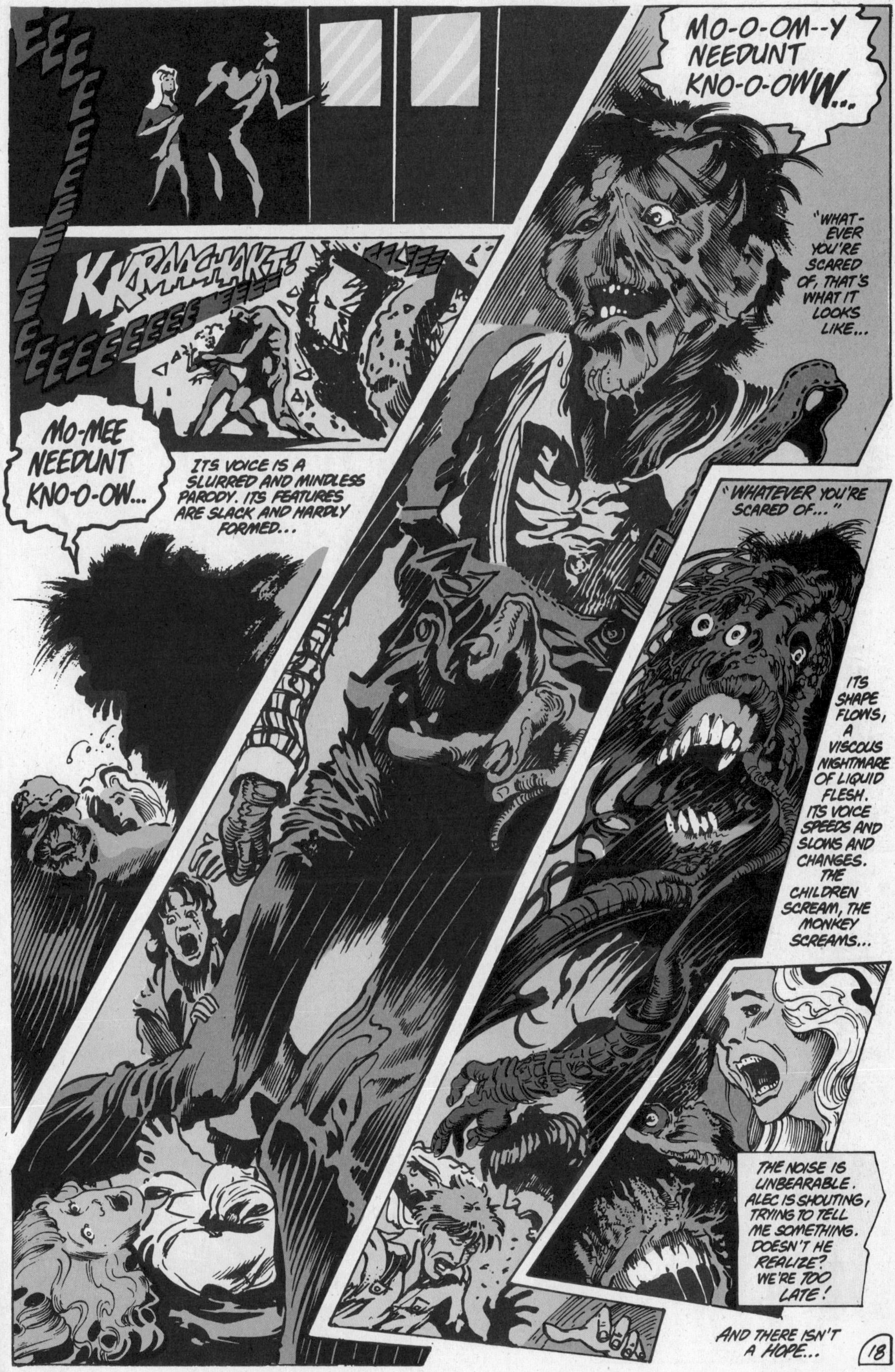
EEEEEEEEEEEEEEEEEE
KRAACHAKT!
EEEEEEEEE
MO-MEE NEEDUNT KNO-O-OW...
ITS VOICE IS A SLURRED AND MINDLESS PARODY. ITS FEATURES ARE SLACK AND HARDLY FORMED...
MO-O-OM--Y NEEDUNT KNO-O-OWW...
"WHAT-EVER YOU'RE SCARED OF, THAT'S WHAT IT LOOKS LIKE...
"WHATEVER YOU'RE SCARED OF..."
ITS SHAPE FLOWS, A VISCOUS NIGHTMARE OF LIQUID FLESH. ITS VOICE SPEEDS AND SLOWS AND CHANGES. THE CHILDREN SCREAM, THE MONKEY SCREAMS...
THE NOISE IS UNBEARABLE. ALEC IS SHOUTING, TRYING TO TELL ME SOMETHING. DOESN'T HE REALIZE? WE'RE TOO LATE!
AND THERE ISN'T A HOPE...
18

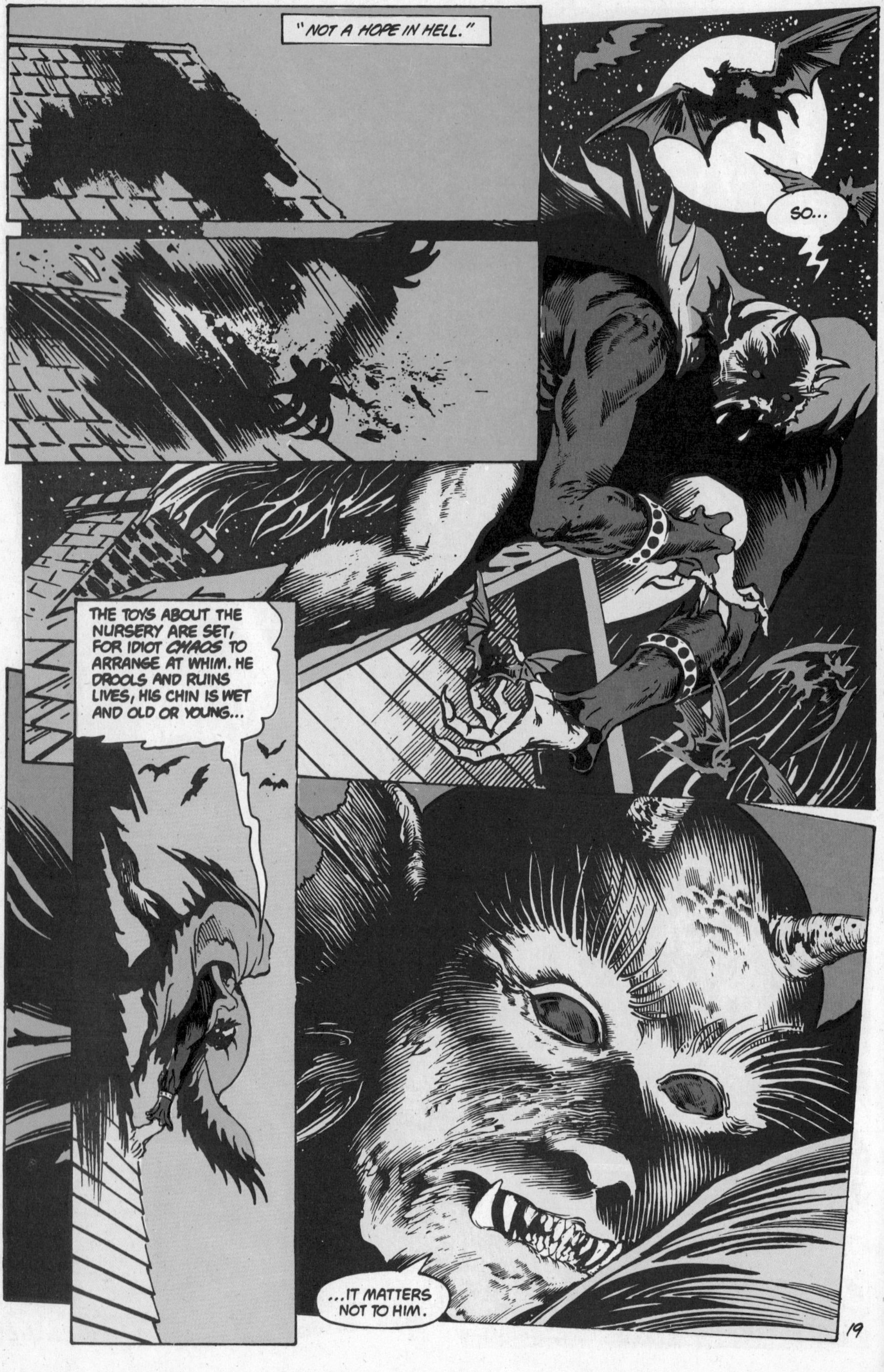
"NOT A HOPE IN HELL."
SO...
THE TOYS ABOUT THE NURSERY ARE SET, FOR IDIOT CHAOS TO ARRANGE AT WHIM. HE DROOLS AND RUINS LIVES, HIS CHIN IS WET AND OLD OR YOUNG...
...IT MATTERS NOT TO HIM.
19

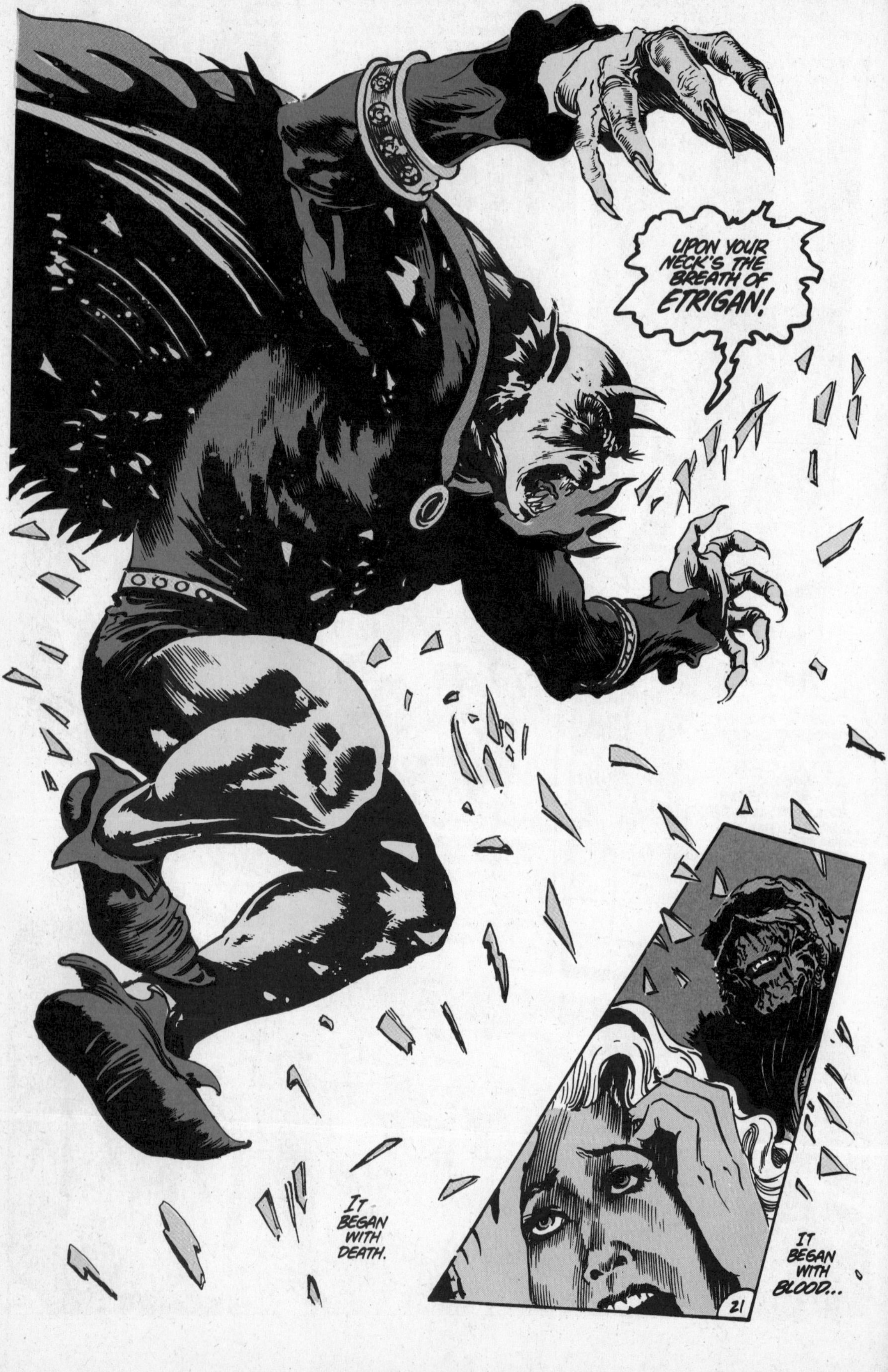
UPON YOUR NECK'S THE BREATH OF ETRIGAN!
IT BEGAN WITH DEATH.
IT BEGAN WITH BLOOD...
21

"... I GUESS IT'LL PROBABLY END THE SAME WAY."

THE NIGHT...

THE NIGHT CAN MAKE A MAN SEE HIMSELF, CAN MAKE HIM LOOK INTO HIS OWN INSIDES...

...AND THE NIGHT CAN MAKE HIM HONEST ENOUGH TO ACCEPT WHAT HE FINDS THERE.

ALL THE WEAKNESS, ALL THE SELFISHNESS, THE CLAMMY DESIRES AND THE SMALL CRUELTIES.

HE'S BEEN THINKING. THINKING SINCE SHE WALKED OUT THE DOOR...

SHE NEEDED HIS HELP, AND HE WASN'T THERE. THE NIGHT...

WILD KINGDOM
OUR INSECT ALLIES

...IT CAN BLOODY UP A MAN'S CONSCIENCE.

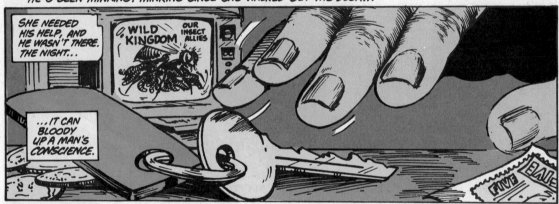

HE BUTTONS HIS COAT AND STEPS OUTSIDE.

HE'S GOING AFTER HER, GOING TO HELP HER, GOING OUT INTO THE COLD...

...THE DARK...

...THE NIGHT.

22

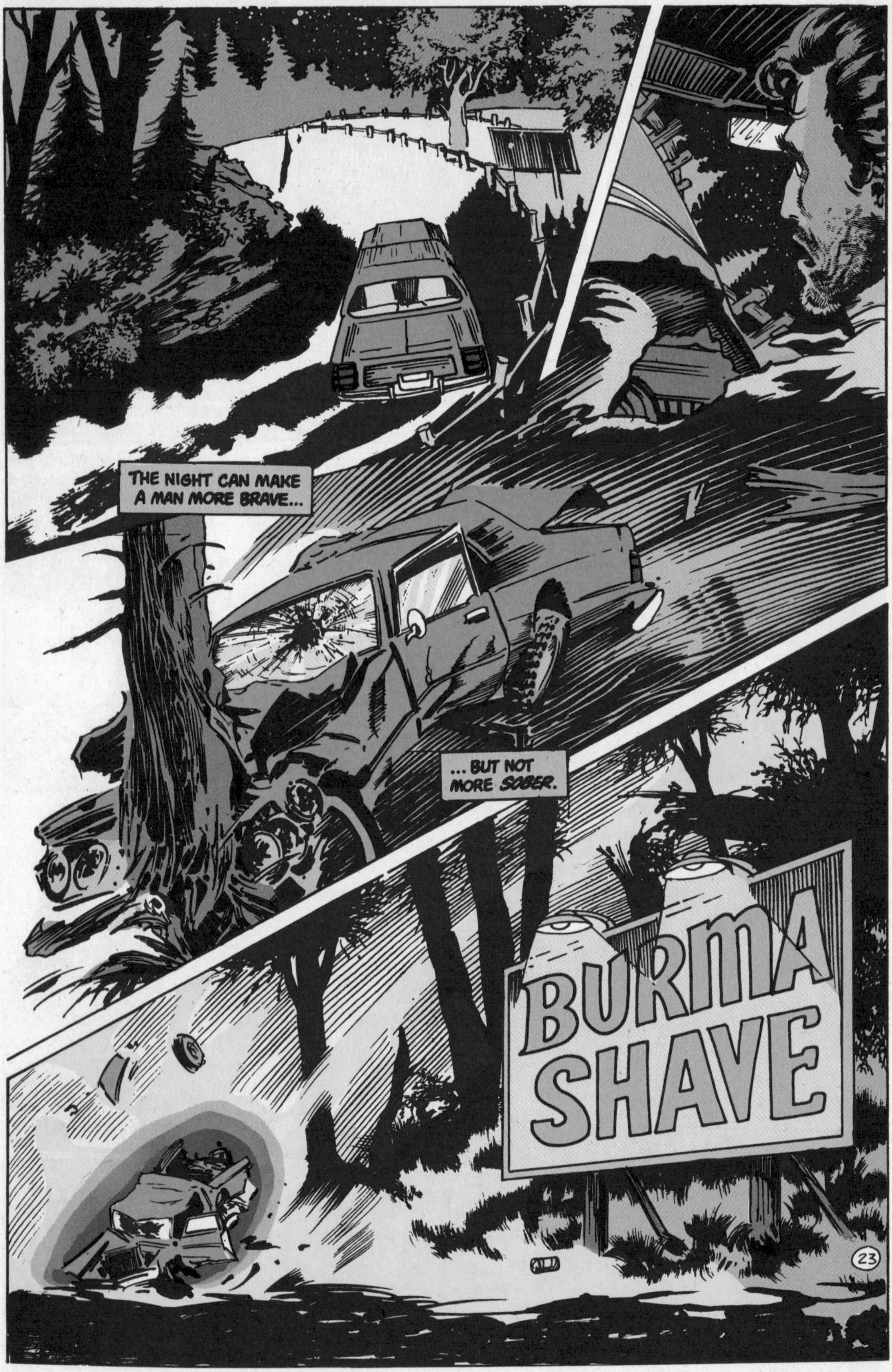
THE NIGHT CAN MAKE A MAN MORE BRAVE...
...BUT NOT MORE SOBER.
BURMA SHAVE
23

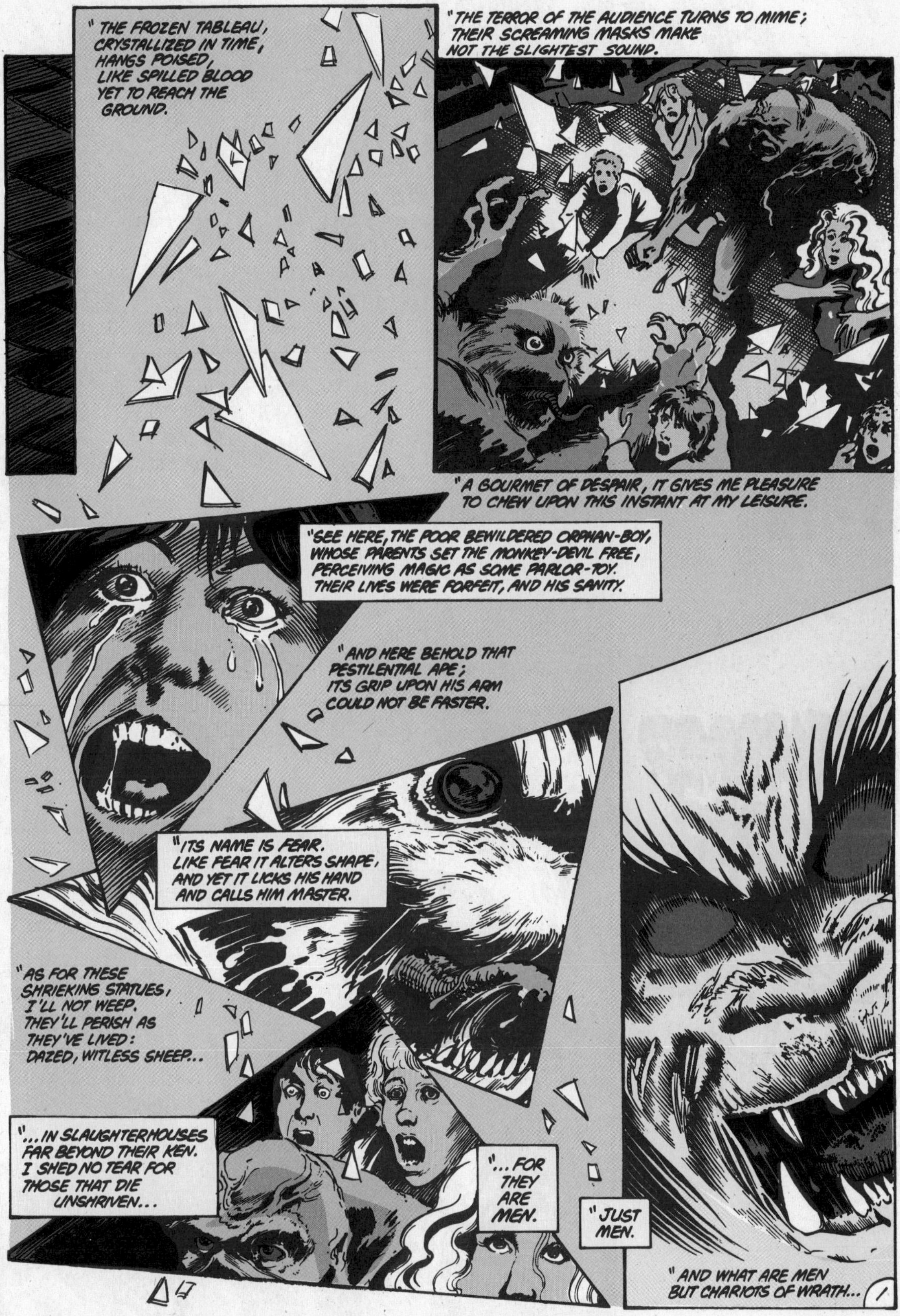
"THE FROZEN TABLEAU, CRYSTALLIZED IN TIME, HANGS POISED, LIKE SPILLED BLOOD YET TO REACH THE GROUND.
"THE TERROR OF THE AUDIENCE TURNS TO MIME; THEIR SCREAMING MASKS MAKE NOT THE SLIGHTEST SOUND.
"A GOURMET OF DESPAIR, IT GIVES ME PLEASURE TO CHEW UPON THIS INSTANT AT MY LEISURE.
"SEE HERE, THE POOR BEWILDERED ORPHAN-BOY, WHOSE PARENTS SET THE MONKEY-DEVIL FREE, PERCEIVING MAGIC AS SOME PARLOR-TOY. THEIR LIVES WERE FORFEIT, AND HIS SANITY.
"AND HERE BEHOLD THAT PESTILENTIAL APE; ITS GRIP UPON HIS ARM COULD NOT BE FASTER.
"ITS NAME IS FEAR. LIKE FEAR IT ALTERS SHAPE, AND YET IT LICKS HIS HAND AND CALLS HIM MASTER.
"AS FOR THESE SHRIEKING STATUES, I'LL NOT WEEP. THEY'LL PERISH AS THEY'VE LIVED: DAZED, WITLESS SHEEP...
"...IN SLAUGHTERHOUSES FAR BEYOND THEIR KEN. I SHED NO TEAR FOR THOSE THAT DIE UNSHRIVEN...
"...FOR THEY ARE MEN.
"JUST MEN.
"AND WHAT ARE MEN BUT CHARIOTS OF WRATH...
1

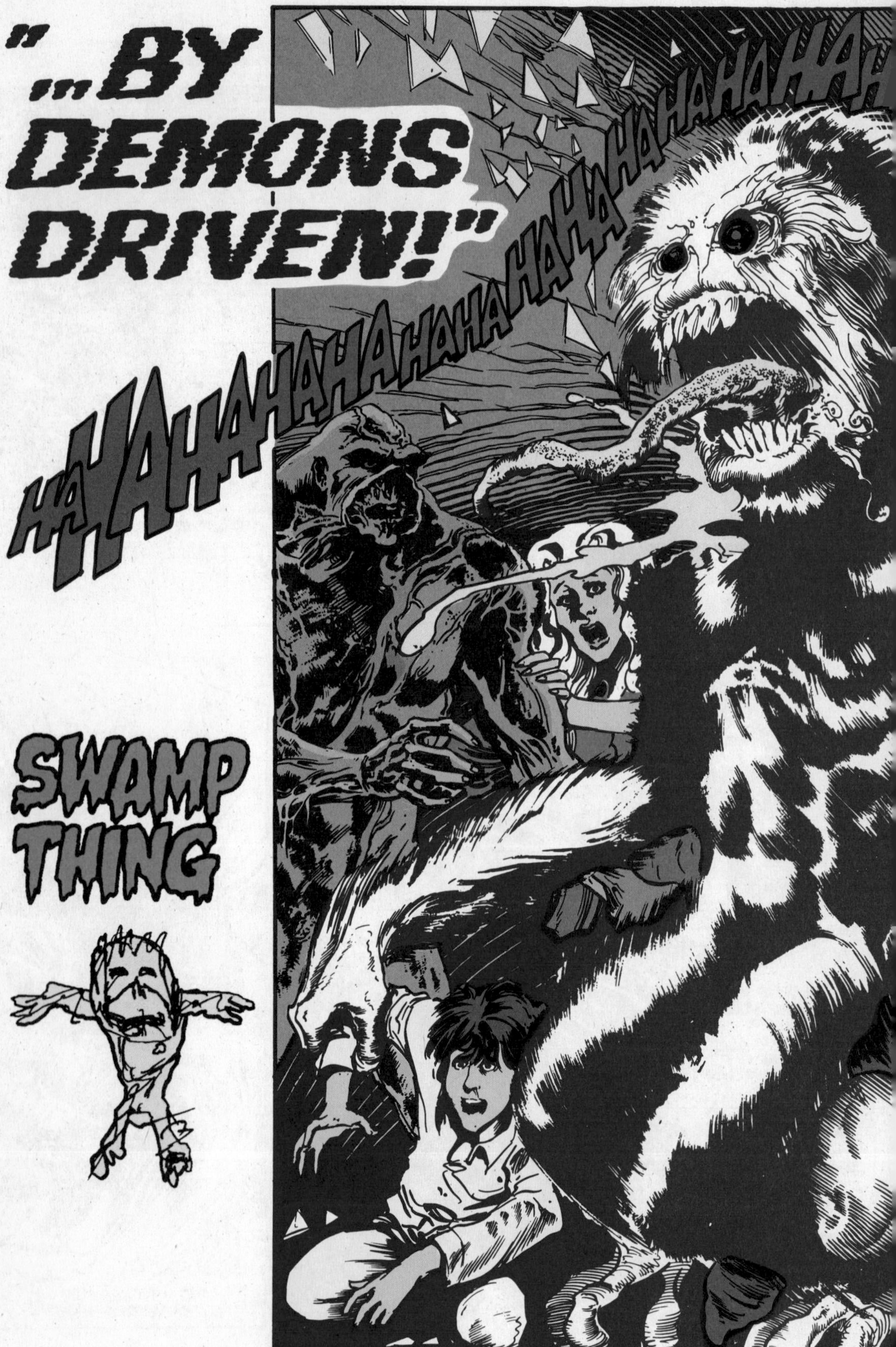
"...BY DEMONS DRIVEN!"
SWAMP THING

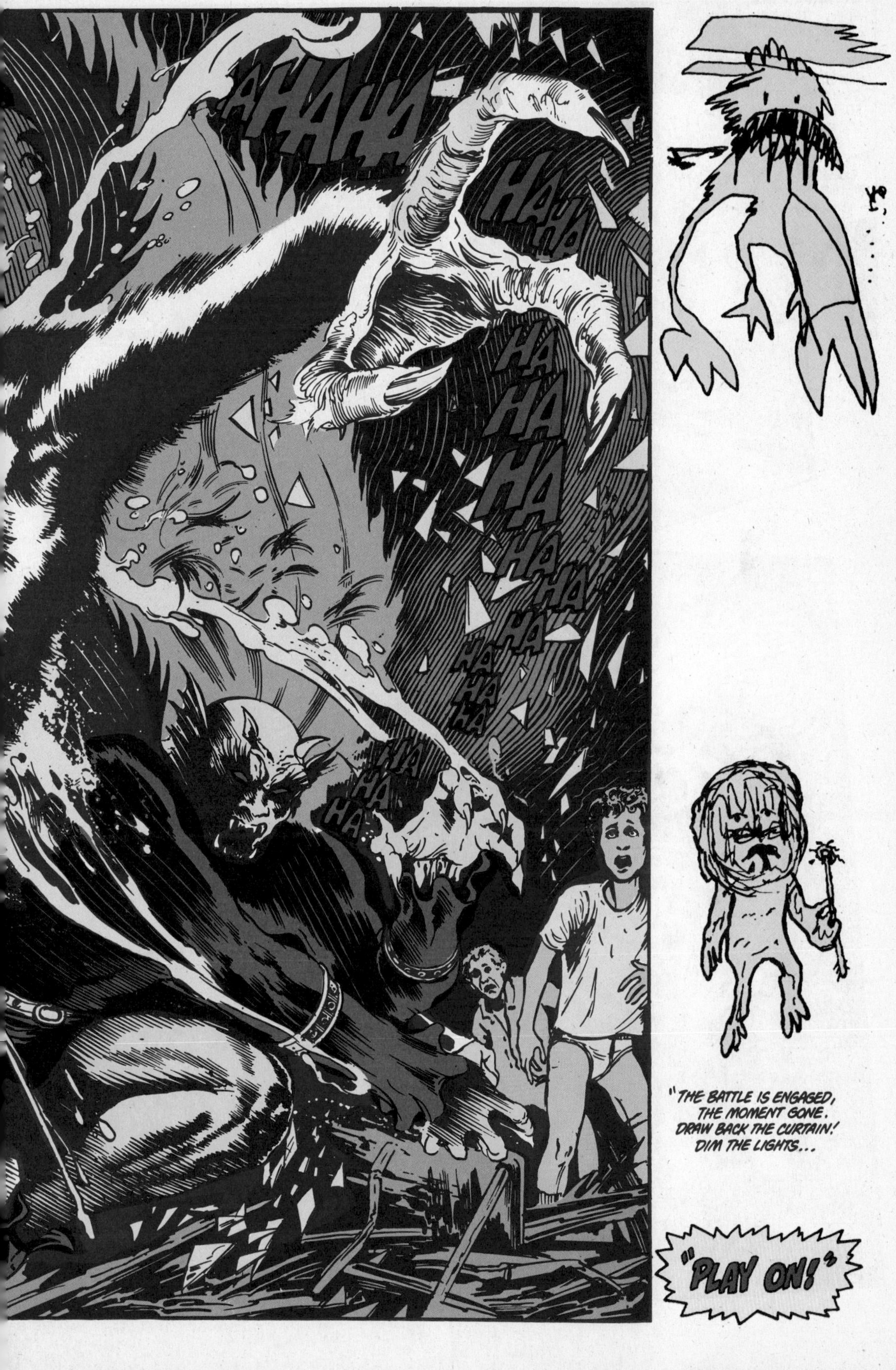
AHAHA-
HAHA
"THE BATTLE IS ENGAGED,
THE MOMENT GONE.
DRAW BACK THE CURTAIN!
DIM THE LIGHTS...
"PLAY ON!"

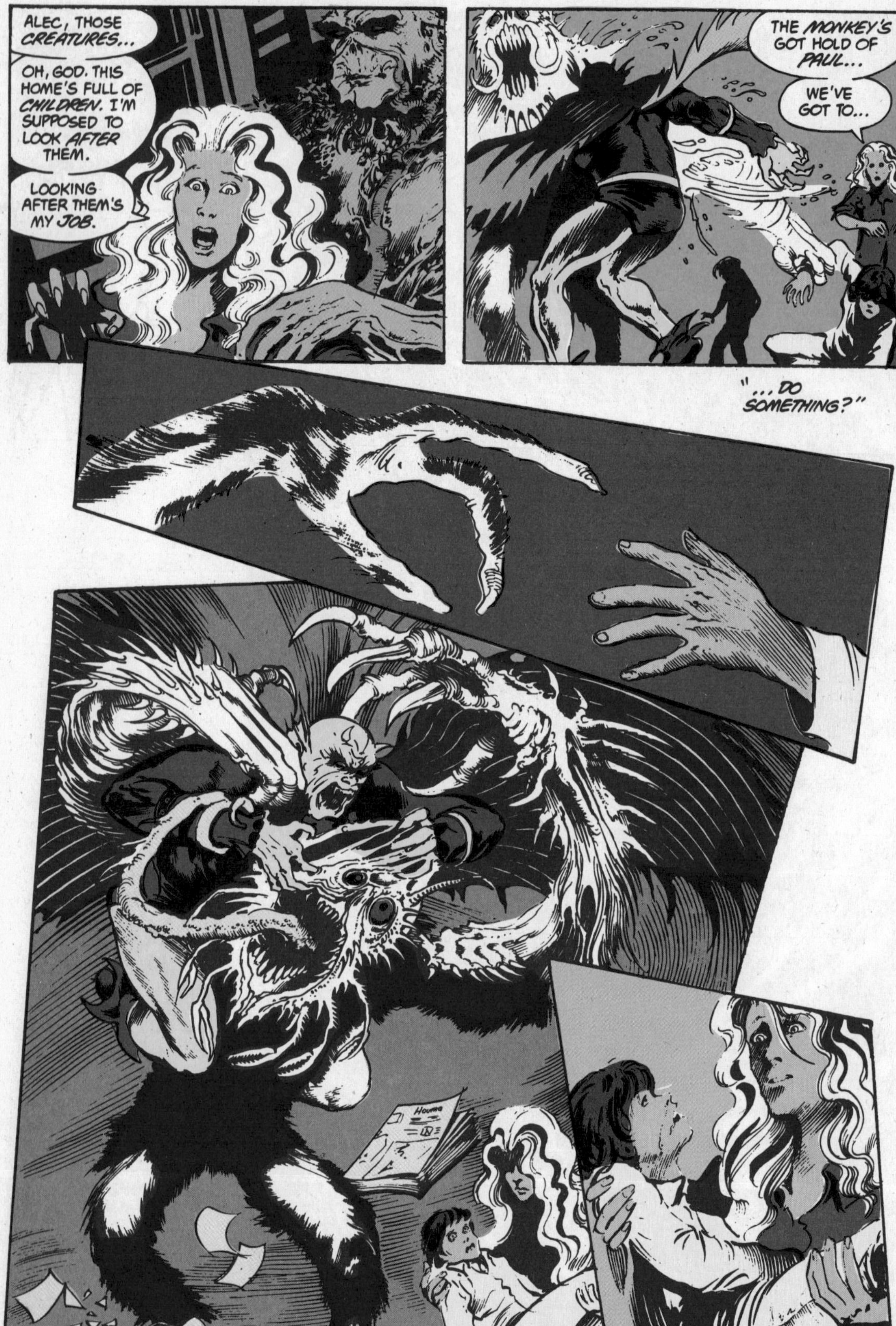
ALEC, THOSE CREATURES...
OH, GOD. THIS HOME'S FULL OF CHILDREN. I'M SUPPOSED TO LOOK AFTER THEM.
LOOKING AFTER THEM'S MY JOB.
THE MONKEY'S GOT HOLD OF PAUL...
WE'VE GOT TO...
"...DO SOMETHING?"
4

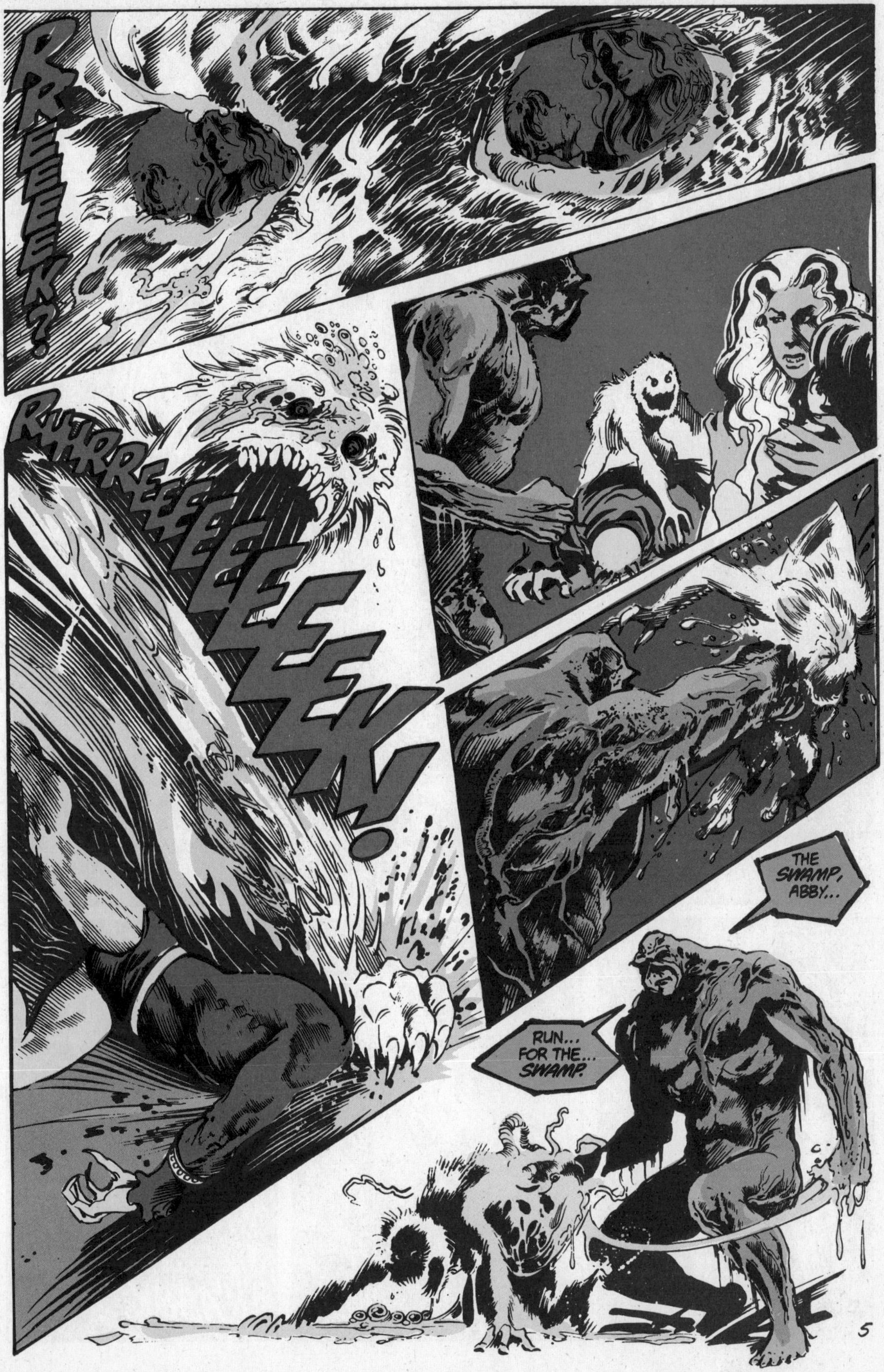
RREEEEK?
RUHRREEEEEEEEEEEK!
THE SWAMP, ABBY...
RUN... FOR THE... SWAMP.
5

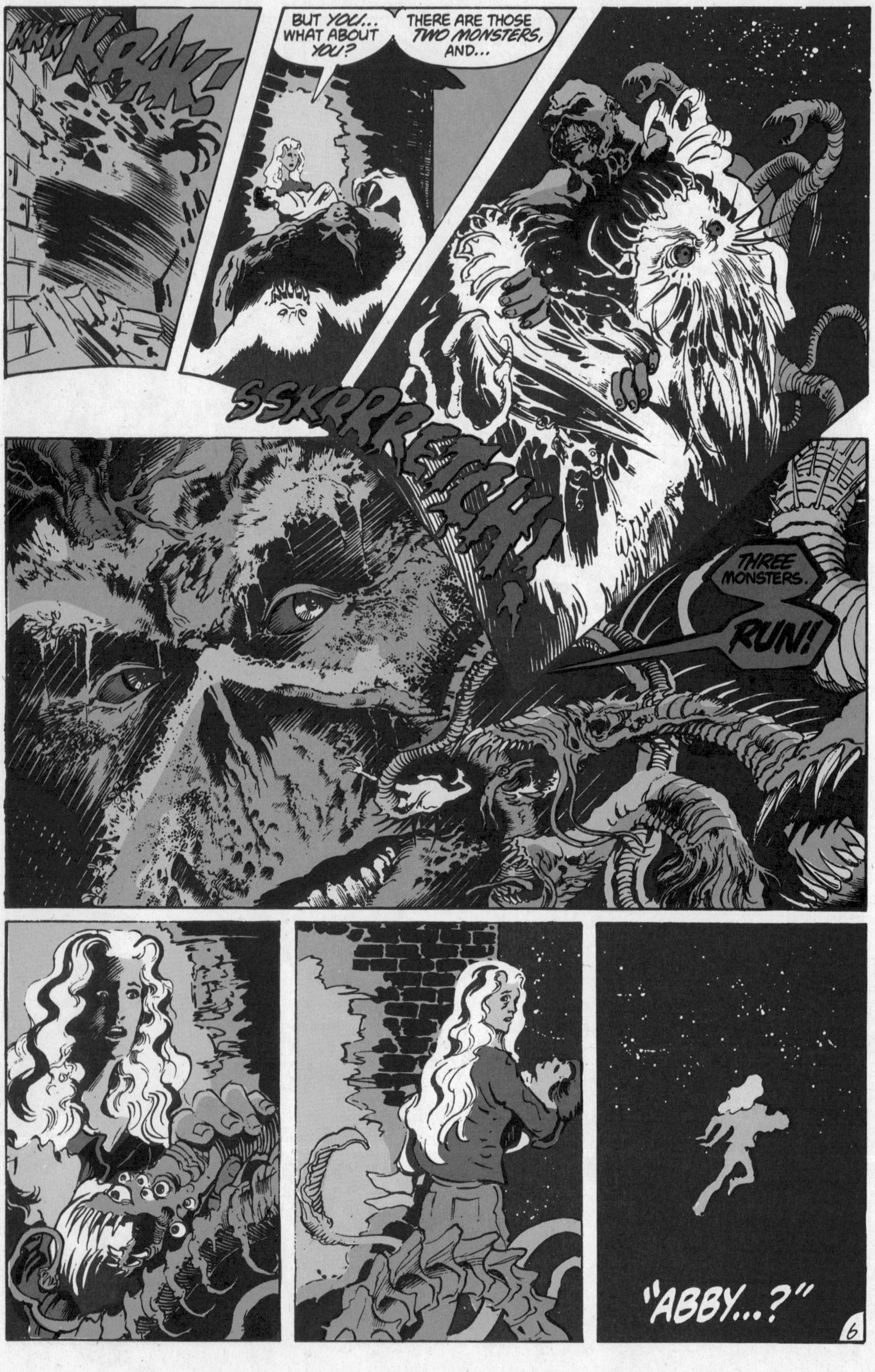
KKKKRAK!
BUT YOU... WHAT ABOUT YOU?
THERE ARE THOSE TWO MONSTERS, AND...
SSKRRRETCH!
THREE MONSTERS.
RUN!
"ABBY...?"
6

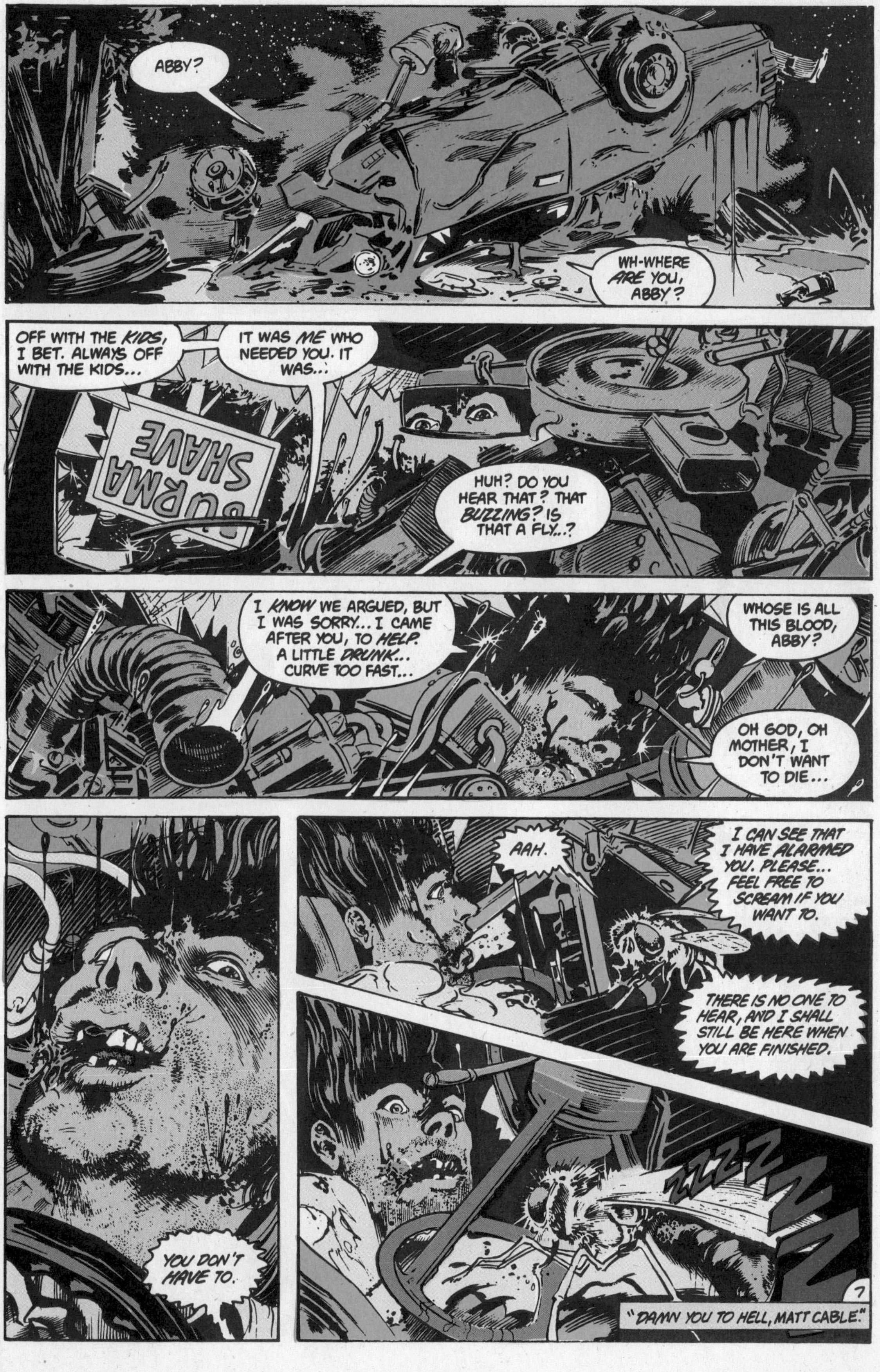
ABBY?
WH-WHERE ARE YOU, ABBY?
OFF WITH THE KIDS, I BET. ALWAYS OFF WITH THE KIDS...
IT WAS ME WHO NEEDED YOU. IT WAS...
BURMA SHAVE
HUH? DO YOU HEAR THAT? THAT BUZZING? IS THAT A FLY...?
I KNOW WE ARGUED, BUT I WAS SORRY... I CAME AFTER YOU, TO HELP. A LITTLE DRUNK... CURVE TOO FAST...
WHOSE IS ALL THIS BLOOD, ABBY?
OH GOD, OH MOTHER, I DON'T WANT TO DIE...
YOU DON'T HAVE TO.
AAH.
I CAN SEE THAT I HAVE ALARMED YOU. PLEASE... FEEL FREE TO SCREAM IF YOU WANT TO.
THERE IS NO ONE TO HEAR, AND I SHALL STILL BE HERE WHEN YOU ARE FINISHED.
ZZZZ
7
"DAMN YOU TO HELL, MATT CABLE."

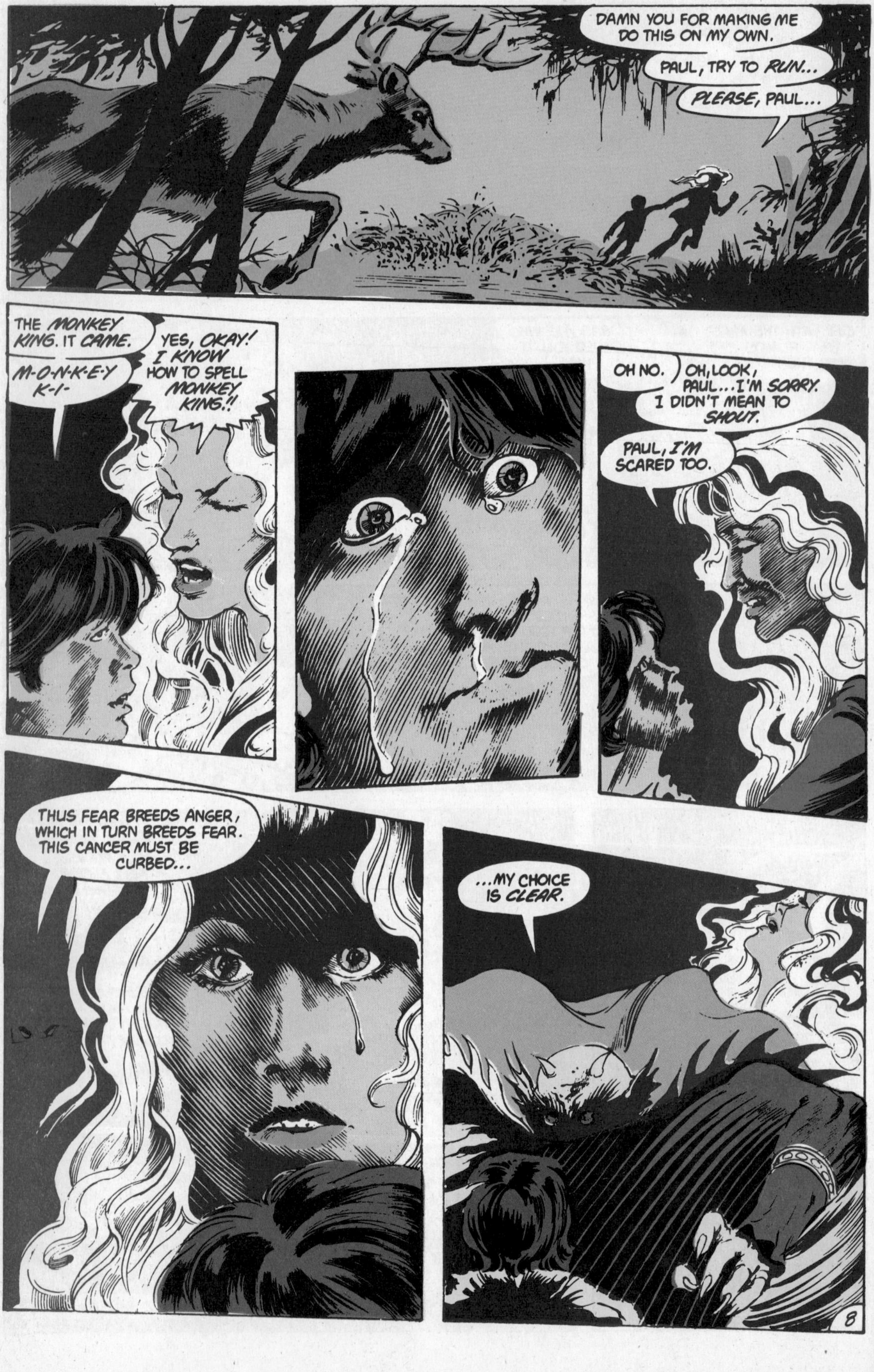
DAMN YOU FOR MAKING ME DO THIS ON MY OWN.
PAUL, TRY TO RUN...
PLEASE, PAUL...
THE MONKEY KING. IT CAME.
M-O-N-K-E-Y K-I-
YES, OKAY! I KNOW HOW TO SPELL MONKEY KING!!
OH NO.
OH, LOOK, PAUL... I'M SORRY. I DIDN'T MEAN TO SHOUT.
PAUL, I'M SCARED TOO.
THUS FEAR BREEDS ANGER, WHICH IN TURN BREEDS FEAR. THIS CANCER MUST BE CURBED...
...MY CHOICE IS CLEAR.
8

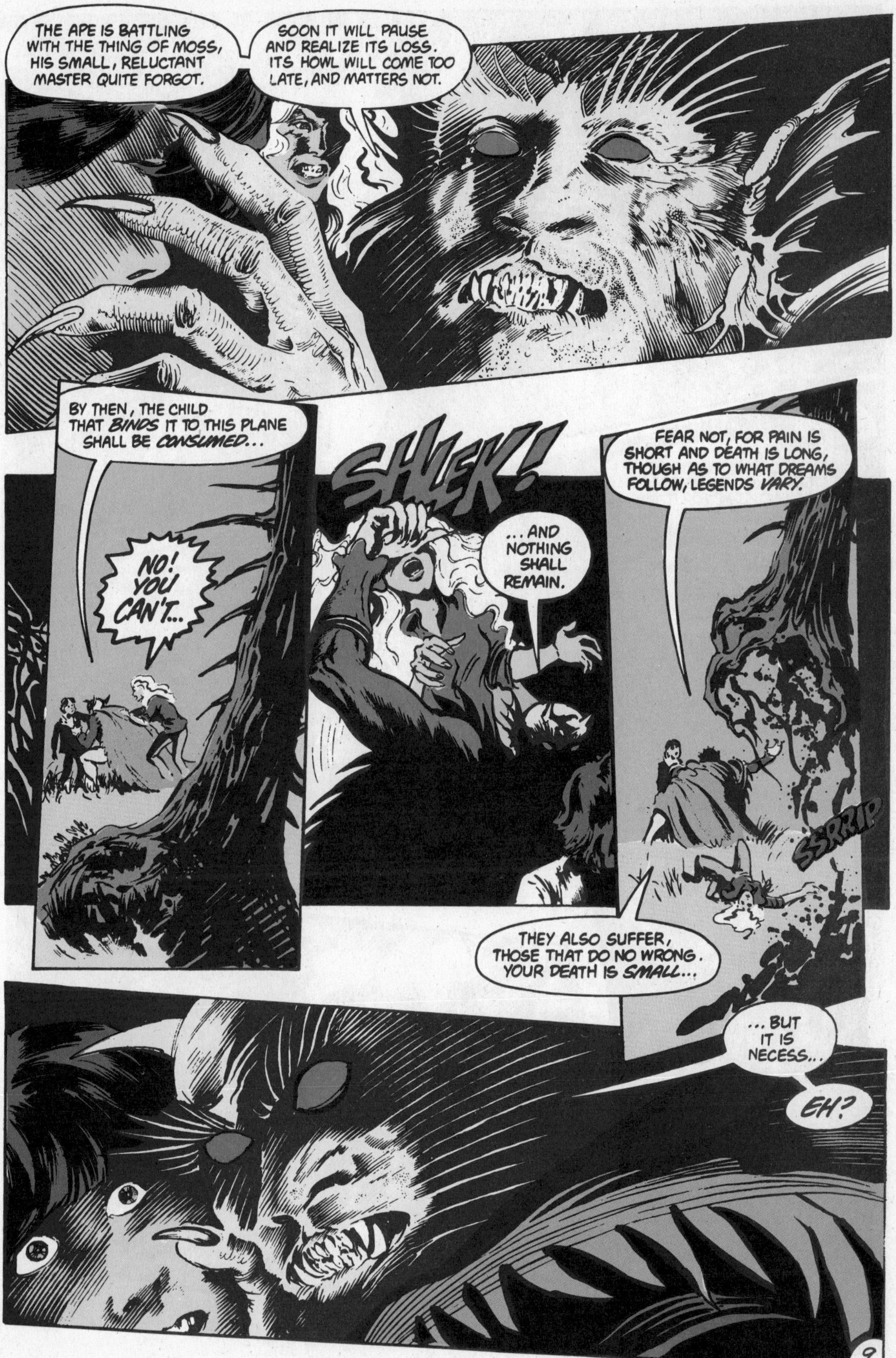
THE APE IS BATTLING WITH THE THING OF MOSS, HIS SMALL, RELUCTANT MASTER QUITE FORGOT.
SOON IT WILL PAUSE AND REALIZE ITS LOSS. ITS HOWL WILL COME TOO LATE, AND MATTERS NOT.
BY THEN, THE CHILD THAT BINDS IT TO THIS PLANE SHALL BE CONSUMED...
NO! YOU CAN'T...
SHLEK!
...AND NOTHING SHALL REMAIN.
FEAR NOT, FOR PAIN IS SHORT AND DEATH IS LONG, THOUGH AS TO WHAT DREAMS FOLLOW, LEGENDS VARY.
SSRRIP
THEY ALSO SUFFER, THOSE THAT DO NO WRONG. YOUR DEATH IS SMALL...
...BUT IT IS NECESS...
EH?
9

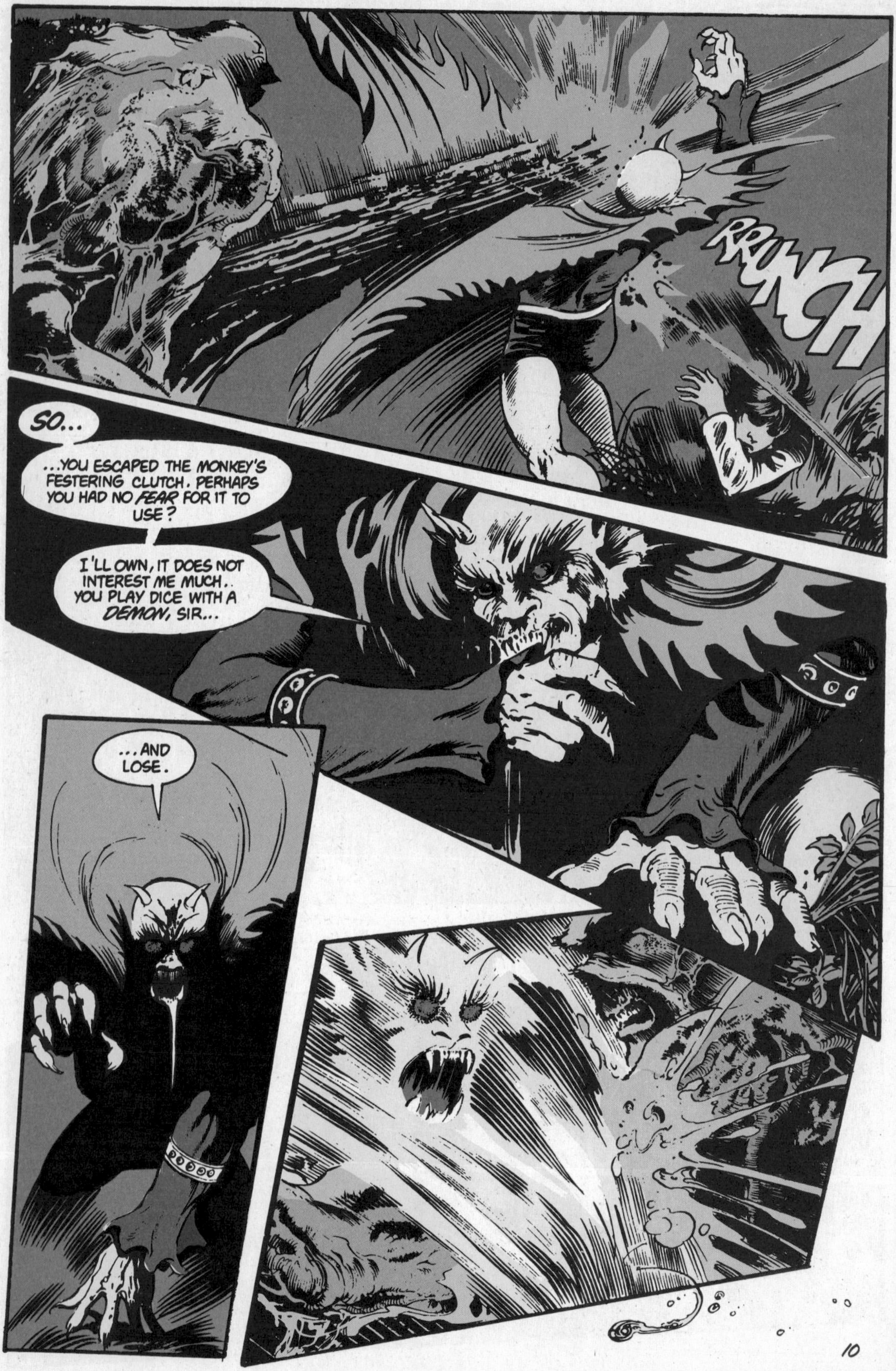
RRUNCH
SO...
...YOU ESCAPED THE MONKEY'S FESTERING CLUTCH. PERHAPS YOU HAD NO *FEAR* FOR IT TO USE?
I'LL OWN, IT DOES NOT INTEREST ME MUCH.. YOU PLAY DICE WITH A *DEMON*, SIR...
...AND LOSE.
10

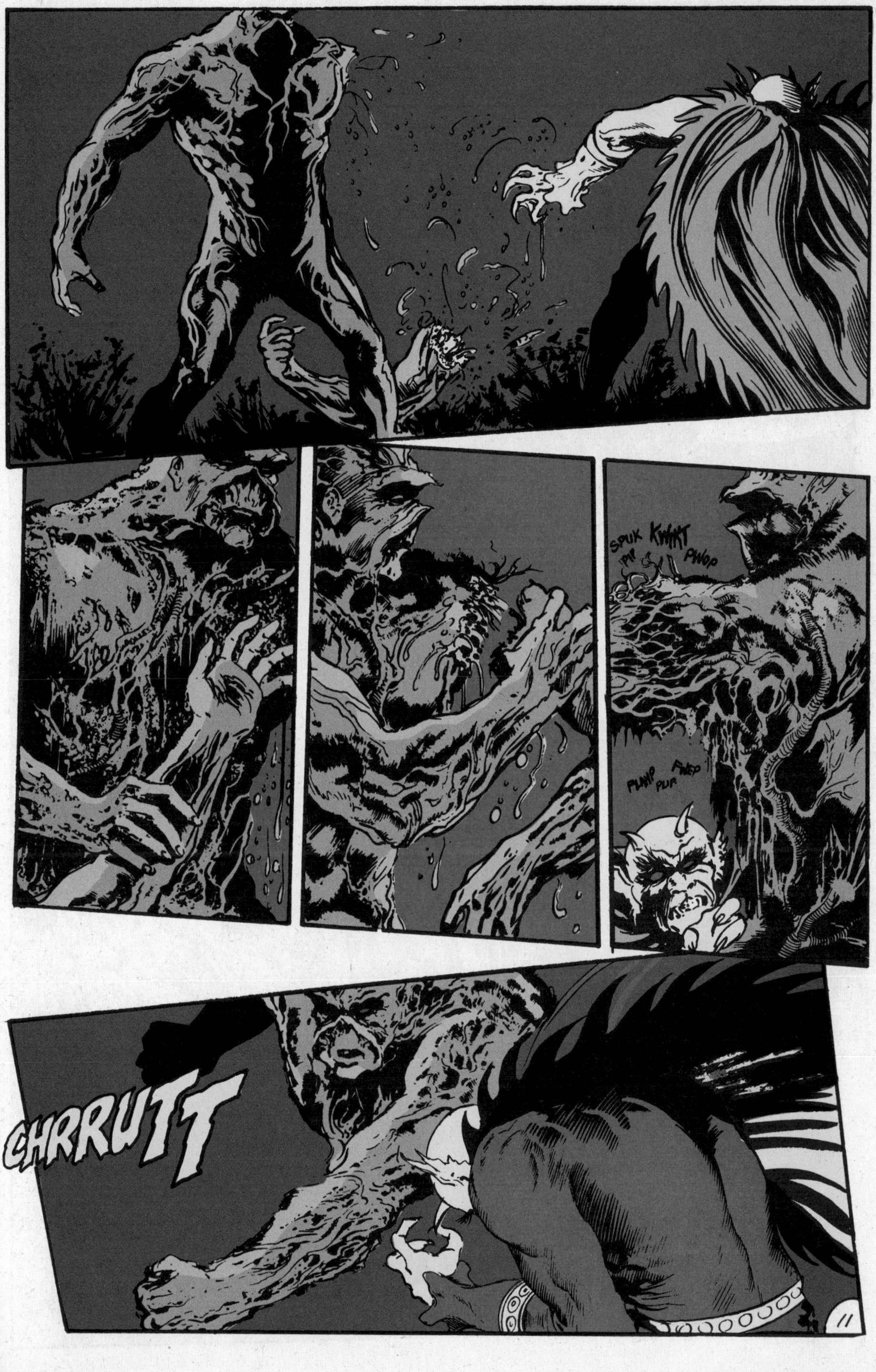
SPUK KWIKT
PIP
PHLOP
PLUMP PLIP FWEP
CHRRUTT
11

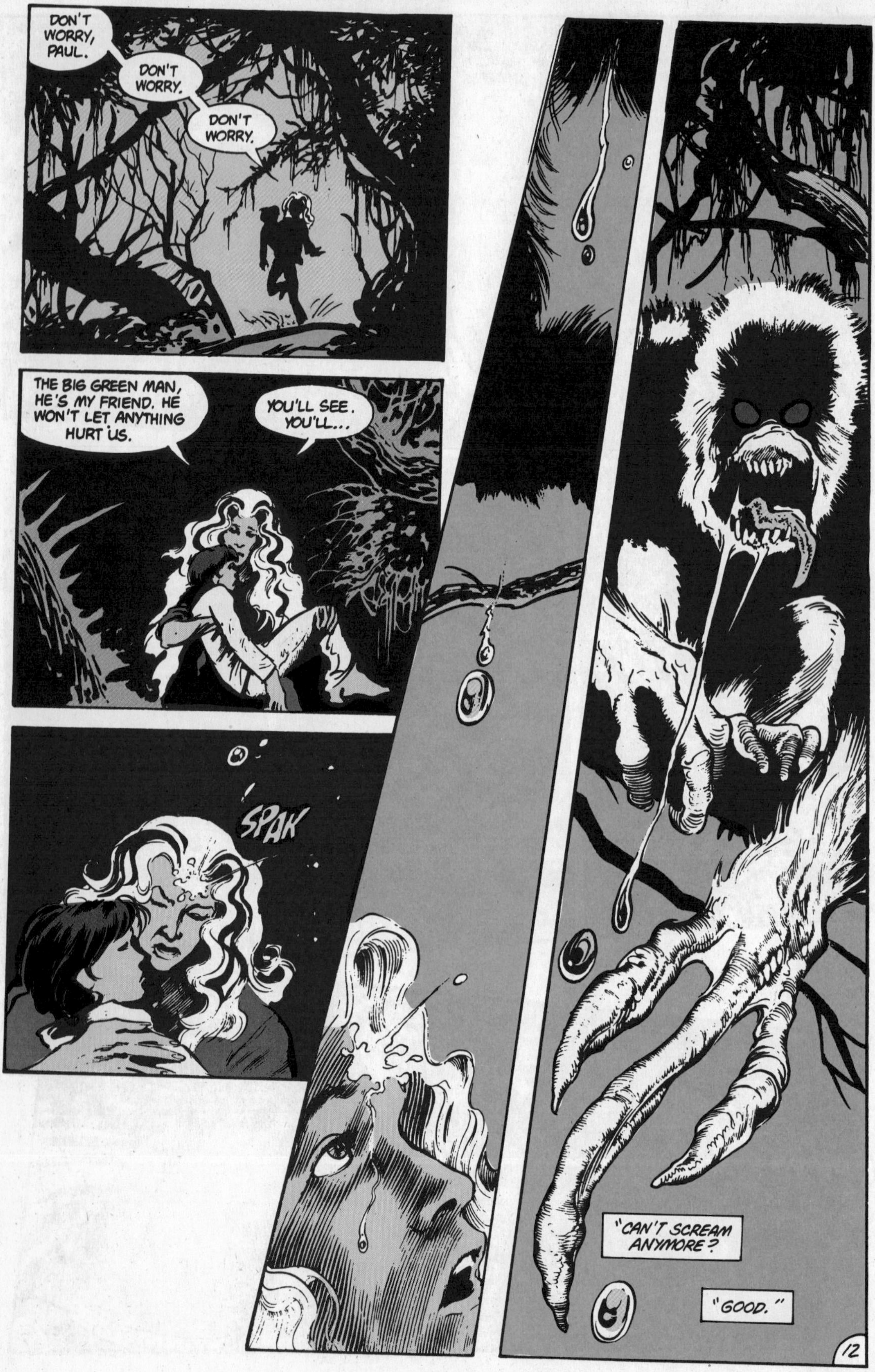
DON'T WORRY, PAUL.
DON'T WORRY.
DON'T WORRY.
THE BIG GREEN MAN, HE'S MY FRIEND. HE WON'T LET ANYTHING HURT US.
YOU'LL SEE. YOU'LL...
SPAK
"CAN'T SCREAM ANYMORE?
"GOOD."
12

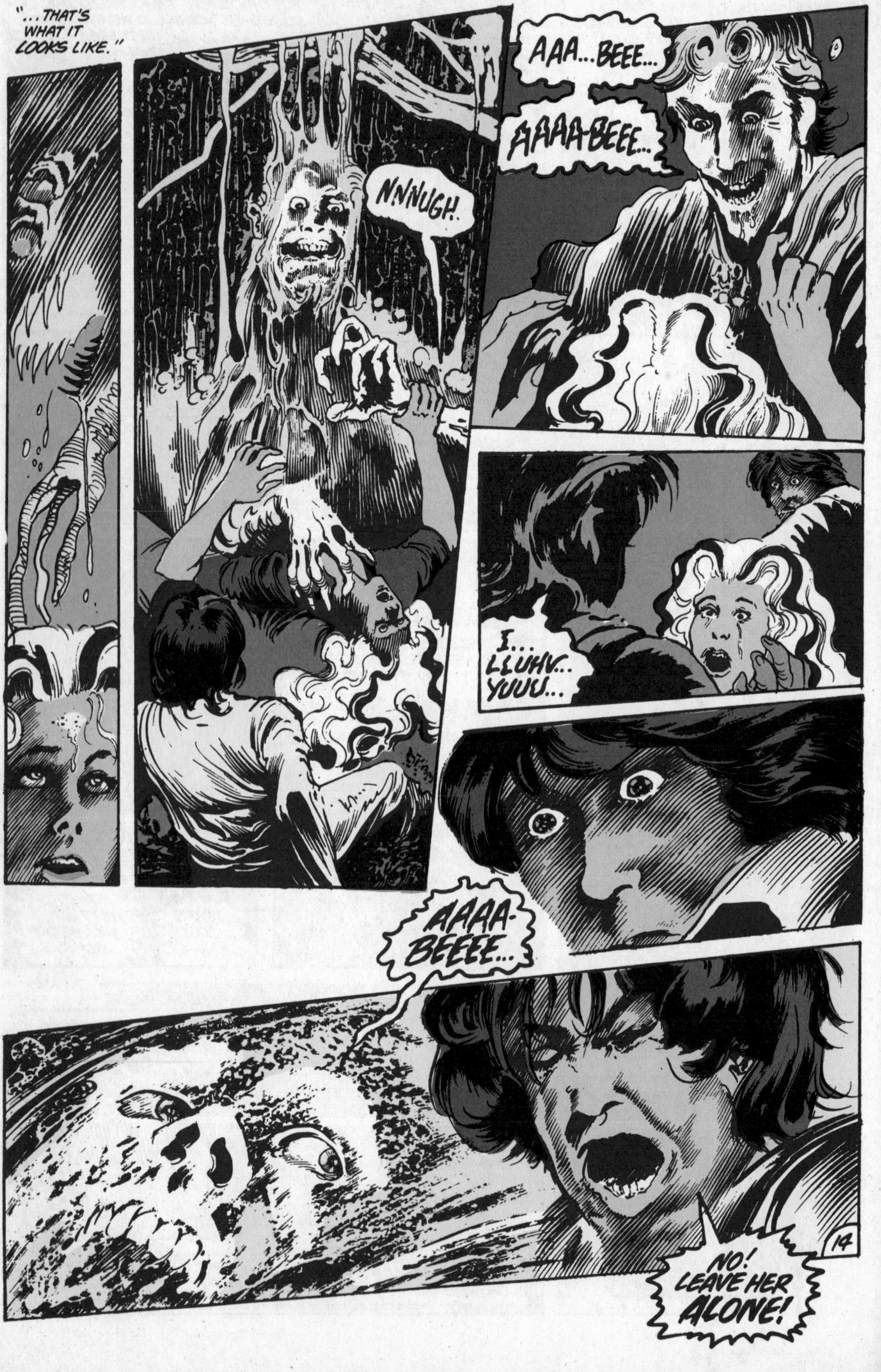
"...THAT'S WHAT IT LOOKS LIKE."
NNNUGH.
AAA...BEEE...
AAAA-BEEE...
I... LLUHV... YUUU...
AAAA-BEEEE...
NO! LEAVE HER ALONE!
14

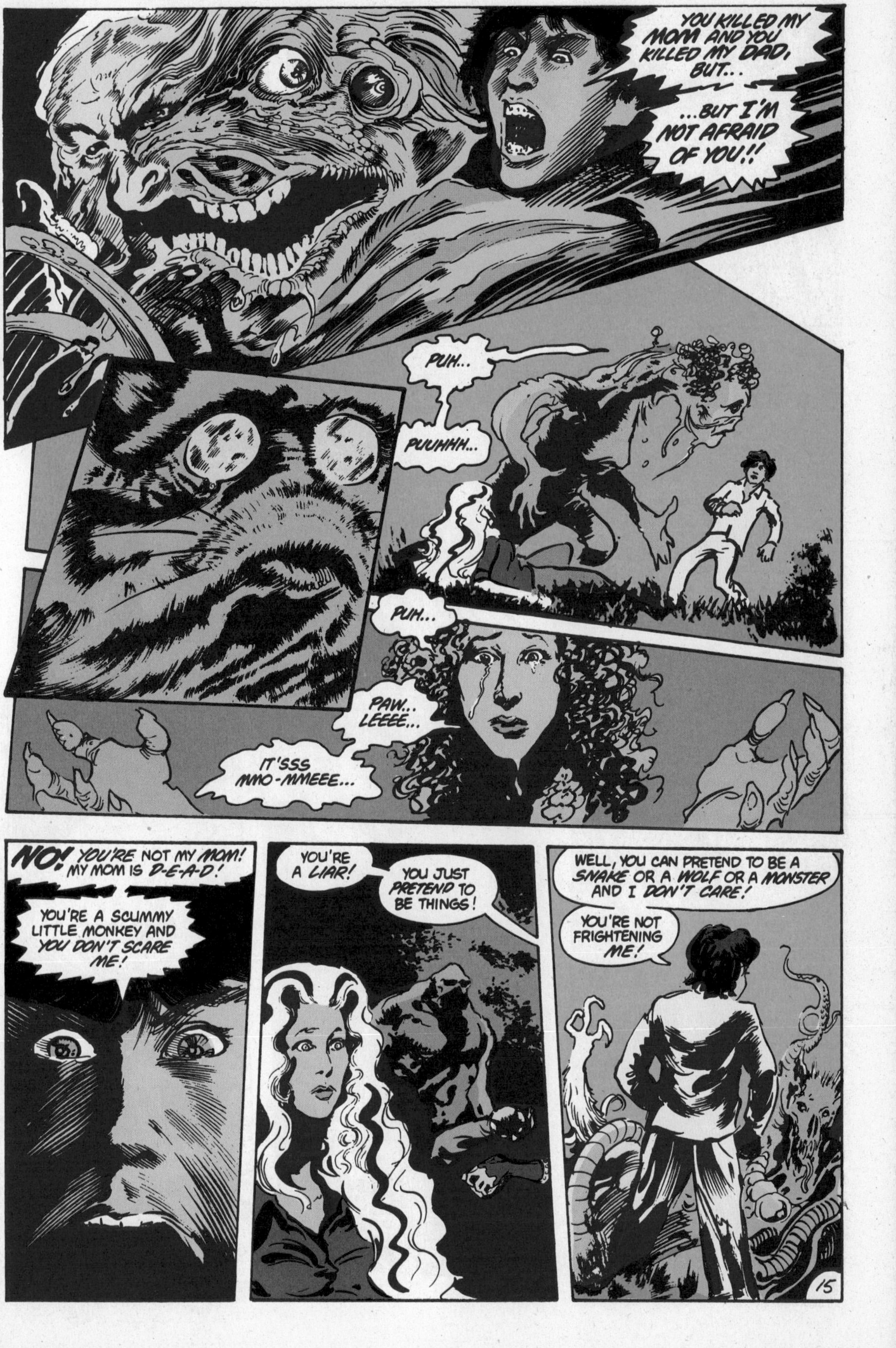
YOU KILLED MY MOM AND YOU KILLED MY DAD, BUT...
...BUT I'M NOT AFRAID OF YOU!!
PUH...
PUUHHH...
PUH...
PAW... LEEEE...
IT'SSS MMO-MMEEE...
NO! YOU'RE NOT MY MOM! MY MOM IS D-E-A-D!
YOU'RE A SCUMMY LITTLE MONKEY AND YOU DON'T SCARE ME!
YOU'RE A LIAR!
YOU JUST PRETEND TO BE THINGS!
WELL, YOU CAN PRETEND TO BE A SNAKE OR A WOLF OR A MONSTER AND I DON'T CARE!
YOU'RE NOT FRIGHTENING ME!
15

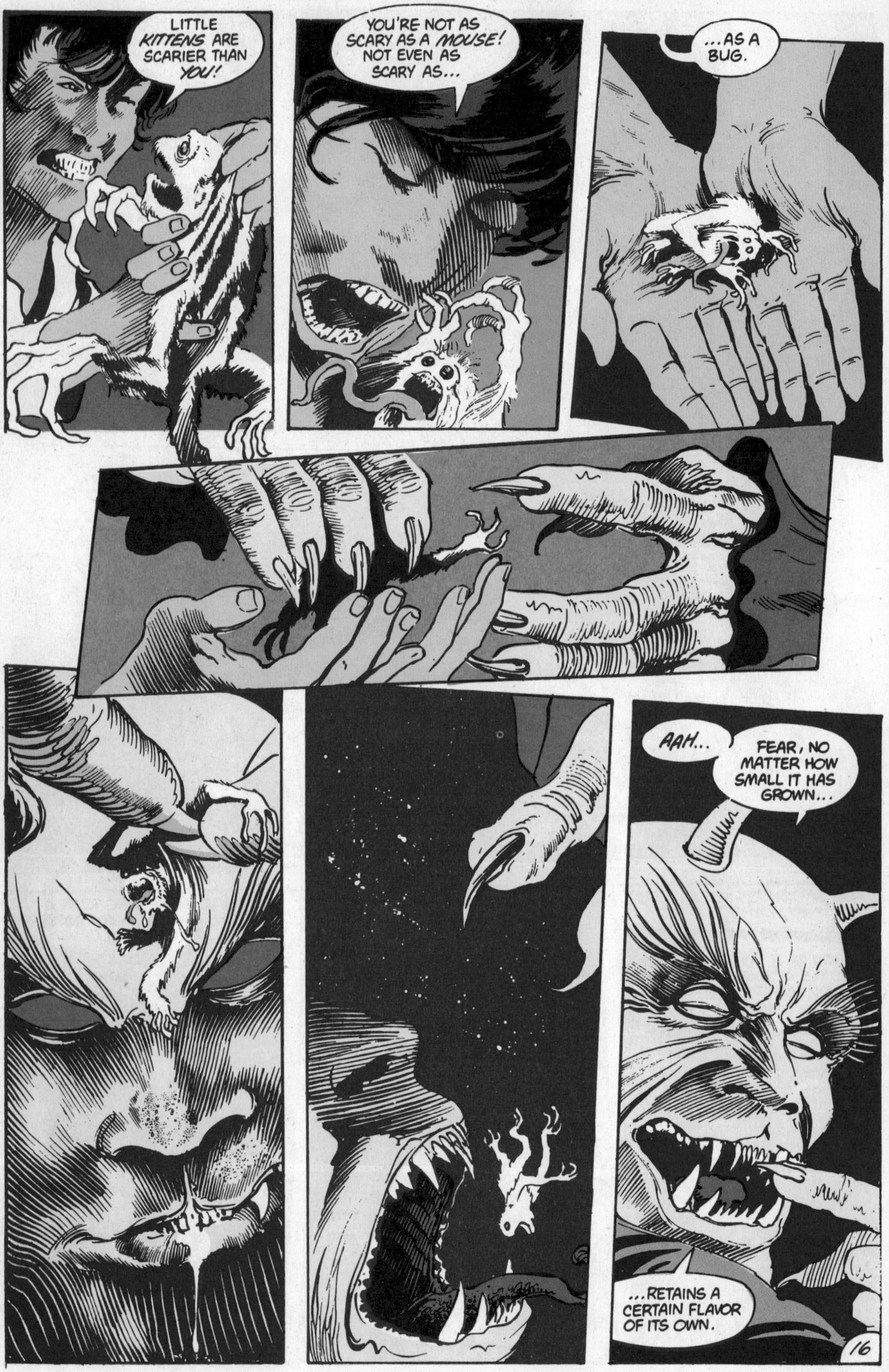
LITTLE KITTENS ARE SCARIER THAN YOU!
YOU'RE NOT AS SCARY AS A MOUSE! NOT EVEN AS SCARY AS...
...AS A BUG.
AAH...
FEAR, NO MATTER HOW SMALL IT HAS GROWN...
...RETAINS A CERTAIN FLAVOR OF ITS OWN.
16

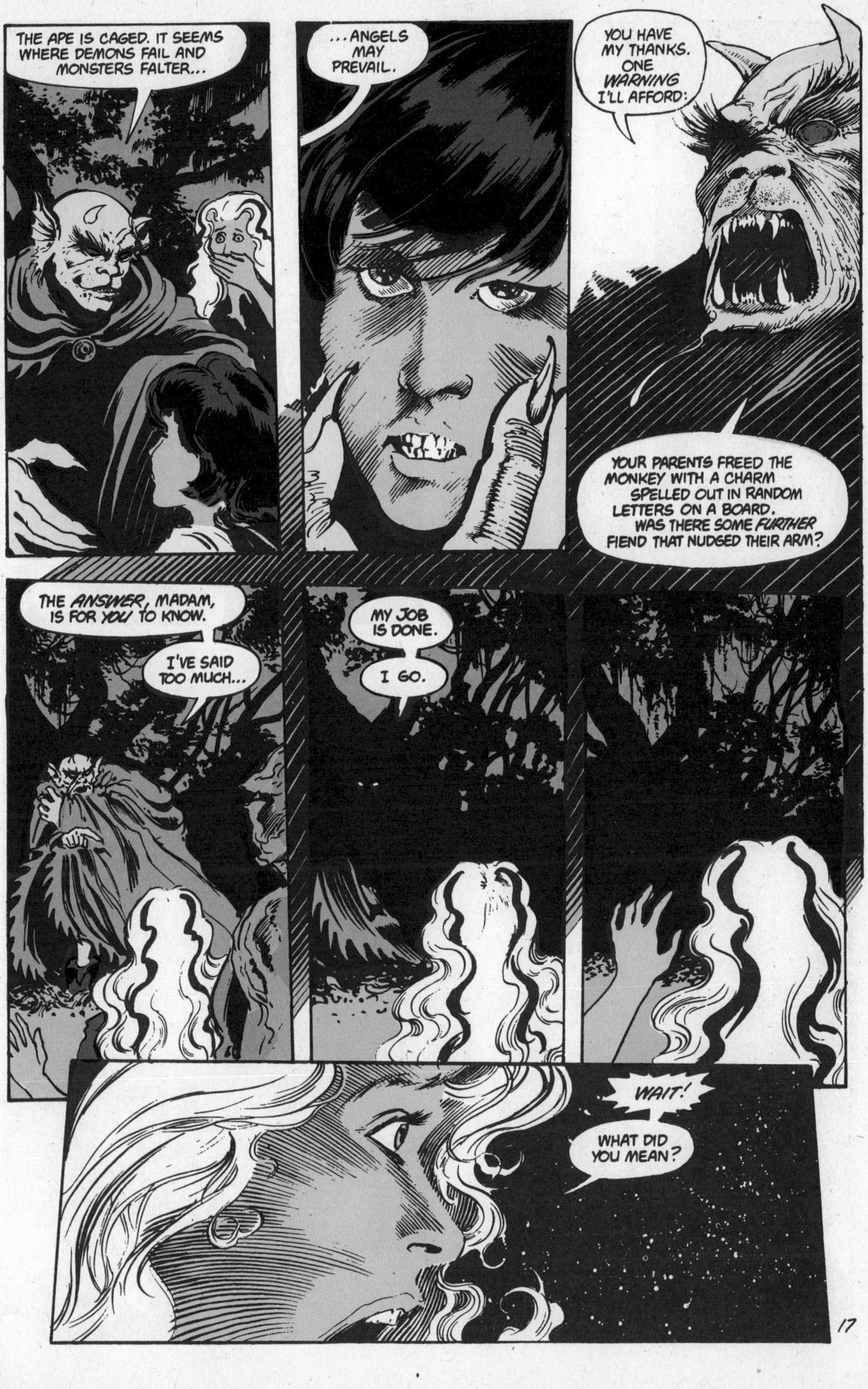
THE APE IS CAGED. IT SEEMS WHERE DEMONS FAIL AND MONSTERS FALTER...
...ANGELS MAY PREVAIL.
YOU HAVE MY THANKS. ONE WARNING I'LL AFFORD:
YOUR PARENTS FREED THE MONKEY WITH A CHARM SPELLED OUT IN RANDOM LETTERS ON A BOARD. WAS THERE SOME FURTHER FIEND THAT NUDGED THEIR ARM?
THE ANSWER, MADAM, IS FOR YOU TO KNOW.
I'VE SAID TOO MUCH...
MY JOB IS DONE.
I GO.
WAIT!
WHAT DID YOU MEAN?
17

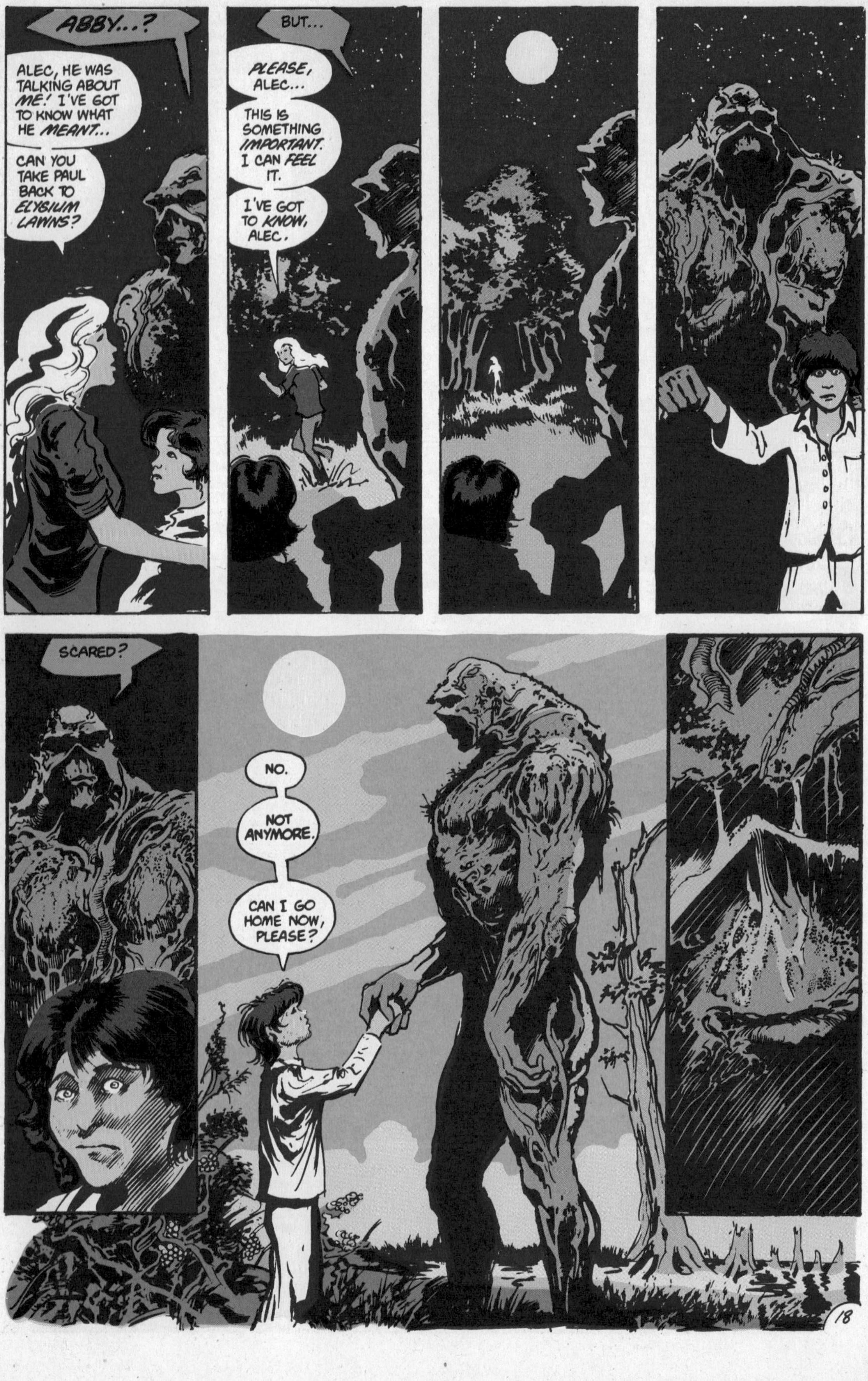
ABBY...?
ALEC, HE WAS TALKING ABOUT ME! I'VE GOT TO KNOW WHAT HE MEANT...
CAN YOU TAKE PAUL BACK TO ELYSIUM LAWNS?
BUT...
PLEASE, ALEC...
THIS IS SOMETHING IMPORTANT. I CAN FEEL IT.
I'VE GOT TO KNOW, ALEC.
SCARED?
NO.
NOT ANYMORE.
CAN I GO HOME NOW, PLEASE?
18

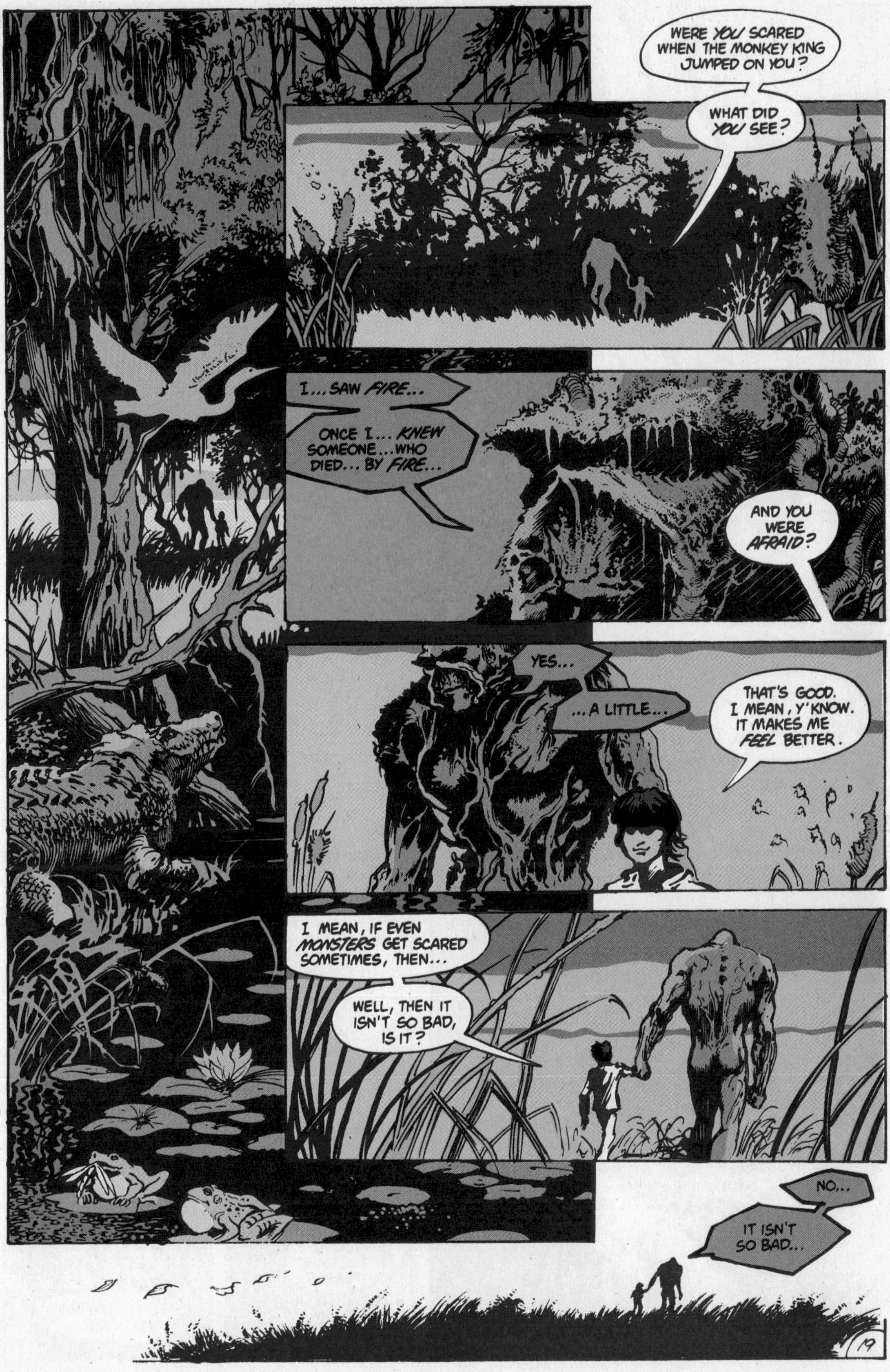
WERE YOU SCARED WHEN THE MONKEY KING JUMPED ON YOU?
WHAT DID YOU SEE?
I... SAW FIRE...
ONCE I... KNEW SOMEONE...WHO DIED... BY FIRE...
AND YOU WERE AFRAID?
YES...
...A LITTLE...
THAT'S GOOD. I MEAN, Y'KNOW. IT MAKES ME FEEL BETTER.
I MEAN, IF EVEN MONSTERS GET SCARED SOMETIMES, THEN...
WELL, THEN IT ISN'T SO BAD, IS IT?
NO...
IT ISN'T SO BAD...
19

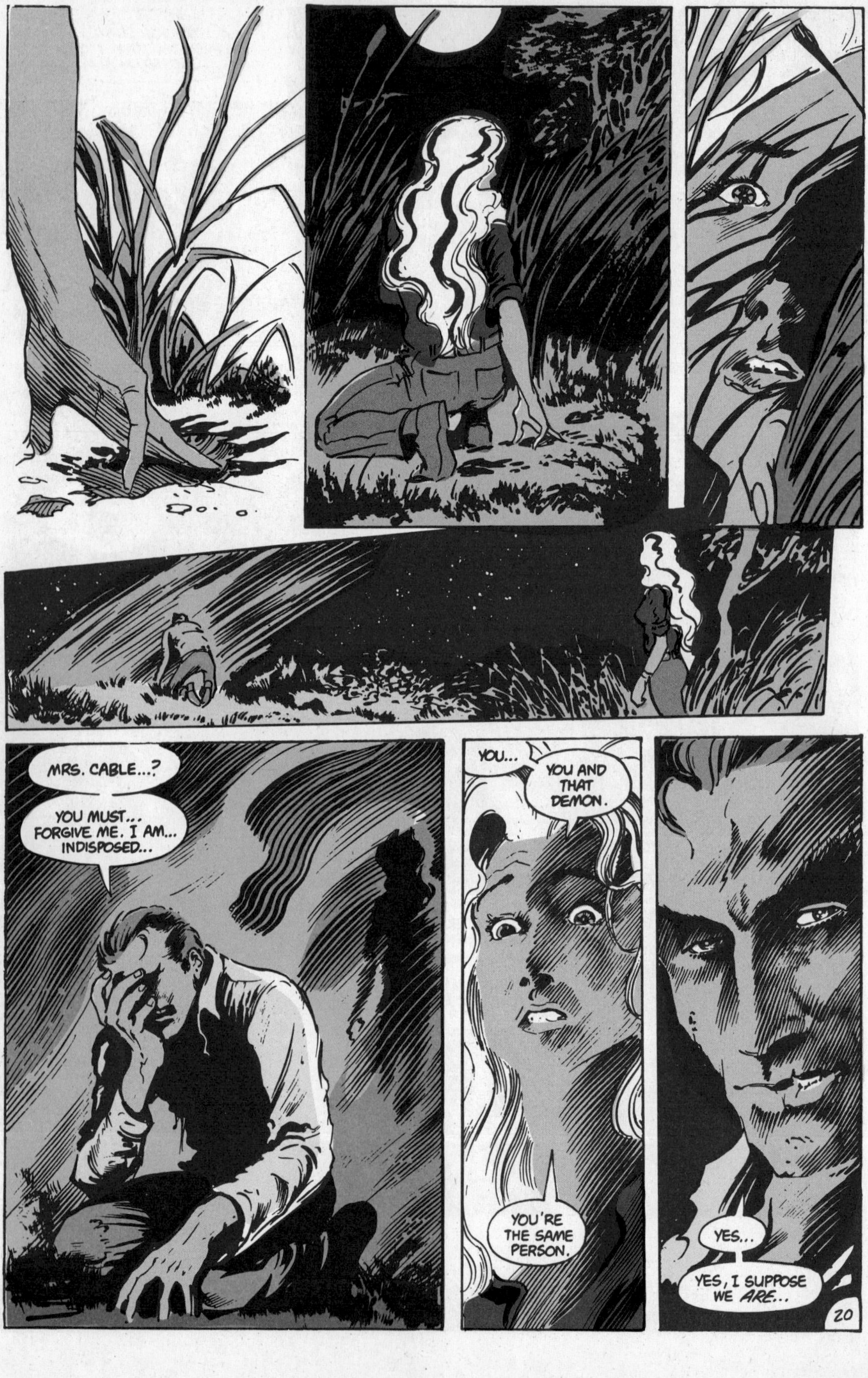
MRS. CABLE...?
YOU MUST... FORGIVE ME. I AM... INDISPOSED...
YOU...
YOU AND THAT DEMON.
YOU'RE THE SAME PERSON.
YES...
YES, I SUPPOSE WE ARE...
20

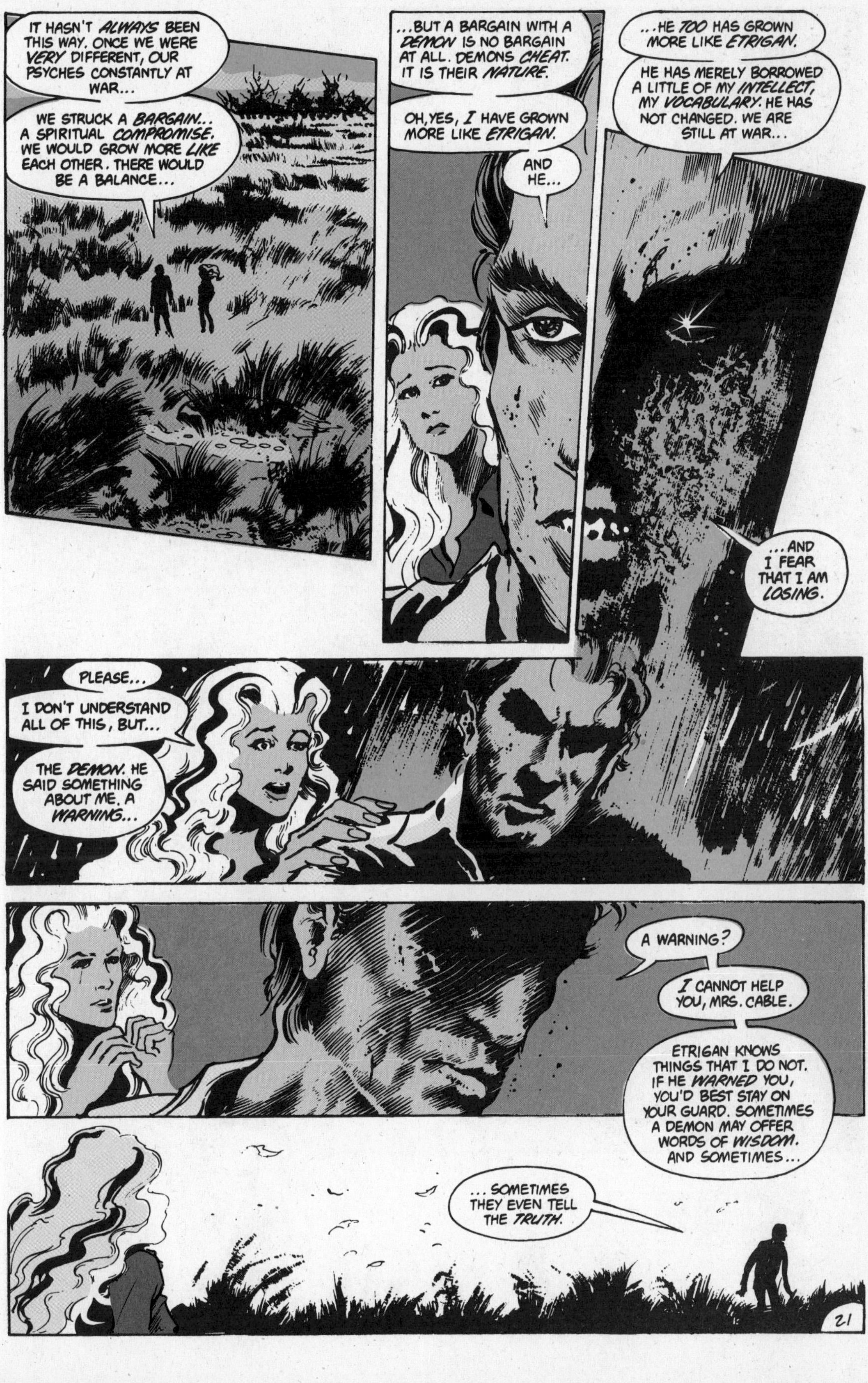
IT HASN'T ALWAYS BEEN THIS WAY. ONCE WE WERE VERY DIFFERENT, OUR PSYCHES CONSTANTLY AT WAR...
WE STRUCK A BARGAIN... A SPIRITUAL COMPROMISE. WE WOULD GROW MORE LIKE EACH OTHER. THERE WOULD BE A BALANCE...
...BUT A BARGAIN WITH A DEMON IS NO BARGAIN AT ALL. DEMONS CHEAT. IT IS THEIR NATURE.
OH, YES, I HAVE GROWN MORE LIKE ETRIGAN.
AND HE...
...HE TOO HAS GROWN MORE LIKE ETRIGAN.
HE HAS MERELY BORROWED A LITTLE OF MY INTELLECT, MY VOCABULARY. HE HAS NOT CHANGED. WE ARE STILL AT WAR...
...AND I FEAR THAT I AM LOSING.
PLEASE...
I DON'T UNDERSTAND ALL OF THIS, BUT...
THE DEMON. HE SAID SOMETHING ABOUT ME. A WARNING...
A WARNING?
I CANNOT HELP YOU, MRS. CABLE.
ETRIGAN KNOWS THINGS THAT I DO NOT. IF HE WARNED YOU, YOU'D BEST STAY ON YOUR GUARD. SOMETIMES A DEMON MAY OFFER WORDS OF WISDOM. AND SOMETIMES...
...SOMETIMES THEY EVEN TELL THE TRUTH.
21

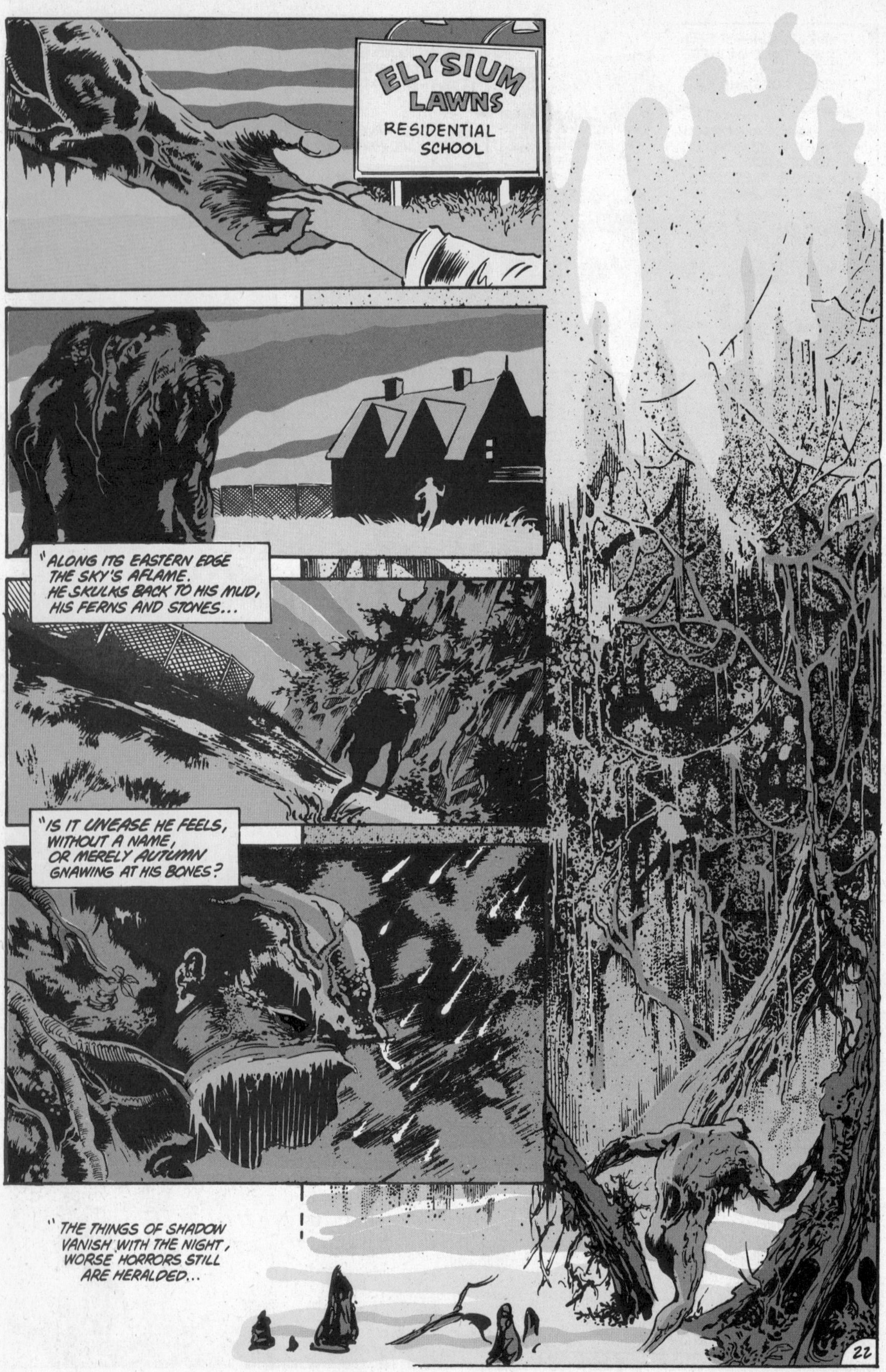
ELYSIUM
LAWNS
RESIDENTIAL
SCHOOL
"ALONG ITS EASTERN EDGE THE SKY'S AFLAME. HE SKULKS BACK TO HIS MUD, HIS FERNS AND STONES...
"IS IT UNEASE HE FEELS, WITHOUT A NAME, OR MERELY AUTUMN GNAWING AT HIS BONES?
"THE THINGS OF SHADOW VANISH WITH THE NIGHT, WORSE HORRORS STILL ARE HERALDED...
22